Making Do

Imagine a world in which clothing wasn't superabundant – cheap, disposable, indestructible – but perishable, threadbare and chronically scarce. Eighty years ago, when World War II ended, a textile famine loomed. What would everyone wear as uniforms were discarded and soldiers returned home, Nazi camps were liberated, and millions of uprooted people struggled to subsist?

In this richly textured history, Carruthers unpicks a familiar wartime motto, 'Make Do and Mend', to reveal how central fabric was to postwar Britain. Clothes and footwear supplied a currency with which some were rewarded, while others went without. *Making Do* moves from Britain's demob centres to liberated Belsen – from razed German cities to refugee camps and troopships – to uncover intimate ties between Britons and others bound together in new patterns of mutual need.

Filled with original research and personal stories, *Making Do* illuminates how lives were refashioned after the most devastating war in human history.

Susan L. Carruthers is Professor of US and International History at the University of Warwick. Much of her work focuses on war and the ways in which individuals, and societies more broadly, have made sense of conflict and its aftermath. She is the author of six previous books, including *Dear John: Love and Loyalty in Wartime America* (Cambridge University Press, 2022) and *The Good Occupation: American Soldiers and the Hazards of Peace* (2016).

Making Do

Britons and the Refashioning
of the Postwar World

Susan L. Carruthers

CAMBRIDGE
UNIVERSITY PRESS

CAMBRIDGE
UNIVERSITY PRESS

Shaftesbury Road, Cambridge CB2 8EA, United Kingdom

One Liberty Plaza, 20th Floor, New York, NY 10006, USA

477 Williamstown Road, Port Melbourne, VIC 3207, Australia

314–321, 3rd Floor, Plot 3, Splendor Forum, Jasola District Centre, New Delhi – 110025, India

103 Penang Road, #05–06/07, Visioncrest Commercial, Singapore 238467

Cambridge University Press is part of Cambridge University Press & Assessment, a department of the University of Cambridge.

We share the University's mission to contribute to society through the pursuit of education, learning and research at the highest international levels of excellence.

www.cambridge.org
Information on this title: www.cambridge.org/9781009464284

DOI: 10.1017/9781009464246

© Susan L. Carruthers 2025

This publication is in copyright. Subject to statutory exception and to the provisions of relevant collective licensing agreements, no reproduction of any part may take place without the written permission of Cambridge University Press & Assessment.

When citing this work, please include a reference to the DOI 10.1017/9781009464246

First published 2025

Printed in the United Kingdom by TJ Books Limited, Padstow Cornwall

A catalogue record for this publication is available from the British Library

A Cataloging-in-Publication data record for this book is available from the Library of Congress

ISBN 978-1-009-46428-4 Hardback

Cambridge University Press & Assessment has no responsibility for the persistence or accuracy of URLs for external or third-party internet websites referred to in this publication and does not guarantee that any content on such websites is, or will remain, accurate or appropriate.

For Patricia Margaret Walton Carruthers (1938–2022)

CONTENTS

FIGURES

NOTE ON THE TEXT

This book, about Britain and Britons' attitudes in the aftermath of World War II, draws on extensive original research. Some of the contemporary sources from which I quote verbatim (in Chapters 1 and 4) contain racist language which is deeply offensive. For people of colour, these slurs were always experienced as profoundly demeaning and hateful. Racist language hasn't only recently become unacceptably hateful. Yet, as I show, many Britons in the 1940s, socialized by an educational system that took Britain's place at the centre of a vast empire for granted, simultaneously took white superiority as a given, employing charged language in a cavalier fashion. I have not amended the original phraseology of these quotations so that readers can appreciate for themselves the tenor of both public and private speech in the 1940s. In quoting from original sources throughout the book, I have not amended grammar, punctuation or spelling.

ABBREVIATIONS

AP	Associated Press
ATS	Auxiliary Territorial Service
BAOR	British Army of the Rhine
BCC	British Colour Council
BCMI	Britain Can Make It exhibition (1946)
BFUW	British Federation of University Women
BMJ	*British Medical Journal*
BoT	Board of Trade
BRCS	British Red Cross Society
BWRS	British War Relief Society
COI	Central Office of Information
DP	Displaced person
EVW	European Volunteer Worker
FRS	Friends Relief Service
HC Deb	*House of Commons Debates*
IRO	International Refugee Organization
IWM	Imperial War Museum, London
JCS	Joint Chiefs of Staff
LSE	London School of Economics and Political Science
MAF	Ministry of Agriculture and Fisheries
MG	Military Government
MO	Mass Observation
MoL	Ministry of Labour and National Service
MRC	Modern Records Centre, University of Warwick

NARA	National Archives and Records Administration, United States
NCO	Non-commissioned officer
NCUMC	National Council for the Unmarried Mother and Her Child
NYT	*New York Times*
PNP	People's National Party (Jamaica)
POW	Prisoner of war
RAF	Royal Air Force
RAMC	Royal Army Medical Corps
RCN	Royal College of Nursing
SEAC	South East Asia Command
SEN	Save Europe Now
SHAEF	Supreme Headquarters Allied Expeditionary Force
TNA	The National Archives, Kew
TUC	Trades Union Congress
UNRRA	United Nations Relief and Rehabilitation Administration
UNRWA	United Nations Relief and Works Agency for Palestinian Refugees in the Near East
UP	United Press
USAMHI	US Army Military History Institute, Carlisle, PA
USHMM	United States Holocaust Memorial Museum, Washington, DC
V&A	Victoria & Albert Museum, London
WAAF	Women's Auxiliary Air Force
WLA	Women's Land Army
WO	War Office
WRNS	Women's Royal Naval Service
WVS	Women's Voluntary Service

INTRODUCTION

When I was thirteen or fourteen, at the very start of the 1980s, my mother made me a long skirt from blackout material. The fabric had a glossy sheen, silky to the touch. With a tucked waistband and generous gathering, my swishing skirt made me feel suitably dressed for the dawning 'New Romantic' era. Duran Duran had just enjoyed their first Top 40 hit, and I longed to show my peers that I, too, was riding this wave on a crest of ruffles and puffs. Back then, I didn't dwell too much on where the material for my skirt came from. But later on, whenever I've recalled a garment I soon outgrew both in size and style, it's struck me as entirely in character that my mother clung onto a length of blackout material from World War II for so many decades before sewing my skirt. It's equally indicative of my own generation that I possess no recollection of when or how exactly I disposed of this skirt. My mother, in contrast, preserved almost every garment or piece of fabric she'd ever sewn, worn or owned until the end of her life in 2022 – her fingers still busy with imaginary stitching, folding, pleating and buttoning as dementia unravelled her.

Born in 1938, my mother grew up under the war's long shadow. In my childhood, I heard stories about hers: the air raid sirens in Belfast and a Mickey Mouse gas-mask intended to make this fearful object less terrifying to toddlers. It seemingly worked. Even as an adult, she still clung to memories of how important and grown-up carrying it made her feel. Her early life coincided with a period of stringent austerity. Clothes rationing persisted until March 1949 – nearly four *years* after Germany's defeat, one month before she turned eleven.[1] Like most girls of that era, my mother learnt to sew, as well as how to alter and repair existing garments. She made her own outfits from an early age. By her late teens, she already had a penchant for chic two-piece suits and elegant dresses, tailoring a unique wedding ensemble, and later running up clothes for her daughters. Many items I wore as a child were passed down from my big sister to me: hems successively lowered then raised, tiers added or subtracted, alterations masked with strategic rows of braid, lace or ric rac. (My first school blouse – red Viyella with cherry buttons! – was her special creation. If this garment contravened school uniform rules that didn't matter so much. 'Mrs Carruthers' wasn't just my mother, she was also my first teacher at Irvine's Bank Street Primary.) Socialized by scarcity, she wouldn't have dreamt of throwing away a perfectly serviceable piece of black fabric merely because its original wartime function was long since obsolete. It's characteristic not only of her but of her generation that she spotted blackout material's potential for refashioning. Rather than shrinking from a reminder of the air raids that required windows to be tightly sealed after dark throughout her early childhood, she made her daughter a skirt.

I grew up surrounded by hints about the importance of fabric to Britons during and after World War II. But even if I hadn't absorbed this message from my mother's recollections or from her dedication to sewing and salvaging, I'd have gleaned something of the significance of clothing to a country at war from the way in which forties styles – padded shoulders, well-defined waists, wide-legged slacks and wedge heels – periodically cycle back into fashion, never far from view. Memories of how wartime Britons dressed are preserved through annual revisitations of VE Day, illustrated books, films and museum displays showcasing 'Fashion on the Ration'.[2] Online shoppers for fancy dress outfits can now readily find Auxiliary Territorial Service (ATS) or Land Girl uniforms – corduroy breeches, Aertex shirts and bottle-green V-necks loathed by many wearers at the time – given a glamorous makeover in keeping with pervasive nostalgia for a time imagined as more exhilarating, purposeful and community-minded than our own.

In a new age of austerity, we perhaps look back at the forties as more democratic and less wasteful than our current era of heightened inequality and heedless consumption. Back then, *everyone*'s clothing was rationed, regardless of income. Although some undoubtedly had deeper wardrobes than others, few could afford to wear a garment only once or twice before jettisoning it. In 1945, average weekly earnings for men aged over twenty-one stood at £6 4s 4d; for women over eighteen, £3 4s 3d. (Male and female workers in the textile and clothing industries typically earnt about one-third less than the national average.) That same year, with prices capped by the government, a woman's coat cost £20; a woollen dress, £15 15s; a blouse or jumper, £6. In 2023, the average price of a new garment bought in Britain was just £16.70, barely more (and some items less) than apparel cost eighty years earlier. Accustomed to treating clothes as a throwaway commodity, Britons now annually discard an average of thirty-five garments each, tossing half of these – amounting to 711,00 tonnes – into general waste, 84 per cent of which is then incinerated.[3]

Those troubled by the ruinous consequences of disposable fashion have recently rediscovered a past when Britons had to 'Make Do and Mend', extending the lifespan of what they wore, as well as other household fabrics, by careful washing, ironing and storing, as well as by artful darning, patching and repurposing. This motto, launched by the Board of Trade in 1942 and publicized by the Ministry of Information, was operationalized by the Women's Voluntary Service (WVS). In addition to running mobile canteens for service personnel and civil defence workers, the WVS set up clothing exchanges to circulate second-hand children's garments and shoes – a service that, like rationing, outlasted the war. WVS volunteers also distributed clothing to people bombed out of their homes, and ran classes teaching women how to sew, alter and mend apparel, restyling 'depressing rejects' donated to the organization into 'attractive garments'.[4] Government posters, booklets and short films pumped out a torrent of practical guidance to help Britons extract 'the last possible ounce of wear out' of 'clothes and household things'.[5] Much of this prescriptive advice, dispensed by the cheery rag doll Mrs Sew-&-Sew, was unmistakably angled towards a female audience. While necessity might be 'the mother of invention', mothers were still expected to possess particular inventiveness. Males weren't let off the hook altogether, though. 'Simple jobs boys can do themselves – and so help win the war', at the Board of Trade's behest, included sewing on buttons and darning holes poked through sock toes and jumper elbows.

Figure I.1 The Board of Trade's cheery rag-doll figure 'Mrs Sew-&-Sew' offers tips on how to 'Make Do and Mend', c. 1943 (National Archives)

Some wartime tips continue to resonate. Other injunctions remind us that, in returning to the 1940s, we're entering less familiar territory – if not a foreign country. 'Now that rubber is so scarce your corset is one of your most precious possessions', a 1943 *Make Do and Mend* booklet cautioned. 'The greatest enemies of rubber are sunlight and grease. Never let your girdle get really dirty.'[6] This was doubtless easier said than done, since soap and other detergents were every bit as elusive as new elasticized underwear. The latter problem might, however, be remedied by improvising a home-made foundation garment. Advertisers of Lux soap, for instance, encouraged women to plunder net curtains for transformation into lacy brassieres with a 'pre-war French accent!'[7] Government ministries and commercial interests joined forces to promote 'Making Do' as a patriotic credo that would help secure victory by ensuring every last scrap of material that might prove serviceable as *matériel* was put to martial use. Long before anyone talked of 'upcycling', Britons in the forties learnt how to turn one piece of fabric or yarn into something else by unpicking or unravelling, taking up scissors and needles, and starting over.

Clothing and footwear were critical to the epic 'starting over' that followed the most calamitous conflict in human history. How textiles contributed to postwar reconstruction is far less well remembered or understood than the history of wartime fashion. Yet material stuff – clothes and shoes, blankets and bedding – was pivotal to the refashioning of relationships within the British Isles, as between Britons and others they encountered at home and overseas: American troops 'over here', British GI brides 'over there', service personnel from Britain's colonies, survivors of Nazi camps, displaced persons and immigrants. *Making Do* traces these entanglements to offer a textured reappraisal of postwar Britain and a world remade by devastating violence.

Today it's easy to forget that fabric is a fundamental human need. We could be forgiven for supposing that dress primarily serves an ornamental function: communicating coded messages about identity, status, personality and style. Anyone lucky enough to possess a well-stocked wardrobe of outer garments and underwear, apparel for different seasons, occasions and activities, along with several pairs of shoes and boots – plus bedclothes and towels, curtains and cushions – is apt to take fabric for granted. Clothing is cheaper than ever before; so staggeringly superabundant that it's hard to recall this hasn't always been, and isn't invariably, the case. When we consider life's basic necessities, we probably think first of food, shelter and medicine before recalling garments and footwear as seemingly second-order, more readily satisfied human needs.[8]

Yet, without material to cover them, exposed bodies are vulnerable to various forms of harm. 'Bare life', quite literally.[9] Humans need fabric to shield us from the sun, to ward off cold and rain, as well as to preserve modesty. While clothes offer insulation against burns, frostbite and disease, footwear is just as crucial to wellbeing. 'A man who has no shoes is a fool,' snapped a well-shod Greek at Primo Levi, whose flimsy foot coverings fell apart as they attempted a hazardous journey from Auschwitz. 'Few times in my life, before or after', Levi recalled in *The Reawakening*, 'have I felt such concrete wisdom weigh upon me.'[10] Sturdy leather footwear enabled escape; bare feet were likely to ensure death. But the possession of garments and footwear does not invariably confer dignity, comfort and protection. In the late nineteenth century, scientists began probing the nexus between clothing and contagion, attempting to understand how highly infectious diseases spread.[11] Although some early hypotheses were mistaken, dirty garments and blankets can and do transmit infection. By the 1940s, epidemiologists had understood for some time that lice find the seams of garments ideal burrows in which to deposit eggs and excreta. Inhaling the faecal matter of lice infected with the bacterium *Rickettsia prowazekii* causes typhus fever. During the war, British scientific journals published recommendations for how to destroy 'lousy' clothing and blankets. In the first instance, this knowledge was applied to the disinfection of bedding in air-raid shelters, but scientists also cast ahead to contagions anticipated in post-Nazi Europe.[12]

Like human life, fabric is perishable – much more so then than now. Mass manufactured from synthetic materials derived from coal, oil and gas, today's 'fast fashions' are disposable in only one sense. Easily discarded, they do not rapidly disintegrate. Clothing ditched by inhabitants of the Global North, when it isn't simply burnt, accumulates in ever-expanding mountains of stubbornly indestructible stuff in landfill sites, primarily in sub-Saharan Africa.[13] In the 1940s, however, relatively few garments were produced from man-made fibres. World War II boosted experimentation in new 'miracle' materials, often touted by manufacturers and political leaders as a dividend that would help compensate for years of sacrifice – once swords could finally be hammered into ploughshares. Servicemen reading the *SEAC News* in August 1944 learnt, for instance, that it was probable women would 'soon be wearing clothes from old milk bottles. Glass is now being woven into a taffeta-like material. A bride has already been married in a glass wedding dress.'[14] The reoriented wartime economy likewise popularized *interwar* innovations such as rayon as an alternative to silk. Perfect for parachutes, rayon could also be fashioned into dresses and stockings. Nevertheless, most wartime clothing continued to be made from natural fibres – cotton, wool, hemp, linen – more susceptible to deterioration. In addition to exhorting Britons to 'Make Do and Mend', the Board of Trade entreated people to 'Fight the Moth' by airing garments regularly and brushing them 'thoroughly and often, especially in folds and seams'.[15] Prone to attack from moths and fur beetles, to say nothing of Britain's mildew-inducing climate, clothes left behind by departing servicemen and women weren't always serviceable on return. Bodies had altered too. War work, variously undertaken in factories, on farms or at the front line, reshaped physiques. Even clothing that survived temporary abandonment might prove unwearable when the owner returned home, more slender or bulkier, and with differently contoured feet.

Figure I.2 'Making do' entailed not only altering and mending garments, but also preserving them from attack, Board of Trade, c. 1943 (© Imperial War Museum, Art. IWM PST 8039)

If war provided an education in perishability, it also delivered inescapable lessons in the symbolic potency of clothing: a semiotic system through which identities were established, allegiances signalled and hierarchies maintained.[16] Commentators on wartime Britain routinely remarked on the ubiquity of uniforms, with one-quarter of the adult population attired in some distinctive organizational apparel. By the end of the war, more than 3 million British men had served in the military, along with over 600,000 women.[17] Uniforms of the armed forces, plus numerous civilian organizations, stamped the wearer as belonging to a particular institution. Differences in the cut and colour of uniforms, as well as in insignia and headgear, simultaneously denoted which rung of the organizational ladder that individual occupied.[18] Whether someone had a civilian occupation or served in the armed forces – their status as ally or enemy – could all be deduced from what a person wore. Or seemingly so, because while clothes might be encoded with meaning, they could of course be swapped. In the war's chaotic final months, garments were often appropriated to confuse and deceive. Individuals looking to escape enemy clutches or, like a large number of Red Army personnel, to evade their *own* officers and flee their homeland at the war's end, sometimes switched uniforms with erstwhile opponents. Others bartered with civilians for unmarked clothing, or simply looted it. In the spring of 1945, British and American soldiers encountered SS officers trying to escape postwar justice by scrambling into the very striped camp uniforms with which they'd branded their victims.[19] Meanwhile, in Belgium's Ardennes region, decimated by the *Wehrmacht*'s final all-out offensive, some Belgians were so hungry in March 1945 that they put on pilfered German uniforms. Such was their desperation that being captured by Allied troops as enemy POWs seemed the best chance of securing regular meals.[20]

Germany's surrender in May 1945, followed by Japan's in August, marked watershed moments in the history of both dressing up and dressing down, as this book's first chapter shows. The very language of postwar brimmed with allusions to fabric. Radical shake-ups effected by nearly seven years of total war required national life and the global order to be 'refashioned'. Peacetime called for 'refurbishment' and 'renovation', but the years immediately following 1945 were also marked by 'unravelling' and 'fraying' – of former allegiances and imperial ties alike. Some of this figurative language was both self-conscious and grandiose. The Allied blueprint for the military government of Germany, JCS 1067, promulgated by the US Joint Chiefs of Staff in September 1944, sternly decreed that the country would 'not be occupied for the purpose of liberation but as a defeated enemy nation'.

General Dwight D. Eisenhower (Supreme Commander of the Allied Expeditionary Force) would preside over the rubble of the Third Reich, 'clothed with supreme legislative, executive, and judicial authority' – military power conjured as a magician's cloak.[21]

On both sides of the Atlantic, politicians and journalists spoke of a need for 'belt tightening' through an extended period of reconversion. Economies would need to reabsorb millions of demobilized service personnel, while factories simultaneously shifted back to civilian production. For their part, ordinary Britons employed homely metaphors to convey an aspiration to 'pick up the threads'. Nella Last, a Cumbrian housewife and WVS volunteer, noted in August 1945 that she felt 'like a piece of elastic that has been stretched and stretched and now has no more stretch – and cannot spring back'. Last's diaries, written for Mass Observation, an organization established in 1937 to amass and preserve 'an anthropology of ourselves', posthumously made her famous, incarnated by Victoria Wood in a television dramatization, *Housewife, 49.*[22]

Although *Making Do* foregrounds the United Kingdom, the canvas is necessarily much wider. Across the world, the textile, rubber and leather industries were in crisis by 1945. Clothes and shoes were in desperately short supply almost everywhere except the United States, and scarcer there too than before the war. How would millions of bodies – many in threadbare apparel or none at all – be respectably clad? This wasn't a peripheral issue, as those who dismissively equate clothing with fashion, and fashion with frivolity, might imagine. Remedying a dire lack of garments, bedding and footwear represented one of *the* pre-eminent challenges of the postwar world. In 1944, the US National Planning Association circulated a pamphlet entitled *Clothing and Shelter for European Relief*, which bluntly stated that in continental Europe 'thousands have died of exposure'. Predicting epidemics incubated amid overcrowded conditions, as unwashed bodies clad in 'foul rags' jostled together without adequate shelter, the authors insisted 'Europe needs warmth almost as urgently as food; it is a medical necessity.'[23] Six days after Japan surrendered, President Harry Truman issued a more expansive warning: 'Without adequate clothing and other necessities of life to sustain victims of war on the long road to rehabilitation there can be no peace.'[24]

A war that enmeshed every continent sundered global supply lines and reshuffled manufacturing priorities, exposing the extent to which Britain's textile industries were not hemmed by *national* borders. An abundance of wool from sheep grazing on the uplands of Scotland, Wales and England may have inspired British inventors to dream up more ingenious ways of carding their fleece, spinning it into yarn and making garments from the resulting fibre, helping catalyse the Industrial Revolution. But Britain's dominant position in world textile markets wasn't an insular phenomenon. It relied on imperial patterns of appropriation, import and export.[25] Revisiting Bradford in 1933, popular author J. B. Priestley mused that his hometown was 'at once one of the most provincial and yet one of the most cosmopolitan of English provincial cities', thanks to the wool trade on which it relied. Textiles gathered 'the ends of the earth together', whether or not Bradford folk perceived these filaments of far-flung connection.[26] British cotton manufacturers likewise sourced raw material from distant territories in east Africa and Asia, as well as former colonies in the American South. When World War II began, Britain's textile and garment industries were important contributors to national wealth, but in comparative global decline. Factory owners had been slow to modernize conditions in dangerous, insanitary and unhealthy workplaces. War accelerated the sector's downward trajectory. As conscription mustered legions of textile workers into uniform, transplanting thousands more into armament factories, wool and cotton mills lost about a third of their workforce. In some places, mills themselves turned into munitions plants.[27]

Wartime textile production in Britain, as elsewhere, primarily served military needs. Factories ran up vast quantities of fatigues, tunics, greatcoats, capes, caps, hats and all the sundry pieces of kit – duffle bags, blankets, tents, parachutes, webbing, netting – that armed forces at war couldn't do without, along with shoes and boots. In 1940 alone, British manufacturers churned out 17,550,000 battle-dress blouses and trousers, 16,558,000 shirts and vests, 3,681,000 greatcoats and 11,592,000 pairs of boots.[28] The same US report on the plight of shivering Europeans noted that Britons' annual civilian clothing consumption, circumscribed by rationing, amounted to just 'one-third of the clothes an average American buys in a year (in terms of yardage of cloth used)'. In 1944, Britain's Board of Trade allocated 500 million yards of fabric to civilian production, 'less than half of pre-war civilian consumption'.[29] A chronic shortfall of civilian apparel thus co-existed alongside, and largely due to, a surfeit of military 'stuff'. Postwar redress would require the reorientation of

British textile manufacturing in tandem with a massive redistribution of repurposed military apparel.

The scarcity of commodities of every type – but particularly of cotton, wool, rubber and leather – gave a pointed edge to decisions about *entitlement.* Harold Lasswell's adage that politics is about 'who gets what, when, how' held particularly true in the aftermath of an unprecedentedly ruinous war.[30] Who owed what to whom exactly? Who would be clothed and shod at whose expense? In a world of shortages, decisions about the allocation of resources often had a zero-sum character. Some would be smartly dressed while others remained tattered. Austerity sharpened awareness of inequity. Was it fair, some Britons wondered, that Princess Elizabeth received 100 extra clothing coupons for her bridal gown when she married Philip Mountbatten in 1947 while other brides got none? And what about those demob suits, sported by many of the younger men who gathered in London for the Victory Parade of June 1946 and the following year's royal wedding? The government's decision to reward demobilized servicemen with a whole new wardrobe (discussed in Chapter 3) wasn't uniformly welcomed by Britons as a fitting token of gratitude towards those who had borne arms and made sacrifices on the nation's behalf. It occasioned a good deal of grumbling. Civilians had suffered too. They'd lost homes to bombing raids and endured separation from loved ones, most anguishingly from evacuated children. Women were compelled after 1941 to join the armed forces, work in an essential industry or volunteer for civic service in a war-related capacity.[31] Yet female veterans received only cash and coupons, not clothes, when they exited the services. They nevertheless fared better than British West Indian veterans, who got neither demob suits nor coupons, just promissory notes. Their stories are told in Chapter 4.

Clothing was not, of course, the only issue to animate bitter entitlement struggles in the war's aftermath. Food did too. The 'textile famine' of the 1940s had a counterpart in the lean years that accompanied and followed the war.[32] Hungry, sometimes starving, people were also often under-clad people. This double helix of distress exacerbated vulnerability to disease, depression and premature death. Food, like clothing, is at once a universal human need and culturally specific in its preparation and consumption. The same raw ingredients yield very different dishes depending on how they're combined, seasoned and cooked. Likewise, fabric can be sewn in many styles. But garments have distinct attributes exclusive to *worn* things. Hugging the wearer's skin, articles of apparel acquire human properties, moulding to the shape of a body through frequent contact and absorbing its particular odours.[33] There is, in short, something singularly *intimate* about clothing. While food can certainly be shared, edibility is finite. What's eaten, in short, can't be exchanged and transformed again and again in the same way that garments and footwear, in changing hands, acquire new guises and significations. Because of both its tremendous variety and its centrality to self-presentation, clothing was a much trickier commodity than food to distribute fairly. Quaker relief worker Francesca Wilson issued a prescient caution in a 1944 pamphlet *Advice to Relief Workers*, based on her experience after the Great War and during the Spanish Civil War: 'More anguish of heart is caused by the injustice of clothing distributions, where every item is different from every other, than by any other form of relief.' And so it proved.[34]

If the story of postwar clothing is bound up with calculations of eligibility, it's also about competing visions of retributive justice. In Britain's quadrant of defeated Germany, military personnel and relief workers had to figure out how to clothe survivors of Nazi camps who possessed nothing, or nothing but those striped uniforms that have come to emblematize genocide (a history traced in Chapter 2). One way to muster up garments was to impose a levy on German civilians, whose clothing appeared conspicuously smart and suspiciously abundant, acquired at the expense of those from whom it had been stripped by *Wehrmacht* troops or SS personnel. British squaddies were often infuriated by Germans' unwillingness to part with garments and bedding, as by the trickery they employed to make it seem as though they were surrendering usable supplies when in fact they were handing over sabotaged material. But, as Chapter 5 reveals, it didn't take long before British attitudes began to soften towards a despised wartime foe.

Changes that occurred soon after the Axis powers' defeat, whether of garments or attitudes, can't be understood as exclusively *post*-war phenomena. Indeed, one of this book's central themes, reflected in the layering of chapters that trace intersecting stories of different protagonists, is how elusive any sense of war's categorical past-ness was to those experiencing its aftershocks. As historian Andrew Buchanan convincingly argues, the war – itself a constellation of local, national and intra- and inter-continental conflicts – had multiple staggered and 'ragged endings'.[35] Although *Making Do* focuses on the refashioning of bodies and body politics after the Axis powers' defeat, many key policies, processes and organizations that shaped clothing distribution in the wake of war began *during* it. In Britain, clothes rationing and a whole slew of government controls over textile manufacture began in 1941. The year 1945 marked the mid-point of coupon books' eight-year existence. Humanitarian relief agencies likewise began planning, and in some areas operating, well before VE and VJ Days.[36]

The enormous task of outfitting distressed people was both a national and a multilateral undertaking. In Britain, the WVS took the lead in domestic recirculation of worn garments, some donated by Britons, others by the American Red Cross. For poorer people, there was nothing novel about wearing second-hand apparel; nor in 'making do'. In 1938, the Pilgrim Trust, dedicated to improving conditions for disadvantaged Britons, found that 'less than 50% of the industrial population was adequately clothed'.[37] A significant proportion of Britain's clothing stock in the first half of the twentieth century, as in previous eras, changed hands via market stalls, jumble sales, pawn shops, door-to-door peddlers and other traders in material collectively known as 'rags'.[38] One wartime shift was the volume of donated fabric and footwear arriving from overseas. In the United States, the British War Relief Society (BWRS) began work in 1939 to assist a beleaguered ally by supplying 'Bundles for Britain'. One bemused Royal Navy seaman, Jack Bamford, found himself during a five-week hiatus in Brooklyn (en route to the Falklands in 1942) assigned to work in a BWRS establishment near Times Square in Manhattan. The premises, Bamford noted, were 'littered with … clothing of all descriptions, boots, shoes, hats, coats and even discarded furs'. Mounds of 'books, games, children's toys, crockery, cheap jewellery', along with 'every conceivable oddment that one would expect to find in a sort of old curiosity shop', added to the Dickensian atmosphere, as did the formidable 'voluntary lady workers nursing sympathies for besieged Britain'.[39]

British officials who evaluated the calibre of incoming American bundles were just as sceptical as Bamford about the practical value of these well-meaning efforts. Many garments appeared 'inferior and ludicrous'; shoes were 'freaks … in very small sizes with very high heels'. Perhaps, Board of Trade personnel mused, these donations could be dispatched to continental Europe. However, off-loading them onto liberated peoples would be 'ungracious and likely to lead to unnecessary trouble if we remind the Allies they are poor relations', by sending 'bad quality clothes or ones of really ridiculous fashion'. 'Beggars can't be choosers', the old adage goes. But these civil servants demonstrated that beggars could be both choosy and bigoted when they ridiculed artlessly hand-sewn American donations as seeming 'to have been made by and for the coloured people of the Southern States'.[40]

Other garments sent to the British Isles came from the Dominions and colonies, though changing tides of battle swiftly reversed flows of aid. No sooner had the Ministry of Information released a set of inspirational photographs in December 1941, showing women volunteers sewing garments in Government House, Singapore – 'whence over a thousand cases of clothes have been shipped to the needy in England' – than this British colony, along with Malaya (as it was then known), was overrun by Japanese forces. The fall of Singapore in February 1942 represented the largest surrender in British military history, while Malaya's loss cut Britain off from its primary source of rubber and principal generator of dollar earnings. In 1939, Malayan plantations yielded 38 per cent of the global rubber supply – a resource vital for military purposes as well as for sundry civilian applications, from car tyres to plimsolls, condoms to corsets.[41] With thousands of British residents of Southeast Asia interned under punitive conditions in Japanese camps, internees' projected postwar clothing needs were added by relief agencies to an ever-expanding list of people who were likely to emerge from the war – *if* they survived it – with nothing to wear. Meanwhile, civic authorities and head teachers in the German-occupied Channel Islands frantically tried to alert Westminster to the crisis of a lack of clothing and shoelessness afflicting the islands' children.[42]

Wartime preparations for postwar reconstruction assumed their most far-reaching institutional form with the inauguration of the United Nations Relief and Rehabilitation Administration (UNRRA) in November 1943. In anticipation of the economic devastation and human misery that would surface as Axis troops receded from territories under their wartime occupation, forty-four members of the Allied coalition began to draw up plans for managing the 'margins of chaos'. UNRRA envisioned provision of food, shelter and clothing as preliminary steps towards the longer-term goal of 'rehabilitating' ravaged places and people. Directed by former New York state governor Herbert Lehman, UNRRA would play a key role in supplying inhabitants of liberated territory and survivors of Nazi camps with clothing and footwear.[43] In the war's final months, UNRRA stepped up its efforts to secure donated clothing, principally from Americans with deeper closets. 'They Can Wear What You Can Spare' ran the slogan for a 'Victory Clothing' drive launched in April 1945.

Figure I.3 As part of a 'United National Clothing Campaign' on behalf of UNRRA, American children solicit donations, April 1945 (New York State War Council agency activities, New York State Archives)

Meanwhile, UNRRA staff negotiated with the US military for vast quantities of battledress tunics, trousers, greatcoats, blankets, underwear, socks and boots. In due course, the agency would become the major artery through which army surplus circulated into civil society. But none of this was seamless. Both the US and the British military establishment were reluctant (sometimes loath) to let non-military personnel acquire their kit: a possessiveness that encompassed destitute refugees and UNRRA relief workers themselves.[44] Some enlisted men shared the top brass's disgruntlement over 'feather-merchants wearing either all, or part, of the uniform of the U.S. Army', as one GI protested to *Stars & Stripes* in July 1945. 'I'm referring to the male Red Cross workers, war correspondents (when there ain't no more war in these parts), people running around with weird-looking red tabs labeling them as UNRRA personnel.' He ended this diatribe with a rhetorical barb: 'To satisfy what apparently is their obvious exhibitionist tendencies, why aren't they issued zoot suits?' This aggrieved serviceman signed himself 'Fed Up With The Set Up', though he was evidently also fed up with the get-up favoured by young Black and Mexican American men.[45]

Prejudiced this GI may have been, but he wasn't alone in thinking that *everyone* sported a uniform in July 1945. UNRRA was no exception. The agency was intent on its own staff wearing military apparel, including a red shoulder flash embroidered with its acronym, also emblazoned on the forage cap that topped the ensemble.[46] One of many paradoxes to mark postwar clothing relief was that the very outfits dedicated to this work imposed their *own* demands on overstretched supplies, insisting that their staff must all be distinctively uniformed – distinguishable not just from the military personnel who provided their kit, but from other relief agencies. UNRRA followed the lead of organizations like the Salvation Army, which literalized its conception of the 'Christian soldier' by adopting a quasi-martial uniform in the 1880s. Free from 'all worldly finery, such as gold and silver ornaments, flowers, feathers, fashionably-cut apparel, and the like', this outfit represented, in the estimation of one 'soldier of Christ', 'a magnificent exercise in self-denial for the wearer'.[47] In contrast, the committed pacifists of the Friends Relief Service looked askance at military apparel, consenting with reluctance to uniforms of 'Quaker grey', adorned with the eight-pointed black and red 'Quaker star' first adopted in the Franco-Prussian War.[48] Similarly, the WVS, which prided itself on its horizontal civic-mindedness, opted to have a uniform designed. (Irish couturier Digby Morton won the commission.) 'Jealousy about clothes [could] cause friction', the WVS's official history noted. But, since WVS volunteers received no extra coupon allowance for these garments, their adoption may well have precluded some poorer women from joining what remained a predominantly middle-class organization.[49]

Relief agencies, having first outfitted themselves, quickly developed networks through which fabric circulated within Britain and traversed the postwar world, passing between multiple different pairs of hands, from one wearer to others, via a string of intermediaries. And while clothing flowed from place to place, people did too. The years immediately following World War II were marked by intense mobility as millions of service personnel returned home or moved to different locations. While many Axis troops were confined as prisoners of war, millions remaining encamped in the USSR until the 1950s, Allied combat troops became armies of occupation, presiding over defeated populations across Europe and Asia. Only gradually did demobilization turn soldiers back into civilians. And all the while, vast masses of refugees fled persecution or were forcibly moved, encamped, then set in motion again.[50] Alterations in status – from soldier to prisoner, veteran to civilian, camp inmate to 'displaced person' – were often mediated by a change of apparel. As millions of soldiers stepped out of battledress, innumerable civilians stepped into military uniform – dyed and stripped of insignia, but unmistakably army surplus nonetheless.

To scrutinize postwar clothing is to look anew at an era we may think we already know well. But, in *Making Do*, familiar landmarks such as the Beveridge Report, industrial nationalization and the creation of the National Health Service form the backdrop to less familiar – more personal and tactile – postwar reconstructions. Between 1945 and 1950, huge transformations occurred at every level: individual, familial, local, national and global. Yet in Britain, even as millions of service personnel returned home, thousands of immigrants came and emigrants went, a welfare state took shape, wartime allies spectacularly fell out, a third world war was repeatedly forecast, and former enemies came to appear more sympathetic, it could feel as though *nothing* was changing. Or not fast enough. Rationing persisted, along with shortages and queues. 'Making do' – a mantra some uttered through clenched teeth, others with more chipper resolution – remained the order of the day far longer than most Britons expected. What did winning a world war *mean* if victory's fruits were so slow to ripen, the harvest seemingly so meagre?

This is a book about *alteration*: lives made over, but not always mended. At the most literal level, it concerns adjustment to, and of, different garments at a time when clothing and footwear were alarmingly scarce. But, since garments provide our 'social skin', it's also about altered self-perceptions and reconfigured relationships between Britons and a variety of others, particularly Britain's primary ally and creditor, the United States, and its most bitterly fought wartime enemy, Germany, as well as those persecuted by the Third Reich. *Making Do* brings into focus Britain's corroded empire and eclipsed hegemony, as the baton of world leadership passed decisively from London to Washington. These geopolitical currents rippled through everyday life, felt at the level of the worn, and the worn-out. Britons surely felt diminished as they encountered American GIs and journalists, not only much better outfitted, but prone to characterizing Brits as threadbare, shabby and dowdy. Readers of *Vogue* who'd internalized the magazine's message (in September 1939) that it would be a 'calamity if war turned us into a nation of frights and slovens', would have been chagrined to read a *New York Times* feature (in September 1945) entitled 'Winning the Peace', which depicted Britons as 'tired, cross and impoverished'. Columnist Anne O'Hare McCormick quoted a returning British officer shocked at how 'down-at-heel' his fellow citizens appeared. 'It takes the light of peace to expose the deadly wear and tear of war', McCormick concluded: grist to her mill that the United States had 'the first responsibility to fashion a structure to fit the new world environment'.[51] Britons weren't just figuratively 'down on their uppers'. Many dreamt of escape, looking to the Dominions, colonies and former colonies as places to which they might flee to escape the drab monotony of postwar Britain, craving but also profoundly ambivalent towards 'colour'.[52]

Clothing brings the unevenness of victory into fine-grained focus. Garments, as this book shows, mattered not only for how they looked, but also for how they *felt*: a source of self-worth and individual expression, but also of anxiety about others' assumptions and judgements. In a world of want, clothing determined what people could or could not do, because of what they did or did not possess. Having no footwear might mean going without work. Barefoot children couldn't attend school. Feelings of disgrace occasioned by shabby attire could also trap and immobilize. For Britons, as for others coming to terms with the war's shattering consequences, adequate garments and shoes were preconditions of postwar recovery.

Swamped as we now are by disposable fashion, *Making Do* reminds us how *indispensable* clothing was – and is – to human existence. Far from being a frivolous sideshow, fabric supplies the essential stuff of life.

1 VICTORS

Between 1939 and 1945, Britons encountered no word more frequently than victory. In its pursuit, citizens were compelled to enlist in the services or take up work in factories churning out tanks, aircraft, munitions and other military *matériel*. The War Office-backed National Savings Movement entreated anyone with spare shillings and pounds to 'Save Your Way to Victory', while the Ministry of Agriculture elevated humble vegetable plots and patches into Victory Gardens. By 'Digging for Victory', gardeners would ease the strain on commercial food production and supplement their rations. Exhortations to dig deeper, work harder, sacrifice more and spend less poured ceaselessly from politicians' lips, amplified by Ministry of Information posters and films. Commercial advertisers eager to turn consumption of their product into a badge of patriotic purpose piggy-backed on the prompts of official propaganda. From press photographs and newsreel cameos, Churchill flashed his signature two-fingered salute, widely copied and universally understood. Meanwhile, from radio broadcasts, the opening notes of Beethoven's Fifth Symphony sounded out victory's first letter, transposed into morse code: dot–dot–dot–DASH. Whether at home, at work or at play, there was no escaping the ubiquitous 'V' – a letter, symbol and sound that spelled collective commitment.[1] But after Italy, Germany and Japan surrendered, then what?

So long as fighting continued, many Britons focused on the *moment* of capitulation – peace! – anticipating a climactic burst of exuberant festivity. Britons old enough to have experienced World War I doubtless had their expectations shaped by recollections of the Armistice announced on 11 November 1918. News that the guns across the Channel had 'fallen silent' came in one momentous proclamation, heralded by a national pealing of bells at eleven o'clock in the morning. This historic declaration, commemorated in the twenty-first century in sombre reverence with wreath-laying and a two-minute silence, was greeted with anything but silent circumspection on the day itself. Most cities, towns and villages across Britain erupted in wild celebration. The bells weren't just pealing to mark the end of humanity's most horrific conflict, after all. They were ushering in a new era of perpetual peace – if this paroxysm really *was* the 'war to end all wars'. A 'night of Mafeking' ensued, so described by journalists who invoked the wild jubilation in Britain that had greeted the lifting of a 217-day siege in South Africa during the Second Boer War in 1900. 'Mafficking' became synonymous with frenzied festivity veering towards anarchy. In 1918, Britons again took to the streets. Women dressed in men's clothes to signal their desire for a reversal of the *status quo ante*. Now things *had* to be different. In some places, violence laced public merry-making. Shops were looted, cars overturned, tyres slashed, buildings attacked and fires started in a delirium of destructive energy.[2]

Government planning for VE Day in 1945 occurred under the rubric 'Preparations for Armistice'. Backward-nodding language betrayed the fear that celebrations might again tip over into lawlessness.[3] London's Metropolitan Police commissioner, surveying his bailiwick through jaundiced eyes, feared trouble in the East End, not only the capital's most heavily bombed area, but inhabited predominantly by people 'either of Jewish extraction or of the working class'. 'Both types' were prone to 'excessive excitement', Leman Street police station in Whitechapel cautioned Scotland Yard. Among these east enders lurked 'evilly disposed persons', poised to take 'advantage of Police being fully occupied to indulge in pilfering under the guise of celebrating the "cease fire order"', as had happened on Armistice Day 1918, when an attempted raid was made on the Anchor Brewery in Mile End Road.[4] Alarmism would prove misplaced. Nothing about World War II's ending followed the same script.

This time, victory arrived in dribs and drabs – not all at once. Allied troops first advanced onto German soil in 1944, before getting bogged down and encircled in eastern France and Belgium. But, by March 1945, as the Red Army advanced on Berlin and with British, US and Canadian troops again on the move through Belgium, Germany's defeat seemed a foregone conclusion. By the time *Wehrmacht* generals surrendered in the west on 7 May, Hitler and Eva Braun had been dead for a week, having committed suicide in Berlin's *Führerbunker*, along with Josef Goebbels and his family. In Britain, speculation was rife about when the Prime Minister would *officially* announce Germany's defeat; which precise day would be anointed as VE Day, followed by a promised second public holiday. Churchill's announcement, finally crackling over the airwaves on 8 May, seemed agonizingly belated. 'What strikes me is that the war's ending in just the same phoney way as it began', one forty-year-old woman remarked to a Mass Observation investigator. '"It's peace", "It isn't peace", "They've surrendered", "They haven't surrendered", It does bring back those first months when there was and wasn't a war.'[5]

In London, anticipatory partying began on 7 May, gathering steam the next day as a rumoured *fait accompli* hardened into official fact. But still no 'mafficking'. VE Day was less exultant than we might imagine from newsreel footage and photographs of street parties and knees-ups annually revisited on 8 May. Fixated on Nazi Germany, British memory culture tends to forget something that was far harder for Britons to ignore in May 1945. Namely, that the Third Reich's collapse did not write *finis* to the war as a whole. Those with sons, husbands, lovers, siblings, friends or neighbours deployed in the Pacific, fighting in Burma, or with relatives interned in Japanese camps, knew all too well that there'd be no peace until Japan, too, had been defeated. 'The reminder from official quarters that the Japanese war still had to be brought to a victorious conclusion had a very sobering and useful effect,' one deputy assistant commissioner of the Met remarked. The worst case of 'wanton damage was the burning of a cask of lard and of a crate full of crockery' at a café whose proprietor had 'taken it in good part'.[6] With the Manhattan Project still under wraps – and Japan's determination to fight on until the bitter end taken as a given – nobody knew quite how long war in the Pacific theatre would drag on. Most projections speculatively put Japan's 'unconditional surrender' months, or even years, later than the date we now mark as VJ Day: 15 August 1945.[7]

Victory advanced, along with Allied troops, in increments. Conjured in fantasies, it was foretold in conjecture. Celebrated before official declarations, the war's triumphant outcome was then marked again – and again – on a series of public holidays. These festivities weren't confined to VE and VJ Days. They spilled over into the following year. Britain's culminating Victory Parade processed through London on 8 June 1946. Over the course of the thirteen months that separated Germany's defeat from this last hurrah, many Britons ceased thinking of victory as a euphoric moment, seeing it instead as the start of an unfolding era whose dispiriting character was becoming ever clearer. Clothing was pivotal to each stage of this progression from anticipation to anticlimax. At home and abroad, dressing up and dressing down were crucial both to enacting the Axis powers' defeat and to celebrating military triumph. But a worsening shortage of garments and footwear soon began tugging apart a bundle of terms – 'victory', 'peace', 'prosperity' – that had been used almost interchangeably in wartime. Postwar exposed the delusion of easy elisions.

'Threadbare Millions'

In April 1945, with Germany's downfall imminent, American reporter Richards Vidmer attuned readers of the *Washington Post* to the expectant mood in Britain. His feature trotted out two well-worn generalizations: that Brits looked decidedly shabby, and that they expected to spruce up again soon. 'To the vast majority the end means that rationing of food and clothing, scarcity of transportation and fuel, curtailment of building and repair need not be endured indefinitely.' After four years of restrictions, 'food has become monotonous and clothes are frayed'. Since the introduction of rationing in June 1941, Britons had been 'making do' with alacrity. From what Vidmer reported, tips issued by 'Mrs Sew-&-Sew' had been widely followed. 'Silk linings of prewar coats have been turned into shirtwaists. Curtains and sheets have been made into summer dresses. Mattress covers appear as spring coats. Blankets have been promoted to dressing gowns.'[8]

Past precedent offered little encouragement that peace and prosperity invariably marched in lockstep. Britons who remembered World War I's aftermath – just a generation ago – probably recalled the dosshouses and dole queues of the thirties more vividly than the fabled flapper girls and frivolity of the twenties. But, at the height of the most catastrophic war in human history, few wanted to believe that the cycle of Great War followed by Great Depression would repeat itself. Veterans of that conflict, who'd endured joblessness, infirmity and social neglect, formed an embittered minority. It was much more enticing, however, to hope that this time around the end of hostilities wouldn't mean only, as one woman put it to Vidmer, 'that nothing is likely to fall from the skies at any moment', but that goods would promptly return to the shelves, coupons consigned to oblivion.[9]

Official propaganda, tacitly or more overtly, encouraged Britons to envision wartime scrimping, saving and salvaging as the prelude to postwar spending, fuelling a belief that *consumption* would be one of the most tangible fruits of victory, hanging within easy reach.[10] There was no mistaking the message conveyed by a 1945 poster, prompting women to make use of the Post Office Savings Bank. Houses, holidays or cars might have to wait. But a new outfit was surely a more afford-able and achievable dream – one shared by civilians and women in the services, such as Betty Finlay.

Betty served as an NCO in the Women's Auxiliary Air Force (WAAF), spending the final months of the war stationed in Colombo. An avid letter-writer, Betty filled notes to her mother and aunt with voluble chatter about her wardrobe woes. Indeed, clothing and dat-ing formed her two staple topics, not always unrelated. Boyfriends-in-uniform, in more abundant supply than new clothes, sometimes supplied scarce items of apparel, such as airmen's stockings that Betty cut down to size as a replacement for socks stolen on the voy-age out. Aside from the difficulty of finding husband-calibre material, Betty's tribulations were many. She decried the expense and dearth of dresses available locally in Ceylon. Cotton frocks sold for 90 rupees, about 120s or £6, Betty explained, yet in terms of quality they were 'nothing!'. Like many other women, she made some of her own gar-ments, lamenting the impossibility of sewing lace-trimmed knickers while surrounded by a circle of gawping sailors. To introduce novelty and variety into their wardrobes, Betty and her fellow WAAFs end-lessly swapped clothes with one another. But these borrowings didn't staunch her desire for exclusive ownership of desirable items, nor did they diminish Betty's fears that her best frocks left behind in Essex were rapidly depreciating assets. 'I think with bitter regret', she wrote home, 'esp[ecially] of my white piqué frock and that green linen one – hanging at home – getting old and out of date!' Even in wartime, the seasonal cycles of fashionability were much shorter than the natural life-span of fabric.

Figure 1.1 Official agencies encouraged Britons to believe that consumer goods, including new outfits, would soon become more readily available once victory had been achieved (National Savings Committee/HMSO; © Imperial War Museum, Art. IWM PST 16368)

Over the summer of 1945, Betty's thoughts turned ever more obsessively to how she'd spend the £12 allowance, along with extra clothing coupons, she'd heard WAAF veterans would receive on demobilization. She made detailed plans for shoes and woollens she hoped to acquire in Ceylon, separately itemizing what she'd buy in England and quizzing her mother and aunt as to the quality, cost and desirability (or otherwise) of the colours of light-weight wool cloth available at home. 'I am looking forward to coming back and going shopping with you Mummy and [aunt] E, because I shall be able to start from scratch and choose things that I really like and want and best of all – I shall know that I can wear them and not have to spend half my time in a uniform,' Betty gushed on 10 August, the day after the Soviet Union entered the war against Japan, and an American aircraft dropped an atomic bomb on a second Japanese city, Nagasaki. 'We are all looking forward to shopping – even if everything is Utility!,' Betty declared.[11] 'Utility' referred to garments sold at state-controlled prices, conforming to Board of Trade specifications as to fabric and design.[12]

Betty and her fellow female veterans may have been disappointed with what they found in British shops on return home a few months later. Fantasies of postwar abundance proved to be exactly that: wish-fulfilment projections. At the height of the war, members of Britain's coalition government hesitated to conjure the dispiriting prospect that an age of austerity lay just over the horizon. But overseers of the national economy anticipated that ongoing privation was more likely to persist for years than mere months, with the textile and clothing industries destined to be among those hardest hit by 'reconversion' to civilian-oriented production. Privately, Sir Stafford Cripps warned that, 'quite apart from any improvement in standards, we are going to be very hard put to it to maintain or preserve our pre-war standards'.[13]

As Germany's defeat edged within sight, public acknowledgement of bleaker postwar prospects began issuing from Westminster. In March 1945, Viscount Simon (a Welsh Liberal who served as Lord Chancellor) wrapped up two days of debate on government controls over industry and prices in the House of Lords with a warning that restrictions on food and clothing would need to remain in place after the Axis powers' defeat. 'I do not think our women walk about with bare legs so much because they think they add to their attraction, but because they cannot buy enough stockings,' the peer mused, before asking and answering a rhetorical question. 'Will that stop when the fighting stops? No.'[14] Less than ten days later, as headlines trumpeted that American troops had taken Koblenz, with Eisenhower warning that Mannheim and Frankfurt faced imminent destruction, a much smaller item on the front page of the *Sunday Times* alerted readers that the current clothes-rationing period would 'almost certainly be extended from the end of July to the end of August'.[15] This stretching amounted to a reduction in the number of clothing coupons by three and a half.

While prospects of victory in Europe brightened, news on the home clothing front grew ever gloomier. With as little fanfare as possible, the Board of Trade acknowledged that 'the end of the war with Germany will not make any appreciable difference for months to come in the supply of goods'. This was, however, hardly the kind of forecast to pass unnoticed. Through the spring, the letters page of *The Times* carried a heated back-and-forth between representatives of different segments of the textile and clothing retail industries about who and what exactly was to blame for an 'acute shortage' of civilian apparel that would only worsen in the latter part of 1945 and 1946. Supplies of raw materials had been interrupted. And yarn stocks were further depleted due to the redeployment of carders and spinners. During the war, one in every three textile workers – from those who transformed raw fibres into fabric to those who turned cloth into finished garments – had enlisted or switched to war-related industrial work.[16] All concerned parties agreed that it would take time to redirect labour back to textile mills when munitions factories shut down and service personnel came home. This transitional phase threatened to be the direst time yet for civilians in search of new clothes. Leaders of the retail trade insisted that a catastrophe had been averted thus far only because a large 'cushion' of stockpiled product, accumulated before the introduction of rationing in 1941, had continued to keep clothiers and department stores supplied into 1945. But, after four years of clothing production primarily oriented towards military needs, this cushion had lost almost all its stuffing. Above all, the sector's vociferous representatives blamed Hugh Dalton, the economist and Labour MP who served as President of the Board of Trade, for prioritizing the need of demobilized servicemen for 'civvies' over those of civilian consumers.[17]

Newspapers confirmed what shoppers already knew all too well. 'Stocks of dress material have never been lower,' one store told Alison Settle, fashion editor of *The Observer*, in April 1945.[18] Under the circumstances, it was hardly surprising that scarcity inspired further black-market ingenuity. Dalton cracked down on a 'Dresses from Dust Sheets' racket, whereby unscrupulous traders sold off-coupon what purported to be mattress covers, dust sheets and pillow-slips – fabric cut into lengths appropriate for the home-sewing of dresses and spring outerwear.[19]

As hostilities in Europe ended with Germany's capitulation, the tempo of the Allied campaign against Japan in Asia accelerated. While British forces, including hundreds of thousands of men mustered from India and African colonies, battled against Japanese soldiers in Burma, their American allies were engaged in far-flung campaigns to regain the Philippines and wrest control of a string of strategically significant Pacific islands – Guam, Iwo Jima, Okinawa – from Japanese troops before assailing Japan's four home islands: an invasion plan later overtaken by events. Following the Soviet Union's entry into the war and the atomic bombing of Hiroshima and Nagasaki, Japan surrendered in August 1945 without Allied invasion. But, before this unexpected dénouement, military planners envisioned a much more protracted conflict that would impose further strain on global supplies of clothing and footwear.[20]

In the Asia–Pacific theatre, Allied personnel required protection not only from Axis armaments but also against a hostile natural environment. Uniformed bodies wilted and chafed under attack from oppressive heat and humidity. Like fabric, bodily crevices that never dried out (particularly between toes and legs) were susceptible to mould and rot. Then there were the many irritants and injuries inflicted by tropical environments' teeming non-human inhabitants – insects and reptiles – as well as plants that poisoned, cut and stung. To shield troops from these many sly nemeses, clothing manufacturers in the Allied countries were required to ratchet up production of specialized apparel and equipment. American columnists alerted fellow citizens in the spring of 1945 that further 'belt tightening' would be required to defeat Japan. Syndicated columnist Thomas L. Stokes warned that, among other shortages, women could expect to find rayon hose disappearing from stores 'because of the need for rayon for mosquito netting for our troops in the Pacific'. Millions of pairs of shoes would be required to equip American GIs, while other supplies were urgently needed for allied Chinese armies battling Japan's occupying forces.[21]

From the vantage point of postwar planners, whether located in Washington, DC, or in Whitehall, it wasn't just Allied legions who required urgent outfitting. Clothing supplies were chronically depleted across much of the world. Far from being a national predicament, this global dearth of garments and footwear loomed as an international humanitarian crisis as profound as it was pressing. The deficit was so severe, warned the US Combined Production and Resources Board in May 1945, that its 'proper treatment' would constitute 'a large factor in the formation of a sound and durable peace for the world'.[22] Planners predicted dire suffering in liberated Europe and even worse conditions across Asia. From Ceylon, *The Times*'s correspondent cabled in March 1945 that some women were 'forced to dress in material made of bark, and many have to stay indoors for lack of clothing'.[23] This revelation placed Betty Finlay's dismay over altogether ordinary, yet exorbitantly priced, Ceylonese cotton frocks in a different perspective.

Over the following year, the shortage of cloth only worsened. British journalists began referring to the country's 'textile famine', gesturing back to the disastrous 'cotton famine' that decimated Lancashire communities in the 1860s, when supplies of cotton from the American South dried up during the Civil War. But fabric scarcity in Britain was far less existential than elsewhere in an empire whose resources had been diverted into servicing the war machine at the expense of local populations. 'Cloth famine', urged Mohandas Gandhi in February 1946, 'can and ought to be averted by telling the millions to spin and weave in their own villages.' His call for self-reliance came too late, though, to save imperilled lives. Devastated by mass starvation, Bengal experienced a 'textile famine' so severe that reports began circulating of corpses unburied for want of shrouds, graves plundered by robbers in search of cloth, and people who committed suicide rather than remain trapped in naked seclusion.[24]

'Victory Clothing'

Preparations to meet this looming catastrophe were most extensive in the country least affected by wartime shortages. As Allied troops liberated swathes of Europe from *Wehrmacht* occupation, prominent American industrialist Henry J. Kaiser (working on UNRRA's behalf and by presidential appointment) launched a 'Victory Clothing' campaign with the goal of amassing 150,000,000 pounds of material.[25]

Times Square, the iconic locale later indelibly associated with VJ Day, played a key role in this carnivalesque campaign. Organizers of 'Clean-Out-Your-Closet week' erected a giant wooden house, twenty feet square and fifteen feet high – 'the world's biggest collection box' – at the foot of a model of the Statute of Liberty installed between Forty-Third and Forty-Fourth Streets. This novelty structure, entered by enormous Dutch-style doors, served as a repository for donations, while Times Square was garlanded with a clothesline from which samples of donated apparel fluttered. On 12 April, thousands of onlookers gathered to enjoy a 'before-and-after pantomime', 'Uncle Sam Comes to the Rescue', in which a clown and stilt artist loaned by Ringling Brothers Circus assumed the lead, bestowing garments on two 'ragged youngsters', played by six-year-old twins from East Forty-First Street.[26]

Other stunts turned the de-accessioning of clothes from a charitable gesture into a titillating spectacle. When Hollywood actors Anne Baxter and Ann Miller posed for photographs during a game of strip-poker intended to raise funds for UNRRA, their disrobing redirected attention from discarded apparel to the stars' own partially nude bodies. No one seemed bothered that their glamorous outfits were hardly the stuff with which victims of Nazi persecution could be respectably reclad. If anything, the mismatch between movie stars' apparel and the needs of war victims elicited sardonic mirth. *Life* magazine, showcasing another photo-op in which movie star Janet Blair peeled off one of her 'famous sweaters', smirked that this donation 'would keep some destitute European girl warm next winter'.[27] The salacious association between women taking garments off and giving them away formed a repeated motif of the 'Victory Clothing' drive, evident in a photograph taken by Weegee (Arthur Fellig) of an unnamed woman's parade through Times Square 'dressed' only in a barrel and sandals. Appropriation of the stripped female body as a fund-raising device becomes all the more disconcerting when we note that April 1945 was also the month in which footage shot at liberated Nazi camps began reaching cinema screens. Unprecedentedly graphic, these newsreels horrified viewers with the sight of barely clothed or nude skeletal bodies; living survivors outnumbered by mounds of naked corpses.[28]

Supporters of UNRRA conceived second-hand clothing collection as a vehicle to promote postwar internationalism, persuading Americans to cast off vestigial isolationism. After World War I, US politicians and a large segment of the population had rejected membership

Figure 1.2 An unnamed woman in Times Square, New York, advertises the United National Clothing Campaign's drive to muster 50,000,000 pounds of material from the city's residents, captured by celebrated street photographer Weegee (Arthur Fellig), 15 April 1945 (Weegee/International Center of Photography/Getty Images)

of the League of Nations, President Woodrow Wilson's blueprint for collective security. Influential opinion shapers, from Wendell Willkie to Henry Wallace and Eleanor Roosevelt, spent the 1940s encouraging fellow citizens to reconceive themselves not as aloof inhabitants of Fortress America but as *world* citizens.[29] Widely criticized for its sluggish start and the vagueness of its rehabilitative mission, UNRRA had some remedial work to do in persuading Americans that it was both fit for purpose and a worthy recipient of federal funding. The Victory Clothing drive, UNRRA enthusiasts hoped, would build support for this new multilateral venture. 'UNRRA will cease to be a boring subject of newspaper debate and become instead an organisation to which Mother has just contributed her old fur coat,' a diplomat at the British Embassy in Washington enthused to Foreign Office colleagues.[30]

Yet, despite its internationalist goal – to muster supplies for UNRRA – the 'Victory Clothing' drive leant heavily on national exceptionalism in its promotional appeals. Stunts, adverts and press stories reinforced the message that Americans alone possessed both the spare inventory and the spirit of charity necessary to clothe the war's myriad tattered victims. 'Many Americans have on hand a super-abundance of essential clothing in good condition, and a not incon-siderable number undoubtedly have a superfluity of currently scarce items, such as shoes and heavy bedding, put away to service a possible future emergency or hoarded for no good reason,' the *Washington Post* reminded readers.[31] Donating to the campaign offered an outlet for tri-umphalism in the garb of altruism. One veteran, reported the *New York Times*, marked VE Day by donating seven pairs of shoes he'd outgrown from 'marching so much'. Offloading outgrown footwear was, he pro-claimed, 'a good way to celebrate'.[32] Tellingly, the Victory Clothing initiative was rolled out under the banner of a United *National* Clothing Collection, Americanizing a forty-four-member organization. British diplomat David Ogilvy noted a 'sad footnote' to the campaign's 'bril-liant success': 'the public is not aware that UNRRA have anything to do with this old clothes campaign, because the UNRRA publicity – very sagaciously – omits any mention of UNRRA. Too bad.' The organiza-tion's US leadership seemingly feared fellow citizens wouldn't endorse the nation's 'rise to globalism' unless reassured that the United States was first among unequals in the new world order.[33]

Asymmetric power relations found reflection not just in the politics of naming, but also in that of giving. As scholars of humani-tarianism have pointed out, 'helping' is a knotty political, ethical and psychological phenomenon.[34] While donating garments may express empathy with others' suffering and a desire for human connection across national boundaries, 'charity' also enshrines relations of depen-dence between those with and those without: between donors who give material goods and indebted recipients whose docile gratitude is anticipated (or required) in return. Ostensibly free, the gift is a form of encumbrance, trailing strings of expectation. That US citizens were better placed than other nationals to shed unwanted clothing reaf-firmed a cherished self-understanding that Americans were 'people of plenty', doubly blessed by uncommon abundance *and* a generous dispo-sition that made them more inclined than others to share their bounty. This generosity was all the more laudable, Eleanor Roosevelt proposed, because 'it is hard to visualize the needs of others when you yourself are not in want'.[35] Like any cliché about national character, this one ironed out wrinkles visible to those outside the circumference of belonging drawn by the stereotype: in this case, the striking (and strikingly racialized) unevenness in national wealth distribution.

Children figured prominently in the Victory Clothing drive, and a follow-up launched in December 1945, as both objects and agents of US humanitarianism. Magazine adverts made manipulative use of a curly haired toddler, dressed in a shapeless garment suggestive of poverty, neglect and need: one among the 'one hundred million children' UNRRA characterized as 'statistically naked'. The accompanying pitch informed readers that 'Your contribution of old clothing means the difference between suffering and relative comfort – the difference between despair and renewed faith – for some unfortunate person. They ask so little: you can help so much.'[36] With collection boxes set up in local libraries and schools, American children were enlisted to chivvy peers and parents into clearing closets and attics of unwanted items. Newsreel cameras captured scenes in which youngsters excitedly caught garments hurled from the windows of New York apartment blocks, retrieving articles of clothing and teddy bears from the gutter, then tossing them into a truck – images more redolent of garbage collection than humanitarian relief.[37] In this festival of decluttering, no one was too young to play their part. Nine-month-old John Muller, presumably with adult assistance, 'turned in all his outgrown baby wardrobe' to the Brooklyn Civilian Defense Volunteer office, the *New York Times* reported.[38]

By early May 1945, pupils in New York City alone had gathered 2,000,000 pounds of clothing, with boy scouts and girl guides meeting or surpassing impressive quotas.[39] Perhaps they had been inspired to redouble their efforts by Frank Sinatra, who hailed a newly invented demographic, 'you teen-agers':

> American high school students are the 'kids with the sleds'. You know, a kid with a sled can be the most liked or disliked in the neighborhood. It all depends whether he shares his fun with the other kids, or selfishly hides his treasure away from those less fortunate.
>
> To the thin, ragged children overseas who survived the terrible war, many of whom saw their mothers and fathers killed, and their homes burned to the ground – Americans are the 'kids with the sleds'.

> Not that it is sleds these war victims want. It's faded sweaters
> that you have replaced with bright new ones, warm socks
> which you have discarded, shoes which are too small, any-
> thing that you have outgrown.[40]

Junior world leaders, American teens were urged to give – but without sacrificing anything they'd particularly miss or couldn't readily do
without, secure in the conviction that recipients of faded and frayed
donations would be grateful for these cast-offs.[41]

Sinatra was geographically vague when he invoked millions of
barefoot children, sleeping on straw 'because bedding that the enemy
didn't steal was long ago made into crude clothing'. When promotional
materials *did* identify more precise destinations, they highlighted countries liberated from Axis occupation, including the Philippines, a US colony invaded by Japan ten hours after the bombing of Pearl Harbor in
December 1941, and beleaguered China, a key arena for American mis-
sionary activity since the nineteenth century.[42] Strikingly absent from the
United National Clothing Collection's appeals was mention of another
intended recipient of American charity: Britain and its empire. Some
Americans might have felt less warmly about supporting the restoration
of British imperialism in colonies soon to be liberated from Japanese
occupation. But Britain was one of the first countries approached – along
with Ukraine, Russia, Belorusia and China – with an offer from UNRRA
of some 45,000 pounds from the total collected thus far.[43]

British officials were torn. To be the recipient of postwar charity
underscored painful geopolitical realities. But with Westminster's coffers
drained by the monstrous cost of sustaining military campaigns across
several continents over more than six years, Foreign Office personnel
and British Embassy staff in Washington, DC, hesitated to turn down
UNRRA's offer flat. Many British colonies overrun by Japanese troops
during and soon after December 1941 – Burma, Malaya, Singapore,
Borneo, Ceylon and Hong Kong – had been devastated by occupation
and battle. Would 'western type clothing' be suitable for 'native[s] of this
area?', queried UNRRA's director of clothing. This question inspired
a flurry of cables between British diplomats in Washington, DC, and
Foreign and Colonial Office colleagues in Whitehall as they debated
whether clothing was universally interchangeable. Adaptability and
ingenuity, key attributes of the 'Make Do and Mend' credo, apparently
had outer limits. Some people's clothing simply could not be made to

do, it seemed, for others. Certain items appeared so intrinsically place- and purpose-specific, such as men's suits or women's two-piece ensembles (then termed 'costumes'), that British civil servants boggled at the incongruous apparition of 'natives' of Borneo or Burma running around the jungle in American cast-offs. Only after several telegrams had been exchanged did Britons accept UNRRA's offer – so long as the consignment contained plenty of lightweight 'cotton and cotton-mixture garments and undergarments' that Southeast Asian populations could put to use. Perhaps, British civil servants persuaded themselves, bathing trunks could serve equally well as shorts for 'coolies'.[44]

First, though, this clothing had to make the trans-oceanic journey. Then as now, it's easy for people who donate clothing to forget how much time, labour and money is required to sort, pack, load, ship and unload these donations before they reach recipients who'll give discarded clothes a second life, if indeed they find new owners at all. Prior to transportation, clothing and bedding was baled. Individual garments lost their distinctive contours when they were compressed into bulky blocks, approximately seven cubic feet in size. This standardized unit made it easier to calculate how much shipping space clothing would occupy, as well as making clothing simpler to load. For their part, shoes travelled in burlap bags averaging forty-two pounds in weight.[45] Securing shipping space presented an even greater obstacle at a time when every available merchant or naval vessel was needed to transport combat troops from the European theatre to the Pacific. Long delays at every stage meant that Victory Clothing reached Europe and Asia many months after the war's end. The arrival in Hong Kong of '219 bales of old clothing and 157 bags of old shoes' in July 1946 proved profoundly anticlimactic. 'From a cursory examination it appears that the quality of the clothing is very poor,' the Governor of Hong Kong cabled London.[46] If it was chastening for elite Britons to find themselves the object of a former colony's charity, it was even more galling to find that American largesse was largely useless. Mother's 'old fur coat', newly liberated from mothballs, wasn't necessarily any good to anyone.

Dressing Down

Victoriousness found expression through clothing in many other ways besides this US campaign. Since ancient times, victory has been associated with particular trappings – accessorized with laurel wreaths, crowns or trophies.[47] 'To the victor the spoils,' a familiar proverb runs. And, it might be added, the *styles*. In the imagination, winners do more than exult in expropriation of defeated enemies' territory and property. Adorned in ostentatious raiment, the victors stand in stark sartorial contrast to the tatters of the vanquished. Victory has a palpable aura, or so it's often supposed. The *Daily Mail* tapped into this reservoir of stock imagery when, on 9 May 1945, it reported Germany's surrender: 'London, battle-scarred but triumphant, dons her gayest apparel for victory. Berlin, in ruins, sits in sackcloth and ashes. Justice has been done.'[48] At its most literal, sackcloth refers to fabric woven from flax or hemp used as sacking. Figuratively, its familiarity derives from the Bible. Instances of 'sackcloth and ashes' litter both the Old and the New Testament, wherein cloth made from black goat's hair signifies abjection or abasement. Wearing this scratchy fabric and sitting in ashes – or being smeared with dust – might be self-chosen to signify the depths of grief. Imposed by some external authority, 'sackcloth and ashes' denote submission and humiliation.

Allied observers on the ground encountered something rather different from the *Mail*'s morally gratifying tale of two cities: resplendent London lording it over downtrodden Berlin. Although large tracts of the German capital had been reduced to rubble, the city's residents, reporters noted, looked better dressed than people brought to their knees had any right to appear, largely because of how pitilessly Nazi personnel had dispossessed their victims (a subject to which Chapter 5 returns). Now it was Berliners' turn to experience the vengeful rapacity of occupation troops who gleefully styled themselves the 'Lootwaffe'.[49] Paul Mattick, a German-born naturalized American, described in May 1945 how Soviet servicemen prised Berliners' closets open with bayonets, ransacking cupboards and dressers. Red Army soldiers made no secret of their success: 'They sometimes wore two or three sweaters or suits under the military shirts and pants. Hardly able to walk, they advanced from street to street, tommy-gun in one hand and a suitcase of loot in the other.'[50]

Expropriation of others' possessions was one way to enact victors' justice. Victory parades provided another demonstration of who enjoyed the upper hand. Everywhere Allied troops entered in triumph – along with cities from Rangoon to Delhi, which had contributed significant numbers of men to this gigantic mobilization – staged a victory parade at some point, or points. Berlin witnessed a succession. A showy British event on 21 July, attended by Churchill, was followed by a combined Allied parade on 7 September to mark Japan's surrender. Allied commanders hoped to impress Berliners with the finery of their dress uniforms as well as a triumphal show of armoured strength. The brainchild of US General Floyd Parks, the parade sent tanks and guns thundering through central Berlin, while phalanxes of Allied troops marched past a reviewing stand for inspection. Parks may have come to regret his idea, however. The procession down Unter den Linden, recently the scene of climactic skirmishes between Red Army troops and the city's last-ditch defenders, turned into a competition between Berlin's four increasingly fractious occupying powers: the United States, Britain, France and the Soviet Union. 'This parade was really to be a spectacle to impress ourselves, as well as the Germans,' American General Frank Howley confessed in his diary. Not surprisingly, Berliners showed little enthusiasm for watching their conquerors' bids to out-perform one another with displays of heavy weaponry, medals, spit and polish. But, if the victors were primarily attempting to dazzle themselves, their efforts smacked more of animosity than mutual admiration.[51]

In the absence of the most senior American, British and French commanders, Soviet Marshal Zhukov presided, to the undisguised chagrin of the ranking US officer, General George Patton. The Russian looked 'magnificent in his robins-egg blue uniform with fancy red trimmings and decorations hanging almost below his hips', Howley conceded. By Zhukov's right thigh dangled 'something of gold as big as a saucer'. 'The goddamdest Roxy doorman I've ever seen', one GI reportedly quipped.[52] For his part, Patton lacked such showy ornamentation, but surpassed his Soviet rival in finesse. 'Very sharp looking in his riding trousers, highly polished riding boots and helmet liner, together with his pearl-handled pistols', a fellow American admiringly noted. Not content with cutting a snappier figure, Patton was determined to upstage Zhukov on the reviewing stand. 'When the U.S. contingent passed, he took one step, not forward but at the right oblique, so that he half cut off the Marshal's view, and returned General Gavin's salute with a salute to end all salutes.'[53] Not only was Zhukov's line of vision obscured; he was also left in the undignified position of having 'some of his tummy hanging over the front rail', Howley chuckled.[54] But Zhukov may nevertheless have enjoyed the last laugh. The Red Army used the occasion to unveil its new IS-3 'Stalin' tanks, heavier than anything in the American arsenal. Not only that, the Soviets exceeded the agreed quota for vehicles in the procession, determined to make the most impressive showing.

Half a world away in Tokyo Bay, US General Douglas MacArthur, Supreme Commander of the Allied Powers, adopted just the opposite tack when he choreographed Japan's formal surrender on board the USS *Missouri*. Overshadowed by the battleship's enormous guns, a party of Japanese delegates that included politicians, diplomats and military representatives signed the instrument of surrender on 2 September 1945. Every detail of this ceremony was calculated to underscore the ignominy of defeat, although MacArthur insisted that victors and vanquished did not convene in a 'spirit of mistrust, malice or hatred'. Actions, however, spoke louder than words. The very fact that the Japanese party had to clamber aboard the *Missouri* from a smaller vessel that ferried them over from dry land – a particularly taxing manoeuvre for Shigemitsu Mamoru, who wore a wooden prosthetic leg – underscored the power dynamics in play. So, too, did the fact that the Japanese copy of the surrender instrument was covered in humble cloth while the victors' volume was bound in handsome leather.[55]

Figure 1.3 At the surrender ceremony on the USS *Missouri*, 2 September 1945, the Japanese delegates' formal attire stands in stark contrast to the Allied officers' dress with top buttons deliberately undone (Keystone/Hulton Archive/Getty Images)

Above all, though, MacArthur's degradation ritual relied on what one reporter characterized as the 'master dramatist's touch': 'flamboyance in reverse'. The protocol-conscious Japanese dressed in their most formal apparel. While the officers wore uniforms garlanded in brocade, the diplomats donned customary morning attire: top hats and tails, black ties and pin-stripes, white gloves and spats. This antiquated 'get up', chortled one American officer, was 'all that was needed to present a completely comic opera atmosphere'. But this was not *The Mikado*. The Japanese delegates were greeted, after a calculated delay, by Allied commanders not in dress uniforms but wearing plain fatigues. MacArthur, the supreme commander, left his top shirt button undone, as did his colleagues. No accidental oversight, this cavalier gesture was intended to rub Japanese noses in Allied contempt – vanquished foes unworthy of the courtesy of reciprocal formality. The Japanese should 'realize at last', another American noted, 'that they had gotten themselves into a jam'. One kind of dressing down delivered another.[56]

Dressing Up

If the symbolic power of clothing was indispensable to the military choreography of defeat, dressing up was every bit as significant to the civilian festivities that marked first VE and then VJ Day. The *Daily Mail*'s conjuring of Berlin in sackcloth and London in 'her gayest apparel' rang truer in the latter case. Victory celebrations saw the animated capital, along with its inhabitants and throngs of visitors, decked out with flags, streamers and other patriotic insignia. London's iconic landmarks were floodlit for the occasion – a dramatic illumination not only of architectural facades but also of the night sky itself after years of tightly policed blackouts. Even some Londoners who hated crowds, fled from urban revelry and wanted nothing to do with victory parties defiantly pulled back their curtains at home as dusk descended. 'We and our neighbours switched on all our lights again for an hour or two, notwithstanding the injunctions to save fuel and light, but one must celebrate in some way,' Rose Cottrell wrote to her sister in Switzerland from the family home in Bromley, Kent.[57]

For those drawn to collective forms of jubilation, wearing something special, going out, joining a crowd, linking arms, forming impromptu conga lines, dancing, singing and drinking were among the most obvious ways to mark the war's end, stamping it as something *different* – less hemmed in by restrictions. Rationing, whatever people may have hoped, was not about to end. Service personnel would not be instantly demobilized. Nor would shattered cities be rebuilt overnight, or for many years to come. How, then, could victory be appreciated as something that yielded an immediate, meaningful improvement in day-to-day life? Dressing for the occasion allowed individuals to feel part of an historic moment – authors of victory, not just passive bystanders. Partying also served, at least temporarily, to stave off the incipient threat of anticlimax. After six years in which every aspect of national and individual life had been oriented towards one goal, VE and VJ Day quivered with both promise and peril: punctuation marks shadowed by death and loss, uncertainty about what would come next, and a collective desire for, but also fear of, change. 'At this particular time', remarked one observer, 'many folk felt that under our present system having a job, and having a war go together.'[58]

Mass Observation (MO) reports capture the ambivalence that preceded and accompanied VE Day. Anticipation of Germany's impending defeat, 'more or less a fact since March', meant that 'interest in the news had consequently been on the decline for some time'. By early May, with speculation rife about surrender, expectancy jostled with frustration and uncertainty. 'Victory' appeared to be a moving target. Not so much a marker of the *actual* day when fighting stopped, the official announcement of VE Day instead seemed a matter of political wrangling between Washington and Moscow. Or perhaps of more mundane calculation. 'I don't suppose it'll be until Sunday. It'll be better at the weekend. More convenient for everyone,' one woman speculated on 3 May, associating 'victory' with the two days of public holiday promised by the government.[59] Some Britons suspected Churchill was hanging back because officialdom didn't entirely trust people to respond to the news appropriately.[60] This cynicism wasn't misplaced. Cabinet ministers, like Met officers and military commanders overseas, were preoccupied with the spectre that Britons would go wild, forgetting that the Pacific war had yet to be won. In Germany, British officers busied themselves with preparations for sombre, *sober* 'Thanksgiving' ceremonies and prayers. At home, too, the government struck a rather muted note for VE Day, respectful of what had been lost and mindful of sacrifices still to come.[61]

After protracted exertion and amid mounting uncertainty about what would follow the war, Britons grew 'apathetic' – a characterization that recurs in numerous reports on the home front in the war's final phase and immediate aftermath. Mass Observation observers detected a certain aimlessness and perplexity. Spontaneity was stifled by an expectation that someone, somewhere, ought to have planned everything in advance. This hesitancy apparently marked the first eddying swirls of people to take to London's streets on 8 May. Reticent revellers seemed unsure of quite what to do with themselves. 'At first', MO noted, 'hilarity was extremely self-conscious.'[62]

Despite reports of popular apathy, many communities planned elaborate festivities that weren't dependent on 'authorities' laying on victory events. Indeed, one of the most widespread ways of celebrating the war's end skirted official injunctions not to waste anything of 'salvage value' in celebrations.[63] In villages, towns and cities up and down the British Isles, people made effigies of Hitler, dressing him in whatever could be spared, regardless of whether further active duty might yet be teased from these garments. Some communities clubbed together to ensure that different households each contributed an item to the Führer's ensemble. 'Everybody participated in the making of Hitler,' MO observed in one London district. 'One lady gave the jacket, another the trousers and so on until Hitler's rig-out was assured. A dressmaker living in the road gave the dressing up a professional touch. Hitler's clothes fitted to perfection.'[64] Fabric Führers – more or less recognizable, often accompanied by swastika flags – were then dangled from windows, strung up from trees and lampposts or ignited, blazing atop bonfires that had sometimes taken weeks to build. In real life, Hitler may have cheated the Allies by taking his own life before they reached Berlin, but, fashioned from *papier mâché* or straw-stuffed sacking, his likeness didn't evade retributive justice so readily. Crowds around one bonfire, fearing that Hitler was 'starting to burn too quickly', cried out, 'Don't let him end up so soon, let him linger.' If VE Day festivities transposed bonfire night, with its ritual immolation of Guy Fawkes, from November to May, they also jumbled vernacular traditions. In some places, pantomime prevailed. In a Coventry suburb, the send-off of Hitler's effigy spanned two days of merry-making, presided over by a self-appointed 'Mayor and Wife'. The latter was a builder, 'the fattest man in the street, and the jolliest' (according to MO's witness), dressed in 'a very tight dress, with white frillies showing, and with a wig made from pulled out rope'.[65]

Figure 1.4 A group of children in Lambeth, South London, hang an effigy of Hitler on VE Day, 8 May 1945 (Westwood/Popperfoto via Getty Images)

Although officialdom appeared oddly inert, or actively repressive, in the run-up to VE Day, the government nodded towards festivity by ensuring that copious supplies of red, white and blue bunting would be available 'off coupon'. Shoppers could buy as much decorative material as they wished (or could afford) without having to sacrifice any precious clothing coupons. Department stores and independent small traders were keen to cash in on people's eagerness to *wear* their feelings of joy, pride and relief when victory was announced. Mass Observation's report *Victory in Europe* documented that along Oxford Street, in the period leading up to VE Day, 'Victory scarves, streamers, ribbons, rosettes, even hairslides, were on display in the shops, and featured in elaborate counter and window displays.'[66] Some shoppers were so intent on acquiring these gewgaws that they joined snaking queues 150 or 200 people long. Selfridges took the prize for most impressive array of flags. Meanwhile, 'victory scarves' touted triumphal slogans or motifs, such as Jacqmar's silk square printed with a bouquet of Allied flags. Commemorative novelties were not to everyone's taste, however. One woman weighed up, and then against, this purchase: 'It's ever so pretty, but after the war you can't wear that. You'll want to get away from the war.'[67] This anonymous shopper expressed a widespread desire to forge ahead into a resolutely *post*-war era, but she may also have worried about expense. Victory scarves had a particularly short shelf-life, and women without much disposable income had to calculate whether the cost was worthwhile for a souvenir destined to spend far longer folded in a drawer than draped round their neck.

Cheaper options abounded. By early evening on 8 May, observers recorded not only that Trafalgar Square was filling up with revellers, but also that patriotic regalia was becoming more commonplace. Although GIs had been early adopters of the undignified paper party hat, English reserve was being jettisoned. 'Girls pass wearing victory rosettes and hats worded: "Adolph you've had it", "There'll always be an England", "Thanks Monty" and "Kiss my darling."' Seemingly out of nowhere traders popped up hawking an array of V-themed paraphernalia. '"Don't forget to wear your colours/don't forget your victory wavers/don't forget your victory colours,"' these entrepreneurs hailed passers-by. 'Two buxom cockney women rule the roost,' MO related:

> They do twice as much trade as the others, but then they've got unique methods of salesmanship. Mixing with the crowds they call:
> 'Come on now be sporty. 'Ere yer are luv 'ere's yer Montgomery's beret. A bob a time. 'Ow much with the feathers? Two bob complete luv, an' yer all set ready to 'ave a good time.'
> And women and girls of all ages buy their berets allowing the cockney women to put it on for them at the correct sporty angle.[68]

Field Marshal Sir Bernard Montgomery – hero of the Battle of El Alamein in North Africa that marked the war's first major turning point in the Allies' favour in November 1942, renowned for his peacock tendencies and the élan with which he sported his trademark beret – provided a doubly fitting model for victory fashion.

Black and white photographs of VE Day obscure what was obvious to those present at the festivities in London and elsewhere: the profusion of red, white and blue that bedecked both buildings and partying crowds. 'People were in harmony with the idea of colouration to the extent of wearing emblems (out of 100 people counted in St. James' park, 60 – chiefly women – wore some red, white and blue favour),' according to MO.[69] Donning patriotic colours wasn't confined to 'favours' or accessories. Many women selected their entire ensembles to combine red, white and blue, or to accentuate one or two shades of the Union Jack. 'Of course the paper hats, favours, streamers, whistles and all the rest were there, and combined with the colourful dresses made a kaleidoscope of colour,' Rose Cottrell informed her sister of the West End scene.[70]

Photographs and newsreels shot on VE and VJ Day attest a widespread desire to dress up, particularly evident among women. Equally conspicuous are the numbers of those in uniform. Maybe more unexpected is the *variety* amid uniformity. While men from various Allied forces were distinguishable from one another by peculiarities of national uniform, victory licensed liberties with military dress codes. Two soused Aussie soldiers were spotted cutting the ends off one another's regulation ties, while other servicemen accessorized their standard issue apparel in idiosyncratic ways. A sailor from New Zealand was snapped waving a bowler hat, while another pinned an improvised corsage onto a neighbouring GI's battledress blouse.[71]

Many British servicewomen also took to the streets in their uniforms. Land Girls headed for London fresh from the fields in their regulation corduroy breeches and woollen socks. A *Manchester Guardian* correspondent in London registered surprise at the self-sufficiency of all-female groups of revellers. 'One of the curious things has been the number of parties of girls without a man among them walking along the streets and singing,' noted this anonymous (surely male) reporter. Among knots of ATS and WAAF personnel, a gang of Land Army girls chorused their way along Oxford Street. Other groups of women, not in uniform, but 'young clerks or typists, others apparently of the upper middle class', appeared equally 'content to amuse themselves in their own way without any help from the men'.[72]

Women's pleasure in *female* company is an aspect of victory festivity lost to popular recollection. Instead, many of the most widely circulated photographs accentuate male–female conviviality – interactions charged with latent sexual energy. If Victory Days were

Figure 1.5 A group of revellers celebrate in Trafalgar Square on VE Day (Popperfoto via Getty Images)

occasions for party finery and glad rags, they were also moments of slippage when conventional norms of public decorum crumpled. Several VE Day photographs depict people, men and women, civilians and service personnel, taking garments off or hoisting hemlines to flash a bit of leg. One famous picture, regularly republished on VE Day anniversaries and displayed in the Imperial War Museum's foyer, shows two women, trousers rolled far up their thighs, frolicking in the Trafalgar Square fountains alongside two sozzled sailors.[73] Reporters and photographers recorded numerous similar scenes, including another sailor shimmying to the top of Piccadilly Circus's Eros pedestal in the nude, while a nearby GI performed 'a regular strip-tease act up a lamp-post in Coventry Street'. Mass Observation's informant looked on as he 'threw down everything, beginning with his wrist-watch, and only left himself with a little teeny pair of pants – everything else he threw to the crowd'. Other observers captured scenes of women 'doing the Lambeth Walk' and the 'hokey cokey': 'They are wearing bright colours – general effect Red, white and blue, and whenever opportunity permits, they pull up their skirts to show their bloomers, amid shreaks [sic] from the crowd'. Alcohol no doubt added reckless bravado to this merriment, with performers and audiences delighting in the bawdy vaudeville show.[74]

Some women magnetized attention with a combination of personal chutzpah, patriotic colours and photogenic looks. The watchful (or more prurient) gaze of MO's observer in Trafalgar Square lingered, at around 7pm on VE Day, over a 'very pretty girl about eighteen dressed in a red frock with white polka dots, a blue neck square, and shoeless and stockingless', as she perched on the edge of the fountain:

> She's been fooling around with three pompous looking officers of the Norfolk regiment. Lifting up her skirts, she paddles into the water. Two of the officers, roll up their trousers, and follow suit. They climb to the very top of the fountain carrying the girl. When they reach the top they get a cheer from the crowd, and the pretty girl kisses them. British movietone cameramen take photographs. After a while, they paddle back. Lifting up her skirts she calls 'Oh my, I've never shown so much leg in my life.' Male cries of 'Don't mind us.' The captain … lifts her shoulder high. She puts her arms round his neck and the crowd sing 'For she's a jolly good fellow.' And so perched on the captain's shoulder the party leave.[75]

News outlets annually recycle these iconic images as distillations of pure joy: the exultation 'ordinary people' experienced at the war's being over, and being won. Mainstream national memory culture preserves these snapshots in much the same way that Americans have cherished the 'VJ Day kiss' as emblematic of triumphal ecstasy: a moment restaged in the twenty-first century with mass VJ anniversary 'kiss-ins' in Times Square, and made concrete in computer-generated statues entitled 'Unconditional Surrender'. But images can be deceptive. Historian Brooke Blower has perceptively deconstructed Alfred Eisenstaedt's image, first published in Life magazine on 27 August 1945. Her analysis focuses on details often overlooked: the determined way in which the woman (often mistaken for a nurse because of her white outfit) tugs down her hem; the awkward angle at which she's pinioned in a headlock. Blower's interpretation – that Eisenstaedt documented an assault, not reciprocal rapture – is corroborated by testimony from the woman in the photograph herself. Greta Zimmer, a dentist's assistant, emerged after work into Times Square on 14 August 1945 to find herself assailed by a drunken sailor as onlookers stood by and gawped. This stranger grabbed and restrained her before clamping his mouth onto hers: an act of violence far removed from the romance viewers have determinedly projected onto this image.[76]

Sexual violence stalked victory celebrations, exposed in the small print of American newspapers and hidden in plain sight in photographs like Eisenstaedt's. In San Francisco, VJ Day festivities assumed an especially lethal edge. Women 'had clothes ripped from them', the *Los Angeles Times* reported. In the wake of mayhem, much of it perpetrated by men in uniform, seven people were left dead.[77] Torn clothing sometimes served a forensic purpose. In Haddon Heights, New Jersey, a trail of confetti, among which was scattered a woman's blood-stained underwear and 'orchid slippers', led police officers to a grizzly crime scene. The detritus ended at a well from which a young woman's corpse was dredged. She had been brutally beaten, raped and thrown in, 'while still breathing', by revellers who then dragged a 200-pound iron cover back into place. Alongside other clues lay a 'party skull cap inscribed, "Let's get it over – it's over now"' – an exhortation to defeat Japan charged with a horrific double meaning.[78]

Alert to the volatile undercurrents of victory festivities, it's hard not to feel tremors of unease reading various passages in MO's report on *Victory in Europe*. One cameo features an intoxicated girl, 'hardly over fourteen', stumbling alone from the 'Lord Nelson' in Leicester Square into the arms of three sailors who stopped her and danced for ten minutes. 'I waited to watch what would happen', MO's man-on-the-spot recorded, 'for I thought she was a bit young to go off with them.' She didn't. But would he have intervened if the sailors had whisked her away? And what about the young woman who had 'lost her skirt' – *how* exactly? – clutching her 'little half-length coat' as a searchlight picked her out and pinioned her mortification in its harsh glare? Maybe the kindness of strangers helped shepherd vulnerable women safely home. But the prevalence of exuberant men in uniform – expecting or demanding tokens of female 'gratitude', their sense of entitlement swollen by victory – surely posed hazards to women in Britain, as it did in America.[79]

'A Little Colour': The 1946 Victory Parade

In twenty-first century Britain, VJ Day registers as a faint echo of the national rejoicing on 8 May 1945. Even at the time, contemporary commentators noted a deflationary air of *déjà vu* in the more muted response to Japan's surrender. This momentous event coincided with smaller-scale but nevertheless dispiriting news about continued rationing. Cripps had just warned that *another* cut in clothing coupons was imminent. '[W]e shall have to try to clothe ourselves with these bits of paper for eight months instead of seven,' groaned a *Daily Mail* editorial bluntly headlined 'A Slap in the Face'. The paper found the government's rationale, that priority must be given to making suits for demobilized servicemen, unconvincing. Since each demob suit represented one uniform fewer to be sewn, 'that makes no difference on balance'. 'A nation victorious has a right to expect that restrictions will be relaxed, not increased.'[80]

The disjuncture between 'peace' and 'prosperity' widened as 1945 ended and a new year began. To many Britons looking to rebuild their lives, clothing, food, fuel and housing were all desperately hard to come by. It wasn't just writers and readers of editorials in the *Mail* who expressed disgruntlement. A pervasive sense of gloom, an exhaustion of the spirit accompanying a national depletion of supplies, haunted the Attlee administration's decision to stage a grand celebratory parade in London on 8 June 1946 – a last hurrah for victory, now largely forgotten.[81]

Complaints poured in as soon as the government unveiled this plan in February 1946. Conservative MPs who might have relished a parade had Churchill continued to occupy Number 10, decried the Labour administration's wastefulness. If austerity was the name of the game, they demanded, why squander precious resources on a celebration no one wanted? In March, a dozen Tory MPs tabled a Commons motion urging the government to cancel the Victory Parade and public holiday fixed for 8 June. Their petition cited the strain festivities would place on public transport and the need to concentrate on production, which further bank holidays would necessarily impede. Criticism wasn't confined to opposition back-benchers looking to score party-political points. Many working- and middle-class Britons felt the same way.[82]

As with previous stagings of victory, clothing again came to the fore in 1946. Pre-empting the Tory no-confidence motion, hundreds of typists had already unveiled their intention to 'gate crash' the scheduled parade by marching barefoot – dressed in sackcloth – as a protest against clothing restrictions, reported the *Sunday Chronicle*. Their plan struck a chord, gaining almost 500 adherents in one week alone. 'Unless stopped by the police they will carry banners showing "Mr Chad" querying: "Wot victory?"'[83] Lending further heft to the women's campaign, the National Union of Shopkeepers' Executive Committee asked its 6,000 members to boycott the event because '[i]t would be farcical to hold a victory parade when the people of this country are walking about in patched clothing and repaired shoes, and mothers are sending their children to school in shabby clothes because of the coupon shortage.'[84] Britons who struggled to eke further life from worn-out garments were doubtless unamused by Cripps' quip in response to a journalist's enquiry about when he foresaw an end to clothes rationing. The President of the Board of Trade 'refused to be drawn when asked if it was likely to be within two years, merely remarking, amid laughter, "I hope it will be within our lifetime."'[85]

Mass Observation's survey of public opinion on the 'Peace Parade' registered overwhelming negativity. Some of those canvassed wanted to move on from the war; others whose grief was still raw knew they could not. Neither group welcomed a parade certain to 'bring back memories'. Then there were those who felt that hard-pressed servicemen, who'd already sacrificed so much, deserved a break. If there was to be an additional public holiday in the name of victory, then men in uniform shouldn't have to spend it marching. A parade, by this reckoning, was *work* – a spectacle enjoyable only to those watching.[86] Moreover, the date in question, 8 June, wasn't only a Saturday, but also the start of Whitsuntide, traditionally a week when factories in northern England shut down and workers headed to the seaside. Rather than unifying Britain in celebration of collective pulling-together, the proposed parade strained the seams of a patchwork kingdom. The *Manchester Guardian* noted that most industrial towns and cities, from Lancashire to Sunderland, planned to ignore 8 June as a day of national festivity, lacking either the inclination or funding to mount their own events. 'Blackburn finds that not more than £25 can be spent on an order for fireworks,' the *Guardian* related. Across northern England, there was 'no disposition to celebrate'. The Scottish capital likewise announced that it wouldn't host the children's tea-parties written into Westminster's script for the day.[87]

Fraying became an even more pronounced motif when Moscow announced in May that it would boycott the parade: a major blow that underscored how far and fast the wartime alliance had disintegrated since mid 1945. Fears of another world war, this time pitting the USSR against western Europe and North America, escalated with Churchill's warning (on 5 March 1946) that, 'From Stettin in the Baltic, to Trieste in the Adriatic, an iron curtain has descended across the continent.'[88] Moscow's refusal to participate in the London Parade crystallized a growing sense of pessimism about the prospects for international cooperation and a lasting peace. 'What was planned as a get-together of the victorious Allies is turned by the abstention into an exhibit of their differences,' opined *New York Times* columnist Anne O'Hare McCormick.[89]

Architects of the event had intended it to embody the plurality of a 'people's war'.[90] 'This will not be merely a pompous military parade,' Home Secretary James Chuter Ede told the House of Commons. 'We propose to see that in the marching ranks there shall be representatives of every one of the civil forces and of the industrial forces who unitedly enabled us to achieve the deliverance which we have secured for all mankind.'[91] Civilian organizations, such as the Women's Land Army and Women's Voluntary Service, represented by beloved children's author Noel Streatfield, would march along with members of the armed forces.[92] Female marchers brought up the rear of a procession sent on a two-mile route through west London, while a mechanized column rumbled through the East End.

The Victory Parade was also intended to showcase *imperial* cohesion, spotlighting the contributions of troops from every corner of the empire. Metropolitan Britain had mustered into uniform around three million conscripts and volunteers from its Dominions and colonies, a fact obscured by twenty-first-century nostalgia for a war purportedly waged by a plucky 'island-nation' that 'stood alone' against the rising tide of Nazism.[93] In the 1940s, in contrast, Britons heard constant reminders – from political leaders and royals, as well as the press, newsreels and BBC – of the war's imperial character, and their own location at the heart of the empire. On VE Day, some people travelled to London for the occasion, expecting to feel the imperial pulse beating more quickly there than in the provinces.[94]

In 1946, enthusiasm for the Victory Parade, in those pockets where it could be found, stemmed from a desire for some pageantry that would 'lend a bit of colour to our lives'. 'There are those who do like shouting, flag-waving and fancy dress – so why not?,' one Aberystwyth woman enquired of a journalist.[95] Fancy outfits, ornate headgear, brocade and medals were the *sine qua non* of military parades. Without these martial trappings, a parade was, after all, just a group of people processing in lock-step. But British uniforms alone threatened to make for an uninspiring show. The very name for army khaki, 'olive drab', signalled monotony. Where, then, was the injection of colour to come from? One veteran, confessing 'a weakness', told MO that he should 'like to see the soldiers especially those in kilts'. And kilts there were aplenty on 8 June, imparting flashes of chequered blue and green, red and yellow. Primarily, however, when observers commented on the parade, they ascribed 'colour' to colonial troops. Newsreel commentaries and press reports repeatedly employed the epithets 'colourful' and 'picturesque' to describe their appearance, set apart from the serried ranks of home-grown British personnel by the brilliant panache of their uniforms. What a relief after 'twenty minutes of unbroken khaki' to behold the 'band of the Garhwal Rifles in pale grey with dark-blue sashes', exclaimed one reporter.[96]

The presence of colonial personnel in London gave the 1946 festivities the air of a world's fair from some half-century earlier, when indigenous people from imperial possessions were transported to metropolitan cities and put on ethnographic display, their peculiar customs and costumes to be gawped at in wonder.[97] Expressions of aesthetic admiration were shaded by racial condescension towards people viewed as mired in the primitive past or being hurtled into a more advanced future thanks to imperial interventions. The 1946 parade, announced *The Times*, assembled representatives of 'many stages of civilization'. That some occupied lower rungs on modernity's ladder was further underscored by the rudimentary accommodation arrangements for colonial troops. Twenty thousand servicemen and women from around the Empire, including India, Burma, Ceylon, Fiji, Borneo, Malaya and several African colonies, were billeted in Hyde Park and Kensington Gardens, corralled in what was unfortunately termed a 'concentration area' behind concertina wire – an encampment constructed by German POWs.[98] Photographs depicting the costumes and customs of these colonial troops not only attest a fascination with their 'exoticism', but also hint at the strain of making a dazzling impression while camped in a park.[99]

Written accounts of the Victory Parade make even plainer than black and white images how Britons' empire-mindedness was

Figure 1.6 Sgt Mattlaq Eid makes coffee for fellow soldiers from the Arab Legion of Transjordan in Kensington Gardens while attending the London Victory Day celebrations, 4 June 1946 (AR Tanner/Fox Photos/Hulton Archive/Getty Images)

inseparable from *colour*-consciousness. It wasn't just the bold hues of foreign uniforms that drew white spectators' eyes to scenes they attempted to recreate for those experiencing the parade vicariously. When commentators lauded the colour added to the parade by colonial troops, the allusion was often explicitly racial, referencing more than flashy apparel like the 'white spats and blue turbans' of the Gurkhas. Consider, for example, how reporter Hugh Massingham pictured the scene for readers of the *Manchester Guardian*:

> The fascinating variety of the Empire marched by – white faces, brown faces, black faces, bursting chests showing the ribbons of the Battle of Britain, Burma, and the Pacific. They had come from everywhere and gone everywhere – one was extraordinarily touched by these faces, so deadly serious, each man alone in his mind, representing his country before the eyes of the world.[100]

Fixated on faces and confident he could read the minds behind them, Massingham logged 'bearded poilus, burnt up Mexicans, bleached Danes and Norwegians': skin tone conceived as a palette of shades notable for their gradations of deviance from an imaginary white norm.

This mode of seeing and describing colour on a spectrum from white to black structured civilian spectators' accounts as well as journalistic reportage. Here's how Betty Duignan conveyed impressions of Colombo's victory parade to her mother and aunt:

> The Navy in white. The WRNS in white. Nursing sisters. Air Force. Added to which you must remember all the different shades of brown of the troops – from the white of the newly arrived ATS girls to the jet black of W. Africans, E. Africans, the Singhalese, Tamils, Sikhs with huge beards, Ghurkahs [sic] with great knives, Lascars and Chinese, Dutch, Norwegians, French, S. Africans, Canadians, Americans, Australians, N. Zealanders, men from the heart of Burma, men from the Philippines – every nation and every sort of fighting man. An amazing sight.[101]

The widely employed expression 'lending colour' hinted at profound ambivalence. As Lynda Nead's history of postwar British culture illustrates, many white Britons increasingly associated 'colour' with 'problem' (a tendency probed further in Chapter 4). While a temporary injection of 'borrowed' colour might supply welcome relief from Britain's monotony, this loan was envisioned as an impermanent feature of life in a country whose inhabitants commonly imagined themselves in monochrome. White figures in a grey landscape. As Nead points out, the empire – along with the bundle of assumptions about whiteness, superiority and civilization that simultaneously underpinned and were perpetuated by it – saturated white Britons' very perception of colour, along with the standardized coding and naming of shades undertaken by the British Colour Council (BCC), an empire-wide body founded in 1930. Today, skin tones are sometimes still likened to 'café au lait', 'chocolate' or 'ebony'. In the 1940s, however, the BCC employed not a substance but a particularly vile racist slur as its official designation of the shade adjacent to 'coffee': 'nigger brown'.[102] Informed by the BCC colour chart, fashion industry personnel unblinkingly employed this term. Julia Herrick, reporting for *The Sunday Times* on the shortage of 'good dress materials' in March 1945, alerted women to the 'useful tailored dresses of heavy linen' that could still be found – if they hurried to the shops! – in 'dark tones like nigger brown, navy, blue, black and dark green'.[103] In turn, the female readers for whom Herrick wrote replicated BCC terminology as though it were neutrally descriptive. Schoolteacher Violet Walton, whose army officer husband sent home parcels from Asia and the Middle East whenever he could, sent this guidance in April 1945 about his next purchase: 'It is very sweet of you to suggest a blouse from Palestine. *Crêpe de chine* I think would be best. My costume material is nigger and orange stripes going both ways on a very light grey (almost white) ground, giving a check effect. I suggest beige, pink or peach for the blouse, bust (still) 32".'[104]

The parade's prominent showcasing of imperial troops, meant as a gesture of metropolitan gratitude towards all members of the 'family of Britain', masked more complex dynamics playing out in the colonies themselves.[105] Siblings, in this conceit, were in open rebellion against the postwar reimposition of paternal control. The inaptness of taking victory to be synonymous with peace in 1946 wasn't just a product of the estranged Allies' east–west split. Britain's empire was also unravelling. By June 1946, India was hurtling towards independence and the violent severance of partition that immediately followed Britain's precipitate retreat. Burma (renamed Myanmar in 1989), ravaged by Japanese occupation and the ferocious Allied campaign to dislodge it, became independent in January 1948. British colonial authorities similarly struggled to reassert authority over Malaya, which began a protracted 'Emergency' in the same year as Burma's independence. But the most pressing imperial crisis for Attlee's administration in mid 1946 lay in Palestine, a League of Nations mandate under uneasy British control. Since 1943, Zionist organizations had been waging a campaign of assassinations, ambushes and explosions aimed at dislodging British authority. Just a month after the Victory Parade, the Irgun blew up Jerusalem's King David Hotel: a turning point that hastened Westminster's decision to hand the irresolvable 'Palestine problem' over to UN adjudication.[106]

The Victory Parade emitted mixed signals about what kind of place postwar Britain was: what victory had secured, at what cost, and what lay ahead. Many things people had imagined the Axis powers' defeat would bring about – an end to international conflict, an era of great power cooperation, an elevation of national living standards – remained elusive. 'We're supposed to be such a poor country, aren't we and yet they want to spend – was it 40,000 on celebrations?', one woman plaintively lamented to MO.[107] The Attlee administration's focus on Britain's chronic indebtedness – a balance of payments crisis that required prioritizing export trade over domestic consumption – confirmed the nation's penury. But, at the same time, wasn't Britain *supposed* to be wealthy: an imperial power accustomed to global dominance? A victory that failed to feel convincingly triumphal prompted anxious supposition. What was Britain meant to be now?

After a tour of England in late 1945, Herbert Ellison, associate editor of the *Washington Post*, mused aloud for his American audience that the 'empire job' was perhaps 'too big' for a nation that was 'sicker than leaders think'. He diagnosed this malady on the symptoms of shabbiness, new clothing and footwear having become 'virtually unobtainable':

> England, 1945 is marked by apathy. There is something of the Greek tragedy about it as people queue up for hours to get the numerous things needed for everyday living. There is no revival of national vitality and even personal health is not good … Babies, like mothers, need clothing and good food – even if one gets the very real feeling that England is no longer young.

One consequence of this enervation, as Ellison perceived it, was a disinclination to rebuild the war-ravaged colonies: 'An empire is regarded as a place to emigrate to.' But those who didn't harbour fantasies of escape wanted only 'a progressive liquidation of imperial commitments'. Ellison was mistaken, at least as far as ruling-class intentions went. Attlee's government, like the Conservative administration that followed, was determined to cling onto Malaya for its lucrative, dollar-earning rubber and tin supplies, while Ernest Bevin boasted that development of Britain's colonies in sub-Saharan Africa would have the United States 'eating out of our hand in four or five years'. Yet Ellison's press report nevertheless typified what Americans saw when they looked at threadbare Britons.[108]

An over-determined downpour ensured that the 1946 Victory Parade wasn't merely a figurative washout. Torrential rain left crowds scurrying for shelter, fearful for their best outfits. 'It swamped the crowds right off the street', Rose Cottrell related to her sister, 'and some of them must have been like drowned rats.'[109] Amid the drenched throngs, commentators spotted many men in brand new 'demob suits', giving the crowd a sartorial boost.[110] One year after Germany's defeat, millions of British men had been mustered out of the ranks and back into 'civvies'. But hundreds of thousands of servicemen remained in uniform or were freshly dispatched overseas in an attempt to hold the edges of empire together. *The* war might be over, but others were just beginning or only part-way through.

2 SURVIVORS

We associate the Holocaust with enormity: annihilation of human life on a colossal scale; moral abomination stretched beyond the limits of comprehension. It was, however, something almost microscopically tiny that prompted SS officers in charge of the concentration camp complex at Bergen-Belsen to take an unprecedented step on 12 April 1945. Lice. Typhus was tearing through the camp, daily claiming hundreds of internees' lives.[1] Fearful that contagion would spread into the surrounding German civilian population, Heinrich Himmler authorized his subordinates to contact British commanders with the offer of a truce. If the latter agreed to take responsibility for the area, German personnel would surrender Bergen-Belsen and its environs without a fight. On the evening of 15 April, British forces entered the camp. Over the next days and weeks, they were joined by Royal Army Medical Corps (RAMC) units, Quaker ambulance crews, medical students drafted from London's teaching hospitals and other relief workers representing various humanitarian organizations. In this rural pocket of northwest Germany, the war was over – technically, at least. In its wake came a battle to save thousands of chronically sick people from dying of starvation, tuberculosis, typhus and other infectious diseases. In this campaign, clothing became a key battleground: a matter, quite literally, of both death and life.[2]

Belsen occupied a singular place in the vast constellation of Nazi concentration and extermination camps that radiated out from

Germany across *Wehrmacht*-occupied east/central Europe. Although 'Belsen' and 'Holocaust' would later become synonymous, particularly in Britain, where images of the camp's liberation came to emblematize Nazi barbarity in the spring of 1945, Bergen-Belsen was not constructed as a site of industrialized murder.[3] Unlike Auschwitz, Treblinka and other extermination camps in Poland, there were no gas chambers at Belsen. Established in 1940, its original intended function was as a so-called 'star camp': a place to which certain 'high-value' Jews (in the Third Reich's estimation) would be sent as pawns, then bartered with foreign governments for the release of German nationals. The Bergen-Belsen complex extended beyond this facility, however. A neighbouring POW camp operated from 1940 until January 1945, confining initially French and Belgian soldiers, then, from 1941 onwards, predominantly Russian troops, before the momentum of battle shifted in the Allies' favour with the Red Army breaking the siege of Stalingrad in February 1943.[4]

As Soviet forces swept towards, and then into, Germany in 1944 and early 1945, the SS began relocating inmates from extermination camps in the east to sites further west. For tens of thousands of evacuees, Belsen was the terminus of a gruelling procession from one place of mass death to another. In early 1945, the SS established a large 'women's camp' to accommodate female internees (most of them Jewish) previously incarcerated at Flossenbürg, Groß-Rosen, Ravensbrück, Neuengamme, Mauthausen, Buchenwald and elsewhere. The number of internees at Belsen soared from 7,300 in late July 1944 to around 15,000 at the start of December. Their situation deteriorated calamitously in early 1945. A population numbering around 22,000 in February had ballooned to over 60,000 by the time British forces liberated the camp. By then Belsen was, in one survivor's words, 'hell on earth'.[5] Huts built to accommodate hundreds held thousands, living and dead. Food rations shrank below subsistence levels, reduced to meagre portions of turnip soup and hunks of black bread for those who still possessed sufficient strength to lift a spoon, or hand, to their mouths. In early April, the water supply failed. Sanitation, barely existent hitherto, ceased altogether. Corpses floated in stagnant tanks.[6]

The SS concealed from British commanders just how catastrophic conditions were at Belsen, failing to divulge the enormous number of internees whom they'd consigned to death in recent weeks, and the imminence with which many thousands more would perish without *immediate* medical assistance. German officers admitted just 1,500 typhus cases. The fact that approximately 37,000 people had died at Belsen between January and March 1945 was a horrific reality for which the first British personnel to enter the camp were almost entirely unprepared.[7]

Entering the Camp

'Everything you have read in the papers is true – only more so,' British Red Cross worker Effie Barker informed her father, a retired colonel, on 27 April.[8] The problem for Effie, as for all those who reached Belsen soon after its liberation, was how to make intelligible to distant others a *'more so'* that strained the descriptive capacities of language. Conditions remained 'unbelievable' even to those who ventured into this site of mass death and suffering, concealed behind a pastoral screen of farmland and forest. 'Who would imagine that a Concentration Camp could be hidden in such country,' mused Molly Silva Jones, a fellow Red Cross nurse. 'It seemed fantastic, the peace of the pine woods became sombre and sinister.' Her colleague Jean McFarlane agreed: 'the setting was beautiful. The latter served to accentuate, if anything, the horror of the place.'[9]

For relief workers, the first indication of something seriously awry came in written form. Signs warning 'Typhus Area – Danger' proliferated the closer travellers came to the camp. On breaching the perimeter, incomers' first encounter with Bergen-Belsen wasn't the 'Horror Camp' they'd been braced against, in which some 22,000 women, 18,000 men and 500 children were discovered alive – in overcrowded huts measuring 120' by 20' – amid stacks of dead bodies. Rather, it was a disconcertingly well-built and orderly Panzer (tank regiment) facility. To Silva Jones, its neat rows of housing resembled the council estates that had mushroomed across Britain in the interwar years, but with disconcertingly lavish facilities for officers' entertainment, including marble bath-houses, a cinema and a ballroom, like a scaled-down Royal Albert Hall. What lay ahead, a mere two miles down the road, announced itself by an 'indescribable' stench, and then by what could be glimpsed through ominous swirls of dust and a thicket of double-coiled barbed wire.[10]

Wrenching scenes soon confirmed incomers' suspicions about the constituent parts of this nauseating smell: thousands of unburied corpses; smouldering hillocks of burnt clothing and shoes; everywhere stinking evidence of diarrhoea suffered by thousands of chronically ill internees. One especially surreal sight indicated the stupendous scale on which the SS had annihilated human life. Medical student Michael Hargrave described it thus in his diary:

> It was a pile of boots, made up of the boots taken off the victims they cremated. I don't know how many years it had taken the Germans to build up this pile, but it was about 20 yards long by about 5 yards across and about 12 feet high – the shoes at the bottom were squashed as flat as paper and so you can imagine how many thousands of pairs of shoes there were there, and each pair of shoes had once had an owner, and though the Germans may have destroyed all the records of the Camp, this pile of shoes and boots bore mute but absolutely damning evidence of the number of people who had died in this Camp before the British arrived, because we did not add the shoes of the dead onto this pile, and yet we buried 23,000 people.[11]

Yet somehow – miraculously – human existence persisted. Inside the huts and out, dotting the forest fringe, survivors wandered, sat or lay. Many hovered on the thinnest of margins between life and death.

Britons' written attempts to convey their first stunned encounter with Belsen accentuated jarring contrasts and radical confusion. Incoming relief workers and medical students grappled, as earlier arriving military personnel had, with the chasm between a deceptively tranquil landscape and the grotesque scenes lurking behind a 'dense curtain of black trees'.[12] They also noted the categorical indeterminacy of dead bodies and living beings, discarded rags and worn garments. Several observers characterized as 'scarecrows' the emaciated people, dressed in tatters, who inhabited the camp. Their status as sentient individuals – not stuffed straw figures dressed to resemble humans – took some work, or greater proximity, to determine.[13] In this nightmarish universe, things and beings, flesh and fabric, seemed to switch places. Uncanny reversals and inversions abounded. What at first appeared to be a bundle of filthy cloth might on closer inspection, once the observer's attention had been caught by a flicker of motion, turn out to be a sentient person. But not always. '[P]iles of rags and bits and

Figure 2.1 Women survivors cook, using shoes as fuel, in front of a vast pile of footwear at Bergen-Belsen camp, 15 April 1945 (Popperfoto/ Getty Images)

pieces ... I realised partly concealed corpses in some cases,' noted Jean McFarlane. In certain huts, the 'living propped [the] dead up swathed in blankets so that food would be given, and [the] living could have double share'.[14]

Corpses assumed unfamiliar guises that shocked incoming Britons. Dead bodies doubled as furniture or bedding. Something to lean against, or a makeshift pillow in a world bereft of beds and bedclothes. (Mattresses, sheets and pillows were luxuries reserved exclusively for the SS staff and Panzer officers.) 'What strikes me most were the contrasts in Camp I – how death and life are interwoven – the dead man's body just serving as a rest for the live man's head,' marvelled Dr Arnold Horwell.[15] Corpses could even substitute for blankets, providing a modicum of warmth for a neighbour before life ebbed away completely from the deceased. Lieutenant-Colonel Mervyn Gonin (an Ipswich doctor in civilian life) later recalled that, 'If one died the poor wretch crouching next to the body would crawl on top of it for the sake of a brief spell of warmth.'[16]

That a corpse might serve, however fleetingly, as a comforter was only one reason why British witnesses boggled at survivors' ostensible nonchalance in the face of mass death. Clusters of women heated dollops of who-knew-what in tin pots mere feet from lifeless bodies. Meanwhile, children whose impulse to play had not been extinguished by the engulfing misery roamed unsupervised. Improvised games included throwing stones at corpses.[17] Numbering in the almost uncountable thousands, bodies lay everywhere, shocking not just in their profusion but also in their degree of emaciation. While some had been hastily dragged into a vast pit before British troops took control, others lay piled up, three or four deep, mere inches from the huts – 'like piles of sugar beet you see awaiting carting, except sugar beet does look neatly arranged and it is clean and not rotting', noted Gonin, tapping his Suffolk roots for an apt simile. 'As you watched you might notice four figures shuffling along carrying a blanket out of the sag of which stuck the legs and arms of a corpse, the figures would suddenly slump to the ground and wait there until they had the strength to stagger on till they had tipped their corpse onto the ever growing pile.'[18]

It escaped no one's attention that many of these dead bodies were partially clothed. Some were dressed only from the waist up; others not at all. Horwell, a Jewish German refugee born in Berlin before fleeing to Britain, described 'gruesome bundles of bones held together by tight yellow skin'. And jumbled amongst these prematurely skeletal corpses were discarded garments and rags, promiscuously mingled and sometimes hard to tell apart: 'an almost continuous carpet of dead bodies, human excreta, rags and filth', stated an account of Belsen compiled from British army official reports.[19]

Soldiers, relief workers and medical students invariably noted what Belsen's inmates wore – or did *not* wear – whether they trained their gaze on the living or the dead. All remarked on the prevalence of striped uniforms made notorious by the SS. But what they noticed, and how they described it, differed considerably. Many characterized the outfit as 'pyjamas', a jarring invocation of cosily flannel-clad childhood transposed into the brutal milieu of the camp. 'On the left we caught the first glimpse of barbed wire through which people peered at us, strange figures clad in blue striped pyjamas,' Silva Jones wrote.[20] Her Red Cross colleague, Evelyn Bark, saw something different, more object than human: 'Pitiful wrecks of humanity were still dragging themselves around; their frames, weighing next to nothing, were mere clothes-hangers for the filthy striped pyjamas which appeared to be the uniform of the internees.'[21] Michael Hargrave gave this garb a more carceral stamp when he observed that survivors 'shuffled along in a purposeless sort of way, dressed in their blue and white striped slave clothing'.[22] Revolted by conditions in the camp, some observers' disgust seeped into their descriptions of individuals, as when fellow medical student Alan MacAuslan recorded: 'Most of the women were naked, though some wore the blue and white striped nightshirt of the concentration camps. They were all skeletons, skin over bones, no muscles, no fat. They and the bunks were filthy, covered in excrement, in shit.' One particular woman, squatting on the floor to relieve her scoured bowels, caught his attention: 'black matted hair shimmering with lice ... her shoulder blades like disconnected wings'.[23]

Like many Britons arriving at Belsen soon after its liberation, MacAuslan discerned gendered differences in survivors' appearance and apparel. Women, the majority of survivors, looked to be in worse health than men and more threadbare, if not altogether unclothed.[24] MacAuslan also spotted that the standard issue garb for female internees was not 'pyjamas' but what he termed a 'nightshirt'. Others more accurately called this garment a 'coat', cut from the same vertically striped fabric – described as either blue or grey and white, or grey and blue stripes – sewn into trousers and jackets for men. Photographs taken just after Belsen's liberation by British army photographers depict women in various states of undress and dress, including non-uniform coats with a square swatch of striped fabric sewn onto the back. As historians have noted, the retrospective notion that the SS branded its victims with identikit uniforms – for which 'striped pyjamas' now serves as shorthand – is misplaced. Differentiated clothing, including customizations (like added pockets) undertaken by internees themselves, played an important role in self-fashioning and in the elaboration of power hierarchies within Nazi camps.[25]

The SS intended striped uniforms to stamp their wearers unmistakably as prisoners whose criminality was visible at a glance. Stitched onto the jacket at chest height was a triangular cloth badge indicating the particular attribute that made the wearer odious to the

Third Reich: pink for homosexuals; red for political prisoners; purple for Jehovah's witnesses; green for 'professional criminals'; brown for Roma and Sinti; and yellow triangles for Jews.[26] But, despite stringent regulation, fabric couldn't be made to function as an infallible or indelible marker of identity. Not only could garments be modified, with camp inmates finding surreptitious ways to refashion their apparel; they could also be discarded. One of the many phenomena to confound Britons trying to make sense of Belsen was the difficulty of knowing who was whom by relying on observation of who wore what.

Even the most fateful distinction – between SS personnel and their victims – was not always clear-cut. Some men, whose emaciated bodies suggested they were surely former internees, staggered through the camp in items of SS apparel. 'The SS stores were broken open and clothing distributed. It was common to see internees wandering about naked except for a short grey jacket,' observed Major William A. Davis of the US Typhus Commission.[27] Women's status was also hard to fathom from sartorial clues. Some Britons found it hard to distinguish perpetrators from victims, suspecting that several belonged in an intermediate category of 'collaborators'. MacAuslan was perplexed by the women he encountered in the hut he'd been assigned to oversee:

> Just inside the hut, by the door through which I had first come in, there was a little room with beds, a stove, a wireless, the snuggery of the Blokober and her mates. She and they were dressed in grey skirts and jackets with head scarves and they all wore new shoes. It was possible that their uniforms had been issued by the Germans before the Camp was liberated. At best they might be 'trusties', at worst SS. However the SS clothing store, near the main gate of the Camp, had been broken open by the British and the garments distributed, so the inmates of the small room might be innocents, fit enough to take advantage of whatever had been going. Which ever they were, they were cooperative, they understood our bad German, they worked. They became our orderlies.[28]

On this occasion, MacAuslan and his colleagues decided not to dwell too much on the possible past allegiances of women whose labour they appreciated. But in other cases determining what clothing *really* signified had profound consequences. When the trial of SS guards and others indicted of crimes perpetrated at Belsen began in

September 1945, one defendant, Oscar Schmitz, insisted he had been wrongly accused because of the rumpled green *Oberscharführer* uniform he was wearing when British forces arrested him. A German communist youth movement member who'd fled home rather than serve in the *Wehrmacht*, Schmitz was incarcerated by the Third Reich in 1940 for desertion, spending the war years in a succession of concentration camps before ending up at Belsen. There, on the chaotic night of 16 April, he became embroiled in a fight with Soviet prisoners who stripped him of everything but his underpants. SS guards, with whom he was thrown into a locked room, gave him a uniform for protective cover: a gesture that led to Schmitz's arrest as a suspected war criminal. In a further twist, an SS officer – a representative, in other words, of the very organization that had incarcerated Schmitz for years – corroborated his testimony in court, helping secure his acquittal.[29]

Reverse cases, in which SS personnel stripped off their uniforms and presented themselves in the striped apparel of their victims, hoping to evade arrest as war criminals, also came to light. One female hospital patient became 'demented' when she spotted an SS guard masquerading as a survivor on the ward.[30] It would be easy to imagine that corporeality must have told a more reliable story about identity than garments, for while clothing could readily be swapped, fleshy bodies couldn't be so easily disguised. Less emaciated individuals in civilian garb – and fuller figures in striped uniforms – certainly evoked suspicion that they might be SS personnel posing as internees. Sometimes they were. But not every healthier-looking or better-dressed person at Belsen had belonged to the camp staff.

What, then, *did* smarter attire indicate? Observant British witnesses noticed some markedly better-dressed, more 'respectable', women among the survivors. 'There were a few girls, decently clad walking about, laughing and chatting,' remarked Molly Silva Jones.[31] Private Manny Fisher, a Jewish medical corpsman from London's East End, noted not only that there were 'several young Jewesses from 14 years old upwards with the Star of David on the backs of their coats', but also that some women 'sported slacks and gaily coloured turbans – ironic in the extreme'. These incongruous figures he presumed to be 'recent arrivals' at Belsen.[32] That explanation was plausible, and possibly correct. But different observers entertained another hypothesis. The more presentable women must have been 'kept for the use of the

Germans', Silva Jones concluded: '14 "clients" per day and two days off per week, such is the Germanic order.'[33]

Was Belsen a place of sexlessness or sex? Confronted with mass death, chronic starvation, rampant disease and the startling persistence of 'bare life' amid the corpses, British witnesses struggled with exposure: their own responses to unclothed or semi-clad bodies, and the feelings they projected onto un- or under-dressed camp inmates. In an era when censorship banished nakedness from the cinema screens, Belsen's undressed bodies – encountered not only first-hand by soldiers and relief workers but also by distant viewers of newsreels shot in mid/late April 1945 – perhaps shocked sensibilities all the more acutely by virtue of nudity's unfamiliarity. British film censors (like their counterparts in Hollywood's Hays Office) presumed that nakedness was necessarily erotic. Anything too potently suggestive of sex was duly kept from the screen for fear of arousing viewers. Even Allied filmmakers intent on using footage shot at Belsen, Auschwitz, Dachau and other liberated camps for re-educative purposes, instilling a sense of 'collective guilt' in Germans, fretted that viewers might get 'worked up', as they put it, over the naked bodies.[34] But those who witnessed Belsen for themselves regarded the naked body as anything but arousing: rather an object of horror, fear, pity or disgust – or some inarticulable amalgam of contradictory reflexes.

Several observers insisted that starvation and degrading camp conditions had reduced men and women to a condition of neuter indeterminacy, stripping away self-consciousness along with certain bodily markers of maleness and femaleness. 'They had nothing to wear and were quite unconscious of their nudity,' insisted Myrtle Beardwell.[35] Her claim was echoed by Horwell, who recorded on 30 April that 'All feeling of shame, of "decency" within its conventional meaning has disappeared in the women's Camp. And a thing like "sex" just doesn't exist.' *'The internees were so starved that sex did not exist, and they had no sense of modesty,'* announced an official report on Belsen, italicizing the point for emphasis.[36] Many observers maintained that it wasn't gender alone that had vanished, but any notion that garments might preserve decorum rather than merely providing warmth.[37] 'Clothing is without meaning, for these bodies are no longer people,' wrote news correspondent R. W. Thomson, whose account of Belsen ran in the *Sunday Times*'s edition of 22 April. 'In a sense they are less offensive naked than in the grey-striped filthy rags that hang on them, serving only to accentuate the awful shame,' he opined. Precisely what offended the reporter, and who should feel ashamed of what, remained ambiguous in Thomson's report. But, by insisting that survivors were 'no longer people', he did less to condemn than corroborate that the SS had achieved its aim of dehumanizing its victims.[38]

Others recognized, sometimes to their consternation, that a very human determination to survive – whatever stratagems survival required – persisted. Contrary to assertions that sex had been eliminated at Belsen, both gender identity and intercourse persisted. MacAuslan was appalled to find himself propositioned by one of the women in the hut he oversaw: 'She came close up to me, put a hand either side of my flanks and began to move them slowly downwards whilst looking up ingratiatingly: "Zwanzig cigaretten, zwanig cigaretten". I had no doubt what she was offering for twenty cigarettes. I was shocked to my virginal Scottish Presbyterian immature roots. I was a doctor, she was a patient. She threatened my medical integrity. Angry and flustered, I pushed her away.' MacAuslan was thrown into even greater turmoil when, having confided in a fellow medic, his friend laughed and wouldn't stop laughing: '"Poor girl, perhaps she was desperate for a smoke!" "Didn't she know that doctors don't do things like that with their patients? Anyway sex is for love." "Not in concentration camps it isn't, it's for survival."' The next day this nameless woman had disappeared from the hut. MacAuslan never saw her again.[39]

Clothing and Contagion

For relief workers, the lack of clean clothes, footwear and bedding at Belsen represented an enormous logistical challenge. Where could sufficient supplies be located – *now*? For medical teams, clothing lay at the centre of an epidemiological crisis. Garments played a key role in the transmission of typhus, as Major Davis of the US Typhus Commission (who began work at Belsen on 22 April) explained: 'It is well known that lice seek the temperature which exists under the clothing of the normal human body; those fleeing from the fever of typhus readily found a new host, while those left in the cold bed of one dead from typhus soon found a live person in the bed. Starvation lowered the resistance of prisoners who contracted the disease.'[40]

Through the early months of 1945, lice plagued Belsen's population. One survivor, Dr Fritz Leo, penned a skin-crawling vignette of camp life before liberation: 'As we had hardly any opportunity of washing, let alone of bathing or getting clean clothes, a frightful infestation by lice began in a short time. People lying closely packed, had lice in hundreds, even in thousands. There were pieces of clothing, of which we in grim humour used to say "They wandered about by themselves", there were so many lice inside.'[41] Fear of typhus frenzied some inmates who appreciated all too well the existential threat posed by infected insect bites. Anne Frank, who posthumously became Belsen's best-known victim, reportedly spent her final days unclothed, terrified that her garments might become infested with lice. Anne died, shortly after her beloved older sister Margot, in February or March 1945. Like much else about the Frank sisters' final days, the precise dates of their deaths remain unknown.[42]

Written reports and photographs of Belsen in the middle of April 1945 depict survivors teasing lice from their garments and hair; wrestling clothes from corpses and incinerating these garments.[43] As Davis's report documented, however, the epidemic outstripped internees' Sisyphean efforts. Dire conditions produced lethal chain reactions. 'Clothing and blankets were insufficient. Many were naked. No heat was available in the shacks; this was not important, since the steaming mass of humanity generated considerable heat even on the coldest of days,' Davis observed. 'But clothing was in such demand that it was regularly taken from the dead,' then *worn*.[44] In overcrowded huts, people slept sometimes two abreast in three-tiered bunks, with others lying crammed into the floorspace between. With many internees suffering from diarrhoea, bunks – and occupants too weak to move – became covered in excrement. 'One had to wear rubber boots, the floor was thick with faeces, the hut was raised a couple of feet above ground level, most of the flooring in the corridor had been pulled up and the space beneath used as a latrine and contained in addition many corpses,' Gonin later recalled.[45] No wonder, then, that those with enough stamina to do so tugged less soiled garments from the dead, despite the risk of infection.

And no wonder that Lieutenant Colonel J. A. D. Johnston made the burning of 'rubbish, rags and human excreta' one of the first priorities at Belsen.[46] Work proceeded slowly, however. Medical student Peter Horsey spent 8 May (a sobering three weeks after British troops first arrived) supervising some Hungarian guards in the hut to which he'd been assigned: 'They worked really quite well,' Horsey recorded.

'All the dirty blankets and other filth were carted out, the clean ones shaken and hung in the sun, and in the afternoon they scrubbed the floor, all the beds and the walls with scrubbing powder and water. A fine job.' Amid this whirl of activity, Horsey almost forgot the momentousness of the day, neglecting to tune into Churchill's Victory broadcast at 3pm, instead listening to the King inch his nail-bitingly hesitant way through a speech delivered at 9pm.[47]

Alongside the work of decontamination went the grim task of triage. Medical students presiding in pairs over huts in the 'Horror Camp' had to determine which survivors stood the best chance of survival. Playing god distressed many of these young trainee physicians, barely in their twenties but well aware their decisions would consign to a near-certain death those deemed too weak for evacuation. A 'Belsen standard' of fitness was established: if internees were capable of feeding themselves then they would be removed by ambulance to the newly established hospital area, having first passed through a decontamination facility dubbed the 'Human Laundry'. Since patients were undressed before they were stretchered onto ambulances, people alone – not their garments – were washed in this 'Laundry'. Medical student Michael Hargrave recognized that removal and destruction of clothes, however vital to check contagion, constituted another kind of violence. Patients in the hospital would 'start a new life with no clothes or possessions of any kind, all these being taken outside, when they had gone, and burnt'.[48]

Clearing the huts involved considerable force. Some women, realizing that medics' determination of their unfitness might consign them to death, tore off their clothes and tried to hurl themselves onto stretchers when ambulance crews arrived to transport selected survivors to the 'Laundry'. Orderlies sometimes had to restrain women who had failed to meet the 'Belsen standard'. Emaciated women, in fear for their lives, mustered a furious physical tenacity that took many onlookers aback. 'The excitement was intense and frequently two or three women stripped and tried to put themselves on the stretchers,' an understated British report recorded.[49]

Many people of different statuses and nationalities, wearing all manner of protective apparel or none, took part in the clearance of the 'Horror Camp', transferring patients from hut to 'Laundry' to hospital. British commanders assigned the most dangerous and distressing work, disposing of thousands of corpses, to captured SS personnel: an

Figure 2.2 Members of the RAMC, wearing protective suits, clear bodies from the 'Horror Camp', with garments piled by the door of the hut, 15 April 1945 (Popperfoto/Getty Images)

urgent practical task also intended to chasten. If the perpetrators of atrocity contracted deadly diseases in the process, few British personnel would have considered this anything other than a morally fitting outcome. Not surprisingly, hatred ran high among those who witnessed Belsen first-hand.[50] The distinction between executing war criminals after a trial and placing Germans in the way of harm, for which they themselves bore responsibility, seemed a rather fine one. Numerous photographs taken at Belsen in late April depict SS men and women, in uniform blouses and skirts, with high leather boots, clambering over mounds of bodies in open pits. Meanwhile, British officers assigned German POWs to the 'death cart'. 'Dressed in protective Anti-gas clothing – their job is to go round the Camp, under orders of armed British Guards, calling at each hut to collect all the dead and take them away in the cart to be buried elsewhere – now with a proper burial service,' Hargrave recorded in his diary.[51]

German labour wasn't restricted to collecting and burying bodies. Local civilians played a role in providing medical care. British officers commandeered doctors and nurses from the surrounding area to staff the 'Laundry' and hospital, seeking to alleviate the severe shortage of trained medical personnel at Belsen in the early weeks after its liberation. This arrangement initially discomforted both female patients and German nurses, one group of whom were set upon as they arrived at Belsen – their white uniforms torn, hair sheared off – by enraged survivors.[52]

German nurses had primary responsibility for tending patients brought in for decontamination. Located in a former stable, the 'Human Laundry' had a less than spotless previous function as home to 150 Panzer horses. Repurposed for its new role, this building was equipped with sixty tables, at which worked two nurses from the Germany Military Hospital with two German Medical Officers under the British pathologist of the 32nd Casualty Clearing Station. 'The German nurses were an interesting study,' Gonin recalled. '[A]t the start they laughed, joked and were definitely truculent, made no attempt to get things ready for the job in hand, damned if they were going to work for the something British.' Then the first patients started to arrive. 'I am told by my friend who was in charge of the Laundry that this was one of the most dramatic moments at Belsen, the place of unending drama. Those nurses stood with their mouths open and gazed horror struck as those bodies were brought in, first one then another started to sob until almost the whole sixty were weeping. There was no more truculence after that.'[53]

Gentle sponging was required to lift dirt from epidermis. If proper care wasn't taken in washing and drying patients, skin itself could simply peel off onto the towel. Jean McFarlane cast a compassionate eye over this wrenching scene, focusing not on the German nurses, but on the skeletal survivors under their care. It was 'painfully obvious even to the most inexperienced that most of them were desperately ill, and that practically all were suffering from starvation. How it must have hurt them lying on those hard tables.'[54] Patients, already denuded of clothing, found their own body hair treated as another possible breeding ground to be eradicated. German and British army barbers worked alongside one another to clip and shave patients' heads. They slavered a mixture of 'equal parts olive oil and kerosene' on any remaining hair, leaving this treatment on overnight. After rinsing, a

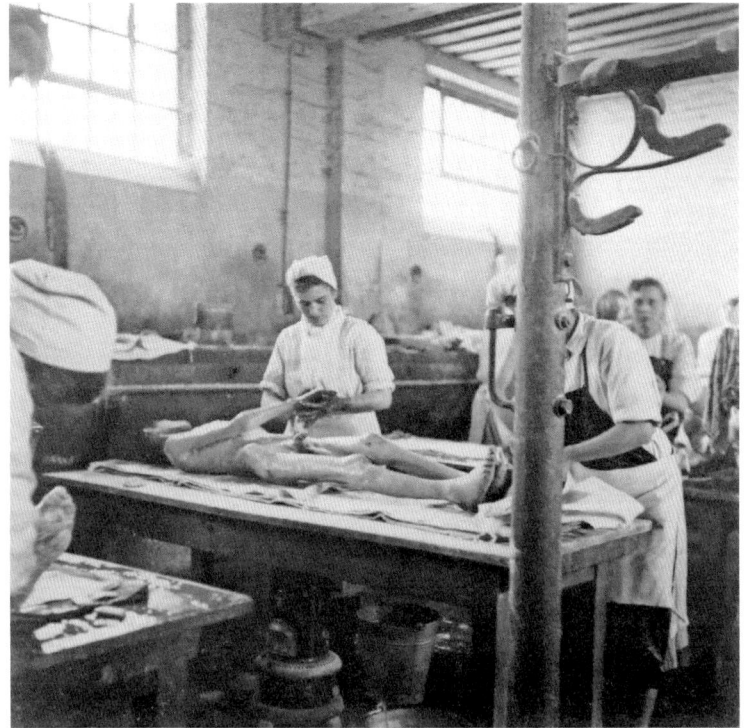

Figure 2.3 German women clean survivors in Belsen's 'Human Laundry', April 1945 (Popperfoto/Getty Images)

fine tooth-comb was pulled through the patient's hair to remove any stubborn lice.[55]

The final stage of this process was disinfection. Survivors brought to the 'Laundry' were sprayed with dichloro-diphenyl-trichloroethane (DDT) in 5 or 10 per cent concentration before being taken to the hospital area. 'The atmosphere was thick with DDT and everything in the building was covered with a film of white – the smell of it will always conjure up the picture of those ex-stables; the near-skeletons lying there on tables; German nurses and orderlies being made to work for those people they so despised; the well-covered German M.O. supervising the proceedings, himself being supervised by [Major] Maxse [Griffen] armed with a revolver and a DDT gun,' noted Silva Jones.[56]

By the early 1970s, DDT had been banned in many countries because of its toxic impact on wildlife and carcinogenic consequences for human life. But at Belsen everyone was constantly sprayed with an insecticide then believed to be miraculously effective: survivors, military personnel, medical students and relief workers, along with the Germans and Hungarians working under British direction. Red Cross worker Effie Barker, boasting that she was a 'good hand with a delousing gun', insisted the procedure was akin to 'being sprayed with talcum and no more unpleasant'.[57] But that was before she reached Belsen, where point-blank dusting surely felt less innocuous. The procedure involved having an 'outsize syringe' with a fifteen-inch nozzle aimed directly into one's clothing, leaving a 'chlorine clean' scent.[58] Medical student Douglas Peterkin later detailed the process in his Edinburgh University doctoral thesis:

> One method of dusting was universally employed throughout the Camp. The subject to be dusted kept his clothes on and the nozzle of the gun was passed up one sleeve next to the skin and two strokes of the gun handle were made. This was then repeated for the other sleeve, each trouser leg from below and above, down the front and back of the neck and under headgear. The outside of the socks and footwear was liberally dusted. It was found that ten persons could be dusted with one pound of powder.[59]

An intensive regime of DDT dusting helped offset the lack of what we'd now term PPE. Protective clothing and equipment was extremely scarce. With the exception of RAMC personnel, who removed blanket-swaddled patients by stretcher from the huts to waiting ambulances, most of the military and civilian relief workers at Belsen during April and May 1945 went without. Instead, they donned a motley assemblage of whichever garments lay to hand and seemed likeliest to offer some insulation from infection. 'I always go about in slacks and battle dress, trousers being a greater protection against the louse!,' Margaret Ward informed her mother with unconvincing bravado. Her colleague Jean McFarlane gave a more elaborate description of Red Cross apparel as modified for Belsen, noting (on 26 April): 'I got into dungarees, army boots, gaiters and tied my head up in a triangular bandage.'[60]

The medical students possessed nothing approaching a distinctive uniform; nor did they receive any protective clothing or masks, just some randomly distributed articles issued prior to departure from England. Peter Horsey inventoried his kit as comprising army battledress and greatcoat, two pairs of long pants, two pairs of under-pants and one pair of pyjamas. These garments had to 'last five weeks', the anticipated duration of their overseas tour in circumstances where access to laundry facilities was likely to be erratic or non-existent.[61] Less than comprehensive, Horsey's wardrobe wasn't standard issue for the entire cohort. MacAuslan tallied 'badge-less forage caps, gaiters, boots and kitbag' among the accessories doled out to his contingent. No greatcoats. 'We looked scruffy', he admitted, 'especially to those of us who had already been in and out of the Army.' He and his peers also received a civilian passport and a document stating that they worked for the Red Cross. This paper offered a different kind of protective cover: 'if captured were to be given the status of sergeants and not shot as spies'.[62]

Adding to the trainee doctors' irregular appearance was the fact that, on reaching Belsen, they received articles of *German* military apparel. Some seemed to relish the transgressive irony: British medics kitted out in *Wehrmacht* garments! Perhaps they regarded these items as collectible curios: mementoes that would later impart a ghoulish shudder of authenticity to Nazi horror stories they'd tell about their time at Belsen. Hargrave revelled in receipt of a camouflage Panzer coat, noting 'we had all wanted one of these since the day we got out here – they were a present from Capt Winterbottom.' MacAuslan expressed even greater enthusiasm for his reversible Germany army camouflage blouse, impressed by its stylishness as well as its functionality: 'These were rather smart, white on one side for snow and brown and green on the other for Autumn. You could wear them either side out.' Horsey, meanwhile, regarded his bounty less as an expression of 'Nazi chic' than as a practical addition to his limited wardrobe. Initially thinking German overalls would make good pyjamas, to be donned after his nightly dousing in Dettol, he later found them 'invaluable' work-wear. His journal entry for 14 May recorded these sartorial recalibrations: 'Have now given up wearing battle dress, and wear the blue cotton German denim trousers with the British denim blouse. Looks queer, but at least is cool, and my khaki denim trousers stink horribly.'[63] None of the medical students seemingly regarded enemy apparel as too ideologically polluted for use.

Royal Army Medical Corps personnel enjoyed the best protective equipment. All but one member of this group had been inoculated against typhus within four months prior to arrival at Belsen. Vaccinations notwithstanding, RAMC members donned elaborate 'typhus suits' before starting their shifts:

> These were put on each morning prior to leaving for the camp and at the same time a dusting with 5 per cent DDT powder was applied. The suits consisted of a one piece garment complete with hood and boots. They were made of a khaki twill material and tied by tapes at the back. It was soon found that with the fabric boots of the suits being worn on top of normal footwear the former rapidly became torn. This was overcome by wearing the normal footwear outside the suit and improvising puttees. Battle dress trousers and blouse were worn under the typhus suit. Gauntlets of a khaki twill material bound in position by tapes were worn by all personnel. Masks were never worn.[64]

Some medical personnel feared the very garments that protected them from contagion might terrify the survivors they treated. The 'typhus suit' gave the wearer a forbiddingly alien appearance. Spacesuits *avant la lettre*. Sensitive medical staff recognized that their traumatized patients – most having lost numerous loved ones, if not their entire families; some having suffered agonizing 'experimentation' by Nazi doctors – had good reason to fear anyone who laid hands on them. When Swiss medical personnel established a hospital a few miles from Belsen to which some survivors were moved in May, uniform regulations for accompanying RAMC staff included mandatory display of the service badge. The 'rod of Aesculapius & the serpent', fashioned in brass, had to be pinned to the head cowl of the protective suit. '[T]his would indicate immediately to our own patients that they were in safe and reliable care,' noted Terence McQuillin. 'This was confirmed to us in sign or common language from the Belsen inmates ... I have never been so proud or affected before or since, on being instantly accepted as a trusted friend, all from the recognition of our cap badge. The overalls were in field grey, very similar to German wear, the only difference it seemed, was in the cap badge!'[65]

McQuillin wasn't the only Briton to impute talismanic properties to medical insignia and other paraphernalia, from Red Cross armbands to badges and stethoscopes. Despite widespread use of garments that weren't just 'very similar' to German apparel but *actual*

German kit, some British medical personnel nevertheless felt that what they wore played a significant role in elevating patients' *esprit*, perhaps even improving their prospects for recovery. Peter Horsey, after feeling rather superfluous once 'his' hut had been cleared, sensed that 'our presence seemed to help keep up morale of patients, chiefly because we brandished stethoscopes and wore British uniform.'[66] Of course, it's possible McQuillin and Horsey exaggerated the psychological potency of symbols that represented not just medical professionalism but Britishness.[67] Horsey implied that the students' aura of efficacy, masking not only their own inexperience but a severe lack of medication at Belsen, functioned as something of a placebo. But, as some medical students came to appreciate, survivors' will to live was a vital sign that defied clinical diagnosis. As easily extinguished as kindled, a determination to cling onto life drew sustenance from diverse places, including the things people wore or pinned to their caps that signified trust and compassion between fellow humans.

Redress

Fresh from the 'Laundry', Belsen's survivors were delivered to the hospital area, a collection of buildings in what had formerly been the POW camp. Operating a facility to treat around 15,000 severely ill patients, survivors of a concentration camp mere metres away, required enormous amounts of expertise and equipment alike. Stockpiling adequate medication took time, as did amassing sufficient beds, mattresses, sheets, blankets and pillows. Uniforms for medical staff and attire for patients also had to be found. Although the ransacked Panzer facility yielded 'blankets, sheets, beds, barracks furniture, soap and scouring powder', quantities fell woefully short.[68] Nurse Molly Silva Jones jotted wearily after her initial shift on 21 April: 'first day in the hospital – no sheets, no pillows, very few B[ed] P[an]s, (augmented by dog bowls), few towels, not enough cups.' These shortages were all the more severe as many patients required frequent changes of bedding. Silva Jones, whose empathy towards survivors extended only so far, didn't hide her exasperation: 'people because of starvation, illness, weakness, apathy and lack of sanitation in camp 1 had become used to defecating and urinating where they lay, or possibly a few yards off if they could get so far … They could not grasp that someone would come if they called. Hard to get the internee staff to empty the BPs often. Almost as difficult to get blankets changed and patients washed. Brown paper took the place of mackintosh sheeting.'[69]

Like many of her colleagues, Silva Jones initially held medical staff recruited from among the survivors in low esteem, believing them too debilitated by illness to undertake arduous work or too focused on their own recovery to tend properly to their patients' needs. But uniforms worked a certain magic in conjuring up renewed professional pride. 'It seemed that to fit them out with decent clothing, to provide the Doctors and Nurses with white coats and overalls, good shoes would help them to regain their self-respect. It did and very quickly,' Silva Jones commented, recording that those working in the hospital area 'received two sets of underclothes, one pair of shoes, one dress and one coat' apiece.[70]

These allocations claimed priority status. However, pervasive shortages threatened to bring evacuation of the 'Horror Camp' to a standstill almost as soon as the operation began. Without enough blankets – wrappers for patients in transit as well as bed coverings – the hospital would be unable to admit new patients. The huts would duly remain choked with those who, given urgent medical attention, stood a fair chance of recovery. This bottleneck had to be unplugged. But how? Red Cross packages found undistributed at Belsen in April 1945 failed to remedy the deficit. Meanwhile, the Victory Clothing drive on UNRRA's behalf (discussed in Chapter 1) remained ongoing in the United States. The fruits of this harvest were weeks away from shipment across the Atlantic, let alone distribution in Germany. Gonin recalled bringing this crisis to the attention of Brigadier Glyn Hughes: '"What's the population of Celle?" he asked. On being told 1600 to what appeared an irrelevant question he said "Go to the Burgomaster and say that I order that each civilian in Celle will hand in one blanket by mid day tomorrow". We got 1800 blankets the following night.'[71] What Gonin recounted as an *ad hoc* improvisation – a short-term stopgap that would let the ambulances start shuttling people from huts to hospital again – anticipated a large-scale military operation to muster garments, footwear and bedding from the German population.

Extensive requisitioning from German residents of Celle, Soltau and Uelzen, communities in the environs of Bergen-Belsen, soon became the order of the day. Military Government (MG) officers imposed a

Figure 2.4 Ilse Kohra (left), daughter of the Burgermeister of Belsen, along with Herr Pfeifer (right) and his daughter Anna, sort clothing for Bergen-Belsen survivors in the Burgermeister's house, June 1945 (National Archives and Records Administration)

'clothing levy' that stretched across British-occupied Germany, persisting over the course of several months into 1946. Lists tallying what was amassed in this way hint at both the scale of the levy and the magnitude of the relief operation in Belsen:

> 15,000 sets of men's clothing comprised of the following articles – Suits, underclothes, socks, boots and shoes
> 25,000 sets of women's clothing comprised of the following articles – Frocks, costumes, underclothes, overcoats, shoes and stockings. 80,000 sanitary towels were also obtained.
> 1000 sets of clothing for children and babies – these included garments, shoes and napkins.
> The following items were obtained and issued to the Hospital Block: 10,000 beds, 25,000 sheets, 40,000 blankets, 15,000 palliases, 1,500 bed pans, 15,000 pairs pyjamas ...

> The following items were issued to the Hospital Block and to
> the concentration camp to clean up the area:—
> 20 tons of soap, 5 tons of scouring powder, 10 tons of cleaning
> rags, 1000 brooms, 1000 scrubbing brushes, 2000 buckets,
> 500 picks, 1000 shovels.[72]

While these numbers alert us to the epic scale of what was required
at Belsen, they don't capture the complexity of the levy operation.
Nor do they reveal where British military requisitioning fitted within
the larger matrix of Allied efforts to extract material *reparation* from
Germany – from the Red Army's wholesale dismantling and removal
of German industrial equipment to myriad individual acts of property
'liberation'.[73]

As soon as the Third Reich's power crumbled in the spring of
1945, survivors of the camps, along with forced labourers brought to
Germany from countries under *Wehrmacht* occupation, sought compensation – sometimes also retaliation – in whatever forms lay most
readily to hand. Appropriation of German clothing lent 'redress' a
particularly literal form. Soldiers and humanitarians alike noted the
ubiquity of looting: seemingly by everyone, everywhere, all at once.
Many British observers deemed liberated Russian 'slave workers' the
most prodigious offenders. 'Altogether this is such an amazing place
that I have forgotten who are allies and who are enemies,' marvelled
Margaret Ward. 'The Russians are the terror of the countryside and
the sooner they are sent home the better for everybody!'[74] MacAuslan
observed that, even though British officers commanded Hungarians to
guard the perimeter of Belsen, nevertheless about 3,000 internees had
escaped. He drily remarked that they had 'set off for home taking their
lice with them. Some were found ill with typhus in neighbouring villages, others raided the countryside and returned to the camp through
the exit hole with their loot – orange pyjamas in one instance.'[75]

Where looting ended and requisitioning began depended largely
on the apparel of the expropriator. Uniformed Britons tended to give
their own procurement methods a more euphemistic label ('organizing') than the ones they pinned on Russians and other displaced persons (DPs). The coinage DP encompassed not only survivors of Nazi
camps but also millions of people uprooted from their former homes
who, as the war ended, were either encamped in liberated German
facilities or attempting to get home – or reach *somewhere* away from

their erstwhile sites of confinement.[76] Ward candidly admitted that Russians didn't enjoy a monopoly over expropriation of German property: 'In Germany anything you want you just go and take, so the looting both necessary and otherwise is terrific.'[77] Civilians and military personnel, men and women alike, routinely 'organized' supplies from whatever portable items could be lifted from German homes and businesses, some taking pride in their entrepreneurial prowess. In a disturbing turn of phrase, Gonin announced that 'The girls were far better in raping the German civilian population for comforts and food for the internees,' leaving no doubt that he felt this violation was entirely justified.[78]

Relief workers' letters home and diaries bear witness to various initiatives to muster all manner of supplies from Germans in Belsen's vicinity. Ward herself embarked on a mission to rustle up wedding rings from the Burgermeister (mayor) in Celle. Though she didn't elaborate on their provenance, wedding bands were perhaps supplied primarily by *Wehrmacht* widows, then redistributed to survivors of Belsen whose own rings had been plundered by the SS: the same organization responsible for murdering many of their spouses. Within weeks of Belsen's liberation, rings were also necessary to solemnize new unions as survivors married one another at ceremonies held in the camp.[79]

Garments, shoes and bedclothes were, however, the primary targets of the British MG's official clothing levy. After an initial round of impromptu house-to-house collections made by British troops, authority was subsequently delegated to local Burgermeisters, issued with lengthy lists of what they must extract from residents. German householders had to deliver the requisite amount of clothes, footwear and bed linen to designated collection points in department stores or civic centres. British troops then collected this material and took it back to headquarters depots for sorting and packing – all under armed guard to prevent 'pilferage and black marketeering'.[80] Wherever possible, clothing was pressed into huge bales with industrial machinery. Compacted fabric blocks required less storage space and facilitated distribution by reducing garments from an unruly mass into a solid bundle of standard size. Over the summer and autumn of 1945, these arrangements became institutionalized across British-occupied Germany, with garments warehoused, sorted, cleaned and disinfected to ensure that the recirculation of clothing didn't simultaneously spread contagion. In some areas where garments were especially scarce, British officers organized their subordinates into search parties, extending the dragnet to *any* type of material. Their efforts garnered usable fabric in the form of bunting, old tablecloths and German parachute silk, which the RAF had hitherto ordered to be burnt.[81]

In this instance, illicit hoarding had an unintended upside. But Germans' circumvention of MG rules was more often an obstacle than an asset. Despite British officers' and German municipal oversight, local residents found ingenious ways to game the system by laundering and folding garments from which material had been filleted at the back, or by artfully presenting apparel that, on closer inspection, proved worn beyond the point of reclamation. 'Much of the commandeered German clothing would go fairly well on a tramp's back,' harrumphed an unusually blunt British MG report on the 'clothing situation'. 'If something isn't done the Germans will continue to be clothed *de rigueur* and the DPs will be the rather drab Cinderellas of the party.' Infuriated by German duplicity, British officers ordered local officials to inspect what people turned in at the moment of handover. But some still worried that Germans couldn't be trusted to supervise other Germans.[82]

'Harrods'

Frustrations experienced at District HQ level, sharpened by a sense that Germans revelled in *Schadenfreude* as their sly civic disobedience unravelled British plans, played out in microcosm at Belsen. There the jumble of locally mustered German garments was sifted, organized and prepared for distribution.

With the arrival of a laundry unit courtesy of Unilever, the hospital situation eased somewhat. But the demand for fresh bedding, pyjamas and nighties continued to outstrip supply until permanent camp laundry facilities became operational. Meanwhile, seamstresses among the survivors were set to work sewing standard nightgowns for the sick.[83] As patients regained strength, the epicentre of the clothing crisis shifted. Mobile people urgently needed footwear, as bare feet presented a vulnerable entry point for infection. In MacAuslan's estimation, shoes posed the biggest challenge when it came to outfitting survivors. Apt to come uncoupled in transit, wayward pairs resisted reunion. From the tonne of footwear harvested from Germans, 'not one shoe was attached to its fellow. Two inmates were given the task of sorting through the pile to match up a pair. As an inducement they were promised one mark for each success. After three days, they gave up with only two pairs to show for their efforts.'[84]

Medics and relief workers fumed not just over mismatched shoes 'of the most depressing variety', but about every aspect of the clothing situation at Belsen: from finding premises for distribution to widespread theft and survivors' 'fussiness' over the quality of apparel on offer. Britons simultaneously regarded clothes as a key agent of patients' psychic resuscitation *and* an enormous headache they could've done without. While Irish doctor Robert Collis identified outfitting survivors as 'one of the most important measures of all', Myrtle Beardwell wrote with some disdain that the garment distribution centre was 'one of the most difficult places to run'.[85]

Initially, relief workers established a clothing depot to outfit convalescent patients in the cellar of a canteen. However, as Silva Jones pointed out, this subterranean venue 'was not suitable because of the stairs and many were afraid to go down through the dark entrance'. Three days later, the operation relocated to a former stable block, where the Red Cross clothing team spent a day 'stocking and arranging' requisitioned German apparel only to find their efforts swiftly undone. 'The place was firmly locked at night but by the morning it had been broken into; that together with the water used in putting out the fire in the fumigating room next door completely spoilt the day's work and it had to be started again from scratch.' Silva Jones' diary recorded that '[t]he following night it was broken into again, but with less damage and some of the culprits were caught.'[86] When it opened for business, this clothing store was dubbed 'Harrods' by British squaddies, deploying their trademark humour with a wry nod to Knightsbridge's most celebrated department store. The name stuck.[87]

On a visit to Belsen in August 1945, British war artist Mary Kessell captured poignant vignettes of 'Harrods'. Using words rather than drawings, she etched impressions of the place, including interactions with survivors eager to quiz her about the latest London styles. One young woman spelt out for Kessell how integral a role clothing had played in camp inmates' debasement by the SS: '"You see for four years the Germans dressed us up like Clowns, they took away all our clothes, and gave us things that did not fit or match, they gave us stockings and nothing to keep them up with, because they took our belts away and there was no string or tape to be had. Our backs were painted because we were Jews." "But even then", said another, "we managed a piece of lipstick and some powder, and before we went to the factory at five am we made our faces up a little!'"[88]

To women intent on reasserting their irrepressible personhood, 'Harrods' could be a place of disappointment as well as discovery. Commandeered German garments dangled from the stable's wooden beams, still marked with names of Panzer horses formerly housed there. Kessell's painterly language, laid out like poetry in elegant script, animates this scene:

> A long grey building, with bales of clothing down each side, old
>   dresses on the table laid out and rows and rows of old old shoes.
> Boxes of odd stockings and young DP girls picking at them
>   frantically trying to find two that make a pair.
> Some come in striped pyjamas from the hospital to choose
>   their first clothes; some very beautiful with hair beginning to
>   grow, some ugly with illness and suffering.
> They hang around to see if any new clothes will come in.
> They all want new clothes.
> They are greedy for dress, these women who nearly died.
> A Polish girl dashed in, hysterical with joy, because she had
>   been given a coat made of rabbit skin, by one of the soldiers.
> A woman came with a child who had no shoes.
> His feet were tied in blankets. 'Shoes, shoes' she kept saying.
>   But there were no shoes.
> There are no shoes in Europe. She can't believe there are no
>   shoes for her child, and she calls again 'Shoes, shoes.'
> They are making new clothes out of old, and Nuns are teaching
>   Polish girls to sew.
> Nuns in full white tunics with black headdress in a grey stable.
>   The windows are blue.[89]

Kessell's depiction is remarkable not only for its vivid evocation of people and place, but also because of the stark contrast it offers with many other British-authored accounts. Where Kessell was present to observe, interact and record, relief workers tasked with organizing 'Harrods' focused more on the endless tribulations of the work and a clientele whose demanding behaviour made an onerous task even more burdensome. Humanitarians had their own views – none too positive – on the nature and calibre of garments collected from Germans or (as time went by) imported through overseas channels. Beth Clarkson, a

Quaker serving with the Friends Relief Service, reserved her most scathing judgement for the 'Victorian drawers' of which German women had apparently been only too keen to divest themselves. Since Russian women alone favoured these voluminous bloomers, they betrayed their nationality with a dowdy preference Clarkson found baffling. Any pairs left unwanted by the Russians, she noted, were 'used for "comic turns" or handkerchiefs'. Although no Britons had anything positive to say about the 'poor and scanty' garments on offer at 'Harrods', relief workers nevertheless expected that survivors should show appreciation, or at the very least that they wouldn't actively hinder operations. Humanitarians often regard themselves as agents of authority, dispensers of benevolence, bound in a hierarchical relationship with the recipients of their good deeds. Gratitude, not money, was the preferred currency of this cashless moral economy.[90]

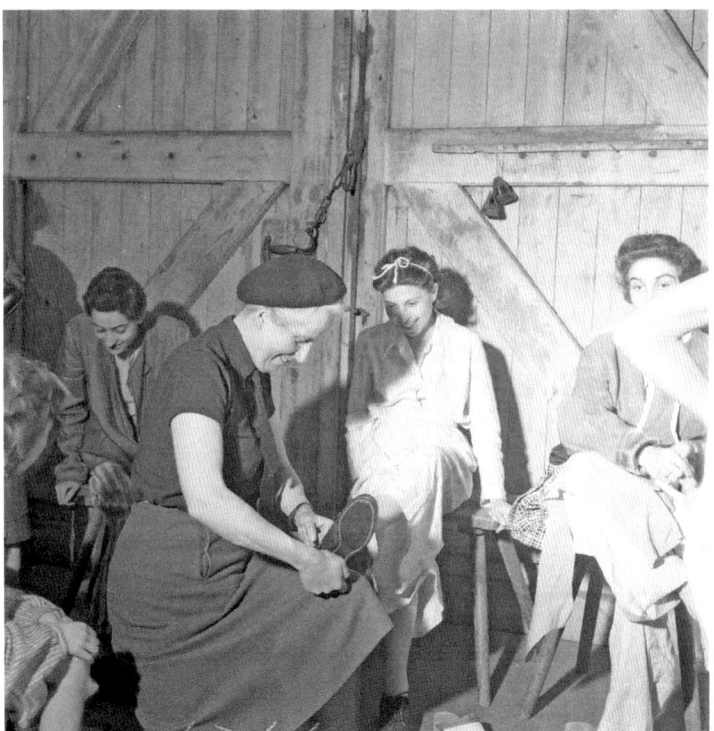

Figure 2.5 Vivian Dantell, an UNRRA relief worker from Aylesbury, helps former camp inmate Livia Crammer select new shoes at 'Harrods', photographed by Sgt CH Hewitt, 16–17 May 1945 (© Imperial War Museum, BU 6366)

Relief workers harboured complex feelings not just about the relationship between 'helpers' and 'helped', but also regarding the character and identity of Belsen's survivors. As several historians have documented, one of the most striking features of liberators' responses to what we now term the Holocaust is how little attention Britons paid to *whom* exactly they had liberated. Few of the first cohort to enter Belsen underscored the singular plight of European Jewry as the primary target of Nazi genocide. That a majority of those killed at Belsen and of those who survived were Jewish often remained unspoken, sometimes actively suppressed. Infamously, the BBC excised references to Jews from Richard Dimbleby's wrenching radio report scripted at Belsen on 17 April and broadcast two days later.[91] But censorship wasn't the reason why many British personnel failed to identify with any specificity – let alone with any specific gravity – who was whom at Belsen. Most reports focused only on survivors' countries of origin, not their faith. British witnesses to the camp rationalized this evasion with the claim that categorizing Jews *qua* Jews was 'playing Hitler's game', setting apart a distinct 'outgroup'. British fair-mindedness, in this self-construction, required people simply to be treated as people, without prejudice or favouritism.[92] As a result, broad and rather misleading descriptors like 'people of every nationality' prevailed. And where relief workers *did* make direct references or indirect allusions to Jews and Jewishness, these weren't always positively coded. Indeed, a strand of latent (or more active) antisemitism ran through some Britons' reports, clouding their perception of what they witnessed at Belsen in general and 'Harrods' in particular.

Take, for instance, this passage written by Effie Barker in a letter on 15 May: 'The main problem now is about 4000 people of all races, most of them in a state of starvation and disease to be got away clothed and healthy ... Into these camps were poured the best (in small quantities) and the worst. The highly cultured failed to exist as one had to be almost criminally minded and tough to get food and remain sane. The exceptions of cultured people who live are fantastically interesting to talk to – although the lack of speaking German is a problem.'[93] Barker reprised a then commonplace notion that the most 'refined' people were those most likely to have perished in the camps, while their more unscrupulous peers survived – at others' expense. (Survivors had reason to experience guilt in this construction.) And, even though she invoked 'all races', her analysis tapped into time-worn antisemitic tropes, in which the wily Shtetl-dwelling peasant triumphed over more genteel cosmopolitan urbanites: people who more closely approximated notions of respectability and deservingness imparted by Barker's aristocratic upbringing.[94]

There was nothing coded about Myrtle Beardwell's complaints about 'grasping' Jews, whom she blamed for hoarding the higher-quality garments that Jewish relief charities started delivering to Belsen a few weeks after liberation. '[T]he Jews (who had by far the most and best supplies – mostly American), refused to share with other nationalities, but they expected their fair share of all other supplies. This caused much unpleasantness, and, to my knowledge, was never satisfactorily cleared up.'[95] That Jews were the sole intended recipients of aid from the Joint Distribution Committee and other Jewish organizations, which also distributed religious apparel vital to Orthodox observance, clearly held no sway with Beardwell. Nor did her remarks convey any compassion for people who had been dispossessed of everything by the Third Reich – homes, communities, loved ones, possessions – then stripped of clothing both on entry to the camps and again on removal to the 'Laundry'. 'Any clothes they had originally had to be burnt,' noted another terse Red Cross worker.[96]

Like hoarding, theft bedevilled workers at 'Harrods'. Beardwell's memoir insinuates that Jews bore primary responsibility for stealing: another manifestation (in her eyes) of selfish possessiveness and chicanery that uncannily mirrored German attempts to withhold wearable garments from the clothing levy:

> When it was first opened the DPs were taken up to the store in ambulances – most of them either swathed in blankets or in striped pyjamas, their only clothing. Each one was allowed to get a certain number of things from 'Harrods' – each one had to be looked over before leaving the store. Nearly all tried to smuggle more clothes – they would tie up the bottoms of their trousers and push all sorts of things such as vests, stockings, etc. down the legs. When they were found they just shrugged their shoulders in a resigned sort of way and shamelessly walked out of the store. This was only one bad trait that was the result of life in concentration camps.[97]

Guards became a fixture at the clothing depot to deter 'shoplifting' and, if deterrence failed, to apprehend thieves. Collis recorded a raid on one hut to retrieve seventeen dresses that a single woman had spirited from 'Harrods'.[98]

Margaret Ward, who became officer in charge of clothing in the middle of June, attempted to bring greater orderliness to distribution. She introduced a ticketed entry system to prevent overcrowding. But deciding who should enjoy priority access was tricky: 'I have about 7000 people to clothe and an allocation of 100 tickets for "Harrods" each day, so the dreadful part is allocating the tickets to the right people,' she fretted. Equally difficult was determining how clothing should be dispensed as equitably as possible, not least when articles varied so wildly in quality. Ward and her colleagues inaugurated a points system, roughly replicating Britain's clothes rationing scheme that assigned different values to garments based on the amount and quality of fabric used in their production. By this reckoning a fur coat – whether at Harrods in Knightsbridge or at 'Harrods' in Belsen – was worth more points than its humbler woollen counterpart. But whether it was fair to reduce the amount of *other* apparel the recipient of a fur coat received was a more ethically charged proposition. A fur coat didn't, after all, substitute for everything else a woman with nothing would need.[99]

In letters home, Ward suggested that her efforts, aided by an international team of sorters and a fleet of interpreters, slowly paid off in terms of streamlining 'Harrods' and assessing people's needs in the camp at large. In the process, she grew attached to 'one particular boy friend aged 8, who is actually a German Jew from Berlin with no known relatives. He and I always do the rounds in the truck together, and also visit the blocks.'[100] But if Ward helped make distribution fairer in the store, she remained furious over the pilfering that remained rampant all over the camp, extending to her very own possessions. 'I am full of rage as my best shoes were pinched from the babies nursery by the Russian women and I am now left with one pair,' she huffed on 22 June. 'I am writing to HQ London about it and hope they'll provide coupons for some more.' The Red Cross went one better. Within a month, HQ had dispatched 'a pair of strong black shoes, which will be quite useful for going around the camp'. But even if the organization hadn't provided replacement footwear so swiftly, Ward possessed a capacious wardrobe at home, plus obliging parents to whom she frequently addressed requests for more garments to be mailed to her in Germany. The same letter that saw Ward raging about her stolen shoes also contained an annotated wish list, ending with a special plea: 'The only thing that is really urgent is my bathing suit and sandals as we have now a super bathing pool here.'[101]

'Back to Life'

Within weeks of liberation, Belsen became a hub of social activity in British-occupied Germany. Drinks parties had been a nightly occurrence from the very start. Senior military and medical officers gulped their way through the Panzer barracks' cellars after their 10pm evening conference, female colleagues first having been ushered out.[102] As more supplies and fresh incomers rolled in, other mixed-sex entertainments supplemented male-only drinking sessions. Dinner parties, film shows, live music, cabaret acts and dances became regular fixtures. Female relief workers soon found that the party dresses they'd packed along with their Red Cross uniforms weren't excess baggage after all, as some had feared. If this exuberant whirl of conviviality seems astonishing with hindsight, not least as the daily death rate remained in the hundreds at this point in May, only some of those present at the time felt troubled by the jarring contradiction between Belsen's former incarnation and its rebirth as what the *Daily Express* dubbed (in August 1945) 'Germany's gayest and happiest city'.[103]

A 'back to life' frame soon surrounded Britons' accounts of Belsen. Just as the British military instituted Christian burial ceremonies with crosses marking mass graves, 'resurrection' structured how many expatriate personnel at Belsen conceived the recovery of people retrieved from the brink of death. Alongside complaints about fussy and light-fingered 'customers' at 'Harrods', another strand of commentary celebrated a transmutation catalysed by clothing. 'It is marvellous seeing the bedridden skeletons of four weeks ago now going about as if they enjoyed life,' gushed Margaret Ward.[104] Colleague Effie Barker waxed similarly rhapsodic, encouraging recipients of her letter to spread the good news with a view to eliciting more donations:

> Stores of clothing have been poured in – tell the [Red Cross] Work Party – that is what they have worked up for and at one corner one meets ambulance loads of female like figures (in a state of starvation sexes become almost non-existent) shrouded in blankets, hollowed tummies and glazed eyes. They are taken in to 'Harrods' and shown dresses, stockings (silk if possible so that they can feel) and immediately some glimmer of hope begins to appear. After much trying on and argument

they totter out with a different outlook on life. To my mind this is one of the most astounding sights. All those who have sent clothes should see it. Our great cry now is for lipsticks and powder etc. It is like living in a town of human beings from another sphere![105]

'Clothes became a medical necessity, a powerful tonic', chimed a British army photographer, 'a strong antidote against the mental apathy of the very weak.'[106] Choosiness itself could be read as an encouraging indication of humanity rekindled. 'Some of our customers, though practically naked, are extremely fussy,' opined Quaker Beth Clarkson. 'Though this is very trying when one is very busy, we feel it is a sign of returning self-respect, for many of these people would once have been most particular about their personal appearance.'[107]

As these remarks hint, relief workers aspired to reanimate not just survivors' humanity, but also their 'sense of femininity', as Barker put it.[108] As many saw it, progress through the 'Human Laundry' – with patients' hair clipped to the cranium – had further accentuated the neutered appearance of Belsen's 'scarecrows'. Helping females become *women*, attractive both to themselves and to others, seemed imperative. Army photographers who captured scenes at 'Harrods' participated in this conflation of dignity with desirability. Captions to some images described Red Cross workers helping women select dresses 'for her next date'.[109] Equally striking in Belsen's gendered scheme of things was the fact that relief workers said very little about the distribution of garments to *male* survivors. Outfitting men was seemingly a bare necessity, not a mystical rite of rejuvenation. Tellingly, Welsh Quaker and conscientious objector Eryl Hall Williams, who briefly worked with Friends Relief Service Team 100 in Belsen's men's clothing store in the middle of May, left just a few terse journal entries about this unwelcome stint. His comments offered no indication of how men responded to their newly received apparel, nor any estimation of garments' role in male survivors' 'return to life'.[110]

More even than clothing, cosmetics promised to redraw gender identities along preferred lines: a clear distinction between maleness and femaleness restored by rouged cheeks and crimson lips. No one spoke more eloquently on the life-altering power of lipstick than the Ipswich doctor-turned-colonel Mervyn Gonin. Concluding a talk on Belsen delivered in 1946, Gonin eulogized the most unexpectedly potent medicine at Belsen – a remedy he personally hadn't thought to prescribe:

> It was shortly after the BRCS [British Red Cross Society] teams arrived, though it may have no connection, that a very large quantity of lipstick also arrived. This was not at all what we men wanted, we were screaming for hundreds of thousands of other things and I don't know who asked for lipstick. I wish so much that I could discover who did it, it was the action of a genious [sic], sheer unadulterated brilliance. I believe nothing did more for those internees than lipstick. Women lay in bed with no sheets and no nightie but with scarlet lips, you saw them wandering about with nothing but a blanket over their shoulders, but with scarlet lips. I saw a woman dead on the post mortem table and clutched in her hand was a piece of lipstick.

'At last someone had done something to make them individuals again', Gonin continued, 'they were someone, no longer merely the number tatooed on the arm. At last they could take an interest in their appearance. That lipstick started to give them back their humanity ... perhaps the most pathetic thing that's ever happened, I don't know. But that is why the sight of a piece of lipstick today makes my eyes feel just a little uncomfortable.'[111]

Other things made fellow Britons feel uncomfortable to varying degrees, and for different reasons. Not everyone rejoiced equally over the refeminization of Belsen's women survivors. Michael Hargrave, pleased in the abstract that women were 'attempting to keep themselves clean and to look nice', took a dimmer view of the efforts of one particular Polish woman, Zosia, to make herself more attractive. Michael had devoted numerous hours to teaching Zosia English when there was little doctoring to be done in his assigned hut. An intense friendship, charged with latent sexual energy, briefly consumed him. Hargrave was entranced by Zosia's intellect and talent as a linguist; their connection distracted and delighted him. But her recovery, rather than gratifying the medical student, curdled his appreciation of her qualities. 'Zosia does not look so nice now that she has tried to make up, as she did in Camp 1,' Hargrave sourly observed. Although he still had time to continue teaching Zosia, he abandoned both the lessons and his pupil. This same journal entry, marking Zosia's final appearance, noted blankly: 'She is still trying to learn English, but has no-one to teach her.' Like many bonds forged at Belsen, this one rapidly disintegrated, cut short by a Briton soon bound for home, and for whom 'helping' had only ever been a temporary calling.[112]

Intimations of intercourse threw Britons off balance all around. With erotic desire energizing 'sexless' Belsen, some celebrated this manifestation of 'normal' human behaviour – a triumph of irrepressible biology over inhuman brutality. Men and women were again doing what men and women typically did. (Same-sex couplings passed unremarked.) British officers soon folded female survivors into social gatherings, as both performers and dance partners. A nightclub, 'The Coconut Grove', was established by anaesthetist Captain 'Frosty' Winterbottom on the top floor of the same block that housed 'Harrods'. The club opened on 21 May to celebrate the climactic incineration of the 'Horror Camp' earlier that day. Jean McFarlane enthused over 'the best party I've ever attended': 'the whole of one big room ... transformed into a Night Club complete with Bar, tables and seating accommodation, shaded lights, band, and during the evening, a Cabaret, the artistes being four of the fit Internees all gotten up in very smart evening dresses made in the Camp sewing rooms ... It was such a surprise to find a place of that kind in Belsen at all.' These 'astounding' dresses were concocted from 'sheets, surgical gauze etc.', a dazzled Effie Barker noted.[113]

MacAuslan's response to the 'Coconut Grove' could hardly have differed more. 'Someone, perhaps the Brigadier, it is the sort of inspiration Brigadiers get, had the bright idea that the fitter female internees needed rehabilitating, would benefit from a return to "normal" life, and that the best way to achieve this would be to give them a dance using medical students as partners,' he recorded grimly:

> The girls and medical students sat around nervously, before partnering each other on the dance floor. The girls, we suspected, thought that they were in the foyer of a brothel and would be expected to go up against the outside of a hut with us later, the Brigadier as an outsize Madame. The students, some of whom [himself included] had been propositioned in the Concentration Camp and did not want a repeat – sex for cigarettes – had not enough German to reassure the girls or even make small talk. Though the Brigadier seemed to enjoy himself, as a party it was not a success.[114]

In MacAuslan's telling, women who were understandably apprehensive about male intentions nevertheless appeared putative aggressors, their sexuality as alarming to the medical student as the Brigadier's misjudged machinations.

Some of MacAuslan's peers were perhaps less squeamish. It seems unlikely that British men who observed the proliferation of sexual activity at Belsen all abstained from participation. Arnold Horwell wrestled with especially conflicted feelings about the thrum of male–female interactions around the camp. As a token of restored female self-esteem, flirtation was all very well and good – up to a point. On 4 May, Horwell confided to his wife:

> It is a heartening sight how some of the women 'pick up', i.e. start caring for their dress etc. I only realized to-day – when checking accomm. in Camp 3 and various houses, where girls employed at laundry and various messes are billeted, how pretty many of the girls look – still, or again. They keep their rooms spotlessly clean, there are flowers on the table, and, the best sign of all – they flirt with the Tommies! If any proof was required that they are gaining self-respect again, this is it.

Just a week later, his observations took a darker turn:

> It looks like 'mating season' – and it probably is. However, this reminds me again of a more serious problem. It is certainly most wonderful that the girls start feeling at ease in male company, take pride in their appearance, and enjoy life, at least its more emotional aspects. But, I'm afraid, it is going too far. I can very well understand the bottled up feelings of a girl, which makes her throw herself at any man, who treats her gently and doesn't maltreat, nor try to rape her. I can also understand that a tommy – sex-starved as he is here in Germany – wouldn't say 'No'. And I don't mind so much if Polish or Gypsie or Russian girls behave like this. But it somehow hurts me if I see Jewish girls – just the finest, cultivated types, even the finest of them all, the German-Jewish girls – behaving like this. It isn't subconscious jealousy on my part only; I have overheard tommies telling each other that most of the girls were probably brought here because they were prostitutes, and that the biggest prostitutes had the best chance of survival and to keep as

fit as many girls appear to be now. It all rather upset me, this entirely wrong interpretation of the girls' behaviour, but I just don't know what could be done about it.

What Horwell *did* do about it was invite a British military Rabbi serving at Belsen to intercede, hoping that he might restore these young women to a more chaste sense of decorum. Perhaps under the Rabbi's tutelage self-esteem could be uncoupled from sexual allure.[115]

Make, Do and Mend

For many Britons, 21 May 1945 marked the dramatic pinnacle of their time at Belsen. Army flamethrowers ignited the 'Horror Camp', along with a swastika flag and large portrait of Hitler strategically positioned on either side of a hut entrance. Sombre words of commemoration were followed by the hoisting of the Union Jack, now able to flutter proudly over space reclaimed from Nazi barbarity. Most British witnesses found this scene a far more cathartic culmination than VE Day, which had flickered past a fortnight earlier like a distant meteor, impossibly remote from the world of Belsen. Dramatic in their symbolism and profoundly moving as spectacle, the burning huts provided an over-determined conclusion to several narratives. Camp eradicated. Chapter closed.

The first wave of liberators receded from Belsen after little more than six weeks or two months in residence, sometimes less. Those who recorded impressions of time working among the camp's survivors tended to represent this period as a uniquely 'gruesome' but also fantastically 'interesting' interlude in their careers as soldiers, doctors or humanitarians, packed with extreme experience. Like human gauze, they soaked everything up. But then they moved on – geographically, if not also emotionally. There were other battles to fight; other camps to organize; other DPs to rehabilitate and repatriate.

Reviewing accounts written in the spring of 1945 at an eighty-year remove is to see history through bifocal lenses, participants' perspectives and the knowledge supplied by hindsight making everything clearer and fuzzier simultaneously. Some key assumptions that structured operations at Belsen in the spring of 1945 were mistaken. Perplexing now, but pervasive then, were the interwoven assumptions that the relief operation would conclude swiftly and that survivors would soon be restored to fitness and then leave Belsen, like their liberators. 'The next and final chapter will be the nursing back to health in the hospitals of the thousands who are sick in mind and body,' announced Colonel Bird on 18 May, anticipating a firm line being drawn under the whole horrific experience in the near future.[116] After recovery would come repatriation. The mass return of DPs to their places of origin formed a bedrock principle of UNRRA's operations.

Only a modicum of hindsight is necessary, however, to appreciate that it was no more realistic to expect most survivors would rapidly 'get better' than to believe that everyone would soon 'go home'. Hundreds of thousands of DPs of different nationalities, especially from the Baltic states, Ukraine and other nations unhappily under Soviet sway, exhibited no desire to return east. Even less susceptible to ready resolution was the plight of the 'surviving remnant' of European Jewry whose communities, homes and families had been destroyed beyond any possibility of reclamation. Stateless people, lacking the protective cover of governmental authority, needed permanent places of sanctuary with particular urgency.[117]

An air of momentum quickens accounts of Belsen – whether official memos, personal letters or journal entries – produced in the late spring of 1945. This sense of propulsion towards an imminent goal pervades reports on the distribution of clothing. 'Approx. 1800 people clothed to date, and on the whole the organisation has worked well,' reported Quaker Beth Clarkson in June 1945. 'Speed is of considerable importance, since it is hoped that the majority of internees will have left Belsen in a fortnight's time.'[118] Two sets of 'new' clothes, a pair of shoes, and everyone would be on their way ... Or so relief workers initially expected.

Severe illness and psychological trauma were, however, no more susceptible to instant cure than the complex geopolitical fracture over where DPs would resettle. Many wealthier countries, the United States in particular, resolutely opposed admitting large numbers of DPs in (and after) 1945. The British government remained equally set against permitting Jewish survivors to emigrate to Palestine *en masse*. But it remained the preferred destination of many, and the number swelled as other doors remained firmly shut. Zionists found an unlikely champion in Harry Truman, whose predecessor, Franklin

D. Roosevelt, died on 12 April 1945: the day SS officers at Belsen made their surrender offer to British commanders. The new president, stung by charges that the American authorities were not doing enough for survivors of Nazi atrocity in US-occupied southern Germany, dispatched special representative Earl G. Harrison (former dean of the University of Pennsylvania Law School) to investigate. Harrison's 8,000-word report, published verbatim in the *New York Times* on 30 September 1945, was damning in the extreme. It made particular reference to the plight of 14,000 Jewish DPs at Belsen. Among other failures, Harrison noted that survivors still lacked adequate clothing. Some were 'obliged to wear German SS uniforms', while others possessed only their 'prison garb', producing a 'rather hideous striped pajama effect'.[119] Truman responded by insisting that Westminster immediately issue 100,000 visas for Jewish DPs to enter Palestine: a proposition Attlee and foreign minister Ernest Bevin rejected, fearing this influx would trigger violent retaliation by Palestinian Arabs. Undeterred, thousands of Jewish DPs attempted to reach Eretz Israel by land or sea, with British forces detaining immigrants whose boats they intercepted in camps on Cyprus.[120]

Belsen remained in existence as a DP camp not just for weeks or months but for years, as did dozens of other camps dotted around Germany and beyond. The last Jewish DPs departed Belsen in 1951.[121] Among the varieties of relief work necessary to sustain existence in these semi-permanent communities, clothing distribution bulked large. As Harrison's report made plain, the business of refashioning 'bare life' was both demanding and ongoing. Jane Leverson, the first Jewish relief worker from Britain to reach Belsen, offered a grim assessment of the clothing situation of Jewish DPs whom she accompanied to a centre at Celle, some twelve miles away: 'Most of them were still in disgusting, dirty, ragged blue-and-white striped outfits from the concentration camp and wore extremely dilapidated, ill-fitting shoes. Only 250 top garments and 177 pairs of shoes had been delivered there (by UNRRA) and no underwear.'[122]

Histories of relief operations tend to treat clothing as a brief prologue to the *real* story of postwar humanitarianism: a one-off distribution of donated garments, re-equipping survivors for life after near-death. Clothes figure as an essential need, yet ancillary to humans' other fundamental requirements: food and shelter. Needless to say, though, one trip to 'Harrods' didn't fully outfit anyone who had nothing. Seasons changed; children grew; needs expanded, as did the contours of bodies and feet. Things fell apart – donated things especially. 'The great problem is shoes,' sighed Margaret Ward, joining the chorus of lamentation over footwear. 'The ones provided wear out in two or three weeks. There seems to be no leather in the country.' Vanquished Germans were even less likely to surrender their higher-calibre items than victorious Americans, scarcely encouraged to dig deep by the 'Victory Clothing' slogan, 'They can wear what you can spare.'[123]

Amid much that continued to be bleak, some relief workers nevertheless discerned encouraging portents. Leverson, whose dispiriting appraisal of the clothing situation at Celle chimed with Earl Harrison's observations, documented the ingenuity that DPs demonstrated whenever they received appropriate materials and tools. In a report written in June 1945, she detailed how much creativity a single parcel could inspire. Her mother had sent a package of sewing materials over to Belsen. These, along with knitting needles and yarn supplied by the Friends Relief Service, had 'made it possible for a small number of people to "Make, Do and Mend"'. 'They are pathetically pleased,' Jane commented, offering three illustrative samples of survivors' handiwork:

> First is of a woman whom I found recently, who had made her dress out of curtains taken from Belsen, with thread drawn from a petticoat she had received at Belsen – and a borrowed needle.
> The second is of a man who was painstakingly unpicking the seams of the wretchedly shabby clothes which his room-mates were wearing, cutting the clothes to fit, with a pair of nail scissors, and sewing them with the thread which he had unpicked.
> The third is of a girl who was making costumes for her friends from blankets which she had brought from Belsen, with thread from my mother's parcel.[124]

Inserting a comma between 'make' and 'do', Leverson altered the sense of this familiar wartime mantra to accentuate energetic activity – 'making', 'doing', 'mending' – rather than the stoic resignation often implied by 'making do'. Not content to passively accept cast-off garments, these men and women took old things and refashioned new ones along lines of their own choosing. The 'mending' had both a practical and a therapeutic dimension.

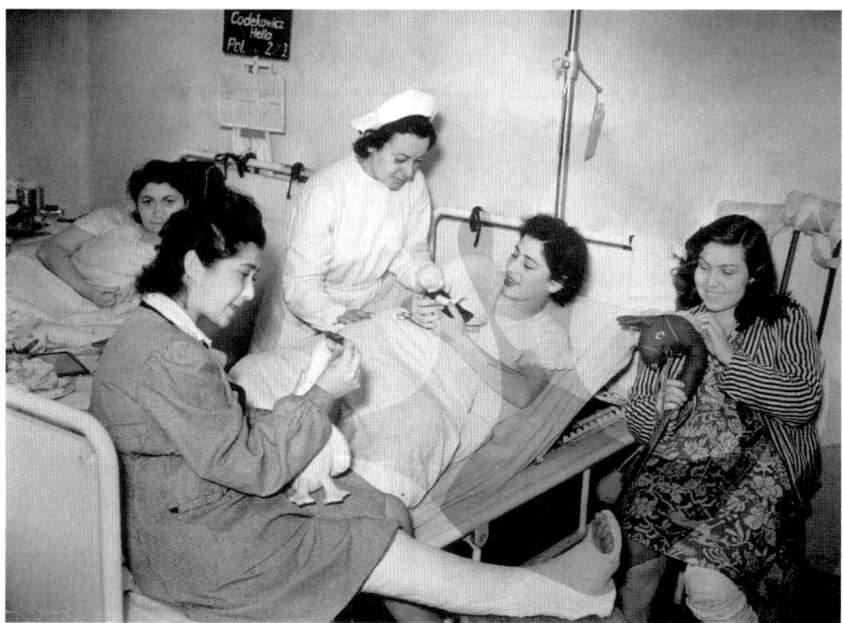

Figure 2.6 Survivors on a hospital ward at Belsen make children's toys from *Wehrmacht* uniforms, 24 December 1945 (Bettmann/Getty Images)

As well as everything from coats and shoes to suits and bridal gowns, survivors of Belsen fashioned toys and dolls from scraps of fabric. No material seemed so irredeemably tainted by its former associations as to be considered fit only for destruction. Remnants of *Wehrmacht* uniforms were reborn as endearing stuffed animals. Most striking of all, though, was the use to which some survivors put their own discarded uniforms. Women sewed dolls, dressed in blue and white striped coats, that represented the liberated inmates of Belsen. Like their creators, these cloth figures bore different expressions: some with exaggeratedly wide eyes, long lashes, crimson lips. Horrifying to outside observers, the striped fabric of the camp uniform signified something more complex to those forced to wear it, yet who'd survived. The abject striped figure was, or had been, *them*: their humanity never entirely stripped away by, or beneath, the camp apparel.[125]

When they left Belsen, some British soldiers and relief workers received these dolls as going away gifts, tangible thank-yous. But more than that. The women who crafted these fabric miniatures wanted their transient friends to take a piece of them home – and cherish it.

3 VETERANS

The evening of 11 August 1944 found Sir Montague Burton, Britain's most successful menswear manufacturer and retailer, revelling in a glorious late summer panorama as he gazed across Blubberhouses Moor from his Harrogate home. Here was a veritable 'Garden of Eden', aglow with 'colourful Floral Schemes'. This paean to North Yorkshire's heather-dappled landscape was penned for the benefit of Burton's son Raymond, then serving as a captain with the 74/23rd Light Anti-Aircraft Regiment, India Command. Not only was the countryside at its most spectacular, Burton senior rhapsodized, but also the residents of this paradise were blessedly free from the 'streaming colds, sneezing and sniffles' that accompanied 'gloomy Northern winters'. 'Everybody seems to be tanned and brimming with health and vigour.' Then the kicker: 'What a happy world this might be, but for the fact that, not far away, children, old men and women are sent daily to be destroyed in Gas Chambers.' How, Burton wondered, could natural beauty co-exist alongside such unnatural monstrosity?[1]

Burton was no stranger to antisemitic hatred. Russian pogroms prompted him to flee his native Lithuania in 1900. Settling initially in Manchester, Burton soon transformed himself from peddler into mass manufacturer following a rags-to-riches arc that might have been scripted in Hollywood. In the 1930s, Burton endowed several chairs in International Relations at British universities and in Jerusalem, hoping to advance the cause of world peace by professorial means.[2]

But Burton's contributions to academia did less to make his name canonical than another piece of business referenced in the same missive to Raymond. At the Ministry of Supply's request, 'all the Plants are being converted from making uniforms for the various Services, to the production of Demobilised Soldiers' suits', Montague informed his son, confident he'd want an update on the state of family business.[3] (Raymond would indeed follow in his father's footsteps, founding the fashion chain Top Shop in 1964.) Although war was still raging across Europe and Asia, Burton's garment factories would be retooled to churn out what soon became known as 'demob suits'. This news was hot-off-the-press. Burton had only just agreed to participate in a government-funded scheme on 31 July, undertaking to produce suits at the rate of 6,000 a week.[4] The brisk note in which he grudgingly agreed to this quota bore no trace of the lyricism and moral outrage that animated Burton's letter to his son. Addressing the Minister of Supply, Burton insisted that higher-quality wool would be needed if these ex-servicemen's garments were to be superior to those currently manufactured for the civilian market. It would take time, he warned, to shift production over to making more durable suits, since 150 different processes were involved, 'calling for expert supervision at every stage'. Then there was Burton's profit margin to consider. Mass production of demob suits would inevitably constrict the company's commercial trade. Each veteran handsomely outfitted with government-supplied clothing was one fewer potential customer for a Burton's high street shop. Moreover, if Burton's manufacturing arm was primarily making demob suits, there'd be precious little stock available to *any* customer, veteran or civilian. In view of this projected hit to his retail business, Burton pressed for more generous compensation.[5]

The Ministry demurred. Nevertheless, over the next few years Burton would manufacture about one-third of all the demob suits supplied to almost four million men as they left the armed forces.[6] The indelible association between Burton and mid-century menswear was confirmed by the ensemble's nickname, 'the full monty'. This phrase nodded towards both Sir Montague himself and the extensive wardrobe given to each demobee as he transitioned from military service back to 'civvy street'. The veteran didn't just receive a suit – or, if he preferred, a sports jacket and flannel trousers. He exited the Demob Centre with a new shirt, two collars, studs and cufflinks, shoes and socks, a raincoat and a hat or cap. Everything, in short, necessary to

Figure 3.1 Sir Montague Burton leaves Claridge's Hotel, London, 16
July 1947 (E. Brookes/Keystone/Hulton Archive/Getty Images)

restart civilian life smartly attired. Only by a curious quirk of pop
cultural fate is the 'full monty' now more likely to conjure images
of stripping former Sheffield steelworkers than veterans' off-the-rack
suits. Thanks to Peter Cattaneo's 1997 hit – 'the year's most revealing
movie' – the phrase's meaning has been more or less inverted, invoking kit's complete removal rather than the whole caboodle's initial
acquisition.[7]

Over time, these 'civvies' became iconic: a staple of postwar
fiction, film, veterans' writings and oral histories. Authors and dra-
matists needed only mention a demob suit to establish a distinctive
milieu in which a man in a shiny new suit, boasting wide pinstripes
and even wider lapels, might be either a veteran or a 'spiv' – or perhaps one and the same.[8] Comedians Norman Wisdom and Frankie
Howerd both made a too-tight suit their sartorial signature, a trademark later adopted by Alexei Sayle. Several museums preserve demob
suits in their collections, including the Leeds Industrial Museum, which

loaned a specimen to New York's Museum of Modern Art in 2017. There, a Burton's demob suit took its place – alongside vintage Levi's, Vivienne Westwood kilts and a Wonderbra® – among the 111 exhibits in a show entitled 'Items: Is Fashion Modern?'[9]

Although the demob suit may look familiar to twenty-first-century Britons, its origin story is not well known. Why did the war-time government choose to bestow this token of gratitude on former servicemen? The decision to compensate British ex-servicemen with clothing and footwear was far from casual. Civil and military leaders haggled for months over a programme projected to cost £21 million (£759 million today): an enormous sum for a country deeply indebted to the US Treasury.[10] Prioritization of demob suits for veterans meant relegating civilians to the rear of an extended queue for new clothes, prolonging the 'period of "make-do and mend"', as Britain's Wool Controller pointed out.[11] Churchill himself weighed in on the subject of clothing priorities. Just three weeks before Germany surrendered, he tersely informed Hugh Dalton (President of the Board of Trade) that it was 'absolutely essential to increase the supply of civilian clothes'. A 'critical shortage after VE-Day' would be 'intolerable'.[12] Moreover, since veterans would have to relinquish uniform apparel on receipt of civilian attire – adding to the stockpile of military surplus for UNRRA to distribute overseas – *subtractions* from servicemen's wardrobes proved just as contentious as the new additions. That some would be attired at others' expense was bound to cause resentment. So, why the full monty? Why, indeed, any monty at all?

'Heroes in Rags'

> When I get my civvy clothes on,
> Oh, how happy I shall be;
> When this bloody war is over
> No more soldiering for me

So ran the jaded refrain of this popular soldiers' song from the Great War. But the heartening prospect of swapping a scratchy uniform for civvies was belied by more dispiriting realities of demobilization after the Armistice finally arrived in November 1918. Men coming home from war received either a suit or a modest cash alternative. Those who accepted the former often found it made of flimsy fabric and doled out with little consideration for whether the garments fitted the recipient. Some men simply got whatever rag-tag oddments could be mustered up at short notice. One veteran was dismayed to find his new cap marked 'Wandsworth Workhouse'.[13]

Shoddy. This word aptly described both government-issued apparel and the larger treatment of Great War veterans by a ruling class that had consigned a generation of young British men to the trenches. Memories of that cataclysm's aftermath shadowed discussions of demobilization as they unfolded over the course of another world war. Middle-aged men in uniform, who'd served in both conflicts, couldn't help but draw comparisons. 'Most of us who remember being released after the first world war have recollections only of shoddy suits, untidy tents and harassed officials, who were so overworked and rushed that we came away with the feeling that they were as glad to be rid of us as we were glad to be rid of them!,' recalled one of the first veterans to be demobilized in July 1945.[14] The spectre of 1919 haunted Westminster too. Discussions of demobilization clothing within each branch of the armed forces – and between their representatives and the Cabinet, Treasury, Ministry of Supply and Board of Trade – almost invariably gestured back to the gloomy past as well as anticipating a brighter postwar future. The suits offered after World War I had been of such poor quality that many men refused to take them, leaving surplus stocks of useless garments on the government's hands.[15] Haphazard fitting compounded the problem of cheap construction. Looking back, one general proposed that the key defect in the Great War's demobilization scheme had been a faulty system for taking and recording servicemen's measurements, as well as the restricted range of sizes on offer. The situation, he insisted, was now much improved in the world of ready-to-wear men's tailoring.[16]

Irrespective of whether cheap fabric, inferior manufacture or slapdash fitting was more to blame for this earlier fiasco, no one in power wanted to repeat any part of the post-Armistice experience. This time around demobilized men must be persuaded that 'we're providing worthily for them', urged a confidential Ministry of Supply memo dated 18 August 1943: 'We have a handicap in the still surviving bad reputation of the demobilised suit of the last war.' This document also candidly noted 'a strong disinclination of most servicemen to believe that anything issued by the state can be better than rough and ready with all the signs of cheap mass production and uniformity upon it'.

Hardly a strong vote of confidence in the civil contract binding the wartime state to its subjects.[17]

For policymakers, far more was at stake than disproving men's assumption that garments offered *gratis* were necessarily sub-par. Politicians, civil servants and military leaders all understood clothing in explicitly political terms, believing that men's attitudes towards the wardrobe they received would influence their larger outlook and collective mood. Veterans who felt adequately compensated for their military service were more likely to endorse the *status quo* rather than challenging it as an earlier generation had. Policymakers intended that demob clothing would be appreciated as a symbolic down-payment on a more prosperous postwar future: a token that the government aspired to raise living standards to a level commensurate with these garments. With a 'first class suit and ancillary garments' veterans would 'return to civil life psychologically and sartorially equipped for the better living conditions which we intend shall prevail', opined Sir Thomas Barlow (the Board of Trade's Director-General of Civilian Clothing) in 1943. An issue of clothing would safeguard Britain's *social* fabric, easing veterans' passage back and forestalling unrest if men struggled to find civilian employment or somewhere decent to live.[18] Moreover, as Mass Observation (MO) warned in 1944, any demobilization scheme was likely to displease men who found themselves waiting longer for release than certain comrades, whether the eligibility criteria favoured older men, decorated soldiers or fathers-in-uniform. The prospect that men with children would be released sooner stirred sectarian animosity in some quarters, one of MO's informants seething at the prospect of 'all the Catholics' getting home first.[19]

The aftermath of 1918's Armistice had been tumultuous. Sluggish in pace and perceived as unfair in its priority categories, demobilization sparked numerous riots and strikes by men impatient to get home and enraged by injustice. Russia's Bolshevik revolution fuelled radical activism, inspiring workers' and servicemen's struggles to seize control over workplaces around the world. Britain experienced its own revolutionary tremors. Over the winter of 1918–19, sections of the Army Service Corps stationed at Grove Park and Kempton Park Mechanical Transport Depots 'formed a Soviet on the Russian model'.[20] Elsewhere, demobilized men's discontent was laced with prejudice. In 1919, race riots disfigured several port cities, notably Liverpool, South Shields, Cardiff and Glasgow, as veterans came home, struggled to find jobs and vented their rage on seamen and dockworkers of colour, often singling out Black men who'd married or lived with white women.[21] All this turbulence in 1919 alone – ten years before the 1929 stock market crash instigated a decade of chronic unemployment, economic distress and labour militancy.

In Whitehall's imagination veterans registered as ambiguous figures: patriotic heroes, perhaps, but also potential trouble. Former servicemen had surely been brutalized by the violence they'd witnessed or enacted – or so nervous civilian leaders feared. Veterans returned from war with psychic scars that found expression in bafflingly misplaced symptoms: mutism or stuttering speech, a halting gait, a vacant stare, all the hallmarks of 'shell-shock'.[22] And with stories of mutinous veterans rife, punctuated with occasional headlines reporting homicides perpetrated by former servicemen, many civilian commentators feared that disturbed returnees might again jeopardize the security of homes, communities and society at large. Conceived in this way, veterans required simultaneous compensation and placation. Rewards would also serve as restraints.

'Not the Austerity Pattern'

Planning for the clothing issue to accompany demobilization began in earnest in June 1943. After the 8th Army completed its drive from Alamein to Tunis in North Africa, the Allies' first major rout of German troops, it became possible to anticipate the war's successful conclusion – untold months ahead.[23] But before full details of how the government would reward this war's veterans were finalized, *ad hoc* arrangements had already been cobbled together for men who exited the armed forces while hostilities were still in progress: some wounded, others discharged as unsuitable for service or for dishonourable conduct. The latter received decidedly short shrift, the state of their wardrobes being a matter of little concern to either civil or military authorities. Men discharged from the army on the grounds of ill health or injury fared somewhat better. Veterans invalided out of service had the option of taking a suit or cash to the tune of £2 15s 10d. A mere four shillings more than the 1919 allowance, this meagre sum provoked Parliamentary questions in December 1942 about men being 'thrown on to the streets with very little sympathy'.[24]

Negative publicity like this, conjuring the phantasm of 1919, influenced Westminster's discussions over clothing for ex-servicemen that gathered pace in 1943. Civilian and military leaders spent count-less hours in committee meetings and exchanging notes, generating hundreds of pages of minutes and memos as they battled over every detail of the demobilization programme. Outfitting veterans was no trivial matter. Accordingly, no item of the proposed ensemble was too inconsequential to inspire heated back-and-forth. Might neckerchiefs save money on collars? Board of Trade officials contemplated this accessory before deciding that, whatever the fiscal merits of such a pro-posal, neckerchiefs 'smacked surprisingly of Charing Cross Road' – too bohemian, in other words, for the average blue-collar Brit. Similarly, from the lofty corridors of Whitehall, upper-class gentlemen pondered whether working men actually wore *caps* any more. Were they, per-haps, an 'anachronism' superannuated by the more modish trilby?[25]

Collars and caps were nothing, though, compared with that most contentious article of all: socks. Long or short? Given the mag-nitude of wartime suffering and devastation, it now seems remarkable that men's hosiery should have been such a hot-button issue during the war. But, like various other items of clothing, socks had been affected by 'austerity regulations', prescriptions established by the Board of Trade in May 1942. Intended to save excess fabric where its use was more a matter of fashion than function, these regulations outlawed turn-ups on men's trousers. Wide lapels and double-breasted jackets met the same fate, along with unnecessary pockets on waistcoats – though not everyone agreed precisely which pockets, if any, were expendable. MPs vented spleen in the Commons about how gents were expected to get by without suitable lodgings for their writing implements, handker-chiefs and fob watches. Even Labour MPs grumbled about the hazards of having to carry a fountain pen 'horizontally in a jacket side pocket and probably find it leaking'.[26] But the truncation of socks – from knee-high to mid-calf – caused the biggest furore of all: a complaint that transcended class. Manufacturers, noted Board of Trade official Henry Lintott, had been 'very touchy and jumpy about these short socks, which indeed, are not popular with the public'. Austerity socks had saved two million pounds of worsted yarn.[27] But, if clothing was to pacify latently disgruntled veterans, reviled articles could form no part of the wardrobe. The Ministry of Supply warned emphatically against 'cheese-paring'.

Utility suits were ruled out on the same grounds. Their 'drain-pipe' trouser-legs were so widely ridiculed that Hugh Dalton emphasized garments for demobilized servicemen would absolutely *not* be hemmed by restrictions when he unveiled government proposals in February 1944. 'Your demobilisation suit will not be the austerity pattern,' the *Air Force News* reassured its readers. 'It will have turn up trousers, a waistcoat with four pockets – and you may have the choice of a double-breasted jacket.' This announcement assuaged servicemen's concerns about the stylishness and longevity of garments they'd receive, as well as the government's *bona fides*. As soon as austerity regulations were lifted, utility suits would appear very much yesterday's war-wear. Cynics feared (not without reason) that the government might try to liquidate stocks of unsold – and unsaleable – utility garments by palming them off on veterans, prioritizing profit above the pride of ex-servicemen.[28]

Various practical concerns underscored the need to issue veterans with a new wardrobe. Personnel stationed in Britain, who'd been able to enjoy furloughs at home, were likely to have 'worn out their mufti while on leave', the War Office warned.[29] Military service tended to remodel bodies, while clothing left behind in wardrobes and drawers was vulnerable to attrition. The home front 'war on moths' proved decidedly less successful than the campaign against the Axis powers. A satirical *Guide to Civilian Life for the Newly Demobilised* cautioned that veterans were likely to find their civvies riddled with holes. Although 'invisible menders' could 'put these to rights' by weaving threads extracted from 'secret parts of the suit' into a 'perfect replica of the previous pattern', authors Dennis Rooke and Alan D'Egville quipped that deft seamstresses were 'at the time of writing … like their mending – invisible'. If wives, daughters and sisters went AWOL when darning had to be done, they were also partly responsible for the dearth of male garments, the humorists insisted. 'Such items as dinner jackets, tails, morning dress for weddings, etc., will, even if they have escaped the bombing, be found to have altered their shape considerably, having been converted by the womenfolk of the house into smart costumes, coatees, hats and so on.'[30]

For policymakers, providing veterans with new clothing wasn't just a matter of practicality, however. Architects of the demobilization clothing scheme constantly stressed its '*psychological*' component as well as its political function. What a man wore profoundly shaped his sense of self-worth. Sporting a smartly tailored suit of clothes, a veteran could hold his head up high in civilian society, feeling proud of his wartime service and properly recognized for it. Whether he needed to make a good impression at interviews or to cut a fine figure at some

Figure 3.2 'Choose wisely': an air cadet helps the RAF fine-tune its arrangements for demobilization at Wembley, 17 October 1944 (Flt Lt S. A. Devon/Imperial War Museums via Getty Images)

special celebration, well-fitting tailored garments were imperative. The provision of high-quality demob suits would also reflect well on the services, for whom clothing was undoubtedly psychological. Veterans, outfitted in new non-austerity styles, would quite literally appear 'a cut above' their peers. And the men responsible for devising the clothing programme were certain that civilians *wanted* veterans to be more handsomely treated, not given stockpiled austerity suits.[31]

Choice would be key to the whole operation. Veterans' self-esteem hinged on a restored sense of 'individuality'. As they re-entered a realm free from the regimentation of life in the forces, men should be offered as wide a range of styles – different fabrics, colours, cuts and trimmings – as national finances and the garment industry's straitened circumstances permitted. In the military, officers alone enjoyed some latitude for personal flair, as they were required to have their own uniforms tailored, paying for them out of their own pockets. This tradition posed a significant obstacle to poorer men's entry into the officer class. In 1945, an officer's jacket cost £8–£9 – one-and-a-half times the average weekly male wage for a single component of an elaborate wardrobe. As John

Berger notes, the pervasiveness of uniforms in wartime Britain failed to erase class distinctions. 'Far from disguising the social class of those who wore them, uniforms underlined and emphasized it.'[32] But though 'uniformity' encompassed numerous variations in service apparel, standardization had to be avoided when it came to demob suits. Whitehall officials were receptive to industry representations that men given iden-tikit outfits would feel they were simply 'stepping out of one uniform into another'.[33] Suits would duly be available in herringbone tweed, window-pane checks, pinstripes or unpatterned wool in shades of grey, brown or blue. Sizing was another vital matter. Myriad fittings (sixty in total) were offered to accommodate different body types.[34]

Months more wrangling went into hammering out what, and how much, to include in the demob ensemble. The various branches of the armed forces had distinct ideas about how *their* veterans should be handled, with the Admiralty initially intent on opting out altogether. Inter-service differences were eventually ironed out in favour of a unified approach that would avoid aggrieved feelings on the part of less well-treated demobees. Divisions also beset the clothing industry. Smaller-scale garment producers and outfitters, along with tailors who made and altered menswear, protested that the big multiples (manufacturers, like Burton, who were also high street retailers) stood to make a kill-ing at the expense of everyone else. After World War I, there had been no outcry from independent men's outfitters only because government-issued 'scarecrow' suits were so pitiful that retailers didn't fear any loss of trade. Veterans, whether they took or rejected the demob outfit, still needed to buy new clothes. In 1943, the National Association of Outfitters vigorously lobbied the Board of Trade, arguing that most ex-servicemen wouldn't even *want* suits they'd barely wear. Instead, men should receive money they could spend at an outlet of their own choos-ing on apparel that fitted their personal tastes and practical needs.[35]

The Board of Trade sympathized, concerned that the demob programme not harm (or, worse yet, eliminate) any sector of Britain's beleaguered garment industry and fearful of provoking 'very serious resentment' from small traders.[36] Initially, the plan was that demo-bilized men should be offered a choice: *either* cash and coupons *or* a new wardrobe. But the monetary alternative was quickly dropped. If 'civvy suits' were to be manufactured within a narrow window, there had to be some certainty as to quantity. It was challenging enough that no one knew exactly when demobilization would begin. (Once the clothing scheme was set in motion in 1944, manufacturing plans were predicated on VJ Day arriving in June 1946, a miscalculation that caused a major production crisis in the autumn of 1945, when the war ended 'early' and sufficient suits weren't yet ready.[37]) If the Ministry of Supply also had to guess how many men would opt for cash as opposed to suits, it might be caught out – either left with a surplus or embarrassingly empty-handed. Logistical considerations pushed in favour of a standard issue of suits, albeit of varied styles and shades. So, too, did financial ones. Cash allowances would need to be offered at *retail* rates rather than the wholesale unit cost at which the Ministry of Supply compensated manufacturers. A mixed-model scheme threatened to add between five and ten million pounds to the cost of outfitting veterans.[38]

More paternalistic concerns also influenced policy. Senior military figures feared that newly demobilized men – armed with cash and coupons but ignorant of their values – would be an easy mark for unscrupulous traders trying to rip them off with inferior garments sold at inflated prices. Returning servicemen had, after all, been spared the privations of the home front. What did veterans know about ration books, clothing coupons and the seasonally shifting number of points assigned to different garments? Betraying a patrician anxiety that enlisted men couldn't be trusted to act in their own best interests, military leaders fretted that demobilized men wouldn't spend their cash windfall *properly*. Some might not invest in new wardrobes at all, squandering their war gratuities at the pub, races or dog track. Feckless types might even sell their clothing coupons on the black market. Were that to happen, the army council secretariat anticipated a public outcry over 'heroes in rags' – with the services (quite unjustly!) blamed for the sorry appearance of ex-servicemen.[39]

So, demob suits all round it would be, plus a substantial number of clothing coupons. But this major decision still left much detail to be thrashed out. Twinned with the question of what new apparel would be supplied was the issue of how much service apparel each man would have to 'surrender' (in the military's redolent term) on demobilization. After the previous Armistice, veterans were permitted to hang onto their army battledress blouses and greatcoats. Although a precedent had been set, the service chiefs were of two minds as to whether it should be observed again. Some generals felt it wasn't quite fitting that battledress should be civilianized along with the men who'd recently worn it. Veterans of the Great War hadn't simply consigned their old uniforms to the back of the wardrobe – an heirloom to be paraded in front of future grandchildren. They donned their old army kit for 'rough work' around the house, painting and gardening. Was it 'seemly', mused the chairman of the army council executive committee, 'for the King's uniform to be worn for such a purpose'?[40]

Another reason why officialdom wanted to retrieve more kit this time had less to do with a feeling that the uniform was somehow dishonoured by humdrum civilian uses than with the need to stockpile clothes for postwar relief. Service apparel such as jumpers, battledress blouses and trousers could be donated to destitute inhabitants of liberated countries after the war. 'We're given to understand that the population of the territories at present occupied by the enemy are in many cases very badly in need of clothing,' observed a Treasury official in October 1943. 'In particular … those living in central and South East Europe for the most part have only one garment and one blanket apiece.' With British civilian stocks dwindling, 'it nearly boils down to Army clothing or nothing for the population in liberated territories'. To meet this crisis, veterans should even be asked to surrender 'articles of underclothing'.[41] Mindful of the cost of manufacturing new clothes for distribution overseas by UNRRA, the Board of Trade and Treasury pushed for as much service apparel as possible to be reclaimed from its former owners.[42] Not all the Service chiefs agreed, however. When it came to deciding priorities, some felt that veterans deserved first dibs on worn military apparel – no matter what they subsequently did with it. British 'troops should not be asked to give up anything which they might find useful merely to provide relief clothing for wretched Europeans', ran the service department line. Some generals proposed that 'a more appropriate source of clothing for relief purposes would be the German, rather than the British, Army'.[43] In the end, as Chapter 5 details, both German and British military surplus would be used to clothe Europeans whose countries had been plundered by the Third Reich, survivors of Nazi camps, POWs *and* destitute German civilians, whose needs figured nowhere in the wartime calculus of 'wretchedness'.

After the generals stopped squabbling, veterans were permitted to keep their underwear and jumpers. The biggest interdepartmental tussle was over service greatcoats and shoes, neither of which ex-servicemen were permitted to retain. This decision seems counterintuitive given that coats and footwear were among the costliest and scarcest commodities in wartime Britain. Overcoats consumed enormous amounts of labour and fabric. In their pre-war glory, men's coats boasted a high-grade wool outer layer and silk lining, with inset sleeves and pockets on the inside and out. Providing coats to all demobbed men would require an estimated fifteen million yards of cloth. Why not, then, simply let veterans keep their greatcoats?[44]

This appeared an obvious solution to the outerwear conundrum, but not one popular with the Board of Trade and Treasury. Both departments were heavily invested in helping Britain regain its historic position as the world's leading exporter of woollen textiles. Broken down, the fibres from army greatcoats could be respun into new fabric, potentially adding twelve to fifteen million yards of wool material to national stocks. One branch of the textile industry, centred in Dewsbury, specialized in producing reconditioned material known as 'shoddy'.[45] 'The battledress of yesterday will reappear next autumn as the fabric of peace-time fashions for civilians,' the *SEAC* (Southeast Asia Command) *News* breezily informed its uniformed readership. Although the author may have been right in predicting that veterans would 'never recognize' their old kit in these new 'stylish tweeds', it was far likelier to be American shoppers who encountered this reincarnation of British army khaki.[46] When policymakers finally agreed that demobilized men would receive a mackintosh rather than an overcoat, the decision had nothing to do with Britain's damp climate and everything to do with rebalancing the national books. A simple raincoat with raglan sleeves required far less labour than a coat, with the additional benefit of needing no woollen fabric.

Shoes also elicited many hours of heated debate. By common consent, the world confronted a 'crisis of leather'. Wartime production of civilian men's shoes had dwindled, leaving an annual deficit of 1.5 million pairs.[47] Again, logic suggested that servicemen who'd been issued with both boots and shoes should simply be allowed to keep one or other pair. But on this point the generals put their feet down. The wrong footwear risked undoing the whole demob scheme. At the first interdepartmental meeting on ex-servicemen's clothing, General Hoare 'pointed out that we were proposing to give demobilised service men a decent suit with which army boots, socks and shirts would not be compatible and would "look quite incongruous"'. Civil servants scoffed at this proposition, amused that generals seemed to consider themselves arbiters of men's style. Indebted Britain couldn't afford to take 'incongruity' into consideration.[48]

But Hoare had a point. Many British women, unable to buy new shoes for years and adjusting to crepe- or wooden-soled footwear, would surely have corroborated his intuition. The wrong footwear could not only ruin the overall effect of an outfit but lead the wearer to experience anything from mild self-consciousness to acute social discomfort. The ugliness of British women's footwear formed a standard trope of American reportage on Britain's home front. Writing for the *Los Angeles Times*, Hettie Grimstead observed that, if British women were well-dressed, that look 'often ends at a woman's knees': 'Her utility stockings are thick and tend to wrinkle at her ankles and her pumps are just something with which she covers her feet.'[49] Shoes *mattered* – for comfort and self-esteem alike. If the government were to invest millions of precious pounds in outfitting former servicemen, then every last detail had to be right. Three-piece suits and combat boots weren't meant for one another. Having lost the battle over surrendered kit for 'wretched Europeans', the generals won the day on footwear. The demob ensemble would include as high-quality leather shoes as Britain could make.

Figure 3.3 To avoid 'incongruity', the War Office insisted that demobilized servicemen be given new shoes with their demob suits (Reg Speller/Hulton Archive/Getty Images)

Selling the Package

One point on which bureaucrats, politicians and generals agreed was that demob suits would need 'good propaganda' if the interwoven symbolic, psychological and political objectives invested in them were to be met. Prominent and positive publicity was all the more imperative as some segments of the garment and tailoring industries might try to torpedo the programme. No one had forgotten the notorious 'workhouse suits' of 1919. Sure enough, detractors began decrying the scheme months before demob suits made their public début. Popular left-wing broadcaster and author J. B. Priestley predicated an entire novel about postwar adjustment, *Three Men in New Suits*, on the premise that the eponymous garments would be of the utility model – expressive of a sclerotic status quo in need of a thorough shake-up. His protagonists, representatives of Britain's tripartite class structure, sport 'horrible' blue, grey and brown suits on re-entry into civilian life, attracting such unwelcome and unflattering comment that even upper-class Alan experiences an epiphany. Ribbed for looking like a 'little insurance tout' by a patrician uncle, Alan realizes that Britons of all stripes must pull together to rebuild a more egalitarian nation.[50] When Priestley spoke, people listened. He was, one critic gushed, 'a minor Tolstoy in his wide human sympathies'. Indeed, Priestley's stature was such that some reviewers billed *Three Men in New Suits* above Evelyn Waugh's *Brideshead Revisited*, also released in June 1945.[51] While *Brideshead* has withstood the test of time, Priestley's novel was outmoded almost before publication. But the author was gracious enough to admit his error. Later editions revoked his presumptuous damnation of the demob suit. The book's third edition contains a preface in which he contritely acknowledges that his lack of faith had been misplaced. On examination, the suits proved 'of excellent quality'.[52]

Priestley wasn't alone in harbouring low expectations. In January 1944, Evelyn Walkden (Labour MP for Doncaster) asked the War Minister for a sample demob suit to be displayed in the House of Commons tearoom: an unveiling which drew considerable press attention. Since the Ministry of Supply had placed its first order for 850,000 suits just one month earlier, even Whitehall officials had no idea where the specimen came from. Whatever its provenance, this 'monstrosity of a suit' was roundly decried by Walkden. 'It is in the ridiculous austerity

style,' he fumed to the *Evening Standard*. 'I want the returning servicemen to have a dignified suit, as well as a full outfit of shoes and
underclothes, not to be branded and made a marked man.'[53] This was
exactly the kind of 'dangerous' publicity Whitehall had feared, invigo-
rating discussion about better presentation.

Far more important than whatever MPs, authors and reporters might have to say in advance about demob suits was the *setting*
in which ex-servicemen selected their new clothes. Where and how
men were issued with their civilian apparel would play a vital role in
cueing responses to the garments themselves. 'No suggestion of the
charity organisation must appear either in garments or in issue procedure,' cautioned the Ministry of Supply in 1943. This remark perhaps revealed more about elite attitudes towards charity than it did
regarding the views of its recipients. The Ministry assumed that those
who wore second-hand clothes must feel demeaned and stigmatized
like Victorian paupers forced into the poorhouse. It's not clear, however, that this shudder of distaste was widely felt. Many working-
class Britons grew up in hand-me-downs and, in adulthood, acquired
second-hand clothes as a matter of course. The war had elevated insti-
tutions like the WVS Clothing Exchanges into a rational, thoroughly
respectable, way of tackling the national scarcity of clothing and shoes,
particularly childrens-wear.[54] Nevertheless, viewed through the eyes
of officialdom, charity hand-outs carried pejorative connotations to
be avoided at all costs. The whole demobilization project would be
imperilled if crowds of servicemen were herded into draughty hangars,
handed crumpled suits and unceremoniously ushered out of service: a
memorable farewell to arms for all the wrong reasons.

Instead, demobilization centres – eighteen dotted about the
British Isles – should have a department-store-like atmosphere, complete with canteens and information bureaus to help men finalize
onward travel arrangements. Before departure, they'd receive train
vouchers and clothing coupons, plus what was then a staple of the military diet: an ample ration of free cigarettes. More unexpectedly, men
drilled to obey orders could offer tips for improvement in 'Suggestions
Books'. Courteous staff, soldiers with prior experience in the slick
realm of civilian retail, would help men pick garments that reflected
their tastes and fitted their physiques. Demobees could try garments on
for size in private cubicles – with heating! Fitting rooms may have been
customary in department stores, but such arrangements were a world

away from the lack of privacy or concern for personal comfort that characterized life in the services. All this needed careful synchronization to ensure that men would progress steadily through the pipeline, selecting suits, shirts, ties, raincoat and shoes without feeling rushed, but nevertheless at a brisk enough pace that (at peak capacity) demob centres could process nearly 100,000 men each week.[55]

The tide of media comment turned in a more favourable direction after a successful dress rehearsal at Olympia in March 1944. Both in servicemen's newspapers and in the civilian press, publicity for demob suits was largely flattering, criticism being restricted to the production bottleneck caused in late 1945 by the war's unexpectedly abrupt conclusion in Asia. While no serviceman was likely to complain that Japan had surrendered 'too soon', some feared that their release from the military might be delayed by the lack of available demob suits. Understandably, no one wanted their return home to be held up by a shortage of civvies, and the Ministry of Supply scrambled to have more labour funnelled into clothing factories. Garment workers found themselves chivvied by union leaders (under pressure from Westminster) to 'make superhuman efforts' for 'the men who have dared so much in our defence'. 'Think how unhappy they would be if for any reason they had to walk about in service dress for even one day longer than was necessary,' prompted Herbert Kay (Secretary of the Wholesale Clothing Manufacturers' Federation) in November 1945. Meanwhile, some ex-servicemen were recruited to deliver motivational speeches aimed at instilling a greater sense of urgency on the factory floor.[56]

For older British servicemen, the cohort eligible for earliest release, demobilization began in earnest in June 1945. The *Manchester Guardian*'s coverage of the first 'batch' to pass through the demob centre at Western Command typified the wider tenor of reportage:

> The making of a soldier entails a long and, it may be, painful incubation: the making of a civilian, it seems, is a blessedly brief transition from khaki or blue into an urban colour scheme of one's own choosing. It is a morning's shopping expedition on which neither money nor coupons matter. Here, at any rate, the clothes make the man – the civilian man.

The *Guardian*'s correspondent acknowledged this might be a 'rather superficial impression' – one that MO ruefully anticipated as early as February 1944. 'Battledress to sports suit; overalls to frocks. For many the future stops there,' MO tutted, before offering its own gen-dered vision of the New Jerusalem to which Britons should aspire. 'If minds are to look willingly forward from sports suits to boiler suits, from frocks to maternity gowns, they must know that the future means something which is theirs to build.'[57]

Both the *Manchester Guardian* and MO intuited that 'recon-version' was unlikely to run as smoothly as the finely calibrated clock-work of the demob centres. But no such caveats marked the jaunty treatment of servicemen's return to Civvy Street by newsreel companies that made heart-warming human-interest stories their stock-in-trade. *British Pathé* incorporated a long segment, 'Demob', in its issue of 28 June 1945, depicting the work of the RAF dispersal centre at Uxbridge to the accompaniment of an upbeat musical score. Most of the story focuses on the selection of clothing: the dramatic highlight of an oth-erwise tedious bureaucratic ushering-out process. As the camera pans across a well-stocked display case – 'better equipped than most civvy stores!' – a veteran delicately tests the quality of a tie between thumb and forefinger, while the narrator expounds the theme that demobees benefit from superior treatment, given 'a complete new outfit, the coupon-clipper's dream!' Viewers tag along as the RAF man proceeds to choose from an array of fabrics, 'everything from pinstripes for bud-ding businessmen to light checks for country gents', and several styles of headgear. He tries a flat cap and trilby before settling on a fedora. 'Gosh!,' the soon-to-be-veteran gasps, observing himself in the mir-ror with acute camera-consciousness. 'I wonder what the missus'll say to this outfit.' *Pathé* left little doubt that she'd be suitably impressed, encouraging viewers to imagine that readjustment really *was* as sim-ple as a change of clothes. When the veteran in his civvies reflexively salutes an officer as he leaves the Uxbridge centre, it's a set-up gag. This muscle memory will surely fade fast, arms encased in the raglan sleeves of gaberdine macs having no business shooting to attention at the sight of officers' stripes.[58]

Nothing in media reports on demobilization broached an espe-cially sensitive topic. Some men would (and did) return from active duty with bodies radically reshaped by war: missing limbs, hands or feet. None of the RAF personnel *Pathé* filmed at Uxbridge bear any vis-ible traces of service. Able-bodied, they're relaxed: smiling, smoking, bantering. That some men would need special outfitting to accommo-date (or disguise) prostheses or amputated body parts – with garments adjusted to make getting dressed easier – was nowhere evident in pub-lic depictions of demobilization. Since wartime censorship rules kept a tight lid on 'upsetting' imagery for home front consumption, this ellipsis is perhaps not surprising. What's more striking, though, is that, among hundreds of pages of declassified documents on demob suits filed in the National Archives, there's no reference to disability either. Officials acknowledged that some men's bodies would not conform to standard measurements, agreeing that unusually proportioned individ-uals would need to have suits mailed to them rather than plucking them from the rails at demob centres. This was a topic the press tended to play for laughs. 'The small fat men, say the trade, often bulge in the wrong places', winked the *Daily Mail*, while 'long thin men baffle predictions on leg and arm measurements.' But the fact that some men had suffered life-changing injuries was never mentioned, even though garment manufacturers themselves had started planning how veterans with disabilities might be reincorporated into the workforce.[59]

If Whitehall preferred not to discuss debility, it couldn't help but acknowledge class. Demobilization saw servicemen quitting one rank-conscious hierarchy for re-entry into another rigidly stratified society. How officers should be treated formed another sticking point. Since officers paid for their own uniforms, there could be no ques-tion of their surrendering any articles. But should they nevertheless get a demob suit? If not, were they entitled to more clothing coupons than enlisted men to help refurbish their wardrobes? Leaving offi-cers empty-handed didn't seem quite right – at least from Whitehall's vantage point. After much deliberation, policymakers decided that it would cause less outcry from coupon-deprived civilians if officers were treated just the same as enlisted men. This proposal had the additional virtue of allowing demobilization clothing to be packaged as an exer-cise in egalitarianism.[60]

The ostensible classlessness of demobilization procedures formed a common motif of media reportage. British squaddies sta-tioned in North Africa who picked up a copy of *Tripoli Times* in early September 1945 could read about the demob of debonair Lt Colonel David Niven, actor-turned-officer-returned-to-civilian, who 'chose a smart single breasted brown worsted suit with a red window pane overcheck. With it, he favoured a fawn raincoat, a fawn shirt with two matching collars, two pairs of brown socks, brown shoes, a brown snap brim hat and brown and red tie.' The motto: 'Any demobilised

Service man can have exactly the same outfit as a famous film star.'
Two months later, much ballyhoo accompanied Monty's appearance at Edinburgh's Redford Barracks. Field Marshal Sir Bernard
Montgomery picked an outfit redolent of David Niven's – a 'nice dark
brown herringbone tweed suit with a thin and not too obtrusive red
stripe' – corroborating the *Tripoli Times*'s point, though not in the way
the paper intended.[61]

'Beware of Sharks'

Alongside congratulatory stories about the seamless operations of the demob centres – 'Colonels really do queue with corporals,'
marvelled the *Guardian* – ran a darker strand that emphasized not
quality and choice but variegation and corruption. Not all demob suits
were created equal. To meet its target output of 35,000 suits per week,
rising to 100,000 in January 1946, the Ministry of Supply issued contracts to several manufacturers.[62] Although Burton was the single largest supplier, other suits came from factories that made both inferior
and superior garments. Word soon spread that Savile Row and Austin
Reed models lurked among the demob centres' wares – accessible to
men willing to slip a 'pound or two' to unscrupulous staff members
who stashed the most desirable apparel 'under the counter'.[63]

Illicit transactions continued to permeate veterans' recollections of demobilization decades later. One former airman, Bill Hunt,
recalled his trip to the demob centre as follows:

> We went to the place where the demob suits were kept, and
> men who looked like tailors, in shirtsleeves and with tape mea-
> sures draped round their necks, made enquiries as to size and
> showed us what was available. I had heard rumours that the
> best clothes were hidden away … A ten shilling note (say, £15
> today) surreptitiously conferred, would, it was said, gain one
> entrance to a back room where the Savile Row stuff was wait-
> ing. It may have been true, or it may have been someone's envi-
> ous fantasy, but I wanted no part in black market dealings, and
> made my choice from what was openly displayed.[64]

Fellow veteran Bert Scrivens recounts being so overburdened with
freebies as he navigated the Aldershot demob centre that he inadver-
tently dropped a carton of 200 cigarettes. Without intending to bribe

the staff, he found himself whisked aside to peruse a rack hidden at the back of the hall. Scrivens duly acquired a suit that a savvier veteran identified as a Simpson's of Piccadilly number.[65] Other men took umbrage at corruption, indignantly asserting a right to something better than the 'horrible things' on the rails. Robert Ellison, demobbed near Chester in April 1946, claims that by kicking up a fuss he secured a 'navy blue one with red striping'. 'Nobody would believe me it was a demob suit!'[66]

Soon 'bribe patrols' of military police were stationed at demob centres to intercept illicit exchanges between servicemen and corrupt assistants, with questions posed about this 'black market' in the Commons.[67] Posters warned men to 'Beware of Sharks' on Civvy Street, as furtive transactions weren't confined to the demob centres.[68] In veterans' storytelling, 'spivs' play a dominant role, prowling nearby railway station platforms, eager to part demobees from their new garments (or coupons) for resale on the black market. William Cowans recalls that at Aldershot train station 'there was always a few that would hassle you, asking "is there anything you want to get rid of?" But all the soldiers would tell 'em what to do, you know, "I fought hard for this, I risked my life for this, you won't be spivving off of this."' Perfectly content with his Burton's suit – 'Top class to come out of the army with that!' – Cowans clung onto it.[69] Likewise, Edward Grey parried the spivs offering £12, satisfied with the 'absolutely beautiful suit' in which he'd later marry.[70] Other men, however, couldn't get rid of their demob suits fast enough, happily pocketing whatever black market operators offered. Thomas Jackson, demobbed at Guildford, sold his 'straight away' for 'four quid', while Monty Fish, who considered his demob suit 'bloody awful', parted with it 'for a fiver'. Other men promptly deposited their suits at pawn shops.[71]

These transactions were arguably victimless crimes. The same couldn't be said, however, for outright thefts of demob suits or material earmarked for their production – new varieties of larceny reported by the civilian press and service newspapers as emblematic postwar morality tales. Like the process of demobilization itself, these crimes persisted long after the war ended. In May 1947, a fifty-nine-year-old bookmaker's clerk appeared in a magistrate's court, accused of stealing a twenty-three-year-old man's demob suit while the latter enjoyed a 'farewell drink with his comrades'. Discovering he'd been robbed, the veteran gave chase, knocking the thief to the ground and giving him a black eye. It was the theft, not the assault, that incurred criminal charges. 'What did you expect him to do?,' the presiding magistrate quizzed the defendant. 'Shake your hand and inquire after your health?'[72]

Veterans' responses to their new outfits varied widely, and not only because certain men emerged better dressed. Some felt that their unmistakably new suits did indeed make them 'marked men'. 'When you walked down the road or down the local pub there were about half a dozen people all with the same demob outfit on,' Don Mitchard, who received his at Uxbridge in July 1946, complained in 2005.[73] Influenced by apocryphal stories of identical suits, veterans' memories may have flattened out variety. Or perhaps they didn't encounter the selection the government aspired to offer, choices narrowing as the tempo of release accelerated. Either way, many veterans' oral histories emphasize that limited choices left men looking 'like bookends'.[74] Few ex-servicemen wanted to wear their veteran-ness on their sleeves, preferring to blend as invisibly as possible into civilian life. Others regretted choices made in haste or, like Priestley's fictional avatars, bristled at disparaging comments civilians made about their new kit, often with the insinuation that it looked 'lower class'. Bill Hunt recalled being told by a fellow student at navigation school that he resembled 'a grocer's boy on his day off' – jumped up above his station, perhaps, or awkward in stiff Sunday best. Whatever this detractor meant to imply, Hunt feared it was true. Negative remarks no doubt ensured that even men who'd hitherto been quite comfortable in their new togs developed inhibitions. Among veterans, complaints about demob suits seemingly outweighed compliments: the fabric (too coarse), the checks (too loud), the cut (too flamboyant), the fit (too haphazard).[75]

Whereas policymakers hoped that attitudes towards demob suits would sway men's disposition towards the postwar state, the direction of influence was perhaps more often reversed. In other words, it was how men felt about wartime service – or *authority* more broadly – that shaped their response to the garments, not the other way around. Men who considered their stint in uniform as so much stolen time, who bristled at military regimentation or felt fobbed off with a flimsy token of appreciation by a government that had no idea what hardships veterans had endured, didn't hesitate to slam the demob suit – at the moment of issue or thereafter. Hunt's memoir contains a revealing vignette about how one 'browned off' comrade carried his sense of grievance into, and out of, the demob centre. 'Convinced that

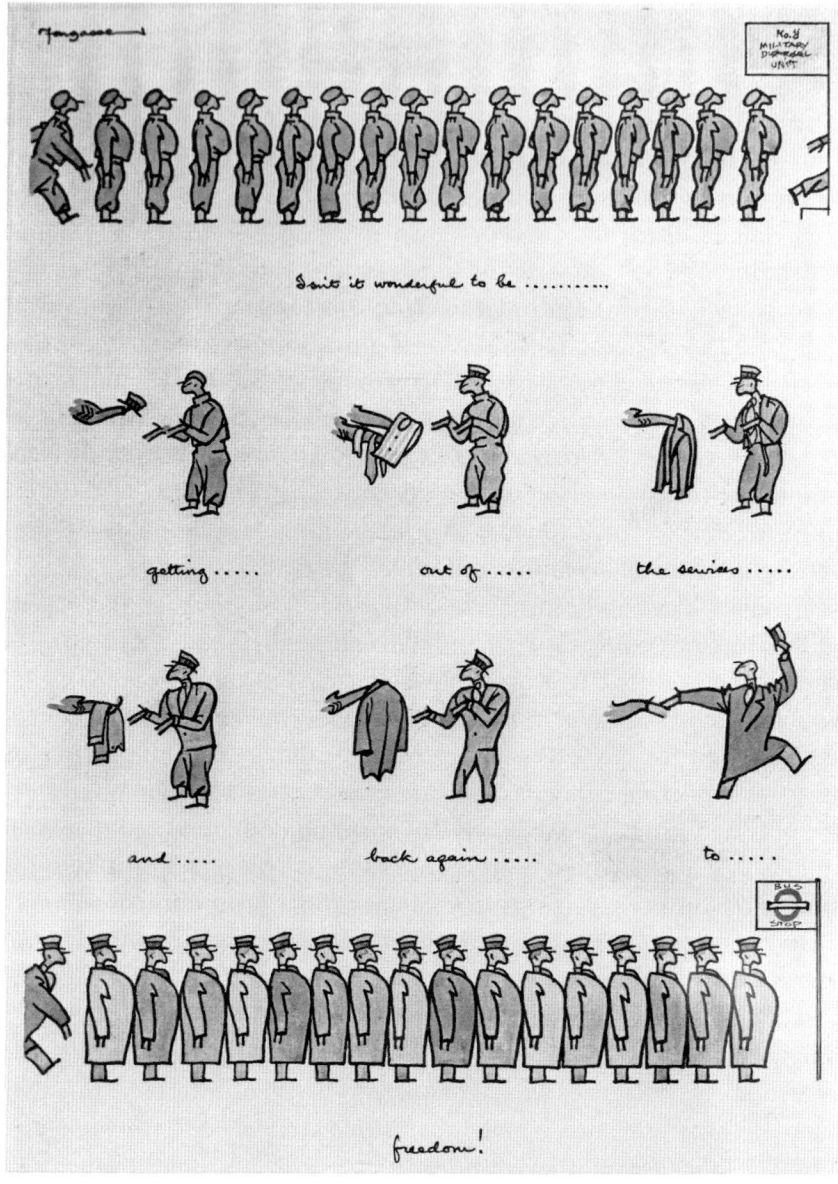

Figure 3.4 Fongasser's 1945 cartoon replicates a widely shared idea that veterans sporting demob suits had simply substituted one uniform for another (Keystone/Hulton Archive/Getty Images)

this whole demob business was a dirty deal', he was 'determined to steal something' before quitting the RAF to 'compensate himself for what he appeared to regard as the inadequacy of what a grateful or perhaps indifferent country was prepared to bestow in return for services rendered'. However, continued Hunt, the 'only thing he could find was a huge ball of sisal string about the size of his head, and he left with it together with the parcel of clothes he had chosen'.[76] What this man felt about the garments themselves Hunt didn't relate. But we could certainly guess.

'Feminine Taste'

While some servicemen groused about their shabby treatment by the state, civilians nursed grievances of their own. What did men who'd just acquired a brand new wardrobe and an issue of *ninety* clothing coupons have to grumble about? (Civilians, in contrast, received just twenty-four between 1 September 1945 and 30 April 1946: the lowest number issued in any rationing period during or after the war, prompting some veterans to redistribute coupons to needy family members.[77]) Policymakers were mistaken in imagining that grateful Britons would patiently accept ex-servicemen's priority status in the wait for new clothes. A wry editorial in *The Times*, following the announcement in October 1945 that even more productive capacity would be turned over to manufacturing demob suits, noted civilians' pangs of 'bitter jealousy' at the sight of 'the demobilized in his new and glittering raiment' – envy 'quickly suppressed'.[78] But not everyone exercised this emotional self-discipline. Demob outfits signalled that, as far as officialdom was concerned, servicemen alone deserved special compensation. Implicitly, *combat* appeared the most meritorious form of service. Not all servicemen had been front-line troops, however. And not all British men served in uniform. Some who'd been conscripted into hazardous work – such as the 'Bevin boys' sent down Britain's mines – raised aggrieved voices about why they, having been paid paltry pocket-money for their service, were denied demob clothing.[79]

Servicemen's exclusive sartorial privilege exposed inequities in how the state evaluated wartime contributions and postwar entitlements. Just as some civilian men took umbrage at their oversight, so too did female war-workers and servicewomen. Government discussions of demobilization clothing almost invariably gendered the veteran male, marginalizing around 640,000 British women who'd served with the Auxiliary Territorial Service (ATS), the Women's Royal Naval Service (WRNS) and the Women's Auxiliary Air Force (WAAF).[80]

Meanwhile, the civilian Women's Land Army (WLA) mustered over 80,000 recruits into corduroy breeches before sending them out into the fields, milking sheds and cattle byres of British farms. Required after December 1941 to undertake some form of war-related work, paid or voluntary, the vast majority of British women had contributed to the war effort, often in uniform.[81]

Servicewomen's feelings about their uniforms tended to be more fraught than men's attitudes towards their kit.[82] This ambivalence was hardly surprising, since women's apparel reflected irresolvable tensions surrounding female service. Could women be mobilized, commentators wondered, without being 'militarized' – sacrificing their femininity and jeopardizing traditional gender norms? For social conservatives, including political liberals like Priestley, the 'female soldier' remained an oxymoronic conceit, a troublingly 'mannish' apparition.[83] To ease such apprehensions, women's service apparel preserved traditional markers of femaleness. Skirts, not trousers, remained the order of the day, at least for dress uniforms. Many women found the A-line cut of their skirts unflattering; the underwear ill-fitting. Yet, since beauty remained an insistently trumpeted wartime duty, with cosmetic manufacturers touting new lipstick shades like 'Auxiliary Red', servicewomen found it all the more galling to be issued with unprepossessing garments. Simultaneously impractical and unattractive, service kit represented the worst of all worlds.[84] 'We were entirely fitted out and I look AWFUL,' one new ATS recruit wailed to her mother. Another woman embroidered the same theme, elaborating on the 'stupid and inelegant' ensemble: 'Thick lisle stockings, which went a sickly yellow colour after repeated washings, balloon shaped khaki knickers and the sorts of vests which our Grannies wore, the sturdy Oxford brogues and that miserable creation, the groundsheet, which doubled as a rain cape.'[85] American servicewomen's uniforms, in contrast, carried such an alluring patriotic mystique that the Women's Auxiliary Army Corps (WAAC) found, to its chagrin, department stores selling convincing knock-off copies to female shoppers. 'This was only the beginning', lamented Colonel Mattie Treadwell, 'of what seemed to be an attempt by every woman in America to get herself into a military uniform without the inconvenience of subjecting herself to WAAC discipline.' (Worse yet, some so-called 'Victory Girls' donned fake uniforms while plying their trade outside military camps and at ports of embarkation, propositioning servicemen by presenting themselves as eager sisters-in-arms.[86])

British servicewomen confronted demobilization with trepidation: an anxious passage to an uncertain future. What educational and professional opportunities would remain open when they exited the forces? As women waited to see whether the elasticity of wartime gender norms would contract after hostilities ceased, they kept a careful watch over exactly how the government intended to reward *their* service with garments, gratuities and coupons. They would be disappointed on all fronts.[87]

For the men in Whitehall who spent innumerable hours debating men's demob apparel, female personnel registered on the outer periphery of their radar. Only fleetingly did they discuss whether women should receive some equivalent to the demob suit. No sooner was this possibility broached than civil servants and service chiefs reminded one another that there *was* no conceivable counterpart. The inaugural meeting to consider demobilization clothing in June 1943 minuted that 'women of the services would be dealt with by a money grant, since the alternative of issue in kind was *fraught with very great difficulties*' (emphasis added). The nature of these prodigious problems remained unspecified, as though everyone fully understood that women's clothing was *terra incognita* – a world apart from menswear. The sexes would necessarily have to be treated differently.[88]

This line never wavered throughout the war. Policymakers insisted that women's fashions and tastes were too varied and evanescent to be distilled into a capsule wardrobe akin to men's demob ensemble. Like many male commentators on clothing, they regarded female dress as decorative, men's clothing as practical – tacitly endorsing the Victorian notion of a 'great male renunciation' of fashion.[89] 'The case of women is different from men and we can't attempt to offer them the wide choice that would be necessary,' opined Sir Thomas Barlow in 1943.[90] Any demobilization clothing initiative for servicewomen would be 'impracticable and unpopular', chimed another memo. In March 1944, Thelma Cazalet-Keir (Conservative MP for Islington East) had the temerity to challenge this article of faith. Would the Secretary of State for War 'consider providing a choice of civilian clothing for women as well as for men on demobilisation?' Sir James Grigg's retort that it would be 'impossible … to satisfy feminine taste' was hurrahed by male colleagues.[91] Perhaps these MPs remembered a trial balloon floated, and hastily shot down, earlier in the war: that some sort of civilian national uniform – like the oversized 'onesie' or 'siren suit' favoured by Churchill – should be introduced to reduce clothing costs. What's clear is that many parliamentarians, while rueing female caprice, considered womenswear primarily in terms of its allure to the appraising male gaze. This eagerness to see femininity restored was articulated most explicitly by John Profumo, who informed the Commons that former servicewomen would get a generous cash allowance, 'affording them the means of becoming once again adequately and gracefully dressed'. 'No one', he announced, 'would venture to prescribe a woman's taste in clothes' – as though the female fashion industry, to say nothing of film studios and spin-off glamour magazines, didn't do exactly that.[92]

Official records indicate that no servicewomen were ever consulted over a possible demobilization clothing issue. Well aware of how scarce new garments were in civilian life, female veterans might have jumped at such an offer, as Cazalet-Keir evidently believed. But it was never made. Instead, the cash allowance, set at £12 10s (raised from the Treasury's original bid of £8 15s after protests), was tabulated on the basis of what women would pay for a hat, costume, scarf, blouse or jumper, stockings, shoes and raincoat. By granting women cash instead of clothing, the Ministry of Supply and Board of Trade ensured that the garment industry could remain focused on manufacturing demob suits along with high-end textiles and tailored garments for overseas sale. To make matters even worse for female shoppers, significantly more womenswear than menswear was exported in 1945 (totalling £1,000,000 as against £34,000).[93]

Discussions about women, demobilization and clothing revolved around how much (or little) service apparel they'd be allowed to retain. Men in Whitehall pored over lists of garments issued to women in the ATS, WRNS and WAAF to decide which items female veterans could keep and what they'd have to 'surrender'. Rarely can women's underwear have received such lengthy, poker-faced and painstakingly minuted discussion in Whitehall. Esoteric debates ensued about how to justify the discrepancy between WAAF policy, which permitted the retention of two bras and one pair of shoes, and the WRNS's more ample allowance of three bras, two corsets and two pairs of shoes. For their part, ATS demobees – the largest constituency of female veterans – would be allowed to keep two corsets, one sanitary belt, three bras, three pairs of knickers and two pairs of stockings.[94] Officials convinced themselves that differences between 'members of the same sex leaving different Services' were more consequential than the glaring chasm between the treatment of male and female veterans.[95]

But women veterans certainly noted these inequities, as did female allies in the press. *The Observer*'s Alison Settle reported on 6 May 1945 – the day before Germany's surrender – that plans for outfitting ex-servicewomen remained 'nebulous', the cash grant 'insufficient considering today's prices'. 'Why', she continued, 'when the girls are "quizzed" on their choice of post-war careers and homes, have they not been asked directly what types of clothing they seek, whether suits and coats, dresses and coats, pinafore frocks, or jumper suits? And what are their colour preferences?'[96] Although depleted stocks of civilian clothing were unlikely to prove equal to demand, some retailers staged fashion shows for servicewomen on the eve of demobilization, aimed at acquainting them with current trends and, less altruistically, promoting their own brands. In November 1945, 300 'girls in WAAF blue' attended a fashion show at Silverstone – 'the first mannequin parade ever held on an aerodrome', marvelled the *Air Force News*. WAAFs watched models from Lewis's Ltd of Leicester parading down a makeshift runway in the NAAFI canteen. The grand finale involved a mock wedding, though Maureen Pilling (reporting on the event) cautioned that the 'groom' was a married pilot who'd merely been loaned for the occasion.[97]

Worse off than their male peers, female veterans were nevertheless more handsomely compensated than women who'd served in civilian organizations. Members of the WLA felt particularly aggrieved. Dorothy Davies of Swansea, who joined the WLA aged nineteen, kept the discharge papers sent her by Glamorgan County Council in December 1945, tersely instructing her to return all 'uniform, badges etc., in a clean condition, as soon as possible, to the Uniform Department, Old Custom House, Cardiff'. She could retain '1 overcoat, 1 pair of shoes and 1 shirt', shorn of the WLA 'shoulder titles'. In a memoir written decades later, Dorothy was still stung that she and fellow Land Girls, unlike ex-servicewomen, got 'no gratuity'. The brusque notice from Glamorgan council hints at another gendered difference in demobilization. Whatever male veterans thought of their new wardrobe, the experience of passing through the demob centre and emerging in civvies (or with a bulky cardboard box) served as a rite of passage: a transition celebrated in the media and shared by cohorts of

Figure 3.5 Land Girls assemble in London to protest against the smaller allowance of coupons they received compared with ex-servicewomen, who also received cash gratuities, May 1946 (public domain)

men in unison. Women like Dorothy, in contrast, came home singly from distant farms without any ushering-out ritual to mark the culmination of their service. Later, a pro forma plopped through the letter-box, demanding the swift return of cleaned uniform apparel – or forfeit their coupon bonus.[98]

May 1946 found disgruntled Land Girls mobilizing. A mass meeting in London of 100 women, representing the organization's 10,000 members, drew up a seven-point charter. This wish list reveals a good deal about their terms of engagement, from unfair clothing allowances to nosy landladies and second-class citizenship in the uniformed scheme of things:

1. More clothing coupons
2. The right to stay out after 10pm
3. Higher pay
4. Protection from prying farmers' wives who read their letters
5. The same gratuities as women's services
6. One week's paid demob leave for each year of service
7. Right to use service canteens[99]

Women's Land Army clothing grievances weren't the result of over-sight on the government's part. Behind closed doors, civil servants can-didly acknowledged that the WLA had 'done the toughest of all the organised women's jobs and had the rawest deal'. However, a whole slew of civilian organizations, including not just the 'Bevin Boys' but in addition civil defence services (immortalized by *Dad's Army*), also aspired to a government-issued wardrobe or compensation in cash and coupons. Weighing up these various eligibility claims in February 1945, the War Cabinet decided that offering more clothing coupons to the WLA would make it harder to reject other claimants. National finances couldn't satisfy every petitioner. Besides, politicians reasoned, many Land Girls wouldn't be demobilized any time soon. The battle for agricultural workers would necessarily continue long after the Axis powers' defeat.[100]

Democratizing Device or Divisive Entitlement?

Full appreciation of the novelty – and generosity – of the demob ensemble requires a transnational perspective. In comparison with other Allied veterans, British ex-servicemen fared singularly well. One Russian soldier, having read about his British counterparts' out-fits, boldly demanded to know why Red Army veterans weren't getting the same.[101] It's hard to imagine his superiors responded sympathet-ically. With the 'Great Patriotic War' over, the USSR confronted the daunting task of rebuilding razed cities and reckoning with the deaths of twenty-four to twenty-seven million citizens.[102] This staggering fig-ure represented the highest proportion of any national population lost in the war. Moscow lacked funds to outfit all veterans in brand new attire, despite promising it to men and women alike. A June 1945 snip-pet in the *Manchester Guardian* related that demobilized 'Red Army girls' were receiving 'a woollen dress, a silk dress, two sets of under-wear, two pairs of silk stockings, and a pair of high-heeled shoes'. Hinted by the story's Moscow by-line, this account smacked of fan-ciful propaganda. The luckiest male Red Army veterans received a fresh summer uniform and some regulation underwear. More often, though, servicemen in tattered uniforms spruced themselves up before release by stripping less-worn clothing and footwear from comrades with months still left to serve. Soon mandatory personnel records included, alongside instances of sickness or absence, notations such as 'without boots', 'without greatcoats', 'without pants'. Red Army veteran Evgenii Moniushko later recalled that, with less than half his regiment fully uniformed, members of the 25th Artillery Division tried to remedy shortages by having locals run up uniforms from commandeered German parachute silk. This was painted blue – 'but only until the first rain'.[103]

According to historian Mark Edele, Soviet leaders objected to singling out service personnel for privileged treatment on ideological grounds. Unlike workers, peasants and intellectuals, veterans did not constitute a special status group under the tenets of Marxist-Leninism. Moreover, in the Great Patriotic War, *every* Soviet citizen had played a vital role in defence of the Motherland, not simply men and women in uniform. Red Army veterans may have been rhetorically lauded as homecoming heroes, but most returnees encountered a dense thicket of red tape and very few (if any) special perks on the far side. Not until the 1970s did the Kremlin begin extending more generous allowances to elderly veterans.[104]

In America, in contrast, neither bankruptcy nor claims of equality dictated the terms of veterans' treatment by the postwar state. In the United States, veterans (male and female) were left to shift for themselves in the nation's diminished civilian clothing market. Although the government urged retailers to reserve stocks for returning servicemen, manufacturers warned in July 1945 that veterans would be unlikely to find garments in stores until 'very late' in the year.[105] Some ex-GIs surely wondered why *they* weren't given something akin to, or better than, their British opposite numbers' demob suits. Since American uniforms were widely regarded as superior in quality and cut to British servicemen's apparel, it might seem surprising that Truman's administration neglected veterans' clothing needs. But in other regards Washington *did* treat former servicemen as a special entitlement group. In a country that, Hawai'i and the Aleutian Islands aside, remained untouched by air raids or combat, members of the armed forces had unquestionably shouldered heavier burdens than their civilian peers, especially those sent into front-line duty overseas. Few Americans would have quibbled with the proposition that service personnel formed a category apart from other citizens. The GI Bill rewarded veterans for their service with free college tuition, business start-up loans and federally backed mortgages, giving a leg-up into middle-class affluence for millions of poorer citizens and their families, although these entitlements were more readily accessed by white ex-servicemen than by their Black or female peers.[106]

A different dynamic prevailed in Britain, somewhere between Moscow's averred egalitarianism and Washington's pronounced favouritism. In the United Kingdom, where service personnel and civilians alike had suffered and made sacrifices, Attlee's administration was fashioning a new social contract, with a more robust network of entitlements and protections, including extended education (to age fifteen), national insurance and free healthcare for all ('from the cradle to the grave'), as its centrepiece. While British veterans might have considered their free clothing rather paltry in comparison with GI perks, Westminster (unlike Washington) didn't funnel public money into construction of a 'warfare-welfare' state to which military service personnel and veterans alone enjoyed access. British civilians might, then, have reached a different verdict on which nation's citizens were ultimately better rewarded by the postwar state.[107]

Received with both gratitude and gripes at the time of issue, the demob suit is now widely considered by dress historians and textile curators as pivotal to the development of twentieth-century British clothing. These garments helped elevate standards of menswear, cementing Burton's reputation as a 'leader in the democratization of men's fashion', writes Miriam Phelan in the book accompanying the Victoria and Albert Museum's landmark 2022 exhibition, 'Fashioning Masculinities'. Although veterans' reactions varied, their strength of feeling about everything from colour to cut attested serious male interest in style and appearance.[108]

Dress historian Geraldine Biddle-Perry characterizes demob suits as emblematic of Labour's aspiration to create a 'fashionable meritocracy': a socialist initiative that equipped around four million British men with well-made, durable clothing.[109] A couple of cautionary notes are necessary, however, before endorsing this celebratory reading of demob suits. Provision of veterans with a new wardrobe was *not* a party-political venture. The decision to do so was taken in 1943 by the coalition government, reaffirmed a year later when Sir Cecil Weir insisted that outfitting veterans was a 'reconstruction policy of far-reaching importance, and its abandonment would create political difficulties of the first order'.[110] From Whitehall's perspective, the suits were intended not only to boost the employability and esteem of veterans, but also to keep men 'contented in the difficult demobilization period'.[111] Churchill would surely not have cancelled the demobilization clothing scheme had he been re-elected that July. Reneging on the promise to outfit veterans risked provoking an aggrieved backlash of the sort Whitehall had spent years trying to avert.

As for the programme's democratizing aspect, this too needs some qualification. The quality of mass-produced menswear did rise after the war. But, in other ways, the issue of garments and footwear to former service personnel was riddled with inequities: between servicemen and servicewomen, between servicewomen and uniformed civilian women, and between veterans and civilians more broadly. Mass production of demob suits meant that the output of civilian clothing necessarily had to be curtailed. And, as many parents pointed out, those who outgrew their clothes and footwear quickest – children – suffered most from this shortfall.[112] There was a direct causal relationship between the production of demob suits and the persistence of clothes rationing far beyond the war. In 1943, the Board of Trade predicted a one-year continuation. Ultimately, though, clothing coupons outlasted the war by four years.

Perceptions of unfairness fuelled Britain's subterranean trade in pilfered or bartered clothing and coupons. Many commentators noted an adjustment in postwar Britons' situation ethics. Scruples about black market dealings were jettisoned as more and more people persuaded themselves that uneven access to supplies justified dubious means of acquisition. This logic generated its own momentum. If everyone was 'at it', what harm could there be in procuring garments – including stockings, the scarcest commodity of all – from traders offering them coupon-free?[113]

An *Observer* story from November 1945 spot-lit this murky transactional realm which many Britons inhabited with less hesitance than during the war, when black market profiteering was more widely condemned, if not always eschewed.[114] Ivor Brown, a prominent columnist, recounted a string of curious thefts: 'A bag with ten pounds in cash and a few clothing coupons was left in a train. It was returned with the money intact: the coupons had gone. Another bag with a good deal of varied and valuable stuff was also overlooked. It, too, was returned – minus only a packet of sweets and a few articles of clothing.' Brown further noted that several dry-cleaners had requested police protection for their premises, 'so strong is the craving for articles lodged on these premises'.

In his view, it was 'especially in the matter of clothes that the public conscience has withered away'. Whereas most Britons accepted food rationing as 'fair, necessary and efficient', they blamed shortages of clothing on 'bureaucratic muddling'. Brown predicted that larceny would cease whenever clothes rationing ended, concluding with a blunt warning to 'our grey-minded Austerity Ministers': 'Every time they tell us that we are to have no fun and no finery for years, they are unconsciously creating new thieves by the score …. We are by no means a nation of criminals: but another year or two of intemperate Austerity may easily put us on that road.'[115]

Provision of demob suits heightened British civilians' and servicewomen's tendency to scrutinize what garments others received and feel cheated in comparison. As a group, male veterans had seemingly been singled out for a unique privilege. But this perception missed something crucial, albeit absent from wartime and postwar commentary on outfits for veterans. Not all British servicemen *did* receive demob suits, as West Indian veterans soon discovered.

4 PROTESTORS

By the spring of 1946, the world's sea lanes – no longer menaced by Axis submarines and destroyers – were again clogged with traffic. With shipping space at a premium, troopships often doubled as passenger liners. Batches of demobilized troops, released prisoners of war and civilian internees freed from Japanese camps had begun to make the long oceanic journey home to Britain from the war's far-flung theatres: India, Burma, China, Australia, North Africa and the Middle East. In May, contingents of distinctively uniformed soldiers from across the empire, lugging their ceremonial attire, disembarked in Liverpool. Bound for newly erected barbed-wire encampments in Hyde Park and Kensington Gardens, these troops would participate in June's Victory Parade through London.

At the same time, numerous vessels were departing *from* British ports. Groups of 'GI brides', some cradling babies or with toddlers in tow, set sail from Southampton for the United States and Canada, while other emigrants struck out for new lives in the Antipodes and Southern Africa. West Indian veterans who had volunteered for wartime service in the RAF were among those ferried *en masse* across the Atlantic in May 1946. It wasn't all plain sailing. One particularly turbulent passage was beset by what British officials and the ship's Norwegian captain deemed a 'mutiny' – a rebellion to which they overreacted, but also one that they underestimated. Long submerged in the British National Archives, the story of the *Bergensfjord* is brought to the surface here for the first time.

Word of trouble on board reached dry land at 11pm on 21 May 1946, when the captain of a liner conveying 1,400 West Indian RAF veterans from Glasgow to the Caribbean, together with about 250 civilian passengers, tapped out an urgent message to a neighbouring frigate, HMS *Ballinderry*: 'Riot aboard can you send craft with boarding party to meet us.'[1] A few hours later, Captain Leif Hansen sounded an even more frantic note: 'Mutiny on board by large number of West Indian air forces. Firearms used by them. Three members of crew and Royal Navy injured.'[2] According to Hansen, an 'organized mutiny' had erupted as the *Bergensfjord* traversed the 800-mile stretch between Port of Spain, Trinidad, and Port Royal, Jamaica, where most of the airmen were due to disembark.

British military authorities responded swiftly to Hansen's distress signals. Upon reaching Port Royal, the captain was 'amazed to see and hear a number of Bren Gun Carriers coming along the road openly visible to everybody on board, and armed troops openly disgorging from trucks and disappear into the bush. This incited the Airmen more than ever and the situation was reaching a climax and all kinds of threats were hurled at passengers and crew.' Hansen aborted his first attempt to put men ashore at Port Royal after some of the airmen threw potatoes, bottles and plates at their peers as they descended the gangplank, demanding they return on board to present a united front in protest. The 'mutineers' issued a threat and an ultimatum. If the *Ballinderry* drew alongside, 'not one' of the women and children on board 'would leave the ship alive'. The protestors demanded that Hansen continue the journey to Kingston, a short distance away. 'I had to listen to this', the captain insisted, 'as reports were continuously reaching me about the arms and weapons these men had smuggled on board in Glasgow, and I could not afford to take any chances.' But no sooner had the *Bergensfjord* set sail than it was chased and escorted back to Port Royal by the *Ballinderry*.[3]

This time, disembarkation proceeded under heavily armed guard. Jamaican reporter Ivorall Davis described the quay at Port Royal as 'like the arsenal for which it was once famous'. Below the 'ugly muzzles' of *Ballinderry*'s guns, groups of RAF men were herded into 'pens' by soldiers of the Suffolk regiment, who hurled even uglier slurs. 'Get out of the bloody truck, nigger,' Davis overheard.[4] Marched into separate rooms in groups of ten, the airmen had their kit searched. The official report on the *Bergensfjord*'s arrival in Jamaica tallied three pistols, ten sheath knives, thirty-one jackknives and three cutthroat razors, plus ten table knives and one pair of scissors 'collected in error'. Seven men were arrested and charged with possessing weapons and insubordination.[5] Only then were the others allowed to reunite with waiting loved ones who'd spent many hours sweltering on the dock-side, trying to cut through the buzz of rumours to establish why this 'troublous day' was such a far cry from the joyful homecoming they'd long anticipated. 'The spectacle', noted Davis, 'was grimly reminiscent of war when the conquerors were subjecting their prisoners of war to close scrutiny.'[6]

An event that 'electrified the entire West Indies' barely regis-tered in the British press. The *Daily Mail* fleetingly reported 'serious rioting' on the troopship, juxtaposed with news that Princess Elizabeth had attended 'Perchance to Dream' at the London Hippodrome the previous evening.[7] Side-lined by reporters, the 'mutiny' inspired a flurry of fretful inter-departmental memos within Whitehall – and between London, Jamaica and Trinidad – as the Air Ministry, Admiralty, Colonial Office and personnel in the Caribbean traded opinions about exactly what had happened on board and what it signified. Senior offi-cials agreed that the disorder had been 'very disturbing'. If not the first manifestation of trouble on a repatriation voyage, the *Bergensfjord* disturbances had been the worst – and, they hoped to ensure, the last. The prospect of losing control over a troopship was bad enough, exacerbated by the presence of white women and children on board, including wives and offspring of army officers posted to the Caribbean.[8] Their safety was a paramount concern, but colonial officials' anxiety extended far beyond the vessel itself, fearful that this violent episode might portend a larger unravelling of imperial order. A 'disaffected rabble', as the Naval Officer in Charge at Trinidad characterized returning veterans, could have 'serious consequences' for British rule in the West Indies, already roiled by unrest in the late 1930s. For his part, the Governor of Jamaica nervously registered the political capi-tal which Norman Manley's People's National Party (PNP) extracted from the *Bergensfjord* 'martyrs'.[9]

Why had these West Indian airmen, returning from service with the British military's most elite branch, rebelled? Contemporary commentators offered discrepant accounts. Predisposed to see these men as trouble, British bureaucrats and officers devoted far less atten-tion to issues of motivation than they did to dissections of mutinous action and projections of what might follow. Turbulence on the *Bergensfjord* confirmed their pre-existing diagnosis of engrained Black male 'insolence' and insubordination. Viewed through the jaundiced eyes of officialdom, this ship-bound coda reprised the same motifs of indiscipline and *ressentiment* that had characterized the Caribbean volunteers' entire service in the RAF. In hundreds of pages of telegrams, situation reports and post-mortem inquiries preserved in the British National Archives, voices of the veterans themselves echo only fleetingly, reported second-hand by white officers and ship's crew members. Jamaican newspapers, for whom the RAF men's 'troublous' homecoming was front-page news for several days in May 1946, likewise paid scant attention to the origins of disorder on the *Bergensfjord*, trivializing the *mêlée* as a skirmish between Jamaican and Trinidadian rivals. Instead, they accentuated the veterans' demeaning treatment *after* disembarkation at Port Royal.

In the absence of detailed accounts produced by the veterans themselves, it's necessary to read official reports largely against the grain – for what they divulge about the prejudices that clouded Britons' ability to make sympathetic sense of West Indians' grievances. But one officer, Squadron Leader Webster, *did* provide a more clear-sighted view of what had animated protest: inequitable clothing allowances. Unlike their white peers, these West Indian airmen did not receive demob suits, despite being British subjects. On demobilization, Jamaican veterans would be awarded £17; Hondurans, £12; and men from Trinidad, British Guiana, Barbados and the Leeward and Windward Islands, £9. Whether they personally stood to gain more or less from these arrangements, West Indians collectively opposed differential payments made '*in lieu of civilian clothing*'.[10] This two-fold injustice – West Indians pitted against one another; Black British subjects treated differently from white veterans – inspired men to rebel.

The long-forgotten mutiny on the *Bergensfjord* braids several strands of postwar experience. The West Indian airmen's rebellion was one of numerous uprisings mounted by veterans across the globe in the months after Japan's surrender. Clothing figured prominently in these protests, emblematic of various forms of injustice, from punitive discipline to racial discrimination and military wastefulness. Apparel could both inspire protest and serve as a potent symbol in campaigns for redress. For the veterans on the *Bergensfjord*, discriminatory allowances meshed with larger patterns of prejudice suffered by colonial volunteers and conscripts who'd lent their labour to Britain's war effort. But a story about clothing, colonialism, racism and resistance also reveals a good deal about postwar mobility, as millions of people travelled between locations, sometimes by choice but often involuntarily: moving or being moved. We can thus chart the *Bergensfjord* protestors – unwilling repatriates, in some cases – within the larger ebb and flow of trans-oceanic crossings that followed the war's end, as white Britons sought to reconstruct a shaken colonial order overseas and British subjects from the colonies tried to find economic security in the metropole.

A Sea of Veteran Protest

A powerful upsurge of transnational militancy followed VJ Day. On the streets of Manila, Tokyo, Honolulu, Frankfurt, London and Paris, on military bases from India to Egypt, as well as on board liners like the *Bergensfjord*, military personnel organized protests and strikes, withholding their labour from armed forces that demanded unquestioning obedience to authority. This radicalism has been largely lost to historical memory. As the war has receded further into the past, many Britons and Americans have preferred to freeze the frame of 'victory' at the moment of its announcement, lionizing the retrospectively anointed 'greatest generation' as the most disciplined, valorous and effective fighting force the world had ever seen. Things looked different at the time. Within weeks of Japan's defeat, Allied military personnel began protesting against the terms of their ongoing postwar service, voicing dissent so loudly that civil and military leaders in far-off home countries jumped to attention.[11]

In late 1945 and January 1946, as this protest wave crested, reports of servicemen's strikes dominated newspaper headlines in the United States. Their key grievance, as American media framed it, related to the sluggish pace of demobilization. The mutinous GIs were men desperate to get home. Enraged by delays in shipping them back stateside, and often disgruntled by the War Department's 'points system' that tabulated eligibility for individual men's release with reference to a variety of factors, from length of service overseas to combat decorations and number of infant dependants, GIs took to the streets. Photographs showed throngs of men in uniform, demonstrating in Manila and other cities that hosted large concentrations of occupation troops. Among the slogans on their placards, 'WE WANT TO GO HOME' predominated.[12]

While US servicemen rallied in the Asia–Pacific region and across Europe, their spouses back home mobilized in parallel. Women eager for their husbands to be demobilized formed Bring Back Daddy Clubs, with chapters scattered across the country. Female activists directed impassioned pleas to their local representatives and lawmakers in Washington, DC, upping the ante by including babies' garments inscribed with messages that purported to be written by infants, some of whom had never even met their servicemen daddies deployed overseas.[13] 'Baby Clothes Used as Threat', ran a *New York Times* headline, reporting on a pair of pink and white crocheted bootees sent to the House Military Affairs Committee with the 'subtle reminder of "No dads, no votes"'.[14] Although the women who orchestrated this campaign hoped to pluck the heartstrings of policymakers, moved by these poignant tokens of fatherlessness, some resisted emotional manipulation. Senator Elmer Thomas (Democrat, Oklahoma), the recipient of some forty pairs of bootees, gleefully announced that the women who'd inundated his office were 'doing destitute Europeans a favor'. He would donate this windfall to a charity that collected clothing for people in 'devastated areas' of the continent.[15] Yet protestations of steadfast commitment to an orderly and measured demobilization schedule notwithstanding, the Truman administration *did* soon accelerate the tempo of troops' repatriation. By mid 1946, millions more US service personnel had been brought home than wartime planning for postwar military needs had envisioned.[16]

Amid all the hullaballoo orchestrated by the Bring Back Daddy Clubs, Americans tended to overlook other issues raised by protesting GIs overseas – a repertoire of grievances as much political as personal. Indeed, for some leaders of the protests in the Philippines, the epicentre of GI activism, the personal and political were inextricably intertwined. Men didn't *just* want to get home; they demanded a more robust justification for their ongoing deployment abroad. Why, they wanted to know, were millions of servicemen still detained overseas months after Japan had capitulated, not least as the subdued Japanese people showed no sign of resisting American occupation? Unnecessary to quell non-existent unrest, many servicemen languished in idleness or were forced to perform busy-work that served little purpose other than killing time.[17]

Servicemen in disparate locations, including growing numbers of aggrieved British troops, noted that after combat ceased some officers made a sudden fetish of spit-and-polish. Never excessively concerned with appearance before, they now insisted their subordinates daily devote hours to the meticulous maintenance of uniforms, shining footwear to a mirror-like state of reflective perfection. Frequent kit inspections and drill parades formed an unwelcome concomitant to all this preparatory frenzy. British servicemen across the Middle East and Asia, from Burma to India, Malaya and Singapore, complained about being made to wear dress uniforms in humidity that weighed oppressively like a waterlogged towel. One newly returned serviceman penned a lengthy description of this predicament, published in the *Manchester Guardian* on 12 December 1945:

> on my own station, in the heat of a middle of a Middle East summer men would be compelled to mount guard in the sun with sleeves rolled down and fastened, collars buttoned up and ties worn, long slacks, and full webbing for four two-hour stretches in twenty-four, at the end of which duty they had two hours stand-off in which to breakfast &c., before resuming work in the hangars.

This demobilized airman noted that the English serviceman was 'notoriously docile compared with troops of other countries'. But placidity had its limits. As weeks went by with no sign of imminent demobilization, men responded angrily to the realization that 'as a result of winning the war they are a lot worse off'.[18] It was perhaps fitting that a large-scale British mutiny, which would escalate into the largest episode of mass indiscipline in Britain's military history, occurred at an RAF base whose name evoked an article of apparel: Jodhpur, in northwestern India. In January 1946, airmen from two maintenance units refused to assemble on the parade ground for morning inspection. Likeminded airmen at RAF Mauripur and Drigh Road, Karachi, also ignored orders to parade in best blues. Before sailing to Glasgow, where the West Indian RAF veterans embarked in early May, the *Bergensfjord* spent some time anchored at Bombay in February. While docked there, riots broke out in the city – with Indian nationalists and activist servicemen swelling the tide of protest. Soon, around 50,000 British airmen and naval ratings were participating in mass shows of disobedience from North Africa to Southeast Asia.[19]

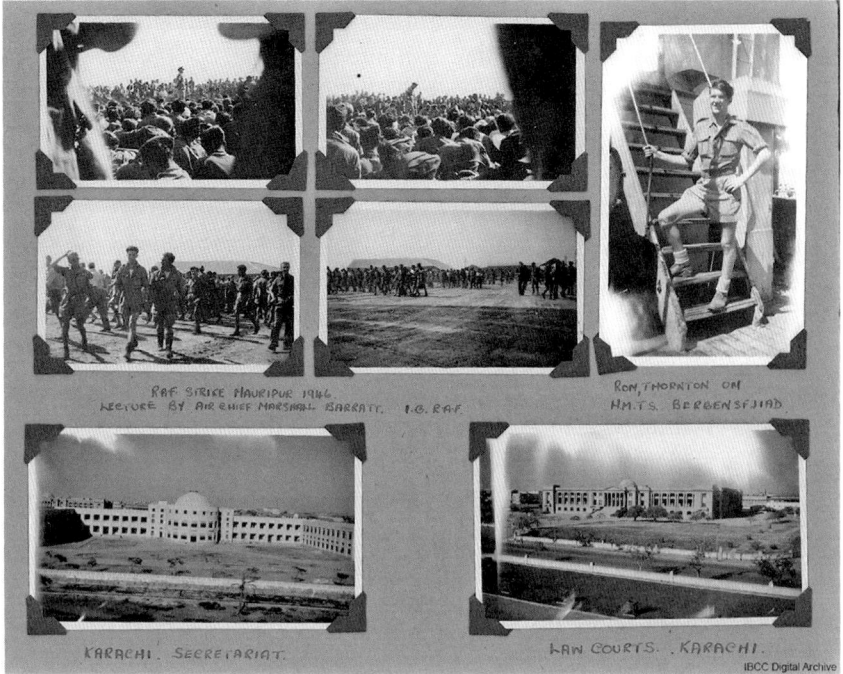

Figure 4.1 John Shipman's scrapbook shows scenes associated with the RAF protests at Mauripur and Karachi; here Ron Thornton stands on the steps of the *Bergensfjord* (IBCC Digital Archive, document/21957)

Servicemen took umbrage at other forms of work besides burnishing their boots, regarding themselves as surplus men guarding surplus *matériel* on behalf of a cavalier military establishment. Soldiers were aghast at the wholesale destruction of property they witnessed in war's wake: an expensive, environmentally ruinous, alternative to selling off or dismantling, repurposing and recycling munitions, vehicles and clothing. In the Pacific, American servicemen witnessed planes being shoved into the sea, while acres of productive agricultural land were ring-fenced to accommodate undetonated ordnance. Despite its global scarcity, clothing was also squandered. Mildew rapidly corroded army field jackets – along with other garments, blankets and shoes – heaped without regard for preservation, leaving a mouldering mess that was then unceremoniously incinerated. In January 1946, a committee of nine servicemen presented their complaints to members of a Senate sub-committee investigating the disposal of surplus materials in the Philippines. The burning of once perfectly serviceable clothing, which could have been given to Filipinos or shipped to 'relieve distress' in Europe, was one of the issues enlisted men raised, only to be shot down by their superiors.[20] Colonel Raymond Oxrieder, commander in Batangas, insisted: 'There has been no destruction of property except by orderly and approved salvage methods.' Oxrieder conceded that 'some clothing has been coming in from New Guinea, which had been stored outdoors and was completely rotted', but he maintained that, following careful inspection of every bale, usable clothing was laundered. Unwearable remnants alone were burned.[21] The GI committee found Oxrieder's explanation spurious. Less than a week later the same men appeared, and levelled the same charges, before an even higher-profile visitor from the States. Secretary of War Robert Patterson, hoping to win over servicemen with assurances that they'd be demobilized and shipped home with all due speed, was caught off-guard by the vehemence with which committee members vented their fury over the imprecise timetable and unconvincing rationales for their prolonged deployment. Again, servicemen decried wanton destructiveness. 'Let us stop burning clothes up!,' fumed Sgt Spitz.[22]

Activist GIs in Manila, like leftist counterparts elsewhere, found the waste of both their time and army resources indicative of larger misuses of power. Washington, as these servicemen saw it, was deploying military force overseas to advance profit-driven American economic and strategic interests, harming prospects for international understanding on which a just postwar order would depend. Sceptical of Patterson's insistence that scarcity of shipping lay behind the tardy pace of demobilization, these men regarded logistics as a smokescreen for imperial geopolitics. If the Philippines were soon to be independent after decades of American colonial rule, why were so many US troops stationed there? And why were American troops aiding Chinese Nationalists, even enlisting surrendered *Japanese* personnel, in a civil war against Mao's Chinese Communists? Other servicemen's protests also expressed opposition to the expansion of US empire and the simultaneous attempt to reconsolidate European colonialism. In the Indian subcontinent, at least some RAF and naval protestors conceived their acts of defiance not as 'we want to go home' protests but rather as shows of solidarity with Asian nationalists in an intensifying campaign for independence.

Terms of Engagement

The *Bergensfjord* 'mutineers' may not have seen themselves staging a wholesale revolt against empire. But, exiting the RAF, they protested against a culminating injustice interwoven with the warp of imperial preference that privileged white subjects over Black as a matter of course. From enlistment to demobilization, West Indian airmen encountered discrimination at every turn. It was particularly galling, however, to find that gratuities issued by the War Office – a monetary token of appreciation – should have been so glaringly differentiated neither by the degree of danger that men had faced nor by the valour they'd shown, but by race. Whereas 'European' privates received ten shillings per month spent in uniform, with this sum rising through the ranks to fifty-five shillings for brigadiers, Asians received 'Sh. 7/50' (regardless of rank) and African privates a meagre 'Sh. 3/50'.[23] And while veterans from the British Isles, including Ireland, received a complete wardrobe on demobilization, airmen from the Caribbean were issued promissory notes to help acquire new clothes, the precise value determined by the island from which a man came. To add further insult to injury, many of the airmen on the *Bergensfjord* didn't *want* to leave Britain. They were effectively cold-shouldered out of the country. By early 1946, the British authorities, eager to rid themselves of what they regarded as an intensifying 'colour problem', sought excuses to repatriate West Indian veterans as swiftly as possible, regardless of the airmen's preferences.[24]

Unlike other British colonial troops, many of whom were coerced into service or lured by deceptive promises about material rewards, these West Indians had volunteered their services to a beleaguered Britain. Several travelled at their own expense to the 'mother country' to enlist in the RAF. Two large contingents of ground crew later underwent training at RAF Palisadoes in Jamaica before sailing across the Atlantic to Britain. On arrival, they were corralled at the windswept site of a former Butlin's camp in Filey, North Yorkshire.[25] Under peacetime conditions, the Air Ministry would have declined these men. Regulations drafted in August 1923 stipulated that recruits 'must be of pure European descent and the sons of natural born or naturalised British subjects'.[26] Since inhabitants of Britain's colonies were, regardless of ethnicity, legally British subjects under the British Nationality and Status of Aliens Act (1914), what the RAF's insistence on European 'purity' meant in practice was that recruits must look white. Senior commanders rationalized prejudice on the subjunctive grounds that exclusion kindly spared Black personnel – *had* they been permitted entry – the social awkwardness of standing out as 'Other' in the rarefied milieu of the RAF. Debarring admission to people of colour was, a self-satisfied internal memo insisted, 'as much with a view to the happiness of the non-European individual as in the interests of the Service'. The RAF clung onto its *de facto* colour bar until November 1940, by which time other branches of Britain's armed forces had already acknowledged the need to enlist colonial recruits. What changed Air Ministry minds was not an egalitarian epiphany but the devastating loss of pilots and crew incurred during the Battles of France and Britain. Together these lethal confrontations with the German *Luftwaffe* claimed around 3,000 airmen's lives. With an estimated 96,000 pilots, observers and gunners required for 1940–2, the RAF grudgingly agreed to accept Black candidates from the colonies.[27]

Over the remainder of the war, the RAF admitted approximately 50 West African and around 6,500 West Indian applicants. A handful were permitted to pilot planes, photographed in winsome poses for propaganda purposes. Most, however, worked in clerical roles and as drivers, technicians, engineers, radar operators and air traffic controllers.[28] Cy Grant, who later became a television personality in postwar Britain, initially trained to be a pilot, but halfway through his instruction was 'switched to navigator'. He later reminisced that, although he hadn't 'made anything of this at the time', he subsequently became aware of 'problems with the English aircrew not wanting to fly with black pilots'.[29] For its part, the War Cabinet was clear that these Caribbean service personnel, like civilian labourers who'd arrived in wartime Britain from elsewhere in the empire, would need to be 'disposed of' after hostilities ended and 're-absorbed' into colonial economies.[30] As in 1919, Whitehall looked to repatriation to resolve the perceived problem of a more ethnically heterogeneous Britain, lauding free passage across the Atlantic as a gesture of governmental generosity – a time-limited offer that colonial recruits would do well to accept quickly before it expired.[31]

West Indian airmen encountered animosity in wartime Britain from both within and beyond the ranks of the RAF. One air force medical officer attracted press attention and questions in Parliament when he barred a young white woman from visiting West Indian airmen on his ward at RAF Tangmere in Westhampnett, Sussex. Other patients, the doctor insisted, had complained about these visits. Her presence had 'lowered white prestige', he asserted, insinuating a violation of boundaries both racial and sexual. A white 'girl' at a Black man's bedside conjured the alarming spectre of miscegenation, or so this physician implied. Such visits, he felt, couldn't possibly arise from the spirit of selfless devotion to servicemen's welfare constantly impressed upon British women in wartime.[32]

Charged encounters were also commonplace off-base. Some American servicemen, like some Britons, bristled at seeing Black men socializing in pubs and clubs they viewed as exclusively *white* enclaves, particularly if women also frequented these spaces. Hostility could quickly escalate from verbal abuse to physical violence. The King George V Club in Manchester, patronized by GIs as well as West Indian airmen, was a particular hotspot for trouble. Tellingly, the Air Ministry seemed less inclined to suspect that GIs habituated to Jim Crow might instigate fights than to pin responsibility squarely on West Indians.[33] Officials tracked an escalation in tense incidents in the months after the war ended. As military discipline relaxed, social disorder increased. In November 1945, air marshals noted 'a very serious clash between white and coloured airmen' at a Maintenance Unit in Heywood, resulting in the hospitalization of seven white airmen and two Jamaicans. Three months later, fighting between Jamaican and white personnel erupted at Blackbushe aerodrome in Camberley, Surrey. 'Trouble had been brewing for some time because of the Jamaicans' alleged lack of discipline and their general behaviour,' the *Manchester Guardian* informed its readers. 'On Thursday, the white airmen decided upon mass action and a general fight is reported in which minor injuries were caused.'[34]

With incidents growing in gravity and frequency, Air Ministry officials broached various paths of action: first, that West Indian non-commissioned officers be given refresher courses in disciplinary methods; second, that those whose 'mentality [was] below the minimum required for service in the RAF' be removed by medical boards; third, that unruly airmen be 'concentrated' in remote locations, preferably without the presence of Women's Auxiliary Air Force (WAAF) personnel; and, finally, that the tempo of repatriation be accelerated.[35] Of these measures, senior commanders favoured expulsion of 'violently anti-British' RAF personnel. 'There is, as you well appreciate, only one solution; and that is, repatriation,' Air Marshal Sir Grahame Donald informed Air Marshal Sir John Slessor on 30 November 1945.[36]

Viscount Stansgate, Secretary of State for Air, then attempted to sell this policy to the Colonial Office. In December, he informed George Hall (a Labour peer briefly serving as Secretary of State for the Colonies) that West Indians who were 'not amenable to discipline' should be shipped back to the Caribbean. Pitching himself as not wholly unsympathetic to these airmen, Stansgate referenced their depression 'by our climate' and invoked nebulous 'events' which had 'not justified the idealistic picture which they had formed of this country' – as though disillusionment were a product of naïveté rather than the relentless Anglophilia of an educational system that portrayed the Mother Country in unrealistically vibrant hues.[37] Echoing the RAF's rationale for excluding Black recruits, Stansgate insisted that early repatriation would be 'in the best interests of everyone – and not least of the West Indians themselves'.[38] The Colonial Office had reservations about mass repatriation, however. Hall countered that the return of airmen in 'small staggered detachments' would 'facilitate reception arrangements'. By this he implied that veterans arriving in smaller numbers over a longer period would be more likely to find work in Jamaica's threadbare job market; or, if they remained unemployed,

Figure 4.2 This school room in Kingston, adorned with posters of British colonies, reveals the imperial character of Jamaica's curriculum as well as the barefoot pupils' poverty in February 1946 (Earl Leaf/ Michael Ochs Archives/Getty Images)

would present a less menacing challenge to colonial government than a bloc of aggrieved, jobless veterans who had served together in Britain, been forced to sail back together, and failed *en masse* to secure employment in Jamaica.[39]

In all their deliberations, British officials remained alert to the optics of policy decisions. Fearful of inciting an anti-imperial backlash, they hesitated to *appear* overtly prejudiced towards Black colonial personnel. '*Concentration*' of West Indian RAF personnel in remote camps was ruled out on the grounds that such a move might 'give rise to criticism of confinement or racial discrimination'.[40] In 1945, with horrific images of liberated Nazi camps fresh in many minds, even the most tone-deaf British officials might have winced at a sentence that placed 'concentration' and 'camp' in such close proximity. Civil servants and commanders also hoped to choreograph repatriation 'unobtrusively' so that voyages like the *Bergensfjord*'s would not arouse 'suspicion' that West Indians were being 'rewarded' for misbehaviour by early repatriation. This risked inspiring copycat troublemakers eager to get home sooner rather than later. Equally, though, no impression should be given that these men were being 'sent home in disgrace', delinquents no longer welcome in the imperial metropole. This, Hall warned, 'would not only be most undesirable for the airmen themselves but almost certainly have unfortunate and far-reaching effects, both politically and otherwise'. In other words, any sign of discriminatory treatment was liable to stoke nationalist sentiment in the Caribbean – another reason to favour 'staggered detachments'.[41]

The Colonial Office lost this argument. A sense of impending crisis, fuelled by the Air Ministry's increasingly hostile appraisals of West Indian airmen as a 'liability' and 'embarrassment', propelled the *Bergensfjord*'s voyage in May 1946. When the ship left Glasgow, it removed approximately one-quarter of the entire cohort of West Indian RAF personnel from Britain. Senior officials told themselves that these men represented 'most of the principal malcontents'. 'They have for the most part turned out unsatisfactory and – resulting from a number of ugly incidents, razor fights and so on – we are packing them off home long before they are due for release,' wrote Slessor: a terse verdict that sounded very much as though these veterans were being sent home in disgrace.[42] During the voyage, the airmen would continue to wear uniform. Despite impending demobilization, they remained subject to martial discipline for the duration, uniforms serving less as a badge of institutional belonging than as a marker of subordination. When the *Bergensfjord* finally docked in Kingston, Jamaica's *Daily Express* printed a front-page photograph showing hundreds of figures in RAF navy, peering down from its decks.[43]

Anatomy of a Mutiny

With West Indian airmen tabbed as troublemakers long before they clambered aboard the *Bergensfjord*, officials effectively scripted a 'mutiny' narrative in advance: yet another example of Black men's truculence, prickly sensitivity to perceived slights and resistance to hard work that had everything to do with obdurate personalities and nothing to do with organized protest. Captain Leif Hansen and Wing Commander Gregory, Officer Commanding the Troops on board, agreed that they were 'in for a tough voyage', and their subsequent accounts – filleted in Whitehall for public dissemination – helped stamp events on board as a mutiny. Both Hansen and Gregory emphasized that many of the Jamaicans and Trinidadians had brought pistols, knives and other weapons on board, either expecting trouble or intent on making it. Within hours of embarkation, the West Indians resisted discipline, refusing to undertake 'fatigues' – chores like stowing away their luggage, clearing up mess kits after meals, disposing of rubbish, keeping the latrines clean – that would have made conditions below decks more tolerable.[44] The situation quickly deteriorated. Hansen viscerally described sinks choked with food waste; ventilator fans interfered with, creating a 'foul smell' below decks; latrines 'ankle deep in water and excreta'. 'If I were a farmer, I wouldn't let my pigs live under these conditions,' Hansen declared. By their refusal to work, the returnees had, in his view, *chosen* sub-human degradation. But it was the captain's decision to let the men 'stew in their own juice' that resulted in 'filth which grew worse and worse as the voyage progressed'. Hansen perhaps hesitated to order white crew members to clean on behalf of West Indians, regarding it as too degrading an inversion of the proper racial order of things.[45]

Tension crackled not just between officers, crew and the RAF men, but also between the 250 paying passengers and the West Indian airmen. For Hansen and Gregory, the presence of white women and children made the men's mutinous behaviour all the more alarming.

Like the Air commanders who feared for the safety of WAAFs in proximity to Black airmen, Hansen and Gregory presupposed that the West Indians represented a sexual menace to white women, reprising an age-old trope of rapacious Black masculinity.[46] It didn't take long for rumours of 'molestation' – euphemistic code for something far worse – to engulf the *Bergensfjord*.

A related threat came from the West Indians' 'infiltration' of areas intended for whites only. Several officials used this term, suggestive of both enemy sabotage and toxic pollution, to conjure a state of anarchy on the *Bergensfjord*. The mere presence of Black bodies intruding where they oughtn't to have been horrified some senior personnel. Army Brigadier Julian Jefferson, commander of the North Caribbean Area, went so far as to announce that the ringleaders' goal was nothing other than to 'humiliate the white man'.[47] Insubordination manifested itself in a refusal not only to work but to accept *boundaries*. West Indian airmen constantly transgressed demarcation lines erected to keep races and classes apart (they had been assigned to different decks, lounges and dining rooms, or debarred from leisure facilities altogether). Captain Hansen reported these violations at length:

> Infiltration of deck space allotted to passengers other than Airmen was bad from the beginning and … got steadily worse and as soon as one group of men were cleared away, another group would appear. Crew recreation space was kept clear with the greatest of difficulty. These Airmen even took over the three swings I had put up on the Tennis Deck for the amusement of the children. Finally it was hardly possible for my 1st Class passengers to find a spot for themselves on their deck. The Airmen would stroll arrogantly along kicking the legs of their chairs, and openly insulting these passengers.[48]

Rude behaviour found a counterpart in vulgar invective. Hansen noted that the RAF men spent their time 'lying around on tables, 90% smoking'. This broke below-decks rules, but when white crew members reprimanded the airmen, the latter reportedly retorted, '"Fuck off", and "we are not taking any orders from you White Bastards"'. Gregory also reported 'insolent remarks' of the same sort, emphasizing that white personnel under his command 'swallowed' these insults 'in the interests of peace' – albeit 'very much against the grain'. This vaunted self-restraint notwithstanding, 'colour feeling', a syndrome that seemingly named affronted Black pride rather than white prejudice, intensified during the voyage. When the ship docked briefly at Port of Spain to let Trinidadian veterans disembark and to pick up more civilian passengers, the airmen allegedly 'were shouting to each other "More White Bastards for us to beat up"'.[49]

Dispatches sent to Whitehall agreed that tension reached boiling point somewhere between Trinidad and Jamaica. While the ship was docked at Port of Spain, some 100 or 200 airmen broke through a police cordon, returned 'intoxicated', and fomented more unrest. The night the *Bergensfjord* set sail for Port Royal, Jamaica, mutineers broke into the Quartermaster's stores, smashing open boxes containing rifles. (Rifle bolts and bayonets had already been removed as a precautionary measure, Gregory reassured superiors.) The following evening, 21 May, a Norwegian sailor was superficially injured by a bullet and a flight sergeant wounded in the lip as synchronized violence erupted at three locations. A siren's blow was 'the pre-arranged signal for mutiny'.[50]

Given the magnitude of what that term implies – a potentially capital offence – a curious vagueness marks accounts of exactly why and between whom fighting erupted. On such a large vessel, Hansen and Gregory couldn't personally have witnessed all the punches thrown, shots fired, bloodied lips and grazed foreheads their reports tried to marshal into coherence. On what grounds, then, did they state with such certainty that violence was co-ordinated in three separate locations? Perhaps they felt confident that precise details were less consequential than the bottom line. 'The only shots fired were by the West Indians and the only casualties were amongst Europeans,' Gregory asserted. His attempts 'to avoid "black and white" trouble' had come to nought.[51]

While Gregory and Hansen were convinced a mutiny had occurred, some of their interlocutors appeared less certain. Strikingly, just one of the seven airmen disciplined for possessing weapons and 'insubordination' was court-martialled. Corporal Alexander had allegedly assaulted a chief petty officer on the night of 21 May. But, since the prosecution could produce no evidence, he was found not guilty.[52] Accounts of what transpired on board oscillate between alarmist visions of a ship on the brink of being 'lost' to a 'howling' and 'snarling' mob of West Indian men – with white women and children cowering in the saloon behind a glass door – and more cautious estimates of unruliness that officers' resolute action safely contained.[53] Testimony gathered from passengers, including the white women whose safety was of such paramount concern, confirmed that rumours of 'molestation' were exactly that: mere hearsay. 'Excepting general unpleasantness and insolence, I have not heard of any molestation of the women passengers who preferred to continue their journey, and those taking passage from Trinidad were given the option of withdrawing,' the Officer in Charge at Trinidad related. 'None did.'[54] Presumably, had any of these female travellers feared for their safety, they would have disembarked at the earliest opportunity.

Yet more revealingly, Hansen gathered evidence of a different racial dynamic on board. On 20 May, the eve of the mutiny, Wing Commander Gregory noted that various women and children on board 'didn't help the situation'. Far from being passive bystanders, helplessly engulfed in strife between Black airmen and white sailors, some civilian passengers inflamed the tensions on board. Gregory observed infants, from their privileged upper-deck location, spitting at the RAF men, throwing down various missiles at them and calling them 'black niggers' – presumably parroting the language and attitudes of parents and other adults.[55] This provocation suggests an alternative account of why the West Indian veterans 'infiltrated' playgrounds, smashed swing-sets and kicked the legs out from under deck-chairs.

British officials, disinclined to acknowledge that the *Bergensfjord*'s white passengers might be responsible for the 'colour problem', were keen to assign blame in the process of learning lessons from this episode. With so many institutional players weighing in – RAF officers and the Air Ministry, the ship's captain and crew, colonial governors and military commanders in the Caribbean, plus their counterparts in Whitehall – it's no surprise that fault was found in multiple locations as buck-passing gathered steam. Why had men already viewed as malcontents been allowed to bring weapons on board in Glasgow? Why hadn't Gregory's men imposed strict discipline from the outset? Why had civilians been permitted to travel on the same liner repatriating 1,400 West Indian airmen? All these questions were posed in the mutiny's wake. But a more exculpatory version of events also lay readily at hand. Air Vice Marshal Sir John Cordingley, anxious lest the governor of Jamaica fault the RAF for 'mishandling or lack of care' of veterans who returned in an 'ugly mood', reassured himself that Sir John Huggins would undoubtedly 'realise that the trouble is inherent in the men themselves'.[56]

The Sartorial Politics of Colonial Service

Amid this torrent of recrimination and self-justification, almost no officers either on the *Bergensfjord* or on dry land paid attention to the injustice that underpinned the RAF men's protest. One commander on the *Ballinderry*, the naval escort summoned to Hansen's assistance, expressly disavowed any interest in what might have provoked trouble. 'I don't care what your grievances are,' he shouted into a megaphone as his vessel drew alongside the *Bergensfjord*. 'I am here to save life. I am coming alongside to take off women and children and 1st Class passengers.' A more ominous coda made clear his willingness to shed blood in the name of preserving life: 'One false move and I will rake you with gunfire.'[57]

One officer alone seemingly appreciated that, whatever animosities had arisen on board the ship, a prior *political* issue motivated the West Indian airmen. Squadron Leader Ronald Webster, senior accountant officer at RAF Palisadoes, Jamaica, noted the 'strong feeling' provoked by 'inadequate' civilian clothing allowances. Having fielded 'numerous complaints', Webster mooted that the 'wide difference' between the amount earmarked for Jamaicans and men from other islands was 'out of proportion'.[58] In his view, it was this grievance that galvanized protest. The airmen had demanded to 'see someone in authority in Trinidad', or they'd refuse to disembark. In an attempt to prevent rioting, Webster announced that all payments would henceforth be to the tune of £17, with a government notice to this effect printed in the *Daily Gleaner* on 25 May. But even as they levelled the field between different islanders, British officials were already calculating how they could claw this expense back through reduced mustering out pay.[59]

Much was at stake for the RAF veterans in the matter of how much – or little – the British government proposed to give them 'in lieu of civilian clothing'. Military apparel bore particular significance for personnel from Britain's empire. Colonial recruitment propaganda emphasized smart uniforms and footwear as alluring material enticements to enlist. Illustrations depicted the make-over of African men hitherto barefoot and clad in tattered shorts or whatever the illustrator construed as 'native dress', such as loin cloths, animal skins and feathers. Recruits were simultaneously Europeanized, militarized and masculinized by their new tailored outfits and leather boots. Both men and women took these sartorial markers of modernity seriously. Enlistees in Sierra Leone refused to go on parade after the relevant authorities failed to issue them with boots.[60] As elsewhere in Europe and North America, both recruiters and recruits endowed military uniform with alchemical properties, capable of transforming the base material of male corporeality into the irresistible gold of sexual desirability. 'Khaki fever', diagnosed as an epidemic among females in wartime Britain and the United States, was similarly believed to afflict women in sub-Saharan Africa. Robert Kakembo, a Ugandan soldier with the King's African Rifles (KAR), noted the magic worked by military apparel both on a man's sense of self-worth and on others' perception of his stature:

> A man leaves his village and goes into the Army; he disappears for some eighteen months, and on return home on leave he is 100 per cent changed. He is fat and strong, clean and clever, with plenty to talk about and lots of money to spend. The young girls of the village worship him; the young men follow him about …. The soldier becomes a centre of worship to everybody except those whose girls have fallen for him.[61]

For West Indians in the RAF, the blue uniform could be a particular source of pride. By common consent, airmen enjoyed the most dashing apparel of any branch of the British armed forces. Their flatteringly cut trousers and wide-shouldered, cinched jackets, together with their jaunty caps and distinctive winged insignia, contributed significantly to the RAF's derring-do mystique.[62] Looking back, some West Indian former airmen ascribed their uniform a further protective function. Signifying membership of an elite outfit, the blue garb eased the wearer's acceptance in British society. If not impenetrable armour against racist abuse, the uniform nevertheless represented far more than the sum of its parts. It was, veteran Robert N. Murray wrote, 'a passport to many privileges', from free travel to admiring female attention.[63] Not all of this appreciative attention was free from condescension, however; nor did the blue uniform necessarily deflect white observers' attention from an airman's black skin. On the contrary, Joyce Egginton noted (in a study of West Indians in Britain) 'something very touching about the sight of a coloured man in British uniform …

Figure 4.3 A West Indian recruit receives his RAF uniform at
No 2 Receiving Centre, Cardington, Bedfordshire, 27 January 1944
(Flight Officer F. J. Brock/Imperial War Museums via Getty Images)

risking his life so that the country which enslaved his ancestors might
remain free'. This poignant spectacle reminded Egginton of 'a child
who offers a kiss after he has been smacked'.[64]

Some British observers anticipated that it would be a challenging rite of passage for demobilized colonial personnel to surrender
their prized uniforms and return to civilian life. One contributor to the
Journal of the Royal African Society (writing in 1944) imagined that
African veterans would particularly regret relinquishing military garb
that symbolized the many horizon-widening experiences, sartorial and
social, afforded them by military service. Former servicemen's aspi-
rations to a 'modern' standard of living, Mrs Fane predicted, would
threaten the colonial *status quo ante*:

> The many thousands of Africans who have served in the
> Forces during the war are not only workers who will want

employment, they are men who have experienced and enjoyed improved conditions of life. They have slept in something better than the malodorous, dark and smoky hut of their childhood; they have used the furniture of house and table; they have known the comfort of clean body and laundered clothes; they have travelled far, met and mingled with men of other races and lands. … Their minds are full of new ideas, and many of them will have acquired new fellowships and new loyalties. Though it is not true of them all, it is true of many to say that they will not want to divest themselves of this new way of life the day they divest themselves of their uniform. They will want – and the articulate express the idea now – a new and better way of life for themselves and their fellow Africans.[65]

Some African veterans, including Robert Kakembo, echoed Fane's premonitory sentiments. He, too, folded superior military-issue attire into a bundle of 'necessary luxuries' which servicemen would resent having to go without. Traditional African garb now represented a retrogression, a step backwards in world-historical time. '[T]he African in the Army will never go back to put on his skins again – not the East African,' Kakembo cautioned. 'The wearing of boots has to them become a necessity, hats and good uniform are becoming a daily wear in their lives.' Petitioning for increased colonial expenditure after the war, he pleaded for higher wages that would afford veterans a more dignified standard of living along modern, western lines. As things stood, African clerks paid just £4 per month – a pittance compared with the £25 salary enjoyed by Europeans – 'have either to go about in rags and be laughed at by Europeans, or to dress respectably and go without some necessities of life' to which army life had habituated them: 'toilet soap, hair cream, razor blades, cigarettes', as well as entertainments like 'cinemas, wireless broadcasts, newspapers'.[66]

Other Africans, leaving no written trace of their attachment to the uniform and what it signalled about enhanced status and aspiration, clung onto items of kit, despite the threat of punishment. Historian Timothy Parsons notes that the British authorities in East Africa were so concerned about veterans retaining their uniforms, which they might employ to swindle or bedazzle peasants awed by military apparel, that they compelled soldiers to surrender all their kit on demobilization. Wastefulness notwithstanding, uniforms were then destroyed to prevent theft. In 1950, with Kenya on the brink of a state of emergency triggered by the Mau Mau freedom movement, illicit possession or sale of military uniform was criminalized as an offence punishable with a 10,000 shilling fine or two-year prison sentence. Despite these draconian penalties, some veterans still kept items of KAR apparel and continued to wear bits and pieces of uniform into the 1950s.[67]

Veterans in Britain, in contrast, were permitted to keep some kit. As we've seen, they also received a complete new wardrobe on exiting the armed forces. This discrepancy suggests a binary distinction between generously compensated servicemen from the UK and empty-handed veterans from the empire. On closer inspection, though, the demarcation line wasn't quite so stark. Some overseas ex-servicemen *did* receive demob suits – volunteers from the Republic of Ireland who'd served with the British armed forces in defiance of Irish neutrality.

Approximately 37,440 men and 4,510 women from Éire enlisted in the British military during World War II – an indication of economic desperation in the Republic as much as, or more than, patriotic allegiance.[68] Irish enlistment was an irritant in the relationship between London and Dublin, barely twenty years after the founding of an Irish free state. In November 1939, the Irish government forbade the wearing of national military uniforms (other than Ireland's own) in the Republic. This policy did not specifically target men in British uniform. Ostensibly, it emerged from the Dáil's more diffuse concern about the militarization of Ireland. The eye-catching presence of foreign service personnel would, Irish leaders averred, undermine the nation's official posture of neutrality. If Ireland was staying out of the war, then foreign soldiers should stay out of Ireland – or, at the very least, appear unrecognizable as such. Behind the general principle, however, lay a more nettlesome issue with *British* uniforms. The prospect of Irishmen wandering the streets in British service kit, 'turncoats' in the eyes of their Republican peers, was far more objectionable than other Allied troops passing through or taking tourist excursions into Éire from bases in the North. British uniforms not only represented a political affront to Irish nationhood, but also placed their wearers at risk. Announcing the ban on foreign uniforms, Stephen Roche, secretary of Ireland's Justice Department, predicted that the 'presence of British soldiers in uniform in this country would lead to breaches of the peace', presumably all the more severe if the 'British soldiers' were in fact Irish citizens.[69] The British Cabinet, satisfied by Taoiseach de Valera's assurances that he didn't plan to hinder Irish enlistment in British forces, agreed to shoulder the expense of ensuring that these men 'proceeding on leave to Éire, should wear plain clothes'.[70]

Mindful of Dublin's sensitivity, the War Office assumed as a matter of course that it would have to equip Irish veterans with civilian garb prior to demobilization. Otherwise newly returned veterans might incur a £25 fine or be liable to a three-month stint in prison, to say nothing of the retaliatory wrath they might encounter from staunchly republican neighbours.[71] As a result, Irish veterans, unlike former servicemen from the West Indies or Africa, received demob suits before going home. While not conceived as such, this policy, born of Britain's peculiarly freighted relationship with Ireland, had the effect of making the demob suit look very much like a privilege of whiteness.

From the RAF to the Raffish

Were the *Bergensfjord* protestors angered that, unlike veterans from Britain and Ireland, they did not receive demob suits? In the absence of records left by the men themselves, we can only speculate whether they took greater issue with the meagre amount of their clothing allowances or with the fact that their treatment diverged from that of UK and Irish servicemen. Like other forms of differential treatment endured by men of colour, separate provisions were invariably *unequal*. In practice, 'different' always meant 'worse'. As some female veterans pointed out, no matter what the monetary value of the clothing allowances awarded them, they were not given the same privileges as men. And, since promissory notes or coupons were only as good as the stock shops happened to possess, the clear message was that the British government did not value the service of those compensated with paper as highly as that of men given garments.

The 'numerous complaints' logged by Squadron Leader Webster indicate shared agreement among West Indian airmen that 'allowances *in lieu of clothing*' would not stretch very far in the economically depressed islands to which they were being returned. As in Britain, the cost of scarce commodities, including garments, had escalated steeply in Jamaica during the war. In contrast to the UK, though, jobs there remained as elusive as they had been throughout the 1930s. A survey of eleven Jamaican towns undertaken in 1946 found 30,000 men and women (around 15.8 per cent of those aged over 14) engaged in a fruitless search for employment. This scarcity of work – and, more especially, of employment that paid a living wage – made some RAF veterans reluctant to go back at all.[72]

Hundreds of West Indian airmen expressed interest in the government's offer of technical training and further education in Britain that would better equip them for skilled, higher-paid positions. But this programme, championed by the Colonial Office, soon proved disappointing. Few applicants won apprenticeships or places on training courses; even fewer were accepted into British universities.[73] While Colonial Office personnel hoped trainees would transport new skills back to the colonies to invigorate postwar development, other departments prioritized ejecting men from the colonies as quickly as possible. Air Ministry officials initially imagined that most airmen from the Caribbean would either show no interest in further training or be rejected as insufficiently qualified. When the Colonial Office judged 50 per cent of West Indian applicants suitable, 60 per cent of the entire cohort having applied, senior air marshals made no bones about their disgruntlement: 'This means that we are going to be inflicted with these men for 2 years or more.'[74] That was another reason to hastily bundle as many airmen as possible onto vessels like the *Bergensfjord*.

Homecoming was perhaps especially fraught for men who'd travelled from a distant colonial society to the imperial metropole, hoping to enjoy accrued social capital on return. These men were highly attuned to the symbolic power of clothing, and not simply because possession of RAF uniforms offered an object lesson in the perception-altering power of apparel. They hailed from societies in which European dress had long served as a marker of Black aspiration to middle-class respectability. As celebrated Trinidadian scholar and activist C. L. R. James noted in 1933, making the case for West Indian self-government, the presence of well-dressed, Black-skinned islanders sometimes shocked newly arrived white British civil servants, armed with a set of disparaging preconceptions about the backward population over whom they would exercise benign trusteeship. 'Here is a thoroughly civilised community, wearing the same clothes that he does, speaking no other language but his own, with its best men as good as, and only too often, better than himself.'[75] Collars and ties, suits and shined shoes represented a bold assertion of individual dignity in a perniciously racialized society. The presentation of a professional appearance required tremendous effort, self-restraint and 'swallowing the bile of poverty', Hazel Carby notes of her Jamaican father, who served in the RAF during the war. His two tropical uniforms helped sustain dignified personhood amid Jamaica's deepening wartime poverty and escalating clothing costs.[76]

Elsewhere in the Caribbean, notably in Trinidad, the politics of respectability lost ground to more transgressive assertions of personal style. During the war, some young West Indian men enthusiastically espoused flamboyant trends that mocked the conservative proportions of conventionally tailored menswear, cocking a snook at wartime restrictions on fabric use into the bargain. In the United States, the zoot suit, with its trademark knee-skimming jacket and ballooning peg-leg trousers spawned competing urban legends as to the style's ultimate originator, from *Gone with the Wind*'s Rhett Butler (as personified by Clark Gable) to the House of Windsor's Edward VIII.[77] But it was young Black and Chicano men who most ardently embraced both the look and the bravado necessary to pull it off. Black entertainers, such as Cab Calloway and Sammy Davis Jr, soon appeared on stage and screen sporting these exuberant styles.

"STORMY WEATHER" with LENA HORNE, BILL ROBINSON, CAB CALLOWAY and HIS BAND
and Katherine Dunham and her Troupe, Fats Waller, Nicholas Brothers

Figure 4.4 Actor and musician Cab Calloway sports an extravagant zoot suit in *Stormy Weather* (1943) (John Kisch Archive/Moviepix/Getty Images)

While some white GIs reviled the zoot suit as 'un-American' in its profligate use of material, Black servicemen more often emulated new trends. Some attempted to modify their government-issue apparel, exporting the look overseas. It found a receptive audience in Trinidad, temporarily home to a large wartime population of US troops who injected much-needed cash into the island's economy. Flush with American money, Trinidad's self-described 'saga boys' claimed the zoot suit as their own. And then some.[78]

In a description as rococo as its subject, Anglo-Irish writer Patrick Leigh Fermor captured the 'slightly raffish' air of these ostentatious Trinidadians, observed during a postwar journey:

> The basis of the whole outfit is the trousers, the saga-pants. They are usually held up by transparent plastic belts, and pleats like scimitars run down to an unusual fullness at the knee, where they begin to taper, reaching almost ankle tightness where the turn-up rests on the two-coloured shoe; peg-top trousers, in fact, but so neat and clean and beautifully ironed that they are nothing like the floppy inexpressibles of *La Bohème*. The jacket, too, the Bim-Bim, or Saga-Boy-coat, has an eccentric and individual cut. There is no padding in the shoulders, a wasp waist, a vent up the back, and lappets that descend in some cases … as low as the voluminously trousered knee. … A broad snap-brim hat is worn with this costume, absolutely straight on the head, or tilted rather forward. The shirts may be severely cut of some pastel-shade material with a high collar and deep cuffs fastened with glittering links, or in patterns of crossed Coca-Cola bottles, mandolines, palm trees, hearts transfixed with arrows, peonies or masks of Tragedy and Comedy. … The ties, secured with gold pins or chains, have the splendour of lanced ulcers.

This formidable ensemble, Fermor declared, was 'elegant and imposing beyond words'.[79] Equipped only with paper promissory notes, how could the *Bergensfjord* veterans possibly compete?

As they cast ahead, returning airmen may well have anticipated the challenge of acquiring either traditionally tailored garments or these expressive new styles. They also surely foresaw how attentively – perhaps apprehensively – scrutinized their appearance would be by family members, neighbours and community leaders on arrival, just as Caribbean seamen shipped from Britain in 1919 chafed against returning in tattered attire.[80] What these veterans wore, and what they could afford to buy with their allowances, signalled whether men who'd voyaged across the Atlantic, courted danger, made sacrifices, and returned home again had been treated well by the Mother Country or shabbily.

The fraught character of homecoming was underscored by Jamaican newspapers' coverage of the *Bergensfjord*'s arrival at Port Royal. If veterans' resumption of civilian life invariably aroused intense and conflicted emotions – anticipation and anxiety in unstable equilibrium – this particular return occurred under an ominous cloud. The violent scenes described by Ivorall Davis demonstrated to veterans' waiting families that the British authorities treated their homecoming sons, brothers, lovers and husbands not with the deference owed to veterans but with contempt as criminal suspects. Instead of a heroes' welcome, the men suffered racist abuse before being roughly searched and marched off, under armed escort, to nearby Camp Gibraltar that accommodated Jewish refugees who'd managed to evade the Third Reich, alongside German and Italian POWs.[81] 'What was done was to punish and humiliate the men,' announced nationalist leader Norman Manley. For his People's National Party (PNP), the *Bergensfjord* episode provided an occasion to excoriate colonial rule; the Suffolk battalion was labelled an 'army of occupation' that must be withdrawn.[82] By emphasizing British brutality *after* the ship docked, however, Manley and the PNP bracketed what had given rise to rebellion on the voyage itself. The returning RAF men were not only objects of blunt colonial discipline, but also political subjects whose protest against inequitable clothing allowances figured nowhere either in Manley's rhetoric or in Jamaican press reportage.

In the *Daily Gleaner*'s estimation, the *Bergensfjord* returnees were 'tired, bitter and enraged at the welcome that had been prepared for them'. As for the rumoured 'disorders', they said it was a 'mere incident which had been caused by the braggings of a Trinidadian aboard'.[83] Eager to burnish the veterans' reputation, the *Gleaner* shrank the 'mutiny' that petrified Captain Hansen to a parochial scuffle between rival islanders. Neither the *Gleaner* nor its competitor, the *Daily Express*, mentioned the returnees' political activism. Voices of protest were almost as muted in the Jamaican press as in the colonial archive, though one returning RAF veteran struck a particularly dolorous note when he informed the *Daily Express* that he would never go back to England. After embittering experiences there, he would 'rather commit suicide'.[84]

Double Crossings

Echoing across subsequent decades, this comment reverberates with especial force. While the anonymous veteran may have held true to his word, some of his fellow travellers returned to Britain not so many months later. If the *Bergensfjord* is forgotten, or perhaps remembered only as the liner that transported the von Trapp family from Nazi Germany to North America, another vessel looms large in recent Black British history. Revisiting the *Bergensfjord* rebellion from a twenty-first-century vantage point, it's impossible not to contemplate this neglected transatlantic passage in tandem with another journey, in the opposite direction, now commemorated as an iconic moment in the making of multiracial Britain: the voyage of the *Empire Windrush* in June 1948.[85]

As they disembarked at Tilbury docks, the *Windrush*'s West Indian passengers attracted much critical scrutiny, not least on account of their attire. Before it docked, the ship's arrival had already been heralded in the British press, while officials hastily readied an Underground air-raid shelter in Clapham as emergency accommodation before longer-term housing and jobs could be found for these work-hungry newcomers.[86] When the *Daily Mirror* pointedly remarked that many of the young men who alighted from the *Windrush* wore 'zoot suits – very long-waisted jackets, big padded shoulders and peg-top trousers – costing £15 to £20', the insinuation was that such ostentatiously attired individuals must have been driven to emigrate by some more nefarious motive than escaping poverty.[87]

Over the course of the 1940s and 1950s, Caribbean migrants' apparel was routinely scrutinized and judged, often being regarded as too fancy for a long ocean voyage and/or inadequate defence against Britain's cool, damp climate. Depending on the observer's perspective, the passengers' 'Sunday best' marked either a commendable bid for acceptance in British society or, by its panache, announced that they would never 'fit in' – too much 'colour' for monochromatic postwar Britain.[88] Ten years after the *Windrush* docked, passengers' ignorance of British conditions, signified by the flimsy attire in which they

Figure 4.5 Original caption: 'Three Jamaican immigrants (left to right) John Hazel, a 21-year-old boxer, Harold Wilmot, 32, and John Richards, a 22-year-old carpenter, arriving at Tilbury on board the ex-troopship *Empire Windrush*, smartly dressed in zoot suits and trilby hats' (Douglas Miller/Getty Images)

landed, was still considered a humiliating demerit – including by some West Indians now settled in Britain. The authors of a BBC pamphlet with the offputtingly interrogative title *Going to Britain?* warned others contemplating the same voyage to outfit themselves sensibly for British conditions: 'Yesterday afternoon in London here a photographer showed me pictures of West Indians he had taken landing in pink cotton dresses, tropical shoes and hats, no coat, no scarf, and that was in the winter. ... Our own West Indians have been very embarrassed when unkind remarks have been made about the simplicity and ignorance of the people coming up.'[89]

Among the other things Britons have come to be taught about the *Windrush* passengers is the prevalence of RAF veterans on the manifest. More than 200 of the 1,027 passengers on board had served in Britain during the war and decided to return soon thereafter. Some of the stowaways, briefly jailed in Chelmsford, reportedly still wore their old RAF uniforms. More recently, 'veteranness' has been foregrounded in a particular framing of the *Windrush* story, mobilized to underscore how unjustly the British government treated the 'Windrush generation'. Former servicemen and their descendants were surely owed better by the Mother Country than to be stripped of citizenship rights and deemed susceptible to deportation.[90]

Today, the RAF publicly celebrates 'the incredible achievements and the enormous contribution made by the RAF black service personnel' in World War II. The introduction to the RAF Museum's online exhibit, punningly entitled 'Pilots of the Caribbean', notes: 'These volunteers fought, and died, for the mother country and for freedom, and thereby helped preserve the values and the heritage they shared with their white comrades.' Obscured in this affirmative vision of interracial solidarity in defence of liberal values is any acknowledgement that racist prejudice structured West Indians' terms of service – so much so, in fact, that there were strikingly few Caribbean pilots. Instead, visitors to the webpage learn that 'the RAF took racism seriously'.[91] The *Bergensfjord* episode offers an instructive reminder that West Indian personnel were demeaned while they served, and as airmen, not just decades later by governments oblivious to these veterans' wartime contributions. Senior air force figures regularly insinuated that, to the extent white people played *any* contributory role in the 'colour problem', the offending parties were either redneck American GIs or 'low class' Britons: racism was disavowed as a product of 'poor breeding' and bad manners. 'There is a continual undercurrent amongst the West Indians that they are being slighted by the white man; and unfortunately a certain class of white airman and airwoman aggravate this feeling,' Sir Grahame Donald lamented to his superior, Sir John Slessor, with no discernible trace of irony. The latter, a man of impeccably aristocratic pedigree, had pontificated in November 1945 on the unsuitability for enlistment in the postwar RAF of a man 'with a name like U-ba or Ah Wong' or who 'looks as though he had just dropped out of a tree'.[92]

The *Bergensfjord*'s turbulent journey between Glasgow and the Caribbean supplies a missing chapter in an often oversimplified *Windrush* narrative, helping explain why West Indian RAF veterans who returned to Britain in the late 1940s didn't simply remain where they'd served (for two or more years) when the war ended. Rarely do

Windrush stories explain why West Indian airmen went back to the Caribbean only to reverse course a few months later. Events that culminated in the 'mutiny' illuminate the British state's attitude towards men they'd come to see as troublemakers to be expelled rather than veterans permitted to stay, study and work in Britain.[93] No wonder the *Windrush's* appearance on the horizon set off alarm bells in Westminster. On its journey *out* to the Caribbean, this ship, like the *Bergensfjord* two years before, had removed another group of 200 demobilized airmen from Britain.[94]

These 'repatriation' voyages can be plotted alongside hundreds of other postwar crossings intended by the Allies to 'un-mix' populations scrambled by German and Japanese imperialism. The war that generations of Britons and Americans have been taught to regard as waged primarily against Nazi racial ideology was followed by a concerted effort on the victors' part to inscribe ethnic homogeneity as the preferred basis of postwar nationhood. In Asia, the US military shipped millions of surrendered Japanese personnel back to Japan's home islands, along with many more ethnic Japanese who had populated the 'Greater East Asian Co-Prosperity Sphere' in Manchuria, Taiwan and Korea. Many of these Japanese colonialists had never set foot in Japan. Similarly, American ships ferried millions more Asians across the South China Sea and Sea of Japan, trying to ensure that diasporic Filipinos repopulated the Philippine Islands; that the two million ethnically Korean residents of Japan resided in Korea, and so on, regardless of whether the people being shuttled about had ever lived in the places Americans imagined as their homelands or where those being 'repatriated' wished to lead their postwar lives. Meanwhile, as Chapter 6 shows, by Allied agreement, millions of ethnic Germans were expelled from their homes in east/central Europe, pushed over the borders of Poland, Hungary and Czechoslovakia into occupied Germany.[95]

This fantasy of a world of nation-states without minorities also prevailed in Britain. In 1942, the Cabinet had already decided that, whenever the war ended, the colonial workforce in Britain would be 'liquidated' and 're-absorbed' by the colonies in the interests – as officials put it – of social order at home and economic development overseas. Setting circumlocutions aside, what they really meant was that Britain's perceived whiteness must be preserved. Attlee's government duly erected obstacles to prospective immigrants from the colonies, while permitting mass emigration *from* Britain. By the lights of imperial racial logic, white Britons' settlement in African colonies such as Rhodesia didn't represent a worrisome dilution of the indigenous population's ethnic integrity, but instead amounted to a reinvigoration of the empire's 'Anglo-Saxon stock'.[96]

Despite a labour shortage so severe that British officials began recruiting 'volunteer workers' from Europe's DP camps, the Attlee administration presided over a mass exodus of Britons heading to the Dominions and North America. Around 50,000 white British veterans took advantage of a free settlement scheme to move to Australia in the decade after 1945. Emigrants heading for tropical destinations even received additional clothing coupons to help them sally forth properly outfitted for warmer climates. In 1947, a huffy Winston Churchill offered a highly partisan reading of these departures when he proposed that two years of socialism had scared off 'half-a-million of our ... most lively and active citizens in the prime of life'.[97]

Congratulatory depictions of the *Windrush*'s arrival as the harbinger of British multiculturalism overlook both the centuries-old presence of Black Britons and the government's active opposition to West Indian migration. While the National Health Service *selectively* beckoned to West Indian women for recruitment as nurses and domestic staff, British officials sought to deter mass migration from the Caribbean. 'As regards the possible importation of West Indian labour', ventured a Ministry of Labour official in 1947, 'I suggest that we must dismiss this idea from the start.'[98] But no amount of intrusive white noise could muffle Jamaicans' awareness that jobs in Britain were plentiful, while unemployment in the Caribbean hovered around 25 per cent.[99] Before the *Windrush* docked in June 1948, the *Ormonde* and *Almanzora* had already brought dozens of West Indians, including many veterans, to Britain in 1947. These voyages were undertaken in defiance of London's cautionary notes and Jamaican administrators' schemes to turn veterans into smallholders or temporary farmworkers in the United States.[100] Like the mutiny on the *Bergensfjord*, these return passages offer another reminder that West Indians would exercise their own agency in the face of racialized injustice. Far from 'answering the mother country's call', as one benign telling of the *Windrush* saga goes, sharply dressed West Indian Britons forced a reluctant metropole to sit up and pay attention.

5 GERMANS

When it came to clothing, the 'German problem', as many Allied observers perceived it in the spring of 1945, wasn't a shortage of garments. It was that some Germans chose to wear too few of them. More specifically, young German women were disporting themselves in their skimpiest attire, angling to attract the lustful attention of young occupation soldiers. So claimed no less an authority on German tactics than Field Marshal Sir Bernard Montgomery. *Fräuleins* were performing a deliberate 'strip tease', Monty announced in June 1945, an 'organized campaign to wear as few clothes as possible'. Their goal was to make Allied personnel 'break the ban' on 'fraternization' between occupying forces and Germans announced by General Eisenhower in September 1944.[1] By outlawing any interaction between victors and vanquished beyond the barest minimum necessary to sustain a military occupation, Ike intended that Germans should feel the sting of social ostracization, recognizing that their complicity with the criminal Nazi regime placed them beyond the civilizational pale. 'This nation is responsible for its leaders,' Monty informed Germans in a radio broadcast delivered on 10 June. 'So long as they were successful you were jubilant, you celebrated and laughed.' As a result, no German hands would be shaken; no sweets would be given to children; no amity could arise between occupiers and occupied. And it went, or should have gone, without saying that a sweeping ban on *social* intercourse also encompassed sexual intimacy.[2]

Widely disregarded by enlisted men and officers alike, the ban proved impossible to enforce. Every stratum of the Allied military engaged in every imaginable form of 'fraternization'. 'Fratting' soon became synonymous with the kind of interaction denoted by a shorter F-word. As such encounters proliferated, the authority of Allied commanders frayed. Rather than attributing this corrosion of the chain of command to an unworkable order, Monty blamed the Germans. Senior Allied commanders had expected resistance after the Third Reich fell, with Nazi partisans retreating to the mountains of Bavaria to mount a last-ditch defence of the fatherland. But instead of *Werwolf* snipers taking pot-shots at Allied soldiers, Monty found instead bands of young German women doing an even more effective job of rendering postwar Germany ungovernable, weaponizing the male libido to torpedo the 'frat ban'. 'Many Allied soldiers', reported the *Manchester Guardian* in June 1945, 'believe that German girls are often deliberately provocative, gloating in the fact that punishment awaits the soldier who attempts to have anything to do with them.'[3] Uniformed Americans concurred. First Lieutenant Daniel Lerner reported in Krefeld that 'German girls seem to have developed the habit of pretending to read the proclamations posted nearby – at the same time flirting furiously with the [American] guard and other soldiers passing through the doorway.' Elsewhere, it was the same story: 'girls, usually in pairs, dressed and rouged prettily, strolling just outside the restricted areas where soldiers are billeted or employed. In the face of this, the behavior of the troops seems little short of heroic.'[4]

If heroic resistance was the order of the day in April 1945 when Lerner submitted this intelligence report, Allied capitulation became more conspicuous soon after Germany's surrender. Numerous newsreels and photographs printed in magazines like *Life* and its left-leaning British counterpart *Picture Post* feature girls and women in translucent cotton dresses, backlit to emphasize the silhouetted figures beneath the sun-filtered frocks, loitering in urban streets or frolicking in shorts, halter-tops and swimwear at the beach or pool – '*Bad*' girls, in a pun Service newspapers found irresistible. Often, flimsily attired German women were pictured in the company of occupation soldiers whose arms lay draped across, or more possessively clutched, the shoulders of bare-legged, sturdily built women, *Fräuleins* now *Freundinnen* (girlfriends).[5]

Figure 5.1 The original caption for this photograph depicting British soldiers with German women pointed out that there wasn't 'anything brotherly about the way these British Tommies and German frauleins fraternize[d] in a Berlin park' on 23 July 1945 (Bettmann/Getty Images)

Under-dressed women, overly fond of sunning themselves, weren't the only stock image to emerge from Germany in its hour of defeat. Allied reports consistently emphasized that the civilian population as a whole was neatly attired, somehow sustaining the Germanic mania for cleanliness even amid panoramic ruination. Lerner noted that 'Most Germans walk around the streets dressed in fairly decent clothes, looking quite healthy, often carrying a brief case – looking as though they were bustling along to a Board of Directors meeting.'[6] His was not a lone observation. Photographs of Germans taken at this time, particularly those that depict Germans being made to inspect newly liberated concentration camps in April and May 1945, capture adults who look strikingly smart. Ordered by Eisenhower to visit camps in their vicinity, forced to confront Nazi atrocity at uncomfortably close quarters, residents seemed to have dressed up for their tours through Buchenwald, Flossenburg and Dachau. Women wore tailored jackets and skirts, floral blouses, scarves tied around their necks and heads.

They walked in heeled shoes and ankle socks. Their 'Sunday best', as contemporary commentators put it, seemed a gesture of respectfulness at once appallingly belated and inappropriate to the grim work that German men and women often had to perform during these mandatory visits, reburying corpses under marked graves.[7]

Descriptions of Germans in early 1945 almost invariably twinned the phrase 'well dressed' with 'well fed'. Both smacked of disdain. 'I saw not one sign of malnutrition among the Germans, who have perfectly nourished bodies and fat-covered nerves,' fumed photographer Lee Miller in *Vogue*'s 1 May 1945 issue.[8] If Germans presented a more plumply upholstered appearance to the world, it was, many Allied analysts agreed, because of what they'd looted from occupied Europe. To discuss German clothes was to invoke German crimes: their abundant possessions were a product of others' dispossession. 'The people look well and amazingly well dressed – the result of raids on all Europe,' seethed a British Red Cross worker *en route* from Holland to Belsen in May 1945, having just crossed the German border. Around the same time, writing from a more southerly location, Marcelle Poirier reported in the *Yorkshire Post* that residents of Bavaria 'lacked nothing'. 'Clothes are not the *ersatz* stuff which has been described to us. They are dowdy but of excellent quality.' He continued: 'Wardrobes in all types of houses reveal no penury of clothes. There are always several pairs of good leather shoes. Every woman wears stockings.'[9] The BBC's Patrick Gordon Walker struck a similar note: 'There are many fur-coats to be seen and more silk stockings than anywhere else in Europe (presumably the last fruits of the plundering of the continent).'[10] Occupied Scandinavia had yielded a steady supply of furs, while *Wehrmacht* soldiers reportedly robbed France of every last pair of silk stockings, sent home to wives and girlfriends – 'a gift from Hans'. Meanwhile, the spouses of Nazi bigwigs swanned around Berlin in the latest Parisian *couture*, even as Nazi Party publications denounced French fashion as un-Germanic and 'degenerate'.[11]

It was not, of course, from occupied countries alone that apparel was stolen. As Nazi extermination and concentration camps were liberated, Allied personnel discovered, filmed and photographed storerooms bursting with garments, shoes, suitcases and spectacles, alongside gold pulled from teeth and hair chopped from women's heads to be used for wigs or woven as padding into garments. Images of stolen goods – accessories of the murdered – heightened awareness

among Allied populations of how the Third Reich had robbed its victims of their livelihoods, wealth and belongings before robbing them of
life itself.[12] 'A horrible sort of calculated exploitation grew up around
the edges of the annihilation – the profitable collection and resale of
the clothes of the dead, the disposal of the ashes for fertiliser and the
like,' explained Gordon Walker.[13] Germans already knew about these
lucrative margins. Some had, after all, directly profited not just from
the plundered possessions of those murdered in the camps, but also
from the prior expropriation of Jewish businesses, including many in
the garment and footwear trades. However, since Germans in the wake
of defeat failed to exhibit appropriate contrition, the horrific nature
and scope of this profiteering was driven home in Allied re-education
films such as *Die Todesmühlen* (*Death Mills*).[14]

Allied observers, familiar with the Third Reich's *modus oper-
andi*, appraised German plenty through the prism of others' penury,
revolted both by this material confirmation of criminality and by
Germans' evasive retreat into fairy-tale fantasy. One British UNRRA
worker, Rhoda Dawson, noted on 15 June 1945: 'I'm not sorry to
be able to fall back on the non-fraternisation order.' (It was, in fact,
relaxed a month later.) 'The Germans look so well dressed and well fed
and they did take so much from the countries they occupied. But they
are so friendly if there is an opportunity. Since I've seen a poor crea-
ture's number tattooed on his body I don't feel so friendly.' A month
later Dawson felt even more embittered: 'I don't like Germany much. I
hate the forest all the same, and the grey and green that gets out of their
landscape into all their clothes; I hate the quaintness and the decorations, the inevitable dirndls, and the short pants and long bare knees.'[15]

Repugnance ebbed, however. Initial perceptions of an enrag-
ingly healthy and wealthy populace gave way to a more durable paradigm: that Germans were alarmingly tattered and hungry, in urgent
need of garments and footwear as well as more calories. By the end
of the Allied occupation in 1949, western Germany had become a
major recipient of international relief. It wasn't meant to be that way.
UNRRA's mandate specifically *excluded* Axis and other 'ex-enemy'
countries from the organization's humanitarian remit. Germans would
be responsible for meeting their fellow citizens' needs, while UNRRA
cared only for those who had endured Axis oppression.[16] The character
of Allied military government was intended to be draconian. Plans for
a protracted *punitive* occupation resonated with a substantial portion

of the British population. An opinion poll conducted in May 1945 found that 54 per cent 'hated the Germans', with 80 per cent favouring a harsh peace.[17] Yet, even before 1945 had ended, some Britons were already concerned by German suffering – a preoccupation that grew steadily over the next two years, transforming Germans from pitiless Nazis into pitiable beneficiaries of aid.

What changed? And why did *fabric* figure so prominently within the matrix of adjusted British attitudes towards vanquished Germans?

Radical Alterations

Access to resources of every sort – accommodation, food, fuel, transportation and clothing – dwindled rapidly in postwar Germany. But, before detailing these shortages, it's first worth noting that most Germans would have failed to recognize their reflection in the mirror held up by the victors in 1945. Far from viewing themselves as well-heeled and amply nourished, many felt degraded and worn down by the escalating sacrifices demanded by the Third Reich as military require-ments cut deeper into civilian life. Curbs on consumption were a feature of wartime German existence from the outset. In the same week that Panzer divisions rolled into Poland, the Nazi regime unveiled a scheme for clothes rationing, becoming more stringent over time, but always more restrictive than the parallel points system Churchill's government inaugurated in 1941. With garment and footwear factories manufactur-ing products primarily for military use, supplies of civilian clothing and shoes available for purchase shrank. Long before the Board of Trade introduced Britons to 'Mrs Sew-&-Sew', German women had been hec-tored by various Nazi Party organizations to repair and remodel gar-ments. Slogans that would become wearisomely familiar, '*aus Zwei mach Eins*' ('From Two Make One') and '*aus Alt mach Neu*' ('From Old Make New'), preceded 'Make Do and Mend' by two years.[18]

Nazi propagandists simultaneously harangued women to donate worn apparel for the war effort. Which newly wed bride would selfishly cling onto her veil when it could be transformed into mos-quito netting for the *Afrika Korps*? And why would patriotic German women begrudge the total absence of sanitary towels from pharmacies when military hospitals so desperately needed cotton wool and gauze? By 1943, period products had disappeared altogether from German shops.[19] But the flow of material aid, from home to fighting fronts, reversed in the war's disastrous final phase. In January 1945, Hans Heck, newly empowered as 'supreme Reich collector of old material', launched a 'total textile mobilization'. At Hitler's command, every officer and soldier of the *Wehrmacht*, as well as members of the SS and police, would give up *all* their civilian clothing – underwear and footwear included – to a national pool. Dead men's apparel too.[20]

Further evidence of Germany's clothing crisis surfaced two months later when the state ordered women into action to concoct uniforms for the *Volkssturm*. This Home Guard organization, mustered from boys too young, and men too old or infirm, to serve with the *Wehrmacht*, would supposedly keep Red Army marauders at bay. In March 1945, SHAEF reported that the Nazis were 'running a salvage campaign for uniforms of any kind: uniforms of Customs officials, firemen, party members, the S.A. [*Sturmabteilung*] – all are well stocked with uniforms of one kind or another, but still there do not appear to be enough'. To remedy this deficit, the Bund Deutscher Mädel, 'roughly the German equivalent of our own "W.V.S."', was making uniforms from plain clothes. Frustrated by pockets of German resistance seemingly deeper than the country's supply of uniforms, SHAEF derived encouragement from a report that, at a recent *Volkssturm* swearing-in parade in Berlin, 'one Volkssturmer turned up in his stage uniform straight from a performance of Lohengrin, and attracted no attention at all'.[21] Allied soldiers entering Germany later expressed amazement at the Third Reich's ragtag defenders. *Volkssturm* members and Hitler Youth barely in their teens wore everything from bellhop boy outfits to school uniforms that exaggerated their extreme youthfulness – indisputably children, not soldiers.[22]

Meanwhile, some German women rued the careworn appearance they presented to conquering Allied troops. Military defeat was chastening enough. But there was something additionally humiliating in appearing in shabby clothes and, quite literally, 'down at heel'. One woman, a journalist whose diary was subsequently published as *A Woman in Berlin*, introduced herself in a detached, third-person entry (dated 20 April 1945) as 'a pale-faced blonde always dressed in the same winter coat – which she managed to save just by chance'. Chance encounters additionally enabled her to barter her 'French soap' for stockings which a male colleague 'had from Prague'.[23] Since soap and detergents of every sort were extremely scarce, bathing presented as great a challenge

Figure 5.2 Thirteen-year-old Hitler Youths, Friedel Rhode (in a hotel pageboy's uniform) and Harold Tersmitten, captured in April 1945 and photographed by Sgt James Mapham (© Imperial War Museum, BU 4363)

as laundering garments. This situation exponentially worsened as the Red Army's onslaught drove Berliners underground. Soviet soldiers' perpetration of mass rape led many German women, including this diarist, to fret less about their looks. Appearing dirty and tattered – 'like lowlifes', as she put it – might even keep Red Army rapists at bay. Or so some women hoped, trying to disguise themselves as men or, with drawn-on crows-feet and talcumed white hair, as elderly grandmothers too old to excite lust.[24]

The diarist herself, despite having undergone a brutal series of rapes, still retained a capacity for shock at how far once-proud Berliners had fallen. Resurfacing from her building's basement on 10 May for a 'first tour of the conquered city', she noted the fluttering hand-sewn red 'flaglets, evidently cut from old Nazi flags – here and there you can still make out the line of a circle, where the white field containing the black swastika used to be'. That German women would dextrously transform swastikas into hammers and sickles with which to welcome the Red Army was startling enough – hardly what the Nazi Party envisioned by 'making new from old' – but not so stunning as the next reversal: a woman 'barefoot and bedraggled'. 'Barefoot? In Berlin? I've never seen a woman in that condition before,' the diarist marvelled.[25] Consternation over the degraded appearance of women in the early days of defeat persisted. For years, Germans debated whether *Trümmerfrauen* – turban-wearing 'rubble women' who (under occupation orders) cleared detritus from bomb-shattered cities – were heroic national saviours or emblematic of Germany's disgrace.[26]

With people unable to buy new clothes, millions bombed out of their homes and numerous parties (including Russian soldiers, DPs and Germans themselves) engaged in wholesale looting of garments, along with sewing machines and every other kind of portable property, how could Allied witnesses have encountered so many 'well dressed and well fed' Germans in the spring of 1945?[27] One answer is that not every part of Germany was so badly damaged as Berlin and the ravaged cities in the Rhineland and Ruhr. British journalists and relief workers whose route into Germany took them through France, Belgium and the Netherlands witnessed stark contrasts between the impoverishment of countries recently occupied by the *Wehrmacht* and the German countryside itself. Many rural communities and small towns appeared almost untouched by war. If anything, some had grown more prosperous. With urban-dwellers venturing into outlying villages on 'hamstering' expeditions to barter their possessions for food, goods circulated in unfamiliar patterns. Another diary-keeping Berliner was surprised (in August 1943) to find farmers' wives – women she'd disdainfully imagined as most susceptible to propaganda pushing the Teutonic 'dirndl look' – instead 'trading bacon for dress goods, eggs for jewellery, butter for silk stockings'.[28] Two years later, British military personnel observed that rural communities appeared substantially better off than urban ones. 'The people who have the best clothing and most bedding are the agricultural districts,' one military memo noted in August 1945. 'Any farmer or man on a cart is usually extremely well dressed.'[29]

Better-off Germans made a presentable impression as the war ended, frustrating Allied observers eager for the enemy to look more unmistakably *defeated*. Others, however, perceived this veneer of respectability as deceptively thin. On the eve of VE Day, Patrick Gordon Walker coupled his observation of smart Germans, strolling in their ill-gotten furs and silk stockings, with a prediction. '[T]hese appearances of comfort are illusory. People already are hungry: they have no work: they will fall prey to the first post-war epidemics.'[30]

Gordon Walker's intuition was borne out. Exacerbating the misery of Germans crammed into bomb shelters, cellars and basements that provided scant protection from the elements was the mass influx of *Volksdeutsche* (ethnic Germans) expelled from east-central Europe. Over the course of late 1945 and 1946, Germany's myriad 'bombees' and 'evacuees' were joined by throngs of 'expellees' ejected from neighbouring countries, eventually totalling around ten million.[31] Prompted by Moscow, the Allies agreed at the Potsdam Conference of July–August 1945 that the postwar presence of ethnic Germans would be intolerable in Czechoslovakia, Hungary and Poland. As Germany's eastern border was redrawn, shunted significantly westwards, Poland incorporated a large swathe of erstwhile German territory. Approximately six million Germans would, the Allies agreed, have to head west as a result. The Potsdam Agreement incorporated a bland assurance that this mass relocation of ethnic Germans would be 'orderly and humane', though sceptics correctly anticipated that the victorious powers had licensed an expulsion that would prove both disorderly and inhumane.[32]

Writing in late 1946, Swedish journalist Stig Dagerman captured forlorn scenes playing out across the British and American sectors of occupied Germany: 'All autumn, trains arrived in the Western Zones with refugees from the Eastern Zone. Ragged, starving and unwelcome, they crowded into dark, stinking station-bunkers or in the giant windowless bunkers that look like rectangular gasometers.' Cold-shouldered by fellow Germans who regarded them not as kin but rather as competitors in the zero-sum game of survival, these 'expellees' brought 'nothing but their hunger and their thirst'.[33] And it was predominantly *these* Germans, forced from their homes in a euphemistic 'population transfer' validated by the victorious Allies, who caught the attention of British humanitarians eager to redeem European civilization.[34]

'This Misery of Boots': Victor Gollancz and Save Europe Now

Two facets of humanitarianism angled at relief of distressed Germans warrant particular note: that the movement's most prominent champion wasn't a life-long Germanophile but a left-liberal British Jew newly evangelical about aiding 'the Germans'; and that this man chose to turn *footwear* into a conscience-stirring symbol of German suffering at a moment when the broken shoe already emblematized Nazi attempts to annihilate European Jewry.

Those who knew Victor Gollancz well, however, mightn't have found it such a surprise that this tenacious champion of unpopular causes should have backed Germany as his preferred 'moral underdog' after the war.[35] Publisher, activist, prolific author of letters, pamphlets and books, Gollancz, at fifty-two, fizzed with crusading zeal. On the left, he was widely credited with having done more than any other individual to secure Labour's victory in 1945, through the immensely popular Left Book Club that operated under the aegis of the publishing house bearing his name. In addition to producing affordable books, Gollancz used this press to disseminate his own polemical writings, including publications that chronicled the horrors inflicted on Jews and others in Nazi camps. More controversially, he coupled denunciations of Nazi atrocity with an insistence that Britons hadn't done enough to interdict the Third Reich's crimes, whereas Germans could be forgiven for not doing more, terrorized into silent acquiescence by knowledge of the fate that awaited the regime's opponents. Britons thus had no claim to the ethical high ground. 'Your case is morally worse than that of the "ordinary Germans,"' he chided in a pamphlet titled *What Buchenwald Really Means*, elaborating a forceful case against the twin doctrines of 'collective guilt' and 'non-fraternization' that underpinned British and US occupation policy.[36]

This polemic, published in April 1945, hinted at Gollancz's first postwar crusade. Over the next two years, he positioned himself as Britain's most energetic champion of treating the Germans humanely – as if they were as worthy of sympathy as any other stricken population, not pariahs to be shunned by civilized international society.[37] 'Civilization' formed the *Leitmotif* of Gollancz's activism on Germans' behalf. Articulated in an explicitly Christian vernacular, his writings on Germany brimmed with New Testament quotations to underscore the necessity of love, forgiveness and reconciliation. 'Love your enemies, bless them that curse you, do good to them that hate you,' Gollancz preached.[38] Save Europe Now (SEN), the organization he co-founded in September 1945, along with MPs Richard Crossman, Eleanor Rathbone and Michael Foot (among others), aspired to a lofty regenerative mission. Aiding impoverished Germans, and pressing

Westminster to halt expulsions of *Volksdeutsche* from Czechoslovakia and Poland, wasn't simply the right thing to do, goodness for goodness' sake. It gave altruistic Britons an opportunity to resurrect European faith in liberal values after a barbarous war that had engendered pervasive apathy, despair and nihilism.[39]

Save Europe Now launched its campaign by inviting sympathetic individuals to complete pre-printed postcards for despatch to Westminster by way of Victor Gollancz's publishing house. These petitions urged the government to increase food supplies to Germans in the British zone from the current level of 1,500 calories per adult per day: an amount rarely achieved in practice, and (even if available) insufficient for subsistence, Gollancz argued. To make the moral case more forceful, senders of these postcards announced their willingness to see their *own* rations reduced. If Germans were to eat more, Britons would consume less, SEN's supporters pledged, swamping Gollancz's office with 75,000 postcards for onward transmission to Downing Street. A packed meeting at London's Conway Hall, with prominent attendees including George Orwell and Rebecca West, further raised the campaign's profile. But Attlee and the various Cabinet ministers to whom Gollancz presented SEN's case remained largely unmoved.[40]

After weeks of strenuous lobbying to little avail, Gollancz set off on 2 October 1946 to witness conditions in Germany for himself. Determined to stay longer than any prior British visitor, Gollancz remained six weeks in the once heavily industrial northwestern quadrant of the country, which had been decimated by the combined consequences of naval blockade, ground combat and aerial bombardment.[41] 'People sometimes say the German public must have been pretty well stocked up at the end of the war, if only with loot from the occupied countries,' Gollancz noted. 'They ought to go and have a look at Cologne and ask themselves how much could have survived there. Of the 5,500,000 pre-war dwelling units in the British zone 1,600,000 were totally destroyed or irreparably damaged, and another 1,400,000 damaged but capable of repair.'[42] By the reckoning of the British military governor of North Rhine, 'hundreds of thousands of people' lived in 'what are nothing more than piles of rubble'. Hamburg, Cologne and Düsseldorf competed for the unenviable mantle of 'most ruined' city in Germany.[43] And it was in these shattered urban wastelands, further strained by the mass influx of 'expellees', that Gollancz spent the bulk of his time: talking to British and German officials, academics, doctors and clergymen; visiting 'ordinary Germans' in their insanitary subterranean hovels; gathering facts; consolidating opinions and penning voluminous epistles to allies, politicians and newspaper editors back home.

'I find myself loving the Germans in general', Gollancz told his wife on day one of the trip, 'just because they're despised and rejected.'[44] Evidence of rejection and its twin sibling, dejection, abounded. Gollancz felt particular compassion for German refugees in the British zone, then estimated at 1.25 million, more than in any other sector. In Kiel, the plight of hundreds of expellees forced to live on a barge docked in the ruined harbour moved him to tears.[45] Malnutrition that bordered on – or constituted – starvation continued to preoccupy Gollancz and SEN. Food has likewise monopolized the attention of historians of postwar Germany, keen to interrogate German claims to victimhood that Gollancz did a good deal to buttress.[46] In contrast, his simultaneous focus on Germany's 'textile famine' has passed almost unremarked, though Gollancz insisted that food was 'by no means the whole story'. As he saw it, food insecurity and clothing scarcity were interwoven predicaments: the warp and weft of an enormous public health catastrophe. Both in his writings and in speeches, Gollancz inveighed against the hopeless inadequacy of Germans' apparel and the lamentable state of their shoes. Or, worse yet, their utter shoelessness.

By the time Gollancz reached Germany, on the eve of its second postwar winter, the country's dire footwear predicament was already a matter of record. One witness to Berliners' woes noted (in July 1946) that a person lucky enough to possess a barterable spare pair of shoes might 'live for a fortnight on the proceeds': 'Shoes are so valuable that they have almost ceased to have a money value: they rank among the real wealth of bread, meat, butter, and tobacco and have a high exchange rate in terms of these necessaries of life.'[47] Gollancz's journals of his six-week tour brim with jottings about garments and footwear. 'I didn't see many German refugees without shoes', he noted on 7 October, 'but canvas, broken down.' School visits became occasions not only to enquire into pupils' malnourishment, but also to inspect their dress and appearance. After quizzing a class of fifty-odd eleven-year-olds in Hamburg, Gollancz tallied twenty-four children with 'good shoes', sixteen with 'no shoes of their own', and just ten who claimed to possess a second pair. In another class, he noted succinctly, 'Girl of eight. 1 pair *kaput* shoes.' On the penultimate day of the trip, he recorded a differently sobering figure, 3,100,000: the number of pairs of shoes immediately wanted for children in the British zone.[48]

Gollancz described all this vividly in letters fired off to British newspapers. These he later assembled, along with other materials such as lavish menus from British officers' messes, in a volume published in January 1947. *In Darkest Germany* also contained 144 photographs, winnowed from significantly more that Gollancz took, or had taken, during his German sojourn.[49] Together, these images would surely have satisfied the precociously polysyllabic heroine of J. D. Salinger's celebrated story 'For Esmé – with Love and Squalor', who pesters a GI to supply graphic evidence of German immiseration.[50] Several of Gollancz's plates depict emaciated Germans, particularly children, some naked or semi-nude to reveal protruding ribs and hunger-swollen stomachs. Others show the squalid cellars in which thousands of urban-dwellers struggled to exist. A few dire lavatories feature, but photographs of footwear loom large.

Gollancz cued readers' responses to this imagery in a chapter devoted to 'Shoes and Other Things', with a subtitle borrowed from H. G. Wells, 'This Misery of Boots'.[51] German pauperization, he insisted, was 'literally indescribable: you can only understand what it means when you actually see it – or, at a long remove, by photographs'.[52] Gollancz deployed a trope that often accompanied photographic images of liberated Nazi camps: an insistence that words alone can never do justice to extreme suffering that has to be seen to be believed. According to this logic, the camera serves as a more credible witness than the pen or typewriter, 'worth a thousand words' in the familiar adage. Yet, despite the vaunted superiority of visual testimony over verbal texts, photography remains fallible as a record of human extremity. Since photographs can be staged and doctored, framed and cropped, they're apt to be mistrusted. So, to corroborate that there was 'no fake about them', Gollancz included *himself* in several of the photographs. In some, his hand holds aloft the scabby leg of an ill-shod German infant; in others, he's a solemnly bespectacled background presence, clad in a buttoned overcoat and hat.[53]

Critics faulted the repetitious nature of Gollancz's footwear photographs. But repetition was precisely the point. And, studied carefully, the images reveal variety within the monotony. There are boots resoled multiple times and still worn through; shoes improvised from torn canvas and frayed string; sandals that are merely thin strips of

Figure 5.3 In Düsseldorf, 1946, items of German children's footwear are photographed at the behest of the British publisher and humanitarian Sir Victor Gollancz (Estate of Sir Victor Gollancz/Modern Records Centre, University of Warwick)

leather nailed to a wooden sole; and, with varying degrees of separation between uppers and soles, many exposed feet with exhausted, clumsily darned, socks slouching around bony ankles. Apart from grinding poverty, Gollancz's photographs hint at how much harder it was to cobble together *ersatz* footwear from remnants of leather, hessian, string and cardboard than it was to fabricate serviceable garments from worn apparel. Whereas sewing took some know-how, it required little equipment beyond scissors and a needle. Pins, patterns and chalk were all dispensable. Making shoes, in contrast, required more of everything: durable materials, specialized tools, and artisanal knowledge.

In a land where *kaput* served as a multi-purpose descriptor for all things busted and bankrupt, from public utilities to the Nazi Party, *kaputten* shoes signified many things.[54] To be barefoot or woefully shod entailed a loss of personal dignity. But more than injured self-esteem was at stake. Threadbare clothing and useless footwear simultaneously increased susceptibility to illness and made certain maladies more visible. Several photographs depict what Gollancz termed the 'ugly skin blemishes that are the stigmata of malnutrition', sores exposed to view on the limbs of bare-legged women and children.[55] Without a protective layer of subcutaneous fat, and living in accommodation that lacked window panes and roof tiles, Germans were prone to infectious diseases such as TB and pneumonia. In underground dwellings, stagnant puddles lapped at the uppers of residents' shoes if they had any, or submerged their feet if they went without.[56]

For children, having no shoes meant missing out on education. In a letter to the *Daily Herald* dated 30 November 1946, Gollancz recounted how teachers in the Rhineland predicted that 'when the really wet weather started, "shoe absenteeism" might amount to 50 per cent'. A single pair of shoes was sometimes family property. Siblings and parents took possession in turns. 'One child said he wouldn't be able to come to school tomorrow "because father would want his shoes": another – "I have Hans' shoes so he's got to stay at home."' And since one size emphatically did *not* fit all, children variously hobbled around in younger siblings' footwear that pinched or 'slopp[ed] about in their mother's or father's shoes', if they did not go 'completely barefoot'.[57] For families with just one pair of shoes, children's intermittent school attendance resulted in parents' intermittent absence from work. Lost wages accelerated the tailspin into deeper abjection.

The broken shoe registered as a singularly pathetic symbol of vulnerability: an index of lost opportunities and heightened risks. Gollancz was far from alone in finding bare or ill-shod feet an evocative emblem of postwar suffering. Allied observers, perhaps especially those whose comfortable lives had never exposed them to the barefoot underclass of their own countries, recoiled from shoelessness, especially when this predicament hinted at a precipitous descent from pre-war comfort. For well-heeled British and American officers and reporters it was one thing to encounter shoeless peasants in southern Europe, another altogether to find members of the professional middle class, such as doctors, going about their business barefoot. For Gollancz, adults and children without footwear in Germany's formerly prosperous industrial cities triggered the same sense of shocked wrongness.[58]

Gollancz evidently felt that poignant images of broken footwear would agitate his audience's moral conscience. Yet, while they may have helped raise funds for SEN, the plates selected for *In Darkest Germany* provoke questions about the ethics of photography as a humanitarian weapon.[59] Images of gaping footwear form a visual counterpoint to the postwar era's pervasive imagery of ruined buildings, opened up like dolls' houses to reveal furniture and fixtures in the three-walled rooms within. Confronted with a *kaput* boot or bomb-damaged home, viewers might experience a prurient twinge, seeing things hitherto enclosed and private – whether a big toe, bedstead or bathtub – unwontedly exposed to public view. But ruined buildings and ruined lives differ insofar as people may, or may not, wish these exposures to be captured on film. How did the children in Gollancz's photographs feel about being asked (or perhaps made?) to strip, or to have their degraded footwear held up for inspection? How, for that matter, did adults respond to their destitution being laid bare? Did they welcome the attention Gollancz drew to their plight or feel that his intrusive camera deepened their shame?

To look at Gollancz's photographs now is, inescapably, to be reminded of images of the victims of Nazi atrocity. Skeletal bodies and ruined shoes have become metonyms for the Holocaust. In a collection of essays on *Jews and Shoes*, the historian Jeffrey Feldman traces the symbolic link between footwear and Nazi genocide to the 1961 trial of Adolf Eichmann in Israel. At one especially wrenching moment in the courtroom, Dr Adolf Berman (an organizer of the Warsaw ghetto uprising) described the impact of a visit to Treblinka. Unwrapping a red silk bundle, he produced a crumpled pair of tiny brown shoes: 'one pair as a token of those terrible days – one pair among one million such children's shoes that are scattered over the fields of death'. 'For seemingly endless seconds', a spectator to this event later recalled, 'we were gripped by the spell cast by this symbol of all that was left of a million children. Time stood still, while each in his own way tried to fit flesh to the shoes, multiply by a million, and spin the reel back from death, terror and tears to the music of gay laughter and the animated joy of youngsters in European city and village before the Nazis marched in.'[60] 'Tattered Sandals Accuse Eichmann' ran the *Los Angeles Times* headline, as though the child's footwear were endowed with the power of speech.[61] With people weeping openly in court, this scene helped solidify the nexus between the orphaned shoe and annihilated life. Piles of footwear have come to form a staple feature of museums and exhibits dedicated to the Holocaust.

We could, however, follow this metonymic association between shoes and genocide back further, recalling how liberators' attention fastened onto the enormous mound of footwear at Belsen in April 1945, testament to murder on a phenomenal scale. Like victims' stolen garments and severed hair, their shoes cried out to be described, filmed and photographed; images that recur in newsreels and documentary records of Nazi camps shown to Allied and German audiences alike. Similarly, when the Oświęcim (Auschwitz) Museum of Martyrology opened in July 1947, its exhibits included 'a vast pile of Russian soldiers' boots and children's shoes', as well as 'mixed heaps of clothing, shaving brushes, penknives and trunks with inscriptions in all languages'.[62]

Gollancz appreciated that some people might take umbrage at his defence of starving Germans when Germans themselves had wrought so much human devastation, and exhibited so little remorse. In a letter to the editor of *The Times* from Düsseldorf, he tried to pre-empt this criticism by making a direct connection between Jewish and German suffering:

> The most horrible of my experiences has been a visit to the camp at Belsen, where I saw the tattoo marks on the arms of the Jewish survivors. I am never likely to forget the unspeakable wickedness of which the Nazis were guilty. But when I see the swollen bodies and living skeletons in hospitals here and elsewhere; when I look at the miserable "shoes" of boys and girls in the schools, and find that they have come to their lessons without even a dry piece of bread for breakfast; when I go down into a one-roomed cellar where a mother is struggling, and struggling very bravely, to do her best for a husband and four or five children – then I think, not of Germans, but of men and women. I am sure I should have the same feelings if I were in Greece or Poland. But I happen to be in Germany, and write of what I see here.[63]

Gollancz's suggestion that humans in extremis were universally worthy of empathy failed to satisfy critics, who objected that his campaign relativized, and accordingly marginalized, the pain inflicted *by* Germans – on European Jewry above all. Gollancz's vigorous advocacy on Germans' behalf alienated some erstwhile allies, including prominent Jewish figures such as the barrister and legal scholar Norman Bentwich.[64] Meanwhile, some British charities were still working intensively on behalf of Jewish survivors in Germany. A small notice placed in the *Manchester Guardian* in December 1946 by the city's Clothing Committee for Relief Abroad plaintively begged readers for

Figure 5.4 Abram Games' 1946 poster, on behalf of the Jewish
Committee for Relief Abroad, reminds Britons of survivors' ongoing
need for clothing (© Imperial War Museum, PST 8325)

donated garments. 'We are continually receiving heartbreaking appeals
for men's, women's, and children's clothes, particularly from Belsen,'
the advert announced. 'They are desperately in need of babies' clothes,
as children are being born at the rate of 50–60 per week and they have
hardly any clothes at all.'[65]

Ties and Binds

After years in which a vocal segment of British society disputed
the very existence of the 'good German', it's unsurprising that some
scorned the notion that generosity was more likely than severity to
resocialize a defeated enemy. 'Is it not the very essence of the German
question that a larger proportion of Germans than of other nations
responds badly to good treatment?,' demanded a testy reviewer of *In
Darkest Germany* in the *Times Literary Supplement*.[66] Viewed against

this backdrop, far more striking than the pushback against Gollancz is the degree of bipartisan support he mustered. Labour MPs were present at SEN's creation. More unexpectedly, some Conservatives endorsed Gollancz's position on postwar German destitution. Major Guy Lloyd (MP for Renfrew East), responding to *In Darkest Germany* in a very different vein, reiterated Gollancz's key claims in a lengthy column for the *Daily Mail* – not known for its softness on Germany. 'Practically no German possesses any clothes but what he stands up in, and among the working classes, at any rate, these clothes are threadbare,' Lloyd wrote. 'Some 75 per cent of German children do not possess shoes, and the rest go about in footwear which would be laughable if it were not so pathetic.'[67]

Even more remarkable is the volume of charitable giving SEN inspired. Although the organization failed to effect a sea-change in British occupation policy, it extracted a signal concession from Attlee's administration: namely, that Britons, along with German POWs living in Britain, could mail parcels of food (up to 7 lb) and second-hand clothing (up to 11 lb) to Germany.[68] Mail service had been suspended since before the war. Now anyone who wished to do so could apply to SEN for a special mailing label to affix to a parcel sent, in the first instance, to Victor Gollancz's publishing house. His staff then shepherded these packages through the tangle of red tape wound around mail service to the British zone. In total, SEN oversaw the despatch of some 60,000 parcels from British citizens. From a population of around fifty million, this number might seem rather unimpressive, but less so when we recall how tightly restricted access to food and clothing remained in Britain.[69]

Between 1945 and 1948, the entire span of SEN's existence, Britons endured their own 'misery of boots'. As in Germany, the situation was worst for those who outgrew their footwear fastest: babies and children. Infants' shoes, limited in availability from 1942 onwards, became even harder to find after the war. (Recall that some civil servants, anticipating this crisis, argued vehemently against veterans receiving new shoes along with their demob suits, only to be overruled by the Service chiefs.) Numerous press stories, supported by agitated readers' letters, attested this predicament. One mother, reported *The Times* in October 1945, had visited ten 'large establishments' in search of new footwear for her eleven-year-old daughter, to no avail.[70] Soon thereafter, the *Daily Mail* launched a campaign against 'The Shoe Scandal', coincidentally alongside the headline 'Keitel Weeps at "Belsen" Film'. Seasonally adjusted, this was also a scandal of the sandal, wellington and plimsoll. Since wartime supplies of leather and rubber for civilian manufacture had dwindled across the globe, footwear manufacturers experimented with alternatives, from rope-and-canvas espadrilles to synthetic leather uppers, clogs carved entirely from wood and wood-soled shoes and sandals. Shoddier substitutes for soles, including cardboard, weren't uncommon.[71] As a result, shoes became not only harder to find, but also quicker to fall apart. In Luton, a member of the town's education committee recommended that parents repair children's footwear with 'old motor and cycle tyres'.[72]

In November 1945, Sir Stafford Cripps, President of the Board of Trade, attempted to defuse criticism by announcing that this ostensible 'scandal' of scant footwear was illusory: evidence of increased *demand*, not diminished supply. Living standards were, he insisted, on the rise. In his own constituency, whereas before the war a 'great many children' possessed no shoes, now none went unshod.[73] So Cripps claimed. Residents of East Bristol furiously begged to differ, confronting journalists with their children's 'gaping and torn' footwear. Across the country, parents, educators and civic leaders added further corroborative evidence to the case against Cripps.

The consequences of scarcity in Britain mirrored those detailed by Gollancz in Germany. Headline: 'No Shoes – No School'. In rural Herefordshire, farm children without wellies slid around barefoot, mud sucking at their ankles, unable to go to school. Three hundred miles to the north in Newcastle, children likewise missed out on education because of flimsy footwear. Heels built out of 'ordinary brown paper' proved no match for the British climate. Sometimes pupils were pulled out of class abruptly by mothers who, having got wind of a consignment of footwear delivered to a local shop, fought to ensure their child got fitted first. Even comfortably middle-class families felt the pinch. One mother in Twickenham, whose businessman husband brought home a 'four-figure income', confessed herself 'reduced to sharing one good pair of shoes' with her fourteen-year-old daughter: 'When she has to go out neatly shod I stay home in my old faithfuls. For my five-year-old son I have the problem of constant search for shoes which do not fall to pieces after the first shower of rain.'[74]

Britain's footwear deficit didn't ease substantially until 1948. Yet, despite these shortages, or perhaps sensitized by them, thousands of Britons – along with 50,000 German POWs – sent parcels via SEN to alleviate Germans' distress. Save Europe Now didn't occupy this humanitarian ground alone. Some chaplains with the British army of occupation encouraged servicemen returning to Germany after home leave to bring parcels of second-hand clothing back with them.[75] In Blackpool, the schoolteacher wife of a Military Government official mobilized pupils into sending twenty-seven parcels of clothing to German children. Several clergymen mounted similar initiatives. An appeal by the Bishop of Sheffield in December 1946 yielded 10 tons of 'gifts for Germans', including 300 overcoats, 200 men's suits and 300 pairs of boots and shoes, plus a 'large collection of underwear'. Even more impressive was the fact that self-sacrificing Sheffielders parted with especially coveted commodities. This consignment included 100 pairs of silk stockings and 800 chocolate bars.[76]

Another such project, led by the Reverend Clifford Pickford of Wood Green (on the northern edge of London) grew organically after a letter he'd sent the *News Chronicle* in support of Gollancz was republished in a German newspaper. Pickford received dozens of epistles from Germans, variously despairing, appreciative or beseeching. 'Most of Germans think, the English want to let us starve. I hope there are some in England, who does not wish it. We do not more know, if there is a God,' wrote Walter Meyer from Hamburg in July 1947. He told Pickford that residents of the port city now consumed just 800 calories a day, since the British authorities had introduced a further ration cut.[77] The idea that Britons *wanted* Germans to perish was reinforced when German newspapers republished, alongside Pickford's letter, opinions like that of A. L. Jones of Westcliff-on-Sea, Essex: 'I don't care two shakes of a duck's feathers if the whole German population in Germany falls down and dies of starvation tomorrow.' Dismayed by this vengefulness, Allbrich Drewitz nevertheless struck a more optimistic note. 'People like Mr Gollancz and you', he assured Pickford, 'do more to prevent the deplorable growing cynicism with which the Germans regard "Western Democracy" than could do all propaganda and pointing at Germany's responsibility and guilt by official members.'[78]

Other correspondents combined notes of thanks with pleas for help. Ada Oestreich, a sixty-six-year-old 'expellee', unmarried and 'living here [in Lachendorf] in a tiny little room amongst people, who do not want Refugees because they have suffered nothing through this war, but rather gained', petitioned Pickford in October, hoping that 'a kind hearted lady' from his church might send 'a little food or clothing':

> The little clothing I have save is worn and torn, shoes are torn and cannot be replaced nor repaired, no stockings for the winter – in summer I went barefoot, no gloves for the winter, I am afraid to think. In the time after the war ceased I lost on weight 15 kilo, so that my personal weight is only 48 kilo – before the war 75 kilo.

If Pickford could facilitate this request, it 'would give me sunshine in my heart and soul in these dreary days of waiting for better ones'. He did. A compassionate female parishioner sent Ada a parcel of food and clothing that reached her within two months.[79]

British charitable organizations approached German clothing poverty from an array of angles. The Association for Moral and Social Hygiene, concerned by soaring rates of sexually transmitted infections in occupied Europe, feared that women without adequate clothing or food would be predated upon by Allied troops looking to 'fraternize'. This concern wasn't misplaced. Sex soon became the most commonly bartered black market commodity, as it had been earlier in Naples and elsewhere in Allied-occupied southern Italy. Stories about what could be procured for cigarettes, a candy bar or pair of nylons proliferated in postwar Germany, memorably dramatized in Billy Wilder's Berlin-set black comedy *A Foreign Affair* (1948).[80]

For its part, the British Federation of University Women (BFUW) sought to assist stricken female graduates in Germany. Correspondence in the organization's archive points to the durability of ties that developed as British female graduates worked to help their German sisters rebuild careers and professional connections shattered by the war. Letters exchanged across borders also underscore how profoundly a threadbare appearance impinged on women's self-esteem, eroding their ability to lead public lives. It wasn't always lack of shoes that kept women trapped indoors. Fear of social humiliation – being seen by others in an unmistakably reduced state – could be just as immobilizing. One older beneficiary of BFUW assistance, Lilli Lilienfeld, who lived in a German DP camp, voiced this crippling fear of others' contemptuous judgement with particular candour. She was 'ashamed' to 'move among people' in her old clothing and bad shoes, 'as I was used all my life to being dressed decently and in good taste'.

The BFUW volunteers stood resolutely by, sending Lilli assistance from 1947 until 1974.[81]

Whether mailed through SEN or other channels, aid parcels contained symbolic significance beyond their material contents. As Gollancz's hard-pressed assistant Peggy Duff put it, they represented 'a tangible token of the sympathy and human understanding which exists in Britain for suffering, wherever it may be' – 'a symbol of friendliness and reconciliation' after long years of hatred and estrangement.[82]

In the Zone

British Military Government (MG) personnel in occupied Germany viewed clothing redistribution in less sentimental terms: not so much a reknitted tie as an impossible juggling act. Over the four-year period of occupation, the population of British-administered northwest Germany remained in flux. Mostly, it expanded. *Volksdeutsche* expellees kept arriving from the east, while only some DPs headed back to the countries from which they'd fled or been forcibly thrust by German personnel during the war. And, as the British government restricted visas for emigration to Palestine, thousands of Jewish survivors remained encamped in Germany. The MG personnel, working alongside UNRRA and other relief agencies, quickly organized DP camps along ethnic lines, believing that this represented the best way to avoid inter-communal tension and facilitate repatriation. But a mass return of displaced populations failed to occur at the pace and scale anticipated by SHAEF before the war ended. Displaced persons whose homelands now lay under Soviet control often fiercely resisted being made to return to places where they feared incarceration as deserters or traitors. As a result, various constituencies – displaced from different places for different reasons during and after the war – jostled for priority status, or any assistance at all.[83]

For British military personnel, keeping these various categories straight, and separate, was a logistical feat. Numbers and locations shifted; and, over time, some groups were reclassified. For instance, Polish POWs who refused to return to Poland were redesignated in late 1946 as DPs, lodged in Germany on an indefinite basis, pending what Allied officials infelicitously termed a 'final solution' of the 'DP problem'. Distinctions weren't merely semantic. Labels that aspired to ring-fence one group of displaced people from another also denoted different material entitlements. Clothing, feeding and accommodating DPs was a responsibility of the MG, in conjunction with UNRRA and other humanitarian agencies. Providing relief for Germans was a German responsibility, albeit under British military supervision. Why, one UNRRA worker wondered, did this organization choose a *globe* for its insignia when it refused responsibility for former Axis areas?[84]

When SHAEF and UNRRA entrenched this binary into policy during the war, it doubtless made sense to differentiate between enemy and allied populations: them and us. But the arrival of millions of destitute 'expellees' simultaneously expanded the boundaries of Germanness while blurring the line between 'deserving' and 'undeserving' dislocated people – all the more so when so many uprooted *Volksdeutsche* arrived with so little. A British military memo (issued on 29 December 1945) noted that 20 per cent of these refugees had 'no other clothes, but those they stand up in'. Their desperation made it hard to sustain the rigid line that German expellees were the 'last priority'. Only 'emergency demands for the completely "naked" individual' would be met by the MG, one unusually blunt memo stated.[85] Even then, covering 'bare life' wasn't so much a humanitarian move as a self-protective manoeuvre. 'People flocking together without sufficient clothing and warmth' posed a 'danger of epidemics', one officer warned, repeating a lesson painfully learnt at Belsen.[86]

Initially, British policy decreed that the textile needs of all groups would be met by *German* supplies, requisitioned from local populations, as was done in the environs of Belsen. A notice issued to the German authorities explained the logic of this levy, further emphasizing that hasty production of new apparel wasn't an option. 'Fuel, power and labour for textile factories must be diverted to other and more essential purposes,' the MG warned. Besides, raw materials for garment manufacture simply weren't available. In the first instance, then, clothing everyone resident in the British zone meant reshuffling garments from Germans to other nationals and between various categories of Germans. 'United Nations Displaced Persons' headed the list of entitled recipients:

> These persons were brought to work in GERMANY by your own Government and the provision to them of the necessities of life is rightly a first charge against your collective or

individual resources. They are being returned to their own countries with all possible speed but while they remain they must be clothed and provided with adequate bedding.

Next in line came Allied 'ex-prisoners of war' temporarily encamped in Germany, followed by 'Wehrmacht awaiting disbandment', 'civil hospitals' and 'essential workers'.[87]

British soldiers assumed the unfamiliar role of parting civilians from their material possessions: everything from pillows to underpants and suspender belts. Even servicemen familiar with the supply management work of the quartermaster corps encountered many unfamiliar items on the docket. The British Army, after all, wasn't routinely in the business of equipping either babies or women. But two of the most urgently needed items that troops had to muster were babies' nappies and sanitary pads. 'Napkins, napkins and again napkins' – this was the cry all over Germany, one Quaker relief worker related.[88] Occupation officers likewise judged the situation in several DP camps 'especially awful' for babies, many of whom were wrapped in 'dirty rags not proper swaddling clothes'.[89] Gollancz noted the use of newspaper in lieu of nappies.[90] The situation was grim for menstruating women, too. In late 1945, MG personnel calculated the requirement at precisely 4,323,000 sanitary towels for the British zone. Since neither cloth nappies nor period products were levied from Germans, manufacture of these essential items had to be authorized, with shredded paper substituting for cotton wool as filling for sanitary pads.[91]

As British officers found in the environs of Belsen, Germans only sometimes fulfilled the quotas set for local districts. Predictably, Germans baulked at handing over especially scarce items. Noting a 'major shortage' of children's vests, a situation report in January 1946 surmised: 'Probable reason is reluctance of parents to surrender at expense of their own children.'[92] That month, British personnel decided to suspend the levy. 'Non-compliance' ran high. But compliance wasn't without its own risk of simply shifting the locus of Germany's intersecting crises. As the memo calling a halt to requisitioning noted: 'Further depletion of household stocks is likely to have an adverse effect on the health of the [German civilian] population, which is already existing on a low food ration scale and with very little fuel.'[93]

Balancing needs and priorities involved both ethical and logistical calculations, matching what was fair with what was available.

Clothing in postwar Germany also had an inescapably *political* dimension. With growing numbers of *Wehrmacht* soldiers returning home, the challenge of 'denazifying' apparel grew accordingly. In Germany, civilian scarcity existed alongside, and largely due to, concentration on military manufacture. 'During the wartime we could very seldom obtain any civil clothes (the soldier uniforms very easily) but nowadays there is to get not anything!,' one young German informed Rev. Pickford. After the war, that same glut of uniforms didn't just represent material subtracted from civilian use, but also constituted an affront to the postwar order. The presence of millions of demobilized men, still outfitted in unmodified *Wehrmacht*, *Luftwaffe* and *SS* uniforms, would be unconscionable under occupation. Demilitarization and Denazification topped the Allies' list of 'D-s' for defeated Germany, along with Deindustrialization and Decartelization – all necessary to achieve the overarching goal of Democratization. With Nazi personnel expunged from public life, swastika banners torn down and street names changed, demobilized servicemen could hardly be left to wander postwar Germany in their service apparel. Nor could the one-and-a-half million German POWs in the British zone be permitted to continue wearing unaltered *Wehrmacht* uniforms.[94] The Allied Control Council (the four occupying powers' coordinating body) agreed in August 1945 that, after 1 December, German veterans would no longer be permitted to wear unmodified uniforms. The following April, Allied authorities announced that Germans caught in military uniforms could be sentenced to death.[95] Even Germans who possessed wearable clothes didn't necessarily possess clothing that could be worn.

In Britain, meanwhile, one stockpile of garments was growing apace: surplus military apparel, including items 'surrendered' by servicemen as they received their demob suits. Importing millions of battledress tunics and trousers, greatcoats and underwear into Germany would alleviate the British zone's clothing crisis. But these items couldn't simply be distributed in their current state. The War Office remained twitchy about kit falling into the 'wrong hands'. Apprehension grew when an investigation into crimes allegedly committed by British soldiers in Germany revealed that the perpetrators were in fact DPs dressed in British uniform.[96] The solution was simple, or seemingly so. Uniforms would be *dyed*: British apparel to avert further cases of accidental or deliberate imposture; German garments to eradicate Nazi associations. British women, frustrated by the lack of new clothes in shops, were simultaneously encouraged to dye their garments so that new colours might satisfy a desire for refreshed wardrobes that couldn't otherwise be met. (Dylon, Britain's leading supplier of dye, still in existence today, was founded in 1946.[97])

Straightforward on paper, this expedient turned out to be time-consuming and wasteful in practice – for women and occupation personnel alike.[98] The War Office initially insisted that dyeing be undertaken in Britain, loath to see any apparel leave the country in its original service shades of khaki, grey and navy. This scrupulousness caused a months-long delay and, with winter approaching, occupation officers pressed Whitehall for a change of policy. The dyeing must, they prompted, be done in Germany.[99] Further delays ensued. Huge quantities of dye, preferably not the *Sturmabteilung* or Brownshirt shade of brown (*Kleiderbraun A*), had to be found. Then German companies were commissioned to carry out the dyeing, which they did with varying degrees of celerity and competence. Woollen garments often shrank in a process that required very hot water to fix the new colour. Tens of thousands of battledress trousers and blouses duly went to waste. One region reported in July 1946 that battledress garments, size 'Small' before dyeing, emerged uselessly tiny 'by reason of shrinkage'. Another deemed 80 per cent of dyed battledress 'virtually unwearable'. Shrinkage wasn't the only defect. When trousers 'with one leg' and torn blouses reached their destinations, 'transportation of such clothing was a complete waste of time'.[100] Dyeing garments also failed to solve the problem of visually distinguishing one group from another, which was a key function served by uniforms. Polish POWs protested bitterly that, in their dyed apparel, they looked the same as ex-*Wehrmacht* personnel in identical dyed garments.[101]

And then there was the familiar dearth of footwear. While it's a truism that an army marches on its stomach, *Wehrmacht* soldiers (like their Allied counterparts) marched *in* their boots. Stocks of ex-*Wehrmacht* shoes and boots commandeered by the MG were in such poor condition that as little as 10 per cent, by one estimate, could be reclaimed for 'refugees etc.', even after 'disinfection and renovation'. Instead, the British military devised a novel variation on the 'swords into ploughshares' theme: 'Tents into Shoes'. German army tents would supply the uppers of canvas footwear, with hundreds of thousands of reconditioned British army boots imported to make up the shortfall.[102]

Footwear increasingly concerned British personnel, less as a result of Gollancz's activism than because sturdy boots were an essential prerequisite of returning German men to heavy industrial and agricultural work. It took just a few months for British civil and military personnel to appreciate that 'deindustrialization' was not a viable foundation for postwar reconstruction – no matter how fervently some critics had wished to 'pastoralize' Germany in perpetuity. If Britons (and their US allies) weren't to expend enormous sums of money over many years on meeting occupied Germany's basic needs, something had to give. Mining, forestry and industrial manufacturing would have to be kick-started in Britain's devastated zone, but that meant recruiting workers and equipping them with appropriate protective clothing and boots.[103]

Fabric and footwear figured twice over in British plans to employ Germans in industry and agriculture. Durable workwear served an obviously practical purpose. Without sturdy boots, men couldn't function as dockers, miners and loggers. Supplied with inferior overalls and boots, men went, or threatened to go, on strike.[104] In addition to securing adequate supplies of hard-wearing apparel for German workmen, British officials tried to instrumentalize *women's* clothing as an incentive to motivate men to undertake arduous, often hazardous, forms of labour. Perhaps men would more readily take up otherwise undesirable employment if they could buy consumer goods with their wages. British officials believed so. And the material 'carrot' they intended to dangle, supplies of women's 'Old Look' garments, had the additional advantage of ridding the Board of Trade of an unwanted surplus.[105]

Whether Ruhr miners' wives actually *wanted* 'Old Look' garments in 1948 was, of course, another matter altogether.[106] Maybe they'd have no choice, but, if Germans' preferences resembled those of many women elsewhere in continental Europe and Britain, the answer was probably not. Christian Dior, architect of the New Look's billowing shapes and elongated silhouettes, staged his first postwar German show in 1947, the year before the Board of Trade decided to offload unsaleable British women's-wear on occupied northwest Germany. After years of straining to 'make new from old', many miners' spouses doubtless shared the desire female consumers expressed elsewhere to replace outworn and outmoded garments with New Look styles. Extravagantly cut skirts and coats quickly swept utilitarian wartime styles aside. Germany's era of threadbare dejection existed, paradoxically, alongside the rehabilitation of its fashion industry.[107]

Judgments at Nuremberg

Dior's 1947 show wasn't the earliest sign of resurgent German interest in high fashion. Foreign correspondents excitedly reported on the first fashion show held in Berlin, Germany's couture capital, in March 1946. Most commentators, except perhaps self-interested staff at the Board of Trade, were heartened by defeated Germans' eagerness to remodel themselves, starting with what they wore. 'Physically, the results were a tribute to their courage and recuperative powers,' opined the *New York Times*' Berlin correspondent. 'Artistically, they produced no competition that need cause insomnia among members of the Haute Couture in Paris or New York.' The same reporter faulted 'clumsiness of design and over-ornamentation', a regrettable Teutonic tendency, while admiring 'an outstanding beach suit of ecru shantung' that included 'a bolero jacket striped with maroon and kings blue and skating-type circular skirt worn over scant shorts which, like the matching bra, were blue on one side and maroon on the other. A huge beachbag of ecru completed the outfit.'[108]

An even more unlikely fashion show was staged the same month in Nuremberg. By March 1946, this rubble-strewn Bavarian city, indelibly linked with Nazi racial ideology, was four months into its new role as the setting for the International Military Tribunal (IMT), at which twenty-four prominent German civilian and military leaders were tried by British, French, Soviet and American prosecutors on novel charges of 'crimes against peace' and 'crimes against humanity'.[109] With grim evidence of Nazi atrocities recounted daily, and sometimes cinematically projected, in Nuremberg's Palace of Justice, a fashion show appears profoundly incongruous in this setting. But seemingly not so to those present at the time, who sought diversion from proceedings that unfolded at an agonizingly slow pace. The courtroom was 'a citadel of boredom', complained celebrated author Rebecca West, reporting on the trial for the *Daily Telegraph* and *New Yorker*. She found the whole city torpid with inactivity; visitors were frustrated in their touristic desire to shop. 'One could not buy a new hat, a new kettle, a yard of ribbon, a baby's diaper. There was no money, there

Figure 5.5 German women model dresses made from curtain fabric at Berlin's first postwar fashion show, 13 March 1946 (Gamma-Keystone-France/Getty Images)

were only cigarettes' – if, that is, one was a civilian. United States military personnel, in contrast, could satisfy their acquisitiveness at a well-stocked post exchange (PX) while 'sightseeing' at the IMT.[110] Attuned to Nuremberg's surreal contradictions, West's gimlet eye might have been drawn to the fashion show, staged for GIs' benefit and billed as a 'television home leave'. As described by a *New York Times* columnist, the catwalk featured 'a display of models ranging from sweater outfits to cocktail costumes, negligees, trailing ball dresses and playsuits characterized by startling economy in the use of material'. These titillating outfits were shown off by women serving with the American Red Cross, along with a secretary from the office of the American chief prosecutor, Robert H. Jackson.[111]

Nuremberg in 1946 may have been an improbable locale for a fashion show, but it's a particularly fitting place in which to conclude an exploration of clothing in occupied Germany. The many functions and meanings assigned to garments as embodiments of status were fully on display in the courtroom. The IMT, a unique multi-national venture in prosecuting indicted war criminals, and the first ever trial to be filmed, was striking not only for the indictments' novelty, but also because of the high degree of forethought devoted to the proceedings' dramaturgy, including what the various protagonists wore.[112] Legal authority often finds expression in material symbols and metaphors: think 'silks' (shorthand for King's or Queen's Counsel), as well as horsehair wigs and black gowns in the British juridical tradition.[113] The proceedings at Nuremberg, however, emphasized the semiotics of dress in singular, sometimes unexpected, ways.

First, as everyone who commented on the IMT noted, the defendants' apparel had been 'denazified' along with other uniforms in occupied Germany. The twenty-one arraigned leaders who appeared in court (three being tried in absentia) did so either in grey-green *Wehrmacht* uniforms shorn of insignia and badges of rank or in 'iron-grey civilian clothes and dark ties'. One, Admiral Raeder, received permission to wear a red tie, 'perhaps as a token of the period he spent in Russian custody', speculated a sardonic *Manchester Guardian* reporter.[114] Hermann Göring alone cut a flamboyant figure, greatly reduced in weight and sporting 'an elegant pale grey Luftwaffe uniform, presumably his own creation'.[115] The former chief of the *Luftwaffe* high command soon emerged as the dominant defendant, striking poses in the dock, attempting to stare down journalists and running rhetorical rings around any prosecutor who'd let him. Göring, noted the *New Yorker*'s Janet Flanner, 'undeniably looked the bravura personality in his vast, sagging, dove-colored jacket and his matching voluminous breeches, with his fine, high, maroon boots and his maroon neckerchief'.[116] West's characterization was more scathing: 'Sometimes he wore a German Air Force Uniform, and sometimes a light beach suit in the worst of playful taste, and both hung loosely on him, giving him an air of pregnancy' – presumably not the effect to which Göring aspired.[117]

Reporters marvelled at how *nondescript* the indicted Nazi leaders appeared, stripped of their erstwhile finery. The perpetrators of heinous crimes looked like they 'might almost have been attending some business convention', one reporter ventured.[118] The celebrated political cartoonist David Low, in attendance as an official artist, captured in a column for London's *Evening Standard* what his courtroom sketches also conveyed: the unimpressive shrunkenness of the 'very ordinary looking' men in the dock.[119] 'I did not look, of course, for a set of puffed-up specimens of the Master Race in fearsome uniforms with padded shoulders, Swastikas and high heels; but, on the other

Figure 5.6 Hermann Göring taking the oath in the dock at Nuremberg, 18 March 1946 (Bettmann/Getty Images)

hand, this lot seemed rather inadequate,' Low remarked. Despite his larger-than-life persona, Göring measured only 'about 5ft. 8in.', 'flapping his pudgy little hands about, patting his hair, stroking his mouth, massaging his cheeks', while the formerly bullying foreign minister Joachim von Ribbentrop seemed 'a meek person, like a family solicitor, with disordered hair, pursed lips, and large spectacles'.[120]

The defendants' appearance retrospectively reaffirmed the vital role of theatrical props – ornate uniforms, insignia, flags and banners – in fabricating fascism's aura of invincible totality. When the American prosecutor Telford Taylor informed the defendants that 'a military uniform' could not 'be accepted as a cloak for criminal misdoing', he gestured towards the way in which the Nazi leadership *had* endowed garments with mystical properties, variously dazzling, distracting and overawing.[121] Now these bullies attempted to hide behind the shell of their uniforms, invoking the defence that they'd merely been 'obeying orders' – as all good soldiers must.

Observers devoted the bulk of their court-room attention to scrutinizing the defendants' appearance, demeanour and body language. But they also noted what the *Allied* judges and prosecutors wore. Flanner admired the cut and panache of the British judges' apparel. Court President Sir Geoffrey Lawrence, the most senior British judge, made a dramatic daily arrival in a 'magnificent black limousine, glistening against the dusty ruins of the bombed walls', resplendent in a 'long, blue broadcloth coat and a bowler'. Flanner ascribed to prosecutor Sir David Maxwell Fyfe the 'same physical dignity and sartorial elegance … impeccable in his Foreign Office attire'.[122] But more striking than this sharp tailoring was the fact that the British lawyers appeared without their customary wigs, and 'in plain gowns like their American colleagues', West observed. She interpreted this unorthodox decision 'as a sign that this was a tribunal above all local tribunals' – an occasion of supranational legal significance.[123]

Through different sartorial cues, the Soviets demonstrated that they did not consider the IMT an ordinary trial either. Unlike their western colleagues in morning suits, the Soviet judges sat in 'a kind of regimental dress – chocolate-brown uniforms with green trimmings'.[124] This stirred a shiver of unease in Rebecca West, as the Soviets' martial appearance lent credence to criticism of Nuremberg as an enactment of victors' justice: a 'show trial' whose end – the execution of all the accused – was written in its beginning. The impression that the Soviets regarded the IMT as 'no tribunal at all', simply a rubber-stamp for a foregone conclusion, was deepened in West's estimation when Andrey Vyshinsky visited Nuremberg in the early months of the trial. At a banquet, the Soviet Minister of Foreign Affairs silenced the room when he 'proposed a toast to the conviction of the accused, a can-trip which would have led to the quashing of the trial in any civilized country'.[125]

The Soviets' cavalier disregard for due process – their failure to entertain the possibility that not all the defendants merited a death sentence (three were, in fact, acquitted; seven imprisoned for life; the others hanged) – deepened pessimism in western Europe and North America about the prospect for postwar cooperation with the USSR.[126] A wartime alliance of necessity, always fraught, frayed more quickly in the absence of a shared enemy. That the allies were now no longer bound together in a common cause was underscored in March 1946 by Churchill's dramatic speech at Fulton, Missouri, urging the West to be on its mettle against Soviet expansionism. Declaring that an 'Iron Curtain' had descended from Stettin to Trieste, he elevated a theatrical fire precaution into the reigning metaphor for Europe's ideological schism.[127] Needless to say, the German defendants revelled in the discomfort that arose when Churchill's rhetoric was relayed to Nuremberg, with *Stars & Stripes* (the only available newspaper) booming: 'Unite to Stop Russians, Churchill Warns.' The former premier's salvo 'exploded over the Allied courthouse in wrecked Nuremberg like a large, postwar bombshell', observed Flanner. The temperature of relations between the former allies plummeted several degrees. Thereafter, as tension escalated, movement between the rival spheres of influence became more hazardous, if not altogether impossible, as though a sheet-metal partition really did sever East from West.[128]

Nuremberg hinted at the shape of things to come during four decades of cold war. From the Soviets' dress and disposition at the IMT, the western powers derived various conclusions: that the Kremlin didn't play by the same rules as London and Washington, but also that, for an emergent 'superpower' (in the new coinage), the USSR was singularly underwhelming, the Red Army's size and strength apart. One feature of the Soviet representatives' appearance that struck both western observers and self-appraising Russians was its sorry drabness. In an arena where clothing was, in one way or another, intended to impress, Soviet dress sent all the wrong signals. Flanner, for instance, pointed to how easily 'Russian female interpreters and typists' could be 'identified, in court or out of it' by their shapeless 'military looking frocks'.[129] More telling, though, was the fact that prominent *Soviet* figures delivered the same verdict. Mikhail Dolgopolov, a senior editor at the Soviet information bureau and 'informal informant' on the IMT, sent a memo back to the Kremlin criticizing how his fellow comrades presented themselves at Nuremberg. Either they under-performed in their roles or, even when doing a competent job, they looked unpolished. Dolgopolov informed his superiors that '[t]he clothing of our female personnel is so bad and looks so poor that the Americans and English make fun of them.' If Soviet representatives were going to be sent all over the world, it would be essential 'to give some attention' to matters of self-presentation.[130]

Drabness was not, of course, a new theme in western representations of Soviet life. Pre-war cinematic depictions of the USSR had already established the trope of androgynous joylessness under communism, with Soviet women forced into 'male' spheres of labour and deprived of the feminine pleasures of consumption. Ernst Lubitsch's 1939 comedy *Ninotchka* – tagline 'Greta Garbo Laughs' – built its plot around the premise that female comrades, oppressed by Soviet austerity, would readily trade the Communist Party line for frivolous Parisian delights, from champagne to lingerie. By the time Rouben Mamoulian transformed Lubitsch's romantic comedy (in 1957) into a musical vehicle for Fred Astaire and Cyd Charisse, *Silk Stockings*, the dowdiness of Soviet women was even more firmly entrenched.[131] In George Orwell's *Nineteen Eighty-Four*, published in 1949, women were required by Big Brother's state to wear functional, unflattering clothes and no make-up. Popularized through film and television adaptations, serialized in magazines and radio broadcasts, Orwell's novel enduringly shaped western visions of the eastern bloc. That 'Air Strip One' bore more than a passing resemblance to postwar Britain was conveniently overlooked by those who preferred to read *Nineteen Eighty-Four* as a factual account of 'actually existing' communism rather than as a dystopian satire.[132]

It became a cold war article of faith that women behind the Iron Curtain craved stylish apparel, and more consumer goods in general, than state-directed economies oriented to other goals could provide. In the 1950s, American cold warriors began to cultivate consumerist dissatisfaction behind the Iron Curtain, waging what eminent sociologist David Riesman satirically conjured as a 'nylon war'. If American 'psy-warriors' didn't *physically* bombard the USSR with nylons, lipsticks, toasters and tampons, as in Riesman's imaginary scenario, they did something not dissimilar, mounting elaborate exhibits of US consumer products with which to dazzle the 'captive nations'. The most famous of these ventures was held at Moscow's Sokolniki Park in 1959. Although best remembered as the site of Nikita Krushchev's and Richard Nixon's notorious 'kitchen debate', the American National Exhibition also prominently showcased American cosmetics, shoes and fashions.[133]

This dramatic event was some thirteen years distant when the Nuremberg trial concluded on 1 October 1946. More imminent than Washington's attempt to detach Soviet citizens from the Kremlin by kindling their acquisitive instincts was the western powers' combined effort to satisfy *German* material needs. In the immediate postwar period, Germans feared that their destitution might persist indefinitely, prolonged by victors who wanted a defeated population to keep suffering. The month after the IMT concluded, one of Gollancz's interlocutors detailed that, on current British projections, it would take nearly a century to equip the adult population of Düsseldorf with coats and shoes, and 266 years to outfit all women with 'one pull-over or knitted waist-coat'.[134] But a radical reversal lay just ahead, hinted by the realignment of power that the IMT exemplified and helped exacerbate.

British and American policymakers became increasingly convinced that earlier plans to deindustrialize and pauperize Germany would not produce stability but enhance the appeal of totalitarianism. Hungry and threadbare Germans would, they feared, prove easy marks for political extremists – whether a resurgent neo-Nazi movement or the German Communist Party, empowered in the Soviet zone and seeking traction in the west. A wartime focus on *reparation* was overtaken by a postwar fixation with *preparation*: for a third world war envisioned as a showdown between 'the West', now including the western zones of Germany, and the Soviet bloc. Politicians in Westminster and Washington thus sought to rebuild German industry, integrating the economy of the new Federal Republic of Germany (established in 1949) with that of reconstructed western Europe.[135] Far from being a non-essential sideshow whose resurrection would have to wait, as British policy initially decreed, Germany's clothing manufacturers were early participants in this boom. Lauding the revitalization of the German fashion industry in 1947, one British columnist's breathlessness conveyed how far the attitudinal pendulum had swung in Germans' favour: 'If they can use what is left of the ingenuity which produced rocket-bombs and jet planes, and artificial rubber and light-weight locomotives to produce the export goods which the world needs so desperately now, they will have gone a little way towards atoning for the terrible crime they committed against humanity.'[136]

In retrospect, what's most striking about Germany's bitterly remembered 'hunger years' isn't their prolonged duration. It's the unexpected speed with which economic misery was supplanted by 'miracle'. Equally remarkable is the swiftness with which Britons who'd so recently cowered at the V-2 rocket's terrifying sibilance came to revel in German technological ingenuity. On the fault-line between the cold war's antagonistic blocs, West Germany became a major recipient of US largesse, channelled through the Marshall Plan for European reconstruction that was launched in 1948. Germany was not, however, *the* major beneficiary of Marshall aid. That prize – or, in some eyes, doubtful distinction – would be claimed by the United Kingdom.[137]

6 WORKERS

The weekend before the Allied judges delivered their verdicts on the German war criminals at Nuremberg, approximately 20,000 Britons joined an enormous throng outside the Victoria and Albert Museum (V&A) in Kensington. They were waiting to see an exhibit titled 'Britain Can Make It' (BCMI), opened by the King on 24 September 1946. Mass Observers, sent to quiz people in the queue on their expectations, found that the crush hadn't deterred potential visitors. If anything, the round-the-block line exerted a magnetic tug. Conditioned by years of wartime shortages, Britons now 'feel that unless there is a queue for something it can hardly be worth having', MO proposed. 'On balance "Britain Can Make It" got a considerable build-up from the publicity of its great queues.'[1] Fear of missing out, then as now, was a powerful motivator. Indeed, so many people wanted to test whether all the ballyhoo about BCMI was warranted that, by the time the exhibition closed in December, nearly one-and-a-half million visitors had jostled their way through the V&A's ground floor to inspect objects that might – one day – fall within reach of the average British consumer.[2]

Organized by the Council of Industrial Design, 'Britain Can Make It' aspired to showcase national ingenuity in the production and promotion of consumer products. In the words of Sir Stafford Cripps, the exhibition would be 'a revelation of some of the better and pleasanter goods for which the people of this and other countries had been waiting patiently since the end of the war'.[3] The exhibit's very name signalled plucky self-confidence: a fresh spin on the defiant wartime motto 'Britain Can Take It' that had shaken an imaginary fist at *Luftwaffe* pilots during the darkest hours of the Blitz.[4] With bombing raids now a thing of the past, BCMI offered a preview of modish lifestyles that, in contrast to the dreariness of late 1946, were aerodynamic, curvilinear and pastel-hued. Visitors could step into model rooms staged with futuristic furniture and fixtures: a television in an oversized cabinet teetering on metal spider-legs; an air-conditioned bed shaped like a giant bob-sleigh; a kitchen boasting an 'atomic cooker'. Some housewives, *Picture Post* reprovingly noted, found this appliance 'a little frightening' – though barely a year after the obliteration of Hiroshima and Nagasaki, cautious women could be forgiven for giving it a wide berth.[5]

Novelty gimmicks formed a minority element of an exhibition dominated by fashion and fabrics. With the government promoting export of British textiles as key to refurbishing national finances, it followed that artfully presented garments and extravagant drapes of material, along with boldly patterned rugs and carpets, would enjoy pride of place. One quarter of the entire exhibition area, extending to 90,000 square feet, was dedicated to dress fabrics, men's and women's apparel and accessories, and infants' and teenagers' clothing. Corsets, observed the fashion columnist Alison Settle, were the only garments conspicuously overlooked. The squeamish men in charge 'concede that feet require shoes, that hands require gloves, but refuse to believe that figures need any support'.[6] Prudish about foundation garments they may have been, but the architects of BCMI weren't reticent about the military origins of some new fabrics. The exhibit proudly touted wartime innovations in the manufacture of synthetic materials – civilian crossovers somewhat less alarming than the 'atomic cooker'. 'A plastic evening shoe', enthused the *Manchester Guardian*, 'emerges as the result of a new plastic moulding process used for gun turrets', while 'a beach bag and shoes are made of a specially treated waterproof cotton used for Commando jackets'. A woman's coat fashioned from 'woven fabric perfected for the protection of gun crews against cold and damp' would surely prove just the ticket for chilly hours spent in queues.[7]

Mannequins displaying women's fashions, everything from sensible Utility garments to sensational evening gowns, assumed their frozen positions on an elaborate revolving stage. With a backdrop painted to resemble Hyde Park, topped by a twenty-five-foot bird-cage, this exhibit was one of BCMI's most frequented areas. Not all comment was favourable, however. *Picture Post* identified the Hall of Fashion as a 'weak point', and female attendees' verdicts were mixed.[8] There were, one middle-aged woman regretted, 'far too many things which seemed to express a frantic straining after design rather than beauty or usefulness'. In her opinion, these were 'clothes which none of our modern women will envy or attempt to copy'.[9] Meanwhile, the *Daily Mail*'s Graham Stanford plucked twenty-year-old Sylvia Wenn from the paper's typing pool so that he could observe how an 'ordinary London working girl' responded to fashions displayed 'against a tanta-lizing background of shimmering nylon'. Sylvia, related Stanford, had spent her young life 'starved of glamour': 'She has one pair of nylons; one pair brown gloves; no evening dress; and her powder puff is made of cotton wool.' Although Sylvia appeared as bewitched as her chaper-one evidently expected her to be, she also wanted to know when – with a boyfriend about to be demobilized and no coupons left – she could expect to acquire such outfits herself.[10]

Sylvia's reaction was so widely shared that the exhibit soon acquired a sardonic new name: 'Britain Can't Get It'. Many visitors bristled at the reminder that Britons couldn't expect gratification of consumerist appetites whetted at the V&A until some deferred moment in the future. 'Well, I am a bit disappointed that we can't buy some of the things <u>now</u>,' confessed one woman to a Mass Observer. 'It's one thing knowing that "Britain Can Make It" but what I want to know is when can Britain <u>get</u> it.'[11] That most of the goods on display were *not* currently available for purchase wasn't something the exhibitors sought to hide. Stickers indicated which items could already be bought, as opposed to products that would only later become available. A third sticker occasioned even greater chagrin: goods currently in produc-tion – but only for export.[12] One masochistic forty-year-old housewife announced that her whole purpose in visiting the exhibit was to 'see what it is we're sending abroad and can't have ourselves. Anything that is good gets sent for export. Only the rotten things remain for us to use.'[13]

This embittered verdict, although unfair to well-made Utility fashions, expressed the frustration felt by many postwar Britons as they waited ever longer for a peace dividend that still seemed unreachably distant.[14] Some doubtless appreciated that a major impediment stood between Britons and the better-quality export goods already enjoyed by wealthy foreigners. The unfortunate reality was that Britain could *not* make it, or not unaided. 'Are we TOO FEW for the job?,' *Picture Post* pertinently inquired in April 1947. Answer: yes. The nation's workforce was dwindling. Thousands of young men continued to be ushered annually into the armed forces while their older brothers were demobilized. A prewar pledge to elevate the school leaving age to 15 was projected to remove 750,000 teenagers from the workforce in 1947, along with about 100,000 freshly minted teachers needed to educate these extra pupils.[15] Meanwhile, many German and Italian POWs, numbering 335,000 by October 1945, were poised to depart. (Coincidentally, the first cohort of repatriated German prisoners set sail just as BCMI opened.[16]) Prisoners, whose labour helped sustain farming, forestry and logging operations in the absence of British servicemen, were not the only ones to leave Britain en masse. All told, between 1946 and 1960, one-and-a-half million Britons – from a total population of forty-seven million – set sail for Canada, New Zealand, Australia and South Africa. Others, including the 'GI brides' discussed in the next chapter, headed for America.[17]

As Attlee's cabinet was well aware, Britain couldn't hope to restore its war-battered fortunes without an immediate influx of workers. The need for labour was particularly acute in the textile industries so crucial to redressing the country's balance-of-payments deficit. 'Britain's Bread Hangs by Lancashire's Thread' was 'no empty catch-phrase', Cripps reminded Britons. It was 'a hard truth that must be constantly before us'.[18] A country that imported fully half its food supplies needed robust export sales to pay for what it ate. But who would spin and weave Lancashire's cotton, along with Yorkshire's wool and Scotland's jute, into the high-quality fabrics that would earn urgently needed dollars overseas? Finding sufficient labour proved a tremendous challenge, not least because Attlee's government was so reluctant to recruit workers from the colonies – as the hasty expulsion of Black RAF veterans on ships like the *Bergensfjord* attested. When British women failed to step up in sufficient numbers, the government began scouring the displaced persons (DP) camps of Germany and Austria to find 'volunteer workers' willing to refashion their lives in Britain.

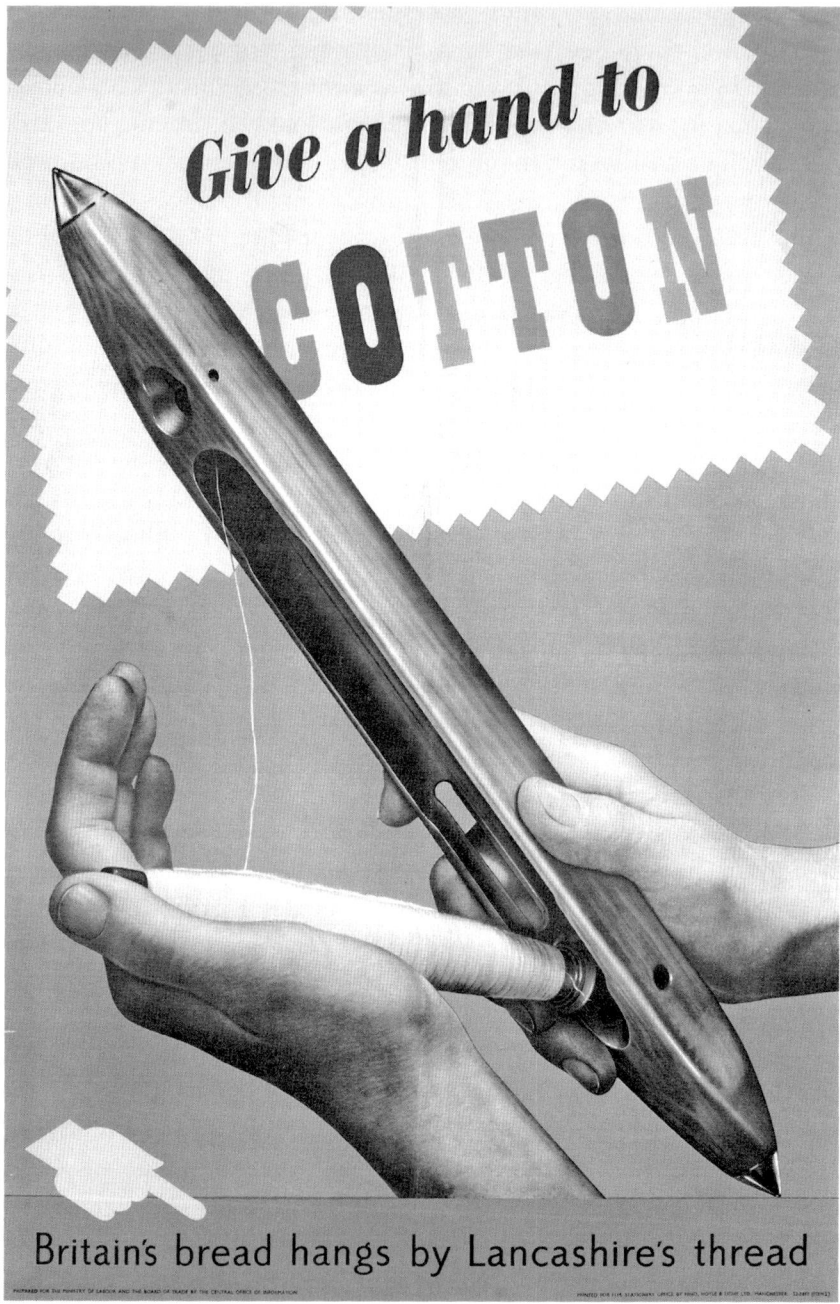

Figure 6.1 Posters like this one, prepared in 1947 for the Ministry of Labour by the Central Office of Information, urged British workers to take up jobs in under-staffed cotton mills (© Imperial War Museum, PST 14943)

'We Can't Get On without the Women'

Today, the very vocabulary of textile manufacturing evokes a long-lost industrial heritage, archaic and alien to most British ears. How many of us could differentiate a ring-mule from a jenny, or specify what tasks strippers, grinders, carders, little piecers, big piecers, doublers or tenters performed? With hindsight, we know that Britain's historic position as the world's leading manufacturer of fabrics, acquired through the Industrial Revolution and sustained up to the outbreak of World War I, would never be regained after 1945. By the 1970s, British textile output lagged far behind foreign competitors. Pakistan and India, whose textile industries British imperialism bankrupted in the nineteenth century, rebounded with the introduction of automatic looms in the 1940s, soon leapfrogging over Lancashire. Postwar Japan also saw its cotton manufacturing capacity rejuvenated under US military government, which preferred to boost light industries over heavier (potentially more militaristic) production.[19]

Even in the 1940s, anyone familiar with the industry wouldn't have needed extraordinary prescience to predict the terminal decline of British textiles.[20] After a slump induced by the Great War, manufacturers proved as slow to modernize machinery as they were reluctant to improve workplace conditions. During the Depression, mass unemployment afflicted Lancashire and Yorkshire. As George Orwell observed, the 'road to Wigan Pier' was littered with human debris generated by an industry that tore heedlessly through its expendable workforce. Despite improved conditions in the late 1930s, long lay-offs and short-time working remained commonplace when orders temporarily slackened, with wages in most branches of textile work lagging well behind those of other industrial workers. World War II boosted the fortunes of makers of uniforms and demob suits, but dealt a further blow to many manufacturers of yarn and fabric. Imports of raw materials stalled as sea lanes closed and the Navy commandeered mercantile shipping. Meanwhile, the government-mandated 'concentration' of industry that took effect from May 1941 funnelled workers away from mills into munitions, where they stood to make substantially more money. All told, British textile industries lost about 200,000 employees, or one-third of their workforce, during the war. Production of cotton yarn and cloth, along with other textiles, contracted even further, halving between 1937 and 1945.[21] In January 1946, a Board of Trade working party on the cotton industry estimated that employment in doubling (the combining and twisting together of fibres), spinning and weaving in Lancashire was 42 per cent lower than necessary to restore pre-war levels of productivity: a shortfall amounting to 175,000 workers.[22] Just as troublingly for the woollen industry in neighbouring West Yorkshire, the number of school-leavers entering that sector plummeted from 40 per cent before the war to 20 per cent in 1945.[23]

Although the writing on the wall was unmistakable, the government set out to resuscitate the manufacture of British cloth and clothing. Textiles comprised 20 per cent of British exports in 1946: a figure the Board of Trade needed to boost. Between 1945 and 1949, the government invested significant sums on publicity campaigns aimed at recruiting more textile workers. Since all branches of textile work relied heavily on female labour – cheaper and more readily hired and fired than better unionized male workers – women formed the key audience for these initiatives. Keen to recapture women who'd left the workforce as soon as 'deconcentration' of industry began in March 1945, the government pressed employers to alter shift-work patterns and introduce more part-time opportunities that would appeal to married women.[24]

Numerous posters, pamphlets, magazine adverts and short films trumpeted a message of national urgency and patriotic duty. The Central Office of Information (the Ministry of Information's successor) pursued every possible angle, from emphasizing the short-term nature of the crisis to conjuring the prospect of restored national prosperity, as well as the less tangible – but more imminent – reward of workplace camaraderie. 'We Can't Get On Without the Women. And that means YOU,' one particularly insistent poster implored. 'We can't win back prosperity without the women's help. Our *man*power is not sufficient, and Britain is up against it.' Concluding with a reminder of the money they'd pocket, this ad tacitly conceded that women were likelier to be tempted into textile work by economic incentives than by abstract appeals to duty. The war years had, after all, seen more than enough of those.[25]

From the very start of 'deconcentration', luring women back from munitions into textiles proved an uphill struggle. As early as April 1945, Alison Settle observed that released female war workers, prodded by the Ministry of Labour to return to spinning and weaving, 'have so far shown little eagerness to do so'.[26] The sources of this unwillingness weren't hard to fathom. 'Women's jobs are mostly repetitive, boring in themselves and widely regarded as monotonous,' remarked Ferdynand

Zweig, a plain-spoken surveyor of Britain's industrial scene.[27] Mill owners, overseers and male-dominated unions ensured that 'women's work', categorized as unskilled, was paid at a lower rate than skilled processes reserved for men. Since the manual dexterity required of female operatives was ascribed not to acquired aptitude but to anatomical difference, a product of nimbler fingers, the gendered division of labour appeared immutable. Employers also regarded women as more prone to absenteeism, less adaptable to change and not worth the cost of training, given their shorter 'shelf-life' in factory work – a 'dreamy interlude between childhood and marriage', in J. B. Priestley's characterization. As a result, female textile operatives were consigned to more tedious tasks and the scantier wages they commanded.[28]

Mills were not enticing workplaces, whatever the worker's role. Hazardous and insanitary, most facilities were noisy, dirty, poorly ventilated and filled with lung-clogging particulate matter. Many lacked indoor lavatories, shudder-inducing 'pail closets' serving as a rudimentary alternative. Oppressed by long hours, low pay and insecure work that exerted a heavy toll on the health and dignity of workers forced to relieve themselves in buckets, some likened their status to that of slaves who, less than a century before, had cultivated the crop on which Lancashire's prosperity depended.[29] While some men described themselves as 'driven like slaves', the status of the 'mill girl' was lowlier still – a function of the consequential distinction between what was perceived as 'clean' and 'dirty' work. 'Many mill girls confessed that when going on holiday they often conceal the fact that they are "mill girls" because of the low popularity of these jobs,' Zweig explained.[30]

Garment workers who cut, sewed and pressed textiles into articles of clothing fared little better than spinners and weavers in conditions and wages. This sector was in decline too. By mid 1944, only 65,000 men and 284,00 women were involved in garment-making.[31] Writing in June 1945 in *The Garment Worker* (the National Union of Tailors and Garment Workers' monthly magazine), Bernard Sullivan of London City Council painted a bleak picture of sweatshop workers' unenviable lot:

> The Garment Worker is not a machine-minder, but an operator. A girl who spends nine to ten hours per day watching the needle of her machine and manipulating the cloth and lining to make a battle-dress or a civilian garment is experiencing a strain that must affect the health of the operator. In addition, few firms have

ideal air-conditioning in the factory, noises wear the nerves, especially when the wireless is abused by programmes that are unsuitable, and bad cooking or an unbalanced diet helps on the sickness that is responsible for a large proportion of absenteeism.[32]

Grim conditions in mills and sweatshops were brought into sharper focus by the munitions plants and light engineering firms to which many textile workers had been redeployed during the war. 'One of the troubles', Hugh Dalton acknowledged to an audience of garment workers in April 1945, 'was that some sections of the textile industries were much less attractive to the workers than the engineering jobs they were on now.' He was, he insisted, chivvying mill owners to modernize their facilities, improving both the conditions and the compensation they offered.[33] This theme – that 'modern' mills weren't what they used to be – occupied a prominent place in government publicity ventures. A half-hour-long film produced under Central Office of Information auspices in 1946, *Cotton Come Back*, staged a familial drama in which the daughters of a hard-bitten Lancashire weaver, laid off in the Depression, try to persuade him that things have changed. They entice him to a town hall screening and discussion, during which the film-within-a-film projects the larger message about the necessity of boosting textile production to pay for Britain's imports. Later taken on a tour around the upgraded facility, the father is impressed by the breathable air and machines humming almost inaudibly. There's even a dance-hall around which smiling pairs of workers contentedly glide. Mills, it seemed, could be not only cheerful workplaces but also conducive to romance.[34]

Embellishing this theme, government propaganda sought to give mill girls a glamorous makeover – more Beverley Hills than Wigan Pier. 'Get your fashion and beauty editors to solve some of the day-to-day problems of women,' Cripps prompted an audience of magazine proprietors in January 1948. 'For instance, how can permanent waves be protected from the steamy atmosphere of a mill? These are important matters to women and they will value your help. The mill girl of today is rightly not content with the clog and shawl, she wants to look and can look as attractive as any other girl in the country.'[35] Women must be encouraged to believe they could work in textiles *and* resemble models or movie stars. Better yet, they could achieve extraordinary feats of productivity while oozing sex appeal, simultaneously Hollywood starlet and Stakhanovite hero.[36]

Figure 6.2 At Brook Mills in Hollinwood, near Oldham, Margaret Colley carries an outsize load of bobbins, 13 April 1948 (Daily Herald Archive/via Getty Images)

Campaigns to recruit more women ran alongside exhortations that existing workers must increase their productivity. Tactics that mightn't have been out of place in Leningrad were transposed to Lancashire. In Nelson, a month-long campaign to drive up output saw the erection of 'Nelson's column' in the town centre, indicating (thermometer-style) rising output of cotton towards an elevated target. Manufacturers bestowed weekly awards on workers with the highest productivity, while the coronation of 'cotton queens' rewarded radiant looks and valiant effort. These stunts found a counterpart in the West Riding's woollen towns and cities. In Bradford, cinemas held fashion shows between screenings, attempting to seduce women with displays of stylish apparel they could wear as a result of their toil, if only they 'got weaving'.[37]

All this effort was, however, to relatively little avail. Those already working in textiles resented the implication that they weren't working hard enough. Many women who had quit after the war, or had just left school, couldn't be tempted by textile work, especially if they didn't absolutely *have* to contribute to household finances. As servicemen came home, some young women longed to marry and start families or to resume a domestic life that had been interrupted by military service. The marriage rate in 1945 rose to 19 per 1,000, with a trend towards not only more marriages but also at younger ages than during the Depression. One in four brides was not yet twenty-one in 1945; in 1938, the figure had been one in six.[38] Running alongside government entreaties to women to lend their support 'a little longer' was an equally plangent counter-message, promoted by Church leaders and other conservative opinion shapers, stressing restoration of family life as *the* pre-eminent postwar imperative. That meant a breadwinner husband and a stay-at-home wife who raised the children and ran the household.[39]

Women didn't necessarily share this vision of divinely ordained domesticity to seek release from factory work sooner rather than later. One fifteen-year-old piece worker offered MO a candid riposte to an enquiry about her postwar employment plans:

> I won't go in for anything after the war. I'll go in for a man and get married and finish with this sort of work. If I could find a man to marry me I wouldn't come out to work, not me. Me and my friend, we'd be the first to be kicked out. They wouldn't keep us on here. We get thrown out of one room after another for cheek and sauce – we do our work all right and earn our money – but they don't like you having a bit of fun. They like keeping you down. If we laugh a bit, or if we sing to the wireless, they're down on us at once. I don't like it. I want a life that feels more free, where you can do what you like.

In her eyes, 'settling down' appealed as another way to defy adult expectations: a lark like exuberant singing and saucing the overseer. Far from being beholden to church-bound tradition, this young woman revelled in her sassy irreverence. And it's not hard to appreciate why the idea of playing at house, being 'kept' by a husband, seemed more appealing than ten hours a day spent inhaling fluff while minding a spinning mule. She could, at least, dream of a more leisurely and pampered existence.[40]

For many wives, however, marriage proved a bitter disappointment. Historians use the term 'double burden' to invoke the dual obligations female workers shouldered when they combined paid employment with the unpaid labour required to manage a household. But 'triple' or 'quadruple burden' would more accurately convey the multiple responsibilities – physically strenuous and often psychologically exhausting – that working wives and mothers assumed. Many communities established exacting schedules for housework, along with high expectations of the rigour with which it would be completed. In Lancashire, Monday was laundry day (without the benefit of washing machines or detergents). Upstairs rooms were tackled on Tuesdays, downstairs on Wednesdays; then there were windows to be cleaned as well as front steps to be swept, washed and polished. Needless to say, socks didn't darn themselves any more than groceries magically materialized in the pantry. The laborious business of managing coupon books and queuing for provisions didn't stop when the war ended. As clothes rationing hit harder, along with more stringent controls over food, queues likewise lengthened.[41]

Maintaining a clean and tidy house was only the beginning. Children had to be clothed, fed and coddled. So did husbands. Many had their own exacting expectations of wifely duty both in the bedroom and in the kitchen. Barrow housewife and diarist Nella Last regretted having to rush home from satisfying work with the WVS to make tea for her ungrateful husband. Infuriated by his unwillingness to do so much as boil a kettle, Nella intuited that men's helplessness, learnt not innate, was a crude mechanism – along with taciturn moods – whereby husbands asserted dominance over wives.[42] For some women, including Nella, marriage was a far cry from the romantic fantasies entertained by teenage girls fed a sugary diet of movies and magazines in which tying the knot represented the pinnacle of feminine achievement and a guarantee of 'ever after' happiness. Labour sociologist Ferdynand Zweig delivered a verdict on the state of postwar marriage even more damning than his appraisal of the demeaned status of 'women's work'. 'Not only in industry itself does woman need a fairer deal but also at home. Often in her home her spirit is crushed and her self-confidence broken. If women are expected and willing to contribute to family livelihood, is it not fair that men should contribute their share to the drudgery of work at home?'[43]

Of course it was fair! But, in the late 1940s, the answer to Zweig's rhetorical question was that, however reasonable women's desire that husbands chip in with chores, many men willingly left all the drudgery to their wives. This included raising children. Lack of childcare seriously impeded women's participation in the paid labour force of the late 1940s. During the war, some mill owners and municipalities opened nurseries that were either free or heavily subsidized for working mothers. But, under conditions of austerity, funding for creches was slashed, despite the escalating urgency of the Ministry of Labour's pleas for married women to 'come back' into the factories.[44] This false economy was one of many reasons why no amount of exhorting or 'glamourizing the mill girl' could cajole as many women to get spinning or weaving as the government wished.

By the end of December 1947, an estimated 6,620,000 women aged 15 to 60 were in paid employment from a total female population (between these ages) of 15,640,000. Women represented just 17.4 per cent of Britain's insured workforce.[45] This statistic makes it all the more revealing that 31 per cent of emigrants (aged twenty to twenty-nine) who departed Britain between 1946 and 1949 were female. Particularly galling to the government was Australia's poaching of women textile workers.[46]

From Displaced Person to European Volunteer Worker

For all these reasons, although Attlee's administration fervently *hoped* that more British women would join the workforce, it anticipated a shortfall. As early as 1946, the Ministry of Labour (MoL) began exploring other avenues. If Britons could not make it unaided, the government would look overseas to plug labour gaps in key industries. One sizeable group of prospective foreign workers was already in Britain: Poles who'd served with the British armed forces during the war and who resisted returning to a Sovietized Poland. In 1946, the government introduced a Polish Resettlement Scheme, permitting former servicemen and their families to remain permanently in Brtain.[47] (Sixty-six of the *Windrush*'s passengers in June 1948 were Polish wives and children of men allowed to settle in Britain under this scheme.) In 1946, the MoL also decided to recruit women from DP camps in continental Europe to work in British hospitals and TB sanatoria and as domestic servants. Operation Balt Cygnet, as this scheme was codenamed, fancifully implied that Latvian, Estonian and Lithuanian young women plucked from German DP camps would be gracefully transfigured by the experience of bed-making, laundering and scrubbing in Britain.[48]

Once British officials had agreed to recruit Baltic DPs for these roles, they soon extended the same expedient to other under-staffed sectors of the economy. In 1947, MoL personnel, with Cabinet and Home Office blessing, devised a much more expansive scheme, breezily named Operation Westward Ho!, which aimed to bring 100,000 men and women from German and Austrian DP camps to Britain as European Volunteer Workers (EVWs). Female recruits would be channelled primarily into depleted tributaries of the textile industries: cotton spinning and doubling, woollens and worsted, hosiery, rayon and silk, flax, textile bleaching, dyeing and finishing, wholesale clothing, plus boot and shoe manufacture. Men, meanwhile, would be dispatched to farms, sent down mines and shunted into steel mills and clay-pits.[49] One version of the scheme's genesis maintains that the idea of recruiting cotton workers from DP camps originated in November 1946 with UNRRA personnel in Germany. The British government apparently dismissed their proposition, deeming it 'as likely as the resettlement of the refugees on the "mountains of the moon"'. But, earlier that autumn, British cotton manufacturers and MoL officials had already visited Germany, returning with a draft plan to recruit 100,000 DP workers, destined not for the moon but for the mills. The Cabinet's Foreign Labour committee duly endorsed a plan in December 1946 to select prospective cotton spinners from Europe's DP camps.[50]

Westminster dressed up 'Westward Ho' in different guises depending on the audience. To Britons, the importation of foreign workers was presented as a necessary – if, perhaps, regrettable – short-term fix to the nation's perilous labour shortage. Addressing UNRRA, in contrast, government officials packaged the scheme as primarily humanitarian. By turning DPs into 'volunteer workers', Britain would contribute to the so-called 'final solution' of Europe's DP problem, helping resettle camp residents so that UNRRA (or its successor organization, the International Refugee Organization) could wind up operations. The MoL needed UNRRA's assistance to facilitate British recruiters' access to DP camps and to support the complex logistics of transporting thousands of 'volunteers' to holding centres on Germany's coast, pending shipment to Britain: a hiatus that, though intended to last mere days, often stretched to several dismal weeks.[51] UNRRA obliged, but staff in the organization's Paris HQ weren't fooled by the charitable framing of 'Westward Ho'. If the British government's goal was to offer a *permanent* home to uprooted refugees, why were officials so intent on negotiating terms with the allied Control Commission in Germany for the deportation of 'unsatisfactory' EVWs back to DP camps?[52] Humanitarian relief workers on the ground were even quicker to detect the whiff of insincerity in British officialdom's boasts of altruism. 'Of course, it's obviously not an emigration scheme at all,' one Quaker relief worker disparagingly remarked when wind of 'Westward Ho' reached her camp. 'It's quite openly just a labour project. Britain wants the workers; the D.P.s want to get out of Germany. But I don't see any guarantee that they'll be allowed to settle in England.'[53]

She had reason for scepticism. Although it later became clear that most EVWs *would* be permitted to stay in Britain indefinitely, recruitment materials failed to clarify the timeline according to which temporary recruits would turn into permanent residents. They were just as hazy on the question of how long 'volunteer workers' would remain tethered to the jobs to which they were first (involuntarily) assigned:

> Workers will enter Great Britain for an initial period of 12 months subject only to good behaviour and to the specific condition that they undertake only employment selected by the Ministry of Labour and National Service, and on the clear understanding that they will only be allowed to change their employment with the consent of that department.[54]

Not unreasonably, many DPs reading this MoL notice in German concluded that, after their first year in Britain, they could choose their own employment: freedom of manoeuvre the Ministry was loath to concede. The permanence or otherwise of these arrangements mattered intensely to potential recruits. Even if prospective EVWs didn't aspire to remain in Britain for good, they feared deportation back to Germany or Austria for whatever offences might be deemed 'bad behaviour'. And if they *did* subsequently leave Britain, former DPs wanted to make their own decisions about onward migratory routes, whether to North America or elsewhere.[55]

Many refugees desperate to escape the desolate futility of DP camps were willing to clutch at available straws, however flimsy. More off-putting than ambiguity surrounding conditions of employment and resettlement was the MoL's stipulation that potential recruits must be either single and childless or willing to be separated from their families for the time being. Bringing over dependants at a later date was an expensive commitment that the government undertook with great reluctance in the first instance, before deciding in July 1947 to abandon any promise to transport family members altogether. Restricting the scheme to single people, or those willing to travel to Britain alone, ensured that 'Westward Ho' never fulfilled its intended quota. Writing in the *Manchester Guardian*, Quaker relief worker Margaret McNeill predicted in October 1947 the impact this policy would have on recruitment. 'Having experienced the agonies of separation and disruption to a degree unknown in most people in England, families cling together with a passionate loyalty. There is ample evidence to show that until the dependents can accompany the workers to England the "Westward Ho" scheme will never become effective.'[56]

In addition to being devoid of – or willing to detach themselves from – family ties, potential volunteers had to be below the age of fifty (if they were men) or forty (if female), fit for strenuous work and free from infection. Recruits were subjected to medical examinations that included lung X-rays as well as tests for sexually transmitted

Figure 6.3 To help assist European Volunteer Workers in Britain, Estonian refugee Helmi Metz is recruited from a German DP camp to serve with UNRRA, wearing an army greatcoat with an UNRRA shoulder flash, 31 March 1947 (Keystone/Hulton Archive/Getty Images)

diseases.[57] In their desperation to leave the DP camps behind, some recruits dissembled in order to squeeze through restrictive eligibility criteria. Mothers presented themselves as childless. Women expecting babies misstated the date of their last periods to obscure pregnancies from doctors working on behalf of the MoL. Married couples, meanwhile, confronted the prospect of long-distance severance made necessary by Britain's geographical division of labour, with men sent to mines and steel plants often far removed from the mills of Lancashire and Lanarkshire or jute works of Dundee. One party of women was dispatched even further afield to Orkney.[58]

Once the Cabinet approved 'Westward Ho', recruitment accelerated with 'dazzling speed' – perhaps even more astonishing by today's dilatory rates of refugee-processing than by the lights of the late 1940s.[59] The MoL recruiters arrived in DP camps on 3 March 1947. In late April, the first arrivals, ferried across the North Sea on the troopships *Empire Halladale* and *Empire Weapons*, disembarked at Tilbury and Hull. A *Pathé* newsreel showed a group of women in headscarves and mangy fur-lapelled coats, waving from the deck with expressions variously grim or cheery, as the narrator reassured viewers about the vital contribution they'd make as 'cooks, canteen hands and waitresses', omitting any mention of mill work.[60] Within two months, 11,500 EVWs had arrived in Britain, with the scheme reaching its peak in March 1948, when more than 1,800 volunteers landed during a single week.[61] This frenetic pace isn't evident only with hindsight. '[T]he days following the announcement of the Westward Ho scheme passed like a hurried dream,' McNeill recalled in her memoir. 'A wave of optimistic urgency swept over the camps; and the first chance to break out of the bondage of dependence and uselessness was grasped with an almost hysterical hopefulness.'[62] Humanitarian workers in the other zones of Germany and Austria witnessed the same frantic expectancy as DPs refashioned their résumés to fit recruiters' preferences. Kathryn Hulme, an American relief worker in Bavaria, described the 'scramble of the DP's to get out of Germany [as] at once heartbreaking and humorous':

> The camp bulletin boards listing all the current avenues of escape made you think of some kind of macabre stock market that dealt in bodies instead of bonds. The DP's read the job offerings and rushed to qualify. When, for example, we posted the advance news that Canada would accept qualified tailors,

everyone who had ever sewed on a pants' button was a master tailor. Our DP nurses with diplomas from Leningrad, Warsaw and Kiev swore they had done a bit of tailoring before they studied nursing.[63]

Hulme was not alone in comparing rival recruiters' ruthlessly instrumental probings with the slave auctions of past centuries: 'markets' that resulted in anguishing family severance as human beings were reduced to tradable units of productive labour. A September 1948 editorial in *The Times* decried the unseemly scramble by various nations, including not just Britain but also Belgium, Australia and Canada, to recruit 'the young and strong and unmarried, leaving behind the women and children and infirm who most need help', regretting 'a touch of the slave market in the methods of selecting refugees'.[64] By 1948, accusations of 'slave labour' loomed large in the rhetorical cold war. Washington and London worked to expose the dense network of forced labour camps scattered across the USSR, the notorious Gulag, as emblematic of the 'slave world' of communism: a damningly concrete reality, not a flimsily figurative device. For its part, Soviet propaganda charged the British government with being a 'modern trader in slaves'. This stinging accusation helped soften the MoL's initial determination to bind EVWs to jobs they wanted to escape after the first twelve-month period. If Moscow's charge of 'slave labour' were to be refuted, the British government could hardly trap indentured 'volunteers' in despised jobs forever.[65]

'Clothed in Prospective Britishness'

In one signal regard, the 'trade' in European migrant workers failed to resemble chattel slavery – an institution dependent on the dehumanization of black-skinned Africans. The architects of Operation Westward Ho!, in contrast, employed a racial schema that favoured impeccably white, and often middle-class, Baltic refugees. In unabashedly eugenicist terms, mixing metaphors of blood transfusion and animal husbandry, government officials hailed European incomers who'd help replenish Britain's depleted 'stock'.[66] Relief worker Francesca Wilson, who, like McNeill and Hulme, spent several months after the war in Europe's DP camps, ventriloquized the logic governing the British government's selection criteria: 'Of all these

DPs the Balts would be the easiest to assimilate in Great Britain or her Dominions. Their standard of living and of education is high – they would never become coolie labour. (The Esthonians [sic] and Latvians are Protestant – this makes assimilation rather easier.) They are nations of small owner-farmers, linking their economy through co-operative societies.' In Wilson's view, some ethnic groups were genetically predisposed towards subjugation. Not so the Balts and Ukrainians. They, Wilson enthused, were 'freedom-loving, sturdy peoples and the proportion of pro-Nazis among them is certainly not high' – a nod to the fact that some DPs had fled *to* Nazi Germany rather than endure Red Army occupation. A number had even served with the German military. Some former SS personnel managed to filter through the coarse mesh of 'political screening' undertaken by the MoL at the TUC's behest.[67]

The government's hierarchy of desirability avoided any appraisal of who had suffered most at the hands of Nazi Germany. This troubled some segments of British opinion. *The Times*, for example, proposed that an ethic of responsibility should shape immigration priorities, not economic expediency alone. An editorial entitled 'An Essential Import' (printed on 10 February 1947) elaborated which refugees should be favoured on 'moral and humanitarian grounds', including 'certain former inmates of concentration camps, non-Fascist political exiles, foreigners who directly helped the British military effort, uprooted Jewish families, and other homeless and Stateless refugees'. 'Westward Ho' not only favoured certain nationalities perceived as 'higher class', but also *excluded* the group of DPs who had survived Nazi genocide: stateless Jews.[68]

The reasons for this omission become clearer if we examine the MoL's efforts to sell 'Westward Ho' to Britons whom they assumed would need educating to overcome objections to imported migrant labour. The very designation 'European Volunteer Workers' was chosen to avoid the pejorative connotations of 'displaced persons'. The *Mail*'s Graham Stanford, who'd accompanied an ordinary London girl around 'Britain Can Make It' a few months earlier, characterized the eight million DPs adrift in Germany at the war's end as 'the human flotsam and jetsam of Europe'. 'The label "D.P." has', he remarked, 'become part of the post-war language', a lexical fact of life the MoL hoped to change.[69] Evaluating the relative negativity of various terms, MoL personnel rejected *'foreign'* as 'repugnant to the British'. Whatever doubts Britons harboured about people hailing from the far side of the Channel, 'Europeans' nevertheless occupied a step up the semantic ladder from 'foreigners'. Likewise, 'volunteer' signified something more elevated than (in Wilson's parlance) 'coolie'.[70] Up to a point, the MoL's terminological fix succeeded. '"Displaced Persons" who come to England to work lose their dreary status of 'displaced' and become, officially, "European Volunteer Workers",' wrote a *Manchester Guardian* columnist, replicating the official line.[71]

Nevertheless, in September 1947, Minister of Labour George Isaacs lamented that 'many people still seem to have the idea that these people were some of the scum of Europe'. A meeting held the following month to strategize how best to 'educate public opinion to acceptance of Foreign Workers' repeated this point in different language. A key goal was enunciated as attempting to 'dispel such views as that the EVWs are the "Jews of Europe"'. The MoL's personnel evidently understood 'flotsam and jetsam', 'scum' and 'DP' as interchangeable slurs.[72] But they were not in the business of tackling antisemitism. The MoL sought to eradicate British hostility towards EVWs not because prejudice was unacceptable, but because prejudicial attitudes were, in this instance, misplaced. In devising eligibility criteria for 'Westward Ho', the MoL did more than choose its terminology with care. It avoided recruiting Jewish DPs altogether. In 1947, British forces were fighting (and losing) a counterinsurgency campaign against armed Zionist groups, while attempting to block unauthorized migration of Jewish DPs from Germany to Palestine. These events fuelled already pronounced antisemitic sentiment in Britain, culminating in rioting and destruction of Jewish property in August 1947.[73] An MO survey conducted the same year found that, despite 'widespread sympathy for DPs in Europe', Britons 'object to anything, from Jews, that sounds insistent or that puts too much emphasis on rights and claims'. Attuned to this widespread prejudice, the government chose not to acknowledge that Jewish DPs had rights or claims that might be satisfied in Britain. *Picture Post* bluntly informed readers that the '11,000 Jews in Belsen are not being recruited'.[74]

As far as some Britons were concerned, despite a centuries-old Jewish population in Britain, Jews remained 'foreigners'. The stubborn insistence that Britain had always been – and ought to remain – a homogeneous 'island nation' was a misconception government personnel sought to overcome (even if they partially shared it) in promotional efforts to create a supportive environment for EVWs.[75] Via press conferences, monthly circulars to trade unions, ministerial statements and collaborations with the BBC and film-makers, as well as through its own publications, the MoL strove to embroider a national tradition of tolerance. According to a booklet titled *Workers from Abroad*, distributed by the thousand to trade unions, refugees had long found a safe haven in Britain. In this account, EVWs joined a lengthy string of oppressed Europeans seeking greater freedom and prosperity in the British Isles. Tellingly, this narrative emphasized incomers' economic contributions, particularly to textile industries, as well as their seamless integration into the fabric of British society: from Flemish weavers in the fourteenth century to the Huguenots who, 300 years later, founded Essex's silk industry.[76] 'So after all we have not forgotten that we were for centuries the asylum of refugees – Flemings, Huguenots and what not – and that far from being losers we gained greatly from them,' Francesca Wilson concluded in a cavalier reprise of the official line.[77]

Immigrants whose ethnic heritage could be blurred to a forgettable 'whatnot' were considered more easily absorbed than others. Perceived assimilability was the price of admission for migrants arriving in, or hoping to enter, Britain in the late 1940s. Balts, Ukrainians, Yugoslavs and (at a pinch) Poles fitted the bill. Jews did not. Nor did West Indians, like the RAF veterans who hoped to pursue further education, vocational training or paid employment in Britain, but found themselves bundled onto liners like the *Bergensfjord* – many soon returning again, as we saw in Chapter 4.[78]

Despite being British subjects, and despite chronic labour shortages, West Indians confronted pervasive discrimination as they searched for employment and housing in postwar Britain. The MoL made no efforts to educate public opinion on the desirability of Caribbean workers settling in Britain, instead pressing colonial officials to deter would-be migrants from undertaking the passage at all. Needless to say, West Indians noticed the glaring disparity whereby white Europeans were welcomed, while Black subjects of the Crown were cold-shouldered.[79] Writing with reference to EVWs, the historian Kathleen Paul observes that the government's 'intention was to transform aliens into citizens by clothing them in a discourse of potential Britishness'.[80] Paul's sartorial figure of speech is striking. The cloak of putative citizenship wasn't conjured from fabric but determined by skin tone. Unlike Latvians, Estonians and Ukrainians, West Indians were *already* British. Yet, because so many Britons conflated Britishness with whiteness, Caribbean settlers were deemed to lack the most essential attribute of citizenship: the pallor that would permit them to meld invisibly into an undifferentiated mass of Britons.

Opponents of Black migration spouted various claims about the unsuitability of West Indians for work in the very sectors into which female EVWs were bundled. Women from the Caribbean, detractors protested, would 'not be able to stand up to the Lancashire climate for any length of time', and, even if they could tolerate damp conditions, they didn't possess 'spinning fingers'.[81] Always specious, these assertions sound all the more discordant now, given the prominence attached in *Windrush* narratives to the profession of the lone female stowaway, Evelyn Wauchope. Like many other women who emigrated from the Caribbean to Britain in the late 1940s and 1950s, including several passengers on the *Windrush*, Evelyn was a dressmaker – work reliant on manual dexterity.[82] But, as far as Attlee's administration was concerned, European migrants alone possessed the nimble digits necessary to 'give a hand' to cotton: a point made clear by Stafford Cripps as he entreated Britons to extend a warm welcome to EVWs:

> They are a most useful if small addition to our labour force. They badly need friendliness and to be encouraged to speak English. Many of them can contribute, if allowed, to the life of a community out of working hours for they are often surprisingly neat fingered and clever with crafts and cooking. They are lonely people in a strange land but have come to help us and we must do our best to help them to fit into our social life.[83]

Although racialized double standards were stark, official messaging on 'Westward Ho' wasn't without hesitancy about 'foreigners' in general. The government White Paper *Economic Survey for 1947* (Cmd. 7046), which laid the groundwork for the anticipated arrival of 100,000 EVWs, made a half-hearted defence of immigration when it proposed that 'There is no danger *for years to come* that foreign labour will rob British workers of their jobs' (emphasis added).[84] To Britons who mistrusted alien interlopers, this phraseology vindicated their fears with its suggestion that, if not now, a time *would* come when immigrants jeopardized British jobs. As a study of EVWs' reception (written

Figure 6.4 Two West Indian women living in Britain browse through
pattern books, 1948 (Keystone/Hulton Archive/Getty Images)

in 1957) pointed out, these migrants were introduced 'somewhat apolo-
getically and subsequently looked upon as a necessary evil, a productive
asset in time of economic need, a liability otherwise'.[85] Cripps embod-
ied this ambivalence. After entreating Britons to befriend and anglicize
'neat fingered' Europeans, he gestured towards anti-immigrant sentiment in averring that 'most of us would rather see the industry manned
by British workers, if it could be managed'.[86] And, even though policymakers privileged Europeans over dark-skinned British subjects, they
also perceived numerous gradations of whiteness – not all as unblem-
ished, in the MoL's appraising gaze, as the Baltic ideal.

Irish immigrants, arriving in Britain in significant numbers in
the 1940s, encountered pervasive hostility: they were demeaned just
as much for their 'popishness' as for visible indices of poverty – like
outdated suits, conspicuously formal for day-labouring.[87] For different reasons, displaced ethnic Germans, a later addition to 'Westward
Ho', were also a hard sell to British trade unionists. The TUC negotiated, more or less grudgingly, with the MoL to accept EVWs. But
this consent was contingent on imported 'volunteers' constituting less

than 10 per cent of the workforce in any setting, and on EVWs being compensated at identical rates to British workers, alleviating the justifiable fear that employers would otherwise jump at the chance to pay foreign labourers less.[88] It took a separate round of negotiations with the Cotton Board, which insisted on political screening of Austrian and German recruits, to reach agreement that Sudeten Germans (who had been driven out of Czechoslovakia) would be hired for the cotton and rayon industries, starting in May 1949.[89]

Hostel Environment

Rhetorically clothed in 'prospective Britishness', EVWs required *actual* garments in order for them to travel from camps in Germany and take up jobs in Britain. Before they could produce textiles, immigrants had to acquire more, and more suitable, attire. A long voyage awaited selected recruits as they journeyed first from German DP camps to Seedorf 'holding centre'. From there, they were 'called forward' to Cuxhaven, near Hamburg on Germany's North Sea coast, when shipping became available. After disembarking in eastern England, they travelled by train to reception centres pending transfer to their final destinations, where new arrivals lived initially in hostels run by their employers or by the National Hostels Corporation.[90]

The MoL sub-contracted the work of outfitting EVWs to various third parties. On the continent, it fell to UNRRA and relief workers operating under its umbrella to ascertain how much clothing departing DPs already possessed and to distribute overcoats and blankets for the journey. On arrival in the UK, EVWs' clothing needs became the responsibility of the WVS: the wartime organization that operated clothing exchanges and ran myriad 'make do and mend' classes. Now, volunteers' expertise in outfitting evacuated children and 'bombees' would be redeployed to aid a fresh set of recipients.[91]

Britons' variegated responses to EVWs, spanning the gamut from warm solicitude to frosty suspicion, were often pegged to what they wore. This was nothing new. Migrants' clothing was invariably read as a barometer of social acceptability. Britons often deemed West Indian migrants' apparel too flimsy and flashy for under-stated, under-heated Britain, 'gaudy' and 'flamboyant' serving as shrill dog-whistle epithets. New arrivals from Ireland, in contrast, were commonly judged to possess too few garments. This verdict wasn't confined to outerwear whose condition observers could readily appraise. Immigrants reputed to have 'only the clothes on their backs' – and no underwear beneath – attracted prurient speculation about the miserable hovels from which they'd escaped: poverty so profound as to render underpants and vests unaffordable luxuries. As they contemplated assisting European volunteers, MoL and WVS personnel recalled problems billeting Irishmen who came to Britain during the war 'without any change of clothing'.[92] Another measure of Irish fecklessness, as unsympathetic Britons perceived it, lay in how these immigrants used their clothing coupons. For municipal authorities, rationing doubled as a surveillance mechanism to track individuals' whereabouts and spending habits, since coupon books were issued in conjunction with identity cards, tethering recipients to particular localities. Irish immigrants in south Wales reportedly treated ration books 'like money'. In other words, they illicitly traded coupons for cash on the black market.[93]

Migrants who amassed too *much* clothing were just as likely to attract the censorious judgement of nosy British neighbours as those with too little. In Barrow-in-Furness, Nella Last used her diary to express perplexity about what exactly Poles were stockpiling and then despatching in bulky brown-papered parcels at the Post Office. Asking a Pole directly, she resolved this mystery. 'They haunt the cheaper wardrobe shops in a rather poorer shopping street in search of garments and shoes to send back to Poland.' These Poles weren't breaking the law. Victor Gollancz's Save Europe Now campaign had successfully lobbied the government to lift a ban on worn clothing being mailed to Europe. Yet she seemed to feel that Poles were stretching the elasticity of host-country generosity too far. Equally expressive of widely shared sentiments was Last's characterization of 'over-decorated' women whom she suspected of 'buying things without coupons': 'They have the Jewish stamp.'[94]

Many hackneyed suspicions about migrants' clothing and black-market activities soon shadowed EVWs. While new recruits were mustering in Germany, relief workers struggled to ascertain precisely how many garments each individual possessed, fearing that unscrupulous customers would conceal items of apparel in order to receive extra clothing before they embarked for Britain. Some UNRRA workers noted that, for people who'd fled – or been torn – from their homes, and who'd then spent years as forced labourers of the Third Reich before becoming DPs, these uprooted migrants had amassed

surprising quantities of *stuff*.[95] Some reportedly set sail lugging disman-
tled bicycles and sewing machines. As they boarded ships at Cuxhaven,
migrants had to present German customs officers with lists of all the
possessions they were taking out of the country, including garments.
The MoL officials proposed that these itemized export dockets should
be preserved and presented by EVWs to WVS staff at the reception
centres to ensure that conniving individuals didn't (again) try to whee-
dle more than their fair share of clothing. Some immigrants, the WVS
regretted, were using 'ingenious artifices in order to obtain a free
issue'.[96]

Mistrust co-existed alongside more empathetic responses to
the challenges EVWs faced, both *en route* to Britain and on arrival.
The 'holding camp' at Seedorf, stripped bare of every portable fixture – from heaters to cooking utensils and light bulbs – by previous
occupants who'd left behind only rats, bugs and mice, was likened
by one British army officer to a 'concentration camp'. He further
recorded that some EVWs were so famished on Seedorf's scant rations
that they resorted to selling coats and suits on the black market to get
enough food.[97] In Rochdale, a welfare officer spoke up on behalf of
one female 'volunteer' sent without a winter coat to join the town's
legion of cotton spinners. Some women shared a single outer garment.
Meanwhile, several EVWs reportedly reached Wigan 'without a change
of underwear'.[98] Others had none at all. The most detailed account of
'Westward Ho' (published in 1957) recorded that 'Many girls arrived
at the textile mills with no underclothes and few outer garments. One
good-looking young woman wore a skirt which she had made herself
from the trousers of a German soldier and a blouse made from old
socks which she had unpicked and re-knitted.'[99] This author shouldn't
have been surprised to find that the 'ambition of the great majority was
to acquire some tangible signs of wealth – first, decent clothing, and
secondly, a house of their own. Money was saved with amazing speed.'
Deprivation fostered both ingenuity and parsimony.

The woman who artfully feminized *Wehrmacht* trousers
would soon have an opportunity to put her skills to use on *British*
army surplus. Much of the apparel distributed by the WVS was new or
reconditioned military stock originally earmarked for UNRRA distribution. The Ministry of Supply issued the WVS with 10,000 battledress
blouses, trousers, greatcoats and boots for men. Women's needs were
to be met with 5,000 overcoats, pairs of underwear (listed as 'new',

suggesting some special privilege), shoes and 'winycette nightdresses' – brushed cotton garments perhaps reclaimed from female veterans.[100] At the MoL's own admission, many ex-military items – like those circulating in occupied Germany – were 'inferior and shrunken', a verdict corroborated by a WVS volunteer at the Preston holding hostel. Free clothing was so 'unglamorous' that women would accept it 'only if in real need'.[101] No matter how undignified their circumstances, many EVWs aspired to high standards of self-presentation. But those sufficiently skilled to transform military garb into new guises didn't necessarily feel pride in accomplishment. Repurposed attire could provoke acute self-consciousness. One EVW later recalled the shame she experienced, a stranger in an unfamiliar country, dressed in a coat made from a blanket. Conceivably, the woman who refashioned *Wehrmacht* kit into a smart ensemble wouldn't have been quizzed about her outfit's provenance – and admired for her artistry – if she hadn't been young and good-looking.[102]

Much was bundled up in clothing distribution. The WVS organizers who liaised with the MoL about plans for EVWs' reception didn't understand the importance of outfitting migrant workers in purely utilitarian terms. As during the war, cast-off garments could do more than equip people with what they lacked. They knitted people together, and, in a chilly new environment, human warmth was as necessary a protective cover as a woollen overcoat. Clothing distribution could help meet what WVS founder Lady Reading deemed the greatest of these newcomers' needs: *friendship*. In supplying garments and explaining coupon books, WVS volunteers would simultaneously deliver informal English-language tuition.[103] But friendship, as Lady Reading conceived it, didn't spring so much from a desire for mutual understanding as it did from a one-way anglicizing mission: to 'help foreigners see with our eyes'.[104] To befriend was to refashion.

Sympathetic employers, as well as women volunteers and paid welfare officers, lobbied the government to see whether EVWs couldn't be given more – and better – clothing to meet distinct needs, as well as a more generous allowance of coupons than the fifteen they received on arrival, along with a miserly five shillings spending money. Women sent into mills required appropriate work-wear. The rationing system awarded industrial workers an extra ten coupons, and some employers argued that EVWs should be instantly eligible for these, rather than having to work for six months to merit the 'Industrial Ten'.[105] Since it wasn't common practice for mill owners to provide workers with boiler-suits or overalls that buttoned at the side or back (to ensure that clothing worn underneath didn't get caught in the machinery), employers had a vested interest in pushing the MoL to do more to help EVWs outfit themselves safely and swiftly for work. Employers typically exhibited less concern for employees' wellbeing *outside* the factory. But WVS volunteers, aware of both the shame shoddy clothing occasioned and animosities provoked by discrepancy in the quality of garments, petitioned the MoL to provide EVWs with a separate set of clothes for 'walking out'. Mrs Pratt, at the Preston hostel, made a forceful case:

> She asked whether EVWs could not be permitted to keep their good top clothes for their leisure, and still obtain working clothes. There were a high proportion of women going into the mills in Lancashire, usually with 3 months' training at low pay, and it would take them a very long time before they could afford to buy another good coat.[106]

Other WVS personnel were particularly concerned that women who lived in dormitory-style hostels, completely lacking in privacy, should have sufficient underwear and nightclothes to preserve modesty as they traipsed to communal bathrooms or bedded down in bunks.[107]

Several aspects of the EVWs' clothing situation shed light not only on the threadbare circumstances of migrant workers' lives, but also on postwar British poverty. The Board of Trade parried requests for 'walking out' garments with the retort that the nation's own clothing situation was currently 'too tight'. In some locations, the sheds and warehouses that held stocks of army surplus and other second-hand apparel awaiting WVS distribution had to be guarded round the clock – protected from potential theft not by EVWs, but by local inhabitants. Perhaps most telling of all is that the hostels which accommodated foreign workers should have stirred such envy in some places. As one MoL officer remarked, there was 'not much danger of any hostels becoming too luxurious, none of them were within miles of this'. But the MoL, the WVS and the press all noted that EVWs' presence in certain communities provoked a backlash, with locals railing against how much these Europeans received: housing, food, clothing coupons and free garments, as well as their wages.[108]

Figure 6.5 Two Austrian EVWs, recruited as cotton mill workers, walk through the streets of Bolton, November 1948 (Paul Popper/Popperfoto via Getty Images)

Postwar Britain was, as historian Jordanna Bailkin has documented, a land of camps. Over the war years, camps, barracks and hostels had proliferated across the country, variously accommodating POWs, 'Land Girls', munitions workers and miners deployed to vital industries far from home, to say nothing of dozens of facilities housing military personnel from Britain, its colonies and Allied nations.[109] As on the continent, many camps were repurposed soon after the war, whether housing new populations or the same residents under different regimes. In Britain, as Axis POWs or Allied personnel moved out of huts and hostels, EVWs moved in. Thus, a former RAF camp at Market Harborough, Leicestershire, became an EVW hostel, as did a decommissioned Navy camp at Bedhampton, Portsmouth. Accommodation for prisoners, soldiers or 'volunteer workers' shared a low common denominator of no-frills functionality, such that 'inhabitants' were barely differentiated from 'inmates'. At one EVW hostel,

MoL inspectors found residents sleeping on army cots with two blankets apiece for bedding.[110] The recreation room boasted one settee and a bare stone floor. Yet even these spartan conditions prompted resentment, as though institutionalized living were a perk that set EVWs apart from ordinary Britons. Rumours swelled in some places that foreign workers received more food and clothing coupons than their British counterparts.[111] But some of the latter lived in hostels too. And one study found that, wherever British and European workers shared the same hostel, conditions were invariably *superior* to those in accommodation reserved exclusively for EVWs: a revealing discrepancy that attracted little publicity.[112]

Xenophobic prejudice fed perceptions of foreign outsiders pitted against, and seemingly winning out over, Britons in a Hobbesian war of all against all. But privation, particularly the nation's chronic housing shortage, also sharpened some disadvantaged Britons' sense of injustice. Accommodation was so scarce that it wasn't just EVWs who moved into former military installations. In various parts of the country, squatters, including several veterans and their families, commandeered vacated Nissen huts and barracks – accommodation, the MoL regretfully noted, that might otherwise have housed EVWs' dependants.[113] One middle-aged woman, struggling to find a home for her family, and whose son had been invalided out of the army in July 1947, wrote furiously to the TUC in February 1948 to demand that it halt the influx of foreigners. The country was being 'invaded by DPs, etcetera', protested Mrs Bernice Dungworth, employing metaphors of inundation that still reverberate through twenty-first-century diatribes against migrants. The imperial tide had, in her view, turned disastrously, with British 'natives' oppressed by colonizing foreigners. 'When the invasion of this country was originally begun by D.P.s, etcetera, it was stressed that as these people were only to be allowed to enter industries here so long as it was not to the disadvantage of the natives here, so there was no cause for alarm on our part', Dungworth persisted; 'but as it is now becoming increasingly apparent this proviso is ignored more and more, cannot your organisation … initiate some action which will stop this ingress and prevent the crowding-out of British workers?':

> Are we to be forced to leave the country to these people, many of whom are the rag-tag and bob-tail of Europe and absolutely undesirable and who are jumping at the chance of getting into

this country which only the late war has rendered possible for them? Cannot you do something to stop it?[114]

Dungworth's interlocutor at the TUC tried to placate her by pointing out that the ratio of foreigners to Britons remained reassuringly low and that, while some Europeans were arriving, others were leaving:

> There are over 20 million workers in this country, and number of DPs that have entered is less than 100,000. Also 74,000 German POWs will have left agriculture by the end of March, so although it may have happened that the presence of some DPs have hit your family, I think you will see from the above figures that the proportion of these workers who have gone into industries in which there is a great scarcity of British labour – mining, agriculture, cotton textiles, hospital ward maids, etc. – is relatively small.[115]

Dungworth remained unassuaged. 'I cannot understand how a body such as the TUC, supposed to represent the workers here can permit such flagrant contempt of them.' She held the government in even greater contempt: 'it definitely produces a determination to, in future, consult one's own interests alone, as one's own Government will help even enemy aliens in preference'. Her fears of enemy invaders had perhaps been stoked higher by the *Daily Mirror*, whose story forecasting the arrival of 30,000 German women to work in textiles Dungworth cited in a second letter.[116]

Dungworth's views and language reflected that of Britain's best-selling tabloid. Although the MoL's publicity committee believed the welter of press stories about European volunteers had mostly been 'very positive', the *Daily Mirror* refused to embrace either the rebranding of DPs as EVWs or the economic logic behind 'Westward Ho'. In the *Daily Mirror*'s opinion, these migrants were not vital workers, but 'black marketeers' and 'criminals'. 'Let Them Be Displaced' railed a July 1948 editorial. 'They live on our rations – and live very well. They add to our discomfort and swell the crime wave. This cannot be tolerated. They must now be rounded up and sent back.'[117]

Other newspapers, without sharing the same editorial line, highlighted persistent tensions between EVWs and locals. Trade unions had misgivings about 'colonies from the Continent' springing up, the *Financial Times* (*FT*) reported in September 1947. These foreign enclaves would make integration harder and set back the cause of unionization.[118] Ten months later, while the *Daily Mirror* called for mass deportation of EVWs, the *FT* registered growing opposition in several mills where workers had voted against accepting more foreigners. Housing remained an especially sore spot.[119] Not surprisingly, immigrants longed to escape austere hostels, moving out as soon as they could. Groups of friends clubbed together to buy Victorian and Edwardian villas that were 'going cheap' in textile towns and cities like Bradford, Rochdale and Oldham, as these sprawling properties were 'too large and inconvenient for an English family without domestic help', one contemporary author noted.[120] But, in the meantime, many EVWs lodged in boarding houses. Relations between tenants and landladies were, the same writer delicately noted, 'not always happy'.[121] A column in *The Observer* reported that female immigrants, 'rather prickly' after 'all they have been through', received short shrift in their lodgings: 'All appear to have met their match in the Lancashire landlady, a formidable and conservative being, whose standing riposte is a chant of "Not in my 'ouse". Coffee for breakfast, hot baths every day, entertaining in bedrooms and the sound of foreign languages are what she most dislikes.'[122] British workers did not like foreigners conversing in their native tongues, 'as they suspect them of talking behind their backs' – a narcissistic assumption still commonly made by English visitors perturbed to find Welsh being spoken in Wales.[123]

In February 1949, as 'Westward Ho' wound down, the *Manchester Guardian* recorded an escalation of tension in Rochdale, where landlords and landladies had set up their own 'protection society' after Poles won an appeal in a local rent tribunal. This society proposed to lay down uniform regulations, including that 'washing of clothes should not be done by E.V.W.s on Sundays, and that all electric light switches in their rooms should be covered and locked'. One landlady, who'd formerly had nine EVWs boarding in her house, evicted them because 'they put my Sunday joint in the oven and deliberately burned it to a cinder'.[124] No doubt there was another side to this beef, but *The Observer* didn't ask the ejected lodgers for their version.

Productive and Reproductive Bodies

Ambivalence, sometimes outright antipathy, flowed in both directions between European migrants and Britons. Many Baltic EVWs hailed from middle-class households. Whatever they may have learnt or believed about Britain in their earlier lives was belied by disillusioning realities that soon became all too apparent, such as row after row of terraced houses with outdoor privies and no indoor hot water. Women who'd anticipated a prosperous destination were in for an even ruder awakening in their new workplaces. One Latvian later recalled her apprehension on being assigned to a textile mill:

> I couldn't even imagine you know what a mill looked like really, and as soon as I walked in – you know all your eyelids were full of cotton and it was terrible dust and noise. And I thought – my God! … I was ready to go back. But then I thought, well, I decided for myself to come over here, and if other people can do this job, definitely I can do it.[125]

Another Latvian volunteer had to be chivvied by her mother to shape up and knuckle down:

> The first day at the mill I wanted to kill myself. I'd never been in a mill before. All the noise and the dust and the people – oh Lordy! After the first day, I got back to the room and I screamed and cried. My mother said, 'you wanted to come to England, so here we are and I don't want to hear another word.'[126]

It wasn't just the ear-splitting din and the eye-watering, throat-obstructing fluff that took some getting used to, so did unfamiliar work that required dextrous fingers and unbroken attention. One woman sent to a woollen mill near Bradford, who'd 'never seen anything like it', was assigned to supervise six looms. In a factory that wasn't automated, she quickly had to master the art of stopping the machines by hand if the yarn broke.[127] Others, working as carders, spinners or weavers, learnt how to put on new spindles and remove full bobbins. All told, 'Westward Ho' placed about 12,000 women in various branches of the textile industry, each with distinct skills to be acquired in a language that was as alien to most EVWs as the equipment.[128]

Some women appreciated the solidarity of co-workers who generously shared food and tips about how to manage capricious machinery. But, in the mills, as in hostels and boarding houses, friendliness was sometimes signally lacking. The EVWs often proved to be exceptionally hard workers, eager to earn as much overtime pay as they possibly could to expedite departure from the regimentation of hostel life. But, while excessive output may have ingratiated EVWs to mill owners, hyper-productivity sometimes antagonized British workers, who feared that bosses would pressure them to toil just as zealously.[129] Some British workers, evidently not reassured by the deals brokered between the MoL and the TUC to ensure that EVWs would be laid off first if orders slackened, took matters into their own hands. Women weavers in Trowbridge refused to teach EVWs their craft, preferring to do more overtime themselves. Their rationale, approvingly reported by the *Daily Mirror*, was that, 'if we taught these foreigners how to weave West of England Cloth, they would one day take away our bread and butter'.[130]

It wasn't as workers alone that some female migrants attracted stigmatizing judgement. Despite all the government's promotional puff that stressed the contribution these fit and healthy Europeans would make to replenishing British 'stock', women who became pregnant after they moved to Britain – or whose pregnancies were discovered only on arrival – provoked a stir among government personnel, WVS representatives and other agencies dedicated to the 'problem' of unmarried mothers. For the Ministry of Health, pregnant EVWs imposed a strain on the new National Health Service, while for the Ministry of Supply, expectant mothers – the recipients of seventy extra clothing coupons – imposed further demands on scarce clothing supplies. What the MoL viewed primarily as a workplace issue, expensively procured labour lost, posed a moral conundrum for relief workers motivated by an interpretation of Christianity that condemned 'illegitimacy'.[131]

The archive of the National Council for the Unmarried Mother and her Child (NCUMC) brims with correspondence between the Council and various church welfare agencies on the subject of pregnant EVWs. Some had conceived before they left continental Europe. 'It seems to me the problem arose because they all had a very wild time just before they sailed to England!,' speculated Barbara Reeve of Manchester's Diocesan Council for Moral Welfare, conjuring not stricken leave-takings but bacchanalian scenes in Germany's DP camps.[132] Other women became pregnant soon after settling in Britain. Scathing characterizations of female migrants as 'wild', 'difficult', 'headstrong' and of 'bad character' – in their attitudes towards both pre-marital sex and reproductive autonomy – found vindication in these out-of-wedlock pregnancies. Documented cases were, however, less prevalent than the clamorous outrage they provoked might suggest. In

1948, the NCUMC tallied eighteen in Oldham, eight in Bolton and six in Rochdale, with fewer pregnancies recorded in Ayrshire, Edinburgh and Dundee.[133]

Labour officials, church agencies and welfare workers debated the merits of various solutions to this perceived problem, ranging from deportation to marriage and the fostering or adoption of babies that unmarried mothers would struggle to raise while still holding down the labour-intensive jobs into which 'Westward Ho' ushered them. Although it wasn't official policy, the MoL tried to engineer shotgun weddings whenever prospective fathers could be frog-marched into the role of lawful husband. Correspondence about unwed expectant mothers favoured a lofty passive voice, as though attempts to force couples into marriage involved no coercion – just nebulous aspiration. 'It is hoped a Latvian will get married,' a representative of the Gloucester Diocesan Association for Moral Welfare Work airily remarked in May 1949.[134] But some letters hinted at the psychological harm done when various concerned parties insisted pregnant immigrants and their partners marry, with the implicit threat of welfare services being withdrawn from recalcitrant women with nowhere else to turn for either shelter or assistance. A member of the Blackburn Diocesan Council recorded (on 11 March 1948) having seen 'one girl who's being pushed into marriage who looked desperately unhappy'. No wonder, perhaps. The prospective groom had spent two years in a 'concentration camp in Siberia' and still suffered from a head injury. His condition didn't 'argue well for the future of the marriage'.[135] The case of another pregnant 'volunteer' resisted conjugal resolution when it became known that the prospective father was in fact married. In some localities, WVS volunteers inserted themselves into EVWs' romantic lives, vetting the men that women brought back to hostels and alerting them if their British boyfriends already possessed British wives.[136]

For the custodians of 'moral welfare', just as vexing as the prospect of unwed immigrants giving birth was the fact that some EVWs had pronounced ideas of their own about reproductive rights – ideas which involved neither marriage nor adoption. Abortion, illegal in Britain until 1967, was a course of action some pregnant women preferred. 'Some girls feel very strongly that this is the best way of dealing with the situation, and cannot understand our attitude towards it,' tutted a worker at the Bolton Deanery.[137] An especially revealing account was submitted to the NCUMC by Mary Elliott (superintendent of a women's hostel in

Figure 6.6 EVW women line up for medical examinations at a hostel in Havant, Hampshire, 4 September 1947 (© Hulton-Deutsch Collection/CORBIS/Corbis via Getty Images)

Rugby), elaborating her tribulations in dealing with one pregnant EVW. Elliott characterized this unnamed woman as 'not really a good specimen'; in fact, 'an extraordinary problem in every way'. 'Most intelligent', she spoke 'five languages and anything but the truth':

> She had no roots, no lodgings, payed [sic] for nothing, refused to do the domestic work for which her permit was issued, and trailed around wearing expensive clothes she had earned in obvious ways. Her main idea in life was to obtain an abortion which she asked a leading Manchester gynaecologist to perform for her.

This scathing portrait exemplifies how readily various strands of anti-immigrant sentiment became entangled. In Elliott's view, migrant workers – no matter how well educated – had no business considering themselves too good for the lowly jobs assigned them in Britain. This woman's rootlessness was held against her, despite displacement being the precondition of eligibility for any 'volunteer worker'. Worse still was the fact that Elliott's nemesis preferred (or seemingly preferred) the 'oldest profession' over domestic drudgery, flaunting the superior wages of sin with her ostentatious finery. Not only did this unmarried woman further flout social norms by becoming pregnant, she then deployed her feminine wiles in pursuit of a termination. In this case, as Elliott perceived it, clothing didn't indicate a migrant's downtrodden circumstances. Its conspicuous extravagance screamed out her true colours.[138]

Judging from her tone, Elliott hoped this exasperating 'specimen' would be booted out of Britain forthwith. Deportation was the ultimate sanction for EVWs who breached the 'good behaviour' clause written into their contracts. Welfare workers weren't certain, however, which misdemeanours incurred this draconian penalty as no concrete language codified the criteria for deportation. This left room for interpretation and divergent application of hazy rules, but records show that some pregnant women *were* deported. Revealingly, welfare workers seemed less worried about the fate of stateless women sent back to who-knew-where in Germany than about the unintended consequences of a strict policy of deporting all pregnant EVWs. Some feared that, if the MoL followed this path consistently, it would prompt *more* women to seek terminations – keen to avoid expulsion back to a DP camp. 'Any supposition that unmarried motherhood, when detected, will automatically lead to deportation is likely to increase the number of cases of abortion and to encourage the women in the attitude, into which it is unfortunately all too easy to fall, that loose behaviour does not matter unless it is found out.'[139] In the opinion of this Edinburgh welfare worker, *abortion*, not pregnancy, ought to be the deportable offence. But how could one discover it?

Several women were shipped back to Germany, whether as punishment for having become pregnant or for having ceased to be. UNRRA's judgement proved correct that 'Westward Ho' was far more concerned with meeting British labour needs than with finding permanent homes for DPs. Productive bodies were welcome; reproductive ones were pushed out. By 1949, some 200 EVWs had been deported for a slew of offences, only some involving pregnancy. (Immigrants with chronic mental health conditions, including those who'd attempted suicide, were also sometimes treated in the same unsympathetic fashion.) The low number of deportations, announced Labour MP Ness

Edwards in the House of Commons, indicated that, 'on the whole, the European volunteer workers have reacted very well to the scheme and have played the game'.[140]

Marriage Plots

What were the rules of a 'game' that ultimately brought around 85,000 former DPs into Britain, including approximately 12,000 female textile workers?[141] The unwritten guidelines for EVWs were much longer than for whoever Ness considered their competitors: work hard (but not *too* hard); stick to the assigned job; dress modestly; never appear ungrateful; avoid 'loose behaviour'; and try to 'fit in' by learning English and adopting local habits. Sometimes, though, the game called for EVWs to showcase their cultural difference. The MoL's efforts to educate British opinion on the virtues of EVWs didn't stop at exhorting journalists to write favourable puff-pieces. Migrants must also promote themselves through displays of their distinctive costumes, customs and handicrafts. In Malvern, where anti-immigrant sentiment had been pronounced, Latvians, Lithuanians and Ukrainians staged a Continental Concert at the town's Winter Gardens – the 'first of its kind in the country', gushed MoL officials.[142] This variety show included dances performed in traditional dress, giving the audience an opportunity to admire not only these migrants' musicality, but also their embroidered blouses, waistcoats, skirts and shawls, all intricately hand-stitched. In a multi-national, ethnically diverse state – imagined as 'homogeneous' by many citizens (or at least by many English inhabitants) – immigrants' displays of ethnic distinctiveness were appreciated so long as they remained quaintly picturesque *performances*. Audiences could enjoy these events, safe in the knowledge that foreigners' nostalgic attachment to 'old country' customs didn't betoken unwillingness to integrate. Difference was merely staged for Britons' admiration. Once the performance ended, the players' costumes would come off.

Strategically deployed, national dress could be very beguiling, attractive as well as artful. So believed some Quaker relief workers who toiled alongside Margaret McNeill in German DP camps. One British colleague, poised to return home to get married, promised to invite three Lithuanian refugees to serve as her bridesmaids, hoping this gesture might enhance their own marital prospects in Britain.

'They will wear their Lithuanian dresses ... and all look so pretty that the Englishmen will fall in love with them.'[143]

Marriage supplied another frame through which British opinion-shapers sought to endear EVWs to a domestic audience. In its issue of 17 January 1948, *Picture Post* illustrated a feature, 'Our Immigrants Are Settling In', with the wedding portrait of Ukrainian textile worker Maria Brozovsky and a Mansfield businessman. Mr Taylor had volunteered to teach migrants English and, in so doing, found a wife. Maria was, in the caption's phrase, 'the exile of eight months ago whose luck has changed'. Extricated from a DP camp near Hannover, she now enjoyed domestic comfort in Nottinghamshire.[144] Film-makers also embellished this theme. A government-sponsored documentary released in 1949, *Code Name: Westward Ho!*, depicted the arrival of an EVW couple in Britain, separated by Stefan's despatch to a mine and his fiancée Alma's posting to a Lancashire cotton mill. Over the course of eleven minutes, the drama portrays how serially displaced persons' alienation could be overcome by locals' kindness: a plea for Britons to invite EVWs to share their homes, rather than banishing immigrants to the lonely isolation of institutional life. The film ends with the couple's reunion and marriage preparations, Alma shyly accepting the thoughtful gifts her fellow mill girls have clubbed together to buy.[145]

In fiction, the marriage plot forestalls further questions, as the couple are presumed to live happily ever after. In reality, not all migrants' marriages began so felicitously or lasted so long. Some male EVWs rushed into hasty arrangements, marrying 'girls met in pubs after a few weeks' acquaintance ... to escape hostel life', noted one contemporary observer. 'The results of such marriages were uniformly bad. Divorce, separation or desertion followed within a few months.'[146] Other couples were shunted by British officials into marriages that one or other party – possibly both – didn't want. Brides were further shoved into garments WVS volunteers deemed appropriate to the occasion, even if the women getting married demurred. With their customary mix of well-intentioned bossiness laced with condescension, WVS staff in Atherton, Lancashire, noted that 'Wedding dresses, veils and shoes have been found for EVW brides. Rehearsals have been held, the girls always choosing the most elaborate dress, whether it fitted or not. Erica, a Ukrainian girl, had to be made [to] wear corsets before we dare to let her walk down the aisle!'[147]

In this jaunty register, everything – including premarital pregnancy – could be made good by a trip down the aisle, just as jiggling flesh could be respectably girdled. The only precondition was that EVWs marry one another or white Britons. Black immigrants from British colonies were deemed impossible marriage material by those who considered sexual crossings of the colour line the least conscionable form of 'race mixing'.[148] European immigrants, however, were not only permitted but sometimes propelled to join a lengthy procession of postwar white weddings.

7 BRIDES

In the autumn of 1947, journalists on both sides of the Atlantic reported an alarming escalation of espionage in London as foreign spies made increasingly frantic efforts to steal what the *Los Angeles Times* dubbed 'Britain's most closely guarded secret since radar'.[1] Other commentators likened the protective cordon drawn around this project to the clandestine preparations for the Second Front. Precisely where on the French coast Allied forces would initiate their amphibious assault on Nazi-occupied Europe in 1944 remained under wraps for months, while various diversionary feints sought to mislead German intelligence about the location of the D-Day landings. For some reporters, however, a better analogy lay in the New Mexican desert of Los Alamos where, under the auspices of the Manhattan Project, a team of scientists had developed the world's first atomic bomb. In October 1947, the *Manchester Guardian* wryly noted a 'new danger to world peace' in cloak and dagger attempts to crack classified plans for Britain's biggest operation since the war.[2]

Despite the proliferation of martial analogies, the riddle wrapped in mystery at the heart of this enigma was *marital*. Headlines' punning references to the 'veil of secrecy' drawn across 38 Bruton Street conveyed a strong hint. At this Mayfair address, said to boast 'direct lines to Scotland Yard', royal couturier Norman Hartnell was creating an ornate wedding gown for twenty-one-year-old Princess Elizabeth, whose betrothal to Philip Mountbatten the Palace announced in July.[3]

With the ceremony scheduled to take place at Westminster Abbey on 20 November, Hartnell and his team had just over three months to produce Elizabeth's bridal gown and going-away ensemble, plus a bouquet of bridesmaids' outfits. Not since Queen Victoria married Albert, 107 years earlier, had any single garment aroused such great excitement as Elizabeth's bridal gown, proposed the *New York Times*. Hoping to steal a march on rivals, 'foreign agents' attempted to steal glimpses through the windows of Hartnell's premises or to winkle details from pliable seamstresses, though the *Times* guessed that, 'like the workers who helped perfect the components of the atom bomb, the seamstresses have no idea what the final product will look like'.[4] To thwart saboteurs who'd reportedly sublet premises on the opposite side of Bruton Street, the couturier 'had the workroom windows whitewashed and curtained with thick white muslin'. 'The tension and speculation over the dress reached such a point, that to be quite sure the secret was preserved around the clock, my manager volunteered to sleep in the room next door,' Hartnell recalled.[5]

The dress was, however, less securely fortified than Hartnell's memoir suggests. To feed the voracious appetite of the world's press for advance titbits, journalists were invited into his premises on 6 October and shown bolts of fabric for Elizabeth's bridal gown and going-away outfit, along with material for a bridesmaid's dress, on a strictly 'don't touch, don't tell' basis. 'The lady in charge said the going away cloth was a new color,' reported a sardonic *New York Times* columnist. 'It was draped across a leopard-skin rug. It can be stated, without violating a confidence, that there was considerable difference between the cloth and the rug.'[6] If this glimpse was intended to forestall further probing, the controlled experiment failed. Hullaballoo mounted. When a newsreel claimed to show work in progress, more feverish guesswork about the gown and its price-tag ensued. On 24 October, the *Evening Standard* published photographs of the fabric for the bridal gown, bridesmaid's dress and going-away outfit. Newspapers around the world trumpeted that the princess would wed in 'lustrous white satin'.[7] (The dress was, in fact, ivory.) Eight days before the wedding, the *Daily Mail* went a step further, publishing sketches of the gown and a bridesmaid's dress, identifying the *Giornale d'Italia* as the source of a leak it felt impelled to further publicize. On the day itself, several papers printed Hartnell's sketches, offering readers a detailed view of the dress before photographs of the princess herself appeared.[8]

The reason for this secrecy (as reported by the press) was Elizabeth's desire to preserve the element of surprise traditionally prized by brides hoping to dazzle wedding guests – and the groom in particular – with the radiant novelty of their apparition at the altar. The princess shared 'the wish of a young girl to keep her wedding dress secret'.[9] In the dramaturgy of the traditional white wedding, the dress as well as the bride is 'unveiled'. What was true of ordinary weddings was magnified in the case of this extraordinary royal event. Most brides, after all, don't have to worry about commercial espionage. Not so Princess Elizabeth. '[T]here allegedly is an overwhelming desire by American women to be married in an exact copy of the Princess' gown – but cheaper,' claimed the *Washington Post*.[10] The royal bride-to-be would have been distraught, anonymous intimates divulged, had pirated copies of her dress become commercially available before she'd even walked down the aisle. Hartnell expressed confidence that all the 'time and money' it would take to replicate his creation's 'complicated embroidery' would thwart any aspiring copycats.[11] His prediction was only semi-warranted. Although no retailer pre-empted the ceremony, it took just three days *after* the wedding for a Fifth Avenue boutique to display a copy of Elizabeth's dress.[12] And, as one Harvard Law School expert pointed out, there was no redress that couturiers and their clients, regal or otherwise, could seek for commercial piracy after a design had been 'published'. Imitation wasn't incidental but intrinsic to a business reliant on speedy dissemination, and equally swift replacement, of up-to-the-moment styles. 'Few higher-priced garments wear out', explained Eli Goldston, 'rather they are discarded as fashion sweeps the "New Look" from Dior's Parisian atelier to the "Klassy Klothes Korner" of Keokuk.'[13]

If rough approximations of the regal gown reached Podunk, Iowa, sooner rather than later, the British establishment wasn't entirely blameless. Royal weddings, then as now, were commercial bonanzas for all in their orbit. Everyone had something to sell – whether newspapers, knock-off dresses or the monarchy itself. Keen to stoke popular excitement, the Palace authorized strategic revelations about the focal source of intrigue, feeding journalists crumbs with one hand while trying to keep them at arm's length with the other. It allowed Hartnell to offer teasing glimpses of fabric at his studio, trusting that a deferential press would respect the non-disclosure agreement. Palace press secretary Richard Colville then granted the BBC's Audrey Russell an advance preview of the gown to ensure she would describe it both thoroughly and correctly in her live radio commentary on the ceremony.[14] For their part, the Board of Trade (BoT) hoped that Elizabeth's dress, modelled in New York soon after the ceremony, would help London designers crack open a market that regarded French couturiers – not more stolid British rivals – as the *ne plus ultra* of high style.[15]

A web of national fantasy and international aspiration was spun around this garment as intricate as the pattern of Hartnell's embroidery and appliqué. At a moment of economic peril, amid escalating global crises, anxieties abounded. Fretful discussion of The Dress channelled both lingering wartime animosities and looming cold war antagonisms. Was it properly *British*?, some commentators demanded. The Palace intended the nuptials symbolically to bind the kingdom's nations together, with a wedding ring crafted from Welsh gold, cocoons for the train hatched in Kent and raw silk woven into dress material in Scotland. (Northern Ireland was, as is commonly the case, overlooked in fabrications of 'Britishness'.)[16] But despite conspicuous nods to three, if not all four, of the kingdom's constituent parts, controversies still swirled around the fabric's provenance, as well as the thousands of seed pearls and crystals that Hartnell's team would painstakingly stitch onto the gown and train. The silk for the dress, woven by Winterthur near Dunfermline, attracted particular suspicion. The weavers may have been Scottish, but what about the silk worms? Critics rumoured that they were 'possibly even Japanese!' 'Was I so guilty of treason that I would deliberately use *enemy* silk-worms?,' Hartnell scoffed. Fortunately for the designer, Winterthur confirmed that the silk worms hailed from China – 'Nationalist China, of course!' (Two years later, after Mao's victory in China's civil war, nationalist silk worms would've required sourcing from Taiwan.) No one seemed to impugn Hartnell's patriotism or politics for borrowing motifs for the gown from an *Italian* artist. Sandro Botticelli's 'Primavera' inspired the embroidered tracery of roses, stars, orange blossom and wheatears that figured prominently on the dress and its fifteen-foot train. (Eyebrows would certainly have been raised had Elizabeth's gown been as diaphanous as the transparent drapery barely clinging to Botticelli's ethereal figures.)[17] Behind the scenes, BoT officials posed their own questions about whether Hartnell had secured the correct import licences for the pearls, noting his poor track record of sourcing overseas what he should have bought in Britain.[18]

Figure 7.1 Princess Elizabeth and Philip Mountbatten at Buckingham Palace after their wedding ceremony, 20 November 1947 (Popperfoto via Getty Images)

In November 1947, the operative concern was only superficially what would – or did – the dress look like; the more pressing question was rather what did this garment *represent*? Was it a symbol of regeneration, a vehicle for restored national fortunes, or an emblem of glaring inequality? Little more than a year after the divisive official Victory Parade of 1946, the royal wedding reopened wounding debates about the relationship between ceremony and parsimony, posing a more acute question about the compatibility of monarchy and austerity. The victory festivities were, ostensibly, for everyone: a celebration of shared sacrifice and achievement. But for whom was a royal wedding staged? Although the Archbishop of York insisted that Elizabeth and Philip exchanged the same vows as humble 'cottagers', lavish pageantry strained credulity as to royal 'ordinariness'.[19] Since a simple plighting of troth did not require such extravagant fanfare, the projected cost prompted Britons to evaluate relationships within the United Kingdom as well as ties far beyond. What would *others* see when they looked at Westminster Abbey? In particular, how would American observers interpret this event?

By late 1947, two countries separated by a common language were bound together, for richer or poorer, in both debt and matrimony. In 1936, Elizabeth's uncle had, notoriously, married an American divorcée, Wallis Simpson – a union that led to his exile from Britain and his brother George's reluctant ascent to the throne. Numerous humbler transatlantic marriages followed as a result of Britain's 'friendly' war-time occupation by American troops. Like Elizabeth's gown, British 'GI brides' – around 70,000 of whom set sail for the United States in the years just after the war – were ascribed an ambassadorial role in making Britain better liked 'over there', with (optimists hoped) ameliorative consequences felt 'over here'.[20]

'Annus horrendus'

The royal wedding occurred towards the end of an especially bleak year, beginning with the coldest winter for decades and plunging into ever deeper morasses after the snow finally melted. Chancellor of the Exchequer Hugh Dalton dubbed 1947 an *annus horrendus* for the Labour administration, anticipating Queen Elizabeth's use of a similar phrase to describe her *annus horribilis* in 1992.[21] Britain's economic plight looked more perilous than in 1945, the dollar deficit having ballooned to £8 billion. Prospects for postwar cooperation had also dimmed. Tensions between Britain, the United States and the USSR escalated over 1946 and 1947, the exchange of rhetorical barbs taking more concrete form in hardened borders between eastern and western Europe.[22]

Meanwhile, Britain's empire was crumbling apace: the 'jewel' was relinquished, symbolically if not literally. (The koh-i-noor remained firmly pincered in the Queen's crown.) Britain's abrupt scuttle from the Indian subcontinent, with India's independence declared on 15 August 1947, led to the simultaneous creation of a Muslim-majority state, Pakistan, itself split in two. (East Pakistan would become Bangladesh in 1971.) In the course of a singularly lethal partition process, millions of people lost possessions, homes and lives.[23] While ethnic expulsions and massacres continued, the royal family embarked on a four-month tour of southern Africa, during which Elizabeth pursued an epistolary romance with Philip and the King's equerry, Peter Townsend, pursued her sixteen-year-old sister, Margaret Rose.[24] The visit, intended to strengthen ties with a key Dominion, boosting the electoral prospects of Jan Smuts, failed to stave off rising Afrikaaner power and its radically segregationist agenda. In 1948, the newly installed Nationalist Party cemented the apartheid system that persisted until the early 1990s.

Palestine remained in turmoil. Escalating attacks on British targets by armed Zionist groups ensured that security arrangements for the wedding were framed in terms of guarding the constellation of European royalty against 'terrorism'.[25] The British empire wasn't alone in facing violent challenge. In Greece, a bitter civil war distilled cold war tensions in microcosm, as the Greek monarchy, with US and British support, ruthlessly suppressed a communist-led uprising aided by the USSR. Some British leftists feared that backing for the forces of reaction was likely to be intensified by closer monarchical bonds between Britain and Greece: this was one of several reasons why the nationality of Elizabeth's fiancé proved as controversial as the provenance of her gown.[26]

Most British newspapers toed the official line assiduously promoted by his uncle Louis Mountbatten that Philip was as English as the next man – provided the next man had been born on Corfu to Greek–Danish/Anglo-German parents and educated in the Scottish Highlands before joining the Royal Navy.[27] But some bridled at this stretching of Englishness beyond credulity's boundary. The *Daily Mirror*, an outlier in its populist anti-monarchism, showcased its scepticism by printing a photograph of Philip as a boy in full-skirted traditional Greek garb.[28] 'It makes me feel terrible to think that she is marrying a Greek,' one forty-year-old man moaned to Mass Observation (MO). 'With Attlee and Bevin being Jews, England will soon be ruled by a lot of foreigners.'[29] His bigotry was misplaced all around. Neither Attlee nor Bevin was Jewish. (Bevin's antisemitism has, in fact, been much debated by historians.[30]) And the Saxe-Coburg lineage was no less Teutonic for having been 'Windsored'. Since Elizabeth and Philip were related by way of Queen Victoria and Albert, others found her fiancé objectionable not because he was Greek, but because he was *German*. Some, hazy about Philip's origins but mistrustful nevertheless, simply didn't like the royal pair. 'It's humbug to say Princess Elizabeth is lovely – she isn't. And I don't much care for these East European princelings. I'd rather she'd married a commoner – or at least somebody as common as her mother!,' opined another middle-aged curmudgeon, before comforting himself with a reassuring prediction: 'I don't suppose she'll ever come to the throne, anyhow.'[31]

International conflict was only part of what made 1947 horrendous for many living in Britain, not just those governing it. The country's indebtedness to the United States grew more insurmountable than ever as negotiations for Marshall Plan aid gathered pace. As inflation soared, austerity bit deeper. Bread was rationed for the first time in 1946, while the number of clothing coupons shrank.[32] Against this bleak backdrop, MO surveyed its thousands of volunteers about the royal wedding. Its 'Directive' issued in December 1947 contained four questions, ending with the nuptials but beginning with an invitation to explain how the cost-of-living crisis affected respondents personally.[33] The answers strike an eerily familiar note in the 2020s. *Everything* cost more: food, drink, tobacco, fuel, travel, entertainment. Cinema tickets had risen in price. So, too, had records and books. Even Allen Lane's modestly priced paperbacks, intended to be universally accessible, were becoming an unaffordable luxury. Younger people as well as old found themselves leading 'quieter lives' with narrower horizons than they would've wished.[34] Students on fixed incomes regretted the soaring expense of both studying and socializing. 'I find I cannot afford to take girls out (regularly, I mean; not to a very occasional party) unless they pay for themselves at least some of the time,' whined one Cambridge undergraduate.[35] His woes, resolved by a more equitable splitting of the bill, were small beer in comparison with the life-altering consequences of financial hardship faced by young couples who couldn't afford a home or to start a family. Babies cost considerably more than Penguins.

Children's constantly expanding clothing needs gobbled up household budgets. Adult garments were also pricey. Indeed, for many, clothes topped the list of sacrifices, along with shoes and (another sign of the times) shoe-repair. 'Clothing prices, on the infrequent occasions when I buy clothing, stagger me,' remarked one respondent.[36] One veteran ruefully noted, 'I've only had one new suit in seven years, apart from one which the State presented to me when I left the RAF. It was a mean shoddy thing too.'[37] Some plugged the gap with army surplus, more freely and cheaply available than civilian apparel. But, after six years of clothes rationing, weariness with 'making do' was palpable. One twenty-five-year-old typist from Heswall, Cheshire, elaborated her weekly routine: 'I economise by ringing the changes of ancient and modern clothing – 2 days I wear old garments, then 2 days for new, then back to the rags for the weekend. I mend & patch & embroider everything until I look like a gypsy queen gone haywire.' She was not alone. 'My underclothes are an embroidery of different patches,' noted a forty-two-year-old teacher in Bruton, Somerset, who practised all the precepts encouraged by Mrs Sew-&-Sew. 'I turn three garments into two. I lengthen the toes of utility stockings that shrink, I remake & reinforce bed socks. I use old stocking tops to mend knickers and my souwester, an old table-cloth to alter a dress, etc, etc, etc. I might almost be Robinson Crusoe,' though she evidently would've preferred not to be shipwrecked on an island that required such endless frugality.[38]

Debates over clothing came into sharper focus in February 1947, when Christian Dior detonated a bombshell over the postwar fashion scene with his 'Corolle' collection, showcasing what Carmel Snow (editor of *Harper's Bazaar*) dubbed the 'New Look'. Named after the petals of a flower, Dior's 'Corolle' styles expressed both his nostalgia for nineteenth-century silhouettes and a desire to break definitively with the boxy rigidity of wartime garments. 'In December 1946, as a result of the war and uniforms, women still looked and dressed like Amazons,' Dior complained. 'I designed clothes for flower-like women, with rounded shoulders, full feminine busts, and hand-span waists above enormous spreading skirts.'[39]

Dior's creations aroused ferocious, sometimes violent, feeling in France and far beyond. Fashion editors squabbled over precisely how 'new' this backward-looking trend really was, while economists and feminists were exercised for different reasons, from the extra yardage needed to produce fuller and longer garments to the physical discomfort of boned corsets and horsehair underskirts required to achieve the Look, to say nothing of its impracticality. *Picture Post* headlined its first feature on the New Look 'Paris Forgets This Is 1947'. Striking a stern note, author Marjorie Backett pointed out that the fifty yards of material gathered into one of Dior's skirts would 'require the hoarded coupons of several years'. Most women couldn't afford these garments, even if they possessed the 'leisure to enjoy' them and 'the strength to support' such excessive quantities of material.[40] But, after years of eking out Utility garments and counting coupons for more modest purchases, some British women, longing to forget the '*annus horrendus*', discerned in the swish of a 'fantastically full' skirt the sound of freedom from want.[41] Others hoped British hems would be lowered for a different reason, countering the economic case against

Dior with a practical point in favour: longer skirts would help women keep warm during future fuel shortages.[42] Some just preferred more coverage. Long skirts were 'much less embarrassing to the wearer in a high wind (or a Tube station corridor)', quipped Molly Cochrane in the *New Statesman*. One self-described 'plump' woman in Dumfries, 'not possessing beautiful legs', favoured less revealing garments – in diametric opposition to those men who preferred the shorter Old Look precisely because they enjoyed ogling women's legs. 'The occasional glimpse of something one shouldn't see is rather stimulating isn't it?,' one Leeds student cheekily proposed to MO.[43]

It wasn't just lascivious males who disapproved of Dior. Some women regretted these styles as a step back from hard-won victories in the long campaign for gender equality. For many feminists, electoral enfranchisement and emancipation from trailing skirts and squeezed ribcages went hand-in-hand. 'Can anyone imagine the average house-wife and businesswoman dressed in bustles and long skirts … running for buses and crowding into tubes and trains? The idea is ludicrous. The New Look is too reminiscent of a caged bird's attitude,' protested Mabel Ridealgh (Labour MP for Ilford). A former BoT official and leading wartime champion of 'making do', Ridealgh also advocated a royal 'austerity wedding' – in conformity with workers' wishes – a few months after inveighing against Dior-derived styles. Historians of the New Look have disparaged Ridealgh as a frumpish kill-joy, imper-vious to women's yearning for glamour, whose primary objection to French fashions was their 'over-sexiness'.[44] But her criticisms reso-nated with many MO respondents, canvassed in September 1947 on the 'skirt length controversy'. 'At the moment when we are told that it is essential to make do and mend, to skimp and to starve, it seems to be perfectly ridiculous that fashion designers should try to introduce a longer skirt,' a female respondent protested. 'Women, they say, are wanted in industry – well, a short skirt is much more suitable than a long one for getting on and off buses, and for work in factories .... I feel that women are very well content with the present length of skirt and that the whole thing is just a storm in a tea-cup from which the short-skirt sisterhood will emerge victorious.'[45] A vocal contingent of American women felt the same way. During the French couturier's visit to Chicago in September 1947, a self-styled 'Little below the Knee Club' picketed his hotel with placards telling 'Mr. Dior – We Abhor Dresses to the Floor'.[46] Passions ran even higher among Parisiennes.

Figure 7.2 A young woman wearing a skirt from Dior's 'Corolle' collection is attacked by older Parisiennes outraged by the New Look's wastefulness (Walter Carone/Paris Match Archive/Getty Images)

In Britain, controversy over the New Look was bound up not only with gender politics, but also with the economics of austerity. Could Britain, at a time of steeply rising prices, *afford* significantly lowered hemlines? The BoT and Chancellor of the Exchequer were determined to hold the line. Harold Wilson (future Labour Prime Minister and then President of the Board of Trade) appeared in a *Pathé* newsreel to make the case for restraint, rather nervously sitting at home. At a time of 'material shortages', it 'just didn't make sense' for skirts to be any longer. With the hint of a smirk, he implied his own preference – for higher hems. Small clothing companies, with margins as narrow as their garments', eagerly complied. And, in a show of solidarity, J. Arthur Rank's film studio announced that its stars would continue to sport 'old look' styles on screen for the duration.[47]

For some critics of the New Look, it wasn't just one designer but an entire system that lay at fault. Many of MO's respondents skewered the fashion industry in terms that anticipate twenty-first-century critiques of a business reliant on manipulation of constantly changing desires: an industry as wasteful of resources as it was demoralizing for those unable to afford seasonal adjustments, doomed to appear dowdily behind the times as one 'new look' swiftly gave way to something even newer. A London man made the case succinctly: 'If longer skirts do become the fashion, a woman's wardrobe of clothes will become useless. People with plenty of money to waste will be able to buy black market clothing coupons and buy longer skirts and coats to go with them, while the less fortunate will not. This will intensify the class antagonism.'[48] Even those who didn't particularly *want* new looks – or the bother and expense of attaining them, either by purchase of new garments or by alteration of old ones – feared the inevitable. British consumers could no more halt the incoming wave of French couture than Canute could hold back the tide. A Middlesbrough woman predicted (correctly) that British hemlines *would* fall, necessitating the annoyance of letting down hems. 'I wish we did not have to adhere to the fashion dictates of Paris, but – and this is written with a sigh of resignation – I expect we all shall give in to their whims after all.'[49]

The young man who foresaw intensified social strife proposed a remedy. 'Perhaps Princess Elizabeth could have her wedding dress length above the knee and that would stop this silly nonsense.'[50] While such an outré abandonment of royal precedent was inconceivable, this playful suggestion points to a hemline controversy Hartnell couldn't skirt. Since Elizabeth's bridal gown was obliged to sweep the ground, speculation buzzed more incessantly around the hem of her going-away ensemble. If Elizabeth wore the longer style, the *Los Angeles Times* predicted, 'many women would resolve to follow her lead at any cost of money or ration coupons. This would result in a far greater demand for cloth than could be met.'[51] Fortunately for Whitehall, Hartnell announced himself unmoved by Dior's *bouleversement*. 'Mr Hartnell thinks long skirts are pretty but this is not the time for him,' *Union Jack* (a newspaper for service personnel) related some six weeks before the wedding. 'I cannot but think that this anxiety for longer skirts is most untimely and regrettable,' Hartnell told a friend.[52] Revealed on the day itself, Elizabeth's honeymoon outfit, a 'love-in-the-mist' blue velour dress and matching coat, hovered at the approved distance 14″ from the ground. But, if BoT officials heaved a sigh of relief, their worries weren't over. It didn't take long before Margaret, widely regarded as both the more stylish and the prettier princess, was seen modelling the New Look – in a coat whose hem Hartnell had lowered.[53]

The Princess and the Coupons

A dress that ignited intense speculation over its design inevitably sparked controversy as to its cost. In hard times, what was an appropriate price for a princess's bridal attire? What, more broadly, was a reasonable sum to spend on a royal wedding? Historians of Britain's 'age of austerity' tend to concur that, despite some carping from the far left, Britons overwhelmingly applauded a pageant that raised national spirits, lending a welcome 'flash of colour' (in Churchill's words) 'to the hard road we have to travel'.[54]

Responses to MO's December Directive reveal a bumpier road over uneven terrain. Asked to record how they felt about the royal wedding, respondents didn't just register markedly different attitudes from one another, but expressed numerous individually conflicted sentiments. Reason and emotion didn't always align. Some avowed republicans confessed to becoming misty-eyed listening to the wedding broadcast, like the Glaswegian housewife who didn't 'care two pins' about the royals but found herself 'moved to tears' as she listened while 'doing a prosaic morning's ironing'.[55] For their part, self-confessed monarchists, though (generally) pleased by the match itself, sometimes regretted the cheapening of the crown by vulgar crowd behaviour. An event that offered some an opportunity to excoriate privilege supplied others with an outlet for snobbish prejudice against the 'lower orders' they regarded as tarnishing their superiors. Numerous respondents voiced strong opinions at either end of an affective spectrum stretching from jubilation to revulsion, with 'nauseated' and 'sickened' forming the most common one-word responses to MO's Directive. But the majority struggled to pinpoint their emotions, professed to feeling nothing whatsoever, or responded in equivocal ways that distinguished negative *personal* reactions from the greater approbation they imputed to other Britons. Bifocal vision and torn feelings prevailed. Together, the questionnaires convey far more nuance, as well as deeper negativity, in British opinion on the monarchy than might be expected if the 'age of austerity' is conceived as a brief chapter within an extended 'age of deference'.

As soon as the Palace announced the princess's engagement, sparring began – in the Commons and across the country – over the ceremony's budget, as well as the couple's marital income and residence. Willie Gallacher, Communist MP for Fife, refused to add his congratulations to those Attlee proposed the House should offer the Palace. 'I cannot forget that on the day that this engagement was announced, thousands of Greek citizens – Communists, Socialists and trade unionists – were thrown into the prison camps of the reactionary Royalist Government.'[56] (Several MO respondents, careful to state for the record that *they* were not communists, cheered Gallacher's defiance.) Appreciating a need for caution, the Palace proclaimed that the event would be pared back in comparison with past royal extravaganzas. In ensuing reports of an 'austerity wedding', bridal attire occupied centre stage in both British and US press commentary. On 18 August, the King and Queen announced that the princess would (in the *Washington Post*'s words) 'go on her honeymoon without a single new travelling outfit, pair of bedroom slippers or frothy negligee'. Other than her freshly anglicized husband, only Elizabeth's dress would be new. The princess's plight, opined a *New York Times* editorial, would 'stir pity in the heart of every bride-to-be in America, who wouldn't dream of being led to the altar without all the new raiment she or her parents can buy'. Alas, the 'Spartan conditions of English life' necessitated economies.[57]

Sympathy for this 'poor little rich girl' extended only so far, however, in Britain and America alike. A subsequent *New York Times* story pointed out that Elizabeth had acquired many new outfits for the recent four-month tour of southern Africa, which, since these clothes could 'hardly be worn out', would help fill her hope chest.[58] This report was correct, though it broached a topic the Palace preferred not to discuss: namely, how much was spent on outfitting the royals for this extended trip. Board of Trade records reveal that the King, Queen, princesses and their entourage together received 8,568 coupons – a figure that stealthily expanded over months of planning. With criticism mounting in the press about rumoured expenditure, the BoT pressed the royal household to agree a form of words to be used in response, stressing not only the need for garments suitable for southern Africa's climate, but also the benefits to the nation's fashion industry that would accrue from the royals wearing British-designed and -made garments. The Palace bridled. When they grudgingly agreed to defend the considerable cost of equipping the royal entourage for the tour, Palace officials elevated monarchical over commercial considerations. The need to maintain the 'dignity of the Crown' outweighed national economic imperatives. 'By far the largest proportion of His Majesty's subjects in South Africa are natives,' Sir Ulick Alexander told the BoT, and 'they look for more than austerity in the clothes of those who embody in their persons all that a native dreams of royalty.' Whether Africans dreamt of Hartnell's tea dresses and tulle evening gowns was, of course, another matter. But BoT scruples notwithstanding, Elizabeth received 400 coupons for the tour, while her mother's wardrobe consumed 2,200.[59]

Although Britons remained ignorant of the precise number of coupons issued, the southern Africa tour began to fracture the monarchy's carefully constructed façade of 'ordinariness'. During the war, palace image-makers cultivated the notion that the royal family shared the same privations as commoners.[60] If supportive press stories were to be believed, the Windsors washed in 5″ of bathwater, with a line

Figure 7.3 During the royal tour of southern Africa, Princess Elizabeth inspects girl guides at Lobatse, Bechuanaland Protectorate, 21 April 1947 (Paul Popper/Popperfoto via Getty Images)

drawn inside the royal tub to mark the permitted high tide. (This theme was so well embroidered that even fictional characters repeated it. In Elizabeth Bowen's 1948 novel *The Heat of the Day*, one character scolds another for running too much hot water, 'when the King himself only uses five inches in his bath'.[61]) Royal access to new clothing was also supposedly regulated by the same coupon allowance as for 'ordinary' Britons, compelling the Windsors to 'make do and mend' like everyone else. Cut-down frocks duly passed from the Queen to the princess royal before ending up with Margaret Rose, last in the line of succession for regal hand-me-downs.[62]

To believe that royalty were ordinary mortals just like their subjects *and* endowed with a divine right to rule over them required practising what George Orwell, then shivering over the manuscript of *Nineteen Eighty-Four* on Jura, termed 'double-think': the maintenance of two contradictory ideas simultaneously. But elimination of cognitive dissonance was too much for MO respondents, who refused to swallow the bitter cocktail of inequality laced with dishonesty. 'Spare us the nauseating suggestion that everything is being done on two persons' ration of food and clothing coupons,' fumed one new father, unable to make ends meet in Winchester.[63] Similarly, the veteran dissatisfied with his demob suit informed MO: 'I'm sure nobody really believes all the rot they read. I have seen in print that the King has no special rations & no more clothing coupons than anyone else! Presumably Elizabeth & Philip are now doing wonders on a few ounces of butter, sugar and bacon!'[64] Like-minded individuals expressed incredulity that fellow citizens, pitying the trousseau-less princess, had mailed her their *own* clothing coupons: a story reported on both sides of the Atlantic, along with the fact that the Palace returned all such offerings with appreciative notes of demurral.[65] 'As for the blind pathetic wretches who gave up their coupons to send presents etc. I find it practically understandable,' one woman exclaimed. 'Oh what misdirected kindness!'[66] Particular bitterness prevailed among Britons whose arms had been twisted into contributing to workplace wedding presents. One soldier divulged that his officer had singlehandedly contributed most of the total when enlisted men flatly refused to pay a second time, as they saw it, for festivities they'd already financed as tax-payers.[67]

The Palace's insistence that there was absolute parity between royals and commoners in matters of coupons, teetering in southern Africa, collapsed before the wedding. Contrary to some accounts,

Elizabeth was *not* forced to save up 'like any other bride'.[68] The Royal Family had, in fact, received far more coupons than anyone else since rationing began, and while ordinary Britons' allowance shrank with each successive year, the Windsors' steadily grew.[69] Behind the scenes, the Palace requested *800* coupons from the BoT for Elizabeth's attire – in addition to the 1,440 she had already received in 1947 (her annual allowance plus extra for the tour). The BoT bristled. It had acceded to the royals' wardrobe allowance for southern Africa with reluctance, and was already beset by complaints about anticipated royal wedding expenditure from trade unionists, the Women's Co-operative Guilds and brides-to-be, who received no additional coupons. Civil servants alerted the Palace to popular unhappiness, pointing out that disgruntled letter-writers tended to quote the 'slogan of "equality of sacrifice"'. A compromise was agreed. On 22 October, Harold Wilson informed Parliament that Elizabeth would receive 100 clothing coupons, with her 6 bridesmaids granted 23 each and 2 page-boys 10 apiece.[70]

Complaints continued. The next day, the BoT received a letter from '20 disgusted young ladies', fuming that it was 'high time that the __PEOPLE__ of this country were considered for a change'.[71] For some, it was the blunt fact of inequity that rankled more than the size of this gift. 'It doesn't really make any difference whether Elizabeth used 100 or 1000 coupons, but it leaves a nasty taste when other people don't have either,' opined a young scientist.[72] As he hinted, there was something both nominal and performative in the government's allocation of coupons to the monarchy, whether reports of newly naturalized Philip having to queue for his coupon book or Wilson's announcement of a number that, while not as eye-popping as 800, was still suspiciously round.[73] By any candid reckoning, Elizabeth's dress required far more material and labour than 100 coupons would cover. Hartnell's preview of the fabric and design sketches inspired a flurry of calculations as to the gown's contours and cost, with the *New York Times* estimating the price at £1,250 (or $5,000) and the coupon value at 300. At current rates of issue, this total would take 'the average girl' six years to amass – though the typical female worker could never have afforded such a gown, even if she saved sufficient coupons.[74] These projections provoked hasty Palace denials. The dress would cost under £200, a royal spokesperson announced. The *New York Times* printed this claim, but added a sceptical rejoinder that it 'was difficult to see how such a dress could be made at that price'.[75]

Whatever the gown's true cost, Wilson's announcement marked a retreat from earlier talk of an 'austerity wedding'. 'After the scarcity, the make-do of the war years, this sudden lavishness was unnerving,' admitted 'Crawfie', the princesses' former governess. Many less privileged Britons agreed – perturbed not just by pearl-encrusted apparel but also by the accompanying discussion of which royal residence Philip and Elizabeth would inhabit.[76] 'What could a man 10,000th on the list for a home think when the papers started talking about the number of London homes those two could choose from,' one man wrote.[77] Another queried, 'Would it have been so terrible for the newlyweds to do as hundreds of thousands of British couples were doing, and living at home.' After all, 'One needn't fall over one's mother in law in a place as large as Buckingham Palace.'[78] Some wished that 'Liz and Phil' had insisted on a ceremony more akin to Britons' everyday experience. 'We would all have thought as much of her in a simple frock she'd made herself like thousands of other girls do,' remarked one fifty-two-year-old 'housewife, orchardist and apiarist'. As during the war, many British brides continued to marry in home-made dresses or loaned garments. And if it was true, as one royal hagiographer put it, that the princess 'wore her happiness like a garment, plainly, for all to see', did her radiance need the amplification of a shimmering gown?[79]

Britons' verdicts on Hartnell's creation were as divided as on everything else. This forty-one-year-old clerk might've been regurgitating a BoT press release when she enthused: 'The Princess' wedding dress was a magnificent example of the best artistry in the world, and shows what can be done in this country if we try.' Few waxed so rhapsodic. After watching the colour newsreel of the wedding, one woman complained that the gown didn't *glitter* as the press had reported. Another female clerk was more troubled by what the embroidered motifs represented: 'if it had been me, I should have been disgusted to have ears of wheat on a dress of mine as a symbol of fertility. We haven't progressed very far from the pagan, have we?' Her observation chimed with other remarks on the prurience of those seemingly more preoccupied with the *consummation* of the royal marriage than the ceremony.[80] A Bradford 'housewife and mother' delivered the most devastating critique of all: 'Why if that Norman Hartnell offered to tailor me a shroud I'd refuse to be buried in it.' As for 'that ghastly coat and hat she wore' for 'going away', it would '[p]ut any one off English clothes – if ever they were on them. Poor Lilibet – she is being turned into a frump.' With this remark, she foreshadowed decades of criticism of dowdy royal fashion, before the octogenarian queen's latter-day reincarnation as a timeless icon of British style.[81]

There were, of course, Britons who exulted in the ceremonial grandeur of the royal wedding, proud that no other country could mount such an impressive spectacle – even if no serious competitors entered this imaginary contest. Some wished that additional money had been spent on a yet *more* sumptuous occasion, suspecting Labour of foisting a fewer-frills wedding on the monarchy by failing to declare a Bank Holiday.[82] Since Elizabeth and Philip married on a Thursday, this ensured that, with most people at work, and most workers being male, women predominated in the London crowds and BBC audience alike. Several MO respondents pointed to the feminized character of the wedding: an event primarily aimed at, and consumed by, women.[83]

Was this intentional, some wondered, to gratify (or pacify) 'housewives' starved of luxury and romance? To whom was royal ceremonial meant to speak, and how? As they contemplated the pageant, Britons weighed their own feelings against reactions ascribed to various others, including the royal pair at the centre of the drama. Several wished for a smaller-scale event, not on the grounds of cost, but because they felt that the couple themselves, ordinarily human, would've preferred something more intimately focused on their exchange of vows. Some suspected Elizabeth, whose voice quavered audibly as she plighted her troth, must've found it all rather an ordeal.[84]

'Was the expenditure justified, was the pageantry wise, the bridal gown absolutely necessary?,' one woman rhetorically enquired. 'The answer sounded from millions of hoarse throats, countless untiring multitudes and (note the question of bridal gown and coupons!) predominantly from housewives and was undoubtedly "Yes".'[85] Yet, for every MO respondent who cheered the festivities as a unifying ritual that consolidated bonds within the United Kingdom, as between metropole and empire, another countered that such excessive expenditure could only exacerbate Britain's domestic and international woes. Austerity demanded not distraction but *circumspection*. 'No one will believe that Britain is up against it when they read of nightdresses at £25 a piece and all the rest of it,' one woman feared. She wasn't alone in fretting that impoverished Britain's claim to sympathy overseas had been squandered, while others weighed the impact on national productivity. 'I think it was a shame that those women spent all those work-hours on that elaborate wedding dress and veil, when such workers are so in demand for our factories …. Damn the Royal wedding.'[86]

For many, though, fixation on bridal finery risked obscuring the bedrock issue. Either one accepted royalty's legitimacy and the public expense entailed in its maintenance or one did not. It was futile to squabble about the 'chicken-feed on the edge of it', as one man put it.[87] So long as the monarchy existed, another woman ventured, it was just 'petty and spiteful' to begrudge the princess her coupons. 'However much the Princess had in the way of clothes, it would in fact make no measurable difference to the national economic situation.'[88] Despite deep dissatisfaction with an inequitable status quo, few seemingly felt the time ripe for abolition.

Something Borrowed

Britain's economic plight structured every appraisal of the wedding. Besides 'colour', 'austerity' recurred more frequently than any other word in the MO responses. Variously an adjective or a noun, this term served as a descriptor, as an explanation or as a lament for 'how things were'. Like poverty, austerity was (and still is) often construed in relational terms – measured against something or someone else. The royal marriage simultaneously prompted consideration of how wealth was apportioned within the United Kingdom as well as how Britain's economy stacked up against other nations. Many respondents, as they imagined distant spectators observing monarchical pageantry amid general poverty, wondered what foreigners would perceive. And when Britons thought in self–other terms, the most frequently invoked 'Other' was the country's major creditor: the United States.

Britons understood the nation's indebtedness to be cultural as well as economic. For some, the 'hysterical' crowds along the Mall exemplified the corrosive impact of American pop culture on more restrained British mores. Frenzied onlookers, one man lamented, behaved like the screaming 'bobbysoxers' who mobbed Frank Sinatra.[89] Many regarded Hollywood as primarily responsible for the rise of celebrity culture, whereby people projected intense emotions onto unknown ciphers, whether inside the picture palace or outside *the* Palace.[90] While cultural elitists bemoaned the degenerative effect

Figure 7.4 Boy scouts sell souvenir programmes to London crowds camping out early on the morning of the royal wedding, 20 November 1947 (J. A. Hampton/Topical Press Agency/Hulton Archive/Getty Images)

of American cultural imports on susceptible masses, leftists regretted that glitzy 'circuses' dazzled people with dreams of unachievable luxury. 'Emotional paralysis' set in, observed a miner living in a Mansfield hostel, hobbling the impetus for 'revolutionary change'.[91] Others, setting aside personal distaste for regal pageantry, tried to derive some comfort from the hard currency that the wedding as 'trade show' might yield – a viewpoint suggestive of how deeply Britain's sterling crisis impinged on everyday consciousness. 'While I am most definitely against having a veritable tribe of duchesses and children all being kept in splendour by impoverished Britain', remarked a shorthand typist in Cheshire (who stated her monthly salary as £30), 'yet I quite realise that the actual Royal family of King, Queen & children is a worthwhile investment as a showpiece to endear us to the Americans (our rich cousins, so fond of their so-called "freedom & non-imperialism", who are yet the most snobbish and monarch-worshipping people in the world).' Other similarly tart remarks attest that many Britons bristled at their economic dependence on wealthier Americans.[92]

Whether they revered or reviled British monarchy, US reporters were dispatched to London *en masse* to cover the pageantry. Britons who envisioned American observers in envious awe at the proceedings might've been dismayed by the extent to which the royal wedding served as an opportunity to register not only ceremonial pomp but 'straitened circumstance'.[93] British journalists didn't need to comment on the backdrop of national impoverishment. For their American counterparts, however, the bleakness of postwar Britain – the proximity of wartime catastrophe, the indelible imprint years of total war had left on the nation's capital and its inhabitants – was in its own right a newsworthy aspect of the proceedings. The contrast between regal splendour and pervasive scarcity was too stark to pass unmentioned. *Life* magazine, which devoted thirteen pages to the wedding, located it temporally not in the second year of peace, but during 'the ninth winter of Britain's austerity'. As American reporters surveyed the scene around and within the Abbey, they noted that 'commoners' weren't alone in appearing decidedly down at heel. Some aristocratic guests' camphor-reeking finery had evidently 'seen much better days'. Tiaras were tarnished.[94] Tellingly, though not atypically, the *New York Times* headlined its coverage of the royal nuptials 'Worn, Shabby Britons Thrill to Cavalry, Bands, Coaches'. Drew Middleton interpreted the event not as a harbinger of national regeneration, but rather as a marker of diminution: 'a joyous day but a sad one, too, for Britain. For a brief moment the pace of the strident terrible twentieth century was slowed to the trot of cavalry horses and the rumbling of coaches and pageantry evoked bitter sweet memories of this island's old, heroic past.' 'Austerity had been pierced by a glimpse of pomp and pageantry,' rallying Britons' spirits, but that didn't mean past glory was poised to return.[95]

The *New York Times* had already alerted Americans to the gift most frequently bestowed on the princess by loyal subjects. 'The riches of the world are ransacked when royalty marries, and of all the precious things that Britons could think of, nylons took first place.'[96] Unlike the clothing coupons sent to the Palace, these eighty pairs of stockings were not returned to sender with polite notes. Instead, they joined an eclectic collection of wedding presents on display at St James's Palace, for those willing to pay the entrance fee.[97] Fabric, along with a thoughtfully donated sewing machine, bulked large: from bathmats, blankets and table linen to furs from Canada, kimonos from Japan, saris from India and a 'fringed lacework cloth', spun by Mahatma Gandhi himself. His 'Quit India' campaign, inspired by American revolutionaries' adoption of homespun fabric, had encouraged Indians to weave their own cloth, *khadi*, to break the dependence on British imports that had decimated India's once vibrant textile sector.[98]

Not surprisingly, American reporters paid particular attention to the largesse of their nation's *own* commercial enterprises and individual citizens who'd helped fill the princess's hope chest. The New York Dress Institute presented a satin-lined trunk with twenty-five dresses, suits, coats, evening gowns and negligees, so that 'the princess will not be denied the right of a bride to a trousseau of pretty clothes'.[99] In deference to Westminster's preferences, hems respected 'old look' conventions, remaining 14″ from the floor. Meanwhile, the *Washington Post* found an endearing local angle for its wedding coverage in the person of Mrs Lois Guerrieri, who'd had the same idea as the New York Dress Institute on a smaller scale. The thirty-two-year-old mother of four, a part-time seamstress, designed and made a dress for Princess Elizabeth. 'I read that clothing was being curtailed in England and that Her Highness' wedding would not be elaborate,' Lois told the *Post*. 'I had this green taffeta material to make a dress for myself .... Then I made up my mind – I'll send it to the Princess.' Guessing Elizabeth's size, Lois allowed sufficiently ample seams that the dress could be adjusted to fit. The garment, sewn in snatched spare time over the course of three weeks, boasted a full skirt, leg-of-mutton sleeves (puffed at the shoulder, pinched at the wrist) and a round collar. Unlike the New York Dress Institute's offerings, Lois' creation was 'new length' – a style she imagined would particularly please the princess. Perhaps she was right. The Palace's thank-you note included an invitation to the wedding party.[100]

Seizing an opportunity to convey the drama of first-time foreign travel, transatlantic aviation and a royal wedding through the wide eyes of a 'Washington Cinderella', the *Post* paid for Lois' trip. In return, she cabled a series of reports on this big adventure, while reporters loitered at the family home to observe another novelty: how a working husband coped alone with four young children.[101] After breathless accounts of air travel, Lois' cables conveyed the details of 'very rigid' clothes rationing in Britain, which meant that, although well-tailored apparel beckoned from shop windows, Britons could buy little of it. Coupon-less foreign visitors were unable to purchase anything at all.[102] The highlight of the trip, its ostensible *raison d'être*, turned out to be rather anticlimactic. Dulled by jet-lag and deterred by the crush of 2,000 guests, Lois elbowed her way out of the royal party early, but not before her improvised head-dress of two lily corsages caught the Queen's admiring eye. Lois found herself introduced to the King. 'He looked as tired as I feel right now,' she divulged on return. But, if she didn't meet the beneficiary of her generosity in person, Lois was rewarded with an even better gift of her own back in DC: a realization, redolent of Dorothy's epiphany in *The Wizard of Oz*, that there was 'no place like home'.[103]

By late 1947, the theme of Americans bailing out British brides was familiar. As early as 1943, well-heeled American 'society ladies' began sending over bridal gowns in tandem with larger efforts to amass 'bundles for Britain'. Their goal was to give women-in-uniform who lacked the coupons to procure a white wedding dress the opportunity to rent American-donated apparel for a nominal fee.[104] Both in Britain and in the United States, it became commonplace during the war for brides in the armed forces to wear their uniform instead of conventional bridal attire. This practice was more pervasive in the United States than in Britain, where an unorthodox sartorial choice was more likely to be interpreted as a marker of poverty than of patriotism. American women's uniforms were also generally considered – on both sides of the Atlantic – to be more flattering than their British counterparts, though, had Elizabeth chosen to wear her ATS uniform to marry Philip, she'd still have sported a Norman Hartnell design. 'I tackled the skirt first, for that is most difficult,' he reminisced. 'It could not be too straight or tight-fitting to encumber the young lady whilst scrambling into Army lorries, or mounting civilian omnibuses. Neither could it be full-swinging, not because of the flirtatious breezes of Salisbury Plain, but because too generous a use of material would add to the cost.' In the design of uniforms, if not royal bridal attire, considerations of utility prevailed.[105]

Various parties professed chagrin at the sight of brides in any uniform other than a flounced white frock. Servicemen were reported to be especially disheartened by the prospect of non-traditional brides. One enlisted man writing for the US army newspaper *Stars & Stripes* wondered 'just how far … this martial spirit [would] prevail into the home life of tomorrow. If the uniform can so easily replace the wedding gown, will we live to see the day when the bazooka gun replaces the rolling pin as the symbol of domestic authority?'[106] Conservative women also mistrusted new bridal customs that threatened to recalibrate the scale of spousal relations in wives' favour. In Britain,

Figure 7.5 Members of the ATS watch a fashion show in which models wear donated bridal attire, 6 January 1944 (Fred Morley/Fox Photos/ Getty Images)

best-selling romance novelist Barbara Cartland spearheaded a campaign to shore up the endangered white wedding, placing an ad in *The Lady* to solicit funds with which to purchase wedding gowns and veils. By the end of the war, she'd amassed a pool of over 1,000 gowns which could be hired by British servicewomen at the cost of £1.[107]

Cartland's efforts were mirrored by American society ladies who banded together under the aegis of the General Federation of Women's Clubs to buy white dresses – with *trains* – for despatch to Britain. Eleanor Roosevelt led from the front by donating a dress. Fashioned from ivory taffeta, with a ruched bodice and full skirt, this gown was drawn by the ATS in a lottery to determine the allocation of dresses between the services. On its debut appearance in Edinburgh, police had to be summoned to preserve order as a mob flocked to see a Scottish bride in the First Lady's dress.[108] In time, each branch of the British women's services, along with the Royal College of Nursing (RCN) and Women's Land Army, was equipped with its own pool of gowns loaned out to brides for a modest fee that covered return postage and cleaning. Swansea Land Girl Dorothy Davies paid fifteen shillings to the Ministry of Agriculture and Fisheries (MAF) for 'hire of American Wedding Dress', as her receipt stated, when she married in August 1945. (In her hazy recollection, this outfit had been 'sent over from the film studios for girls in the forces', though it was in fact a British studio, Gainsborough, that loaned out its bridal wardrobe during and after the war.[109]) Unlike the MAF, the RCN avoided the distraction of administering a bridal wear rental service by recruiting a wardrobe mistress from the Strand Theatre. Cissie Thornton duly oversaw burdensome arrangements for the twenty-three wedding dresses bestowed on the college by the Federation of Women's Clubs of America. All told, the RCN gowns were loaned out 285 times, though they sometimes arrived too late for the ceremony or proved too poor a fit to be worn.[110]

These arrangements, though not the glitches, were favourably reported in both British and American civilian and service newspapers. Young couples could enjoy the romantic wedding of their dreams, or their mothers' dreams, despite adversity. In the United States, club-women's generosity received particularly flattering coverage. With anti-British sentiment at a low ebb, aid to beleaguered Britain acquired a patina of patriotic virtue. Newspapers conjured 'Uncle Sam's club-women' as a 'battalion of fairy godmothers', whose donated gowns supplied 'orange blossom by lend lease': a formula that linked a sentimental gesture to Washington's bankrolling of the Allied war effort.[111] Albeit on a much smaller scale, loaned American dresses underscored altered power relations between the two nations. Like many of the traditional marriages elite British and American women were so keen to preserve, their partnership was not a union of equals, but rather a dyarchy predicated on hierarchy. Bridal gowns figured as one particularly intimate way in which Britons experienced ascendant American power at its softest – in silk and satin, lace and tulle.

Ambassadresses

Well-heeled society ladies weren't the only American women with a vested interest in British bridal apparel. Soon-to-be mothers-in-law, whose servicemen sons were engaged to British fiancées, also figured in this transatlantic matrix. Whatever the couples themselves may have preferred, some mothers (the US press reported) were particularly adamant that their boys' brides should wear white. Not just *something* borrowed, but – if necessary – everything loaned.[112]

No wartime phenomenon did more to accentuate the asymmetric character of British–US relations than Britain's occupation by hundreds of thousands of American service personnel during the war. All told, more than a million GIs landed in the British Isles during the war, staying for varied amounts of time, importing different manners, mores and considerably more money than most British soldiers had at their disposal. In this meeting of unequals, Americans were indisputably the 'rich relations', in the title of David Reynolds's pioneering study.[113] British–US relationships assumed many guises: sometimes fraternal, sometimes fractious, but rarely avuncular. While encounters between uniformed 'Yanks' and 'Tommies' tended towards antagonism, amity – or outright amorousness – was more common between GIs and British women. As Reynolds documents, the latter dynamics exacerbated the former.[114] Despite the US high command's best efforts to deter men (especially enlisted men) from marrying foreign women, by 1950 at least 37,879 marriages had been contracted between American servicemen and British women, with some historians estimating a total of 70,000–100,000.[115] After typically protracted spousal separations, as US servicemen landed in continental Europe and were later demobilized and shipped home from elsewhere, the majority of British 'GI brides' sailed to America in 1946. More followed in 1947. Almost as many women emigrated to Canada in the same period, having married Canadian servicemen stationed in Britain during the war. Wives of North American servicemen thus comprised a significant proportion of the roughly 125,000 Britons who emigrated annually between 1945 and 1960 – departures encouraged by the British government keen to strengthen ties with the Dominions, even as it struggled with a declining birth rate and shrinking workforce.[116]

When Americans contemplated the royal marriage, or when Britons projected themselves into the minds of Yankee 'rich relations' observing this ceremony, they did so in the context of intensified conjugal bonds. For many Britons, transatlantic relations had ceased to be the remote stuff of high diplomacy, statecraft and strategy – the exclusive province of statesmen, consuls and generals. Ties became more personal and proximate as daughters, sisters, friends and neighbours met and married Americans, then waited for shipping to become available to take them to the United States. Underscoring postwar power dynamics, German POWs served as baggage handlers at the holding camp at Tidworth, Hampshire, where brides and babies mustered prior to embarkation at Southampton.[117]

As the first contingent of women and infants disembarked from the *Argentina* in February 1946, a *New York Times* editorial likened the moment to 'the landing of the Pilgrims on Plymouth rock in 1620': an event that would 'substantially affect the American scene'.[118] Latter-day pilgrims these women may have been. Puritans who disavowed personal adornment they were not – or at least not as the US press depicted them. For many American observers, the story of transatlantic relocation was framed by consumption. Assimilation, the desired end-state, could be gauged by garments. How immigrants Americanized their wardrobes and adjusted to abundance were markers on the route to citizenship. If Lois Guerrieri's trip to Britain provided an occasion to revel in the superior comforts of home, 'GI brides' supplied an extended opportunity to admire postwar America, flatteringly refracted through British eyes – as Americans beheld them.

To help prepare British women poised to set sail, the American Red Cross ran classes for brides in London.[119] Avice Wilson, a young woman from Wiltshire, attended one such talk. She later remembered being told that 'in general one wears black or dark blue, summer and winter in big cities, and cotton for all clothes, even "dressy" frocks in summer'.[120] *Good Housekeeping* magazine, at the behest of the US Office of War Information (Washington's counterpart to the Ministry of Information), produced a pamphlet in June 1945, *A War Bride's Guide to the U.S.A.*, 'with vital information on their new life in America'. Avice found this booklet invaluable. Tips covered various aspects of cultural and linguistic divergence between two superficially similar nations. An appendix running to several pages provided a glossary so that British brides would keep their 'trousers' and 'pants' straight, appreciating that babies needed 'diapers', not 'nappies'. Muddled words were one thing; messy appearances quite another. The booklet's opening paragraph concluded with a strict injunction: 'Dress your smartest for first interviews and remember that, except in the smallest villages, lipstick is expected.'[121] In Fred Urquhart's comic novella *The Last GI Bride Wore Tartan* (1947), the Scottish protagonist takes this advice to heart. Jessie wears her 'Stewart tartan skirt' for the passage over, saving the new wardrobe – procured with black market coupons by her GI spouse – for the day when she'll strike out alone for Hollywood, having jettisoned him first.[122]

Figure 7.6 'Lipstick is expected': British GI brides, Joan Mary Strombeck and Laura Tickner, heed advice as the USS *Argentina* prepares to dock in New York City, 4 February 1946 (Bettmann/Getty Images)

Unlike Princess Elizabeth, or Urquhart's wayward heroine, most British GI brides did not possess a trousseau. Emigrants departing Britain for wealthier destinations with more abundant clothing supplies – in contrast to those heading for 'the tropics' to re-stake Britain's colonial claims – received no supplementary clothing coupons. 'Americans Must See You Shabby', the *Manchester Guardian* warned GI brides in October 1945. The 200 lb limit on baggage was superfluous for the majority of women setting sail.[123] Margaret Paroutaud met her American husband while studying at the University of Bristol. A skilled practitioner of 'making do', she married in her sister's modified gown and loaned stockings. 'For my honeymoon I had made an elegant housecoat out of a white heavy brocade bedspread,' she recalled in an unpublished memoir, *Is Your Marriage Really Necessary? (A War-Bride's Story).* 'I took that with me – carefully folded – and the very few clothes that I possessed. For the journey I had a Fair-Isle beret and gloves and a warm coat and slacks. It was going to be cold until I arrived in California and there I supposed that I could buy some cotton dresses.' The rest of her trunk Margaret filled with university notes and essays, her undergraduate thesis and exam papers. Who knew, after all, what might prove indispensable in a foreign land?[124]

Conditioned by years of reportage on threadbare Britain, Americans presumably didn't anticipate that the GI brides who disembarked in New York after a gruelling transatlantic passage would be dressed to the nines. If they'd read that British women sometimes resorted to painting their legs with Bisto and faking 'seams' with eyeliner, they shouldn't have been surprised that some had 'never owned a pair of nylons'.[125] But familiarity with British austerity didn't stop American observers from scrutinizing GI brides' self-presentation, hoping that they would, at the very least, put their best face (if not foot) forward. Lipstick *was* expected. Neat tweeds, classic tailoring, clear complexions and trim figures all garnered favourable comment as the 'war brides' came ashore.[126]

British women's awe at the bounty found in American shops formed a preoccupation of stories explaining 'Why This Is Paradise for GI Brides', with some journalists emphasizing that the American *husband* was himself a superior product.[127] The *War Bride's Guide* advised a methodical approach to wardrobe makeovers: 'Go as slowly as you can in buying clothes until you know the markets and are familiar with what your friends wear. It usually pays to look for quality and good, simple styles that will last. Bows, "froo-froos," and tricky cuts may look appealing in store windows and prices may seem attractively low, but it is always better to be conservatively smart than flashy.'[128]

For their part, American women's magazines promoted more conspicuous and fashion-conscious acquisition. One gushing feature in the August 1946 issue of *Ladies' Home Journal* introduced readers to Max Domina, a veteran paratrooper, and Norma, his British bride. Tagline: 'He came, he saw, he conquered – the heart of an English girl who traveled six thousand miles to make a home for him on a California chinchilla farm.' As told by columnist Jessamyn West, Norma was already an exemplary American wife, blessed with model looks, who self-consciously followed a mythic tradition. 'Women have left their homes and their countries, gone with their husbands to new lands, always. Been pioneers. Particularly after wars,' Norma reportedly declared. Yet there was, West continued, 'nothing remotely pioneerish' in her 'slender', 'fine-boned' and 'lovely' countenance – just something pleasingly familiar, 'for Norma's loveliness is of the kind Americans have come to regard as the unique possession of their own women: a certain length of leg, [...] a verve, a suppleness in her clothes.' To display this lithe physique to even greater effect, Max had given Norma a stupendous $1,000 allowance to California-ize her closet. Photographs and descriptions accompanied the story, albeit without comment on the suitability for farm life of an emerald green coat lined with muskrat or a voluminous off-the-shoulder evening gown.[129]

Stories about acquisitive brides sometimes reflected less favourably on British women. It didn't bode well for the marriage if a bride became so engrossed by window-shopping in Manhattan that she missed the train meant to convey her to wherever an anxious husband awaited.[130] Not all husbands *did* wait. A number of transatlantic marriages quickly fell apart. One twenty-three-year-old 'ex-war bride', her relationship over, briefly blazed an independent trail through New York, robbing wealthy Americans in plush hotels. No weapon was involved in these larcenies. The thief, posing as a guest, simply requested – and received – room keys at the front desk of elite establishments including the Barbizon-Plaza and Hotel Ambassador. Betty Margaret Pitt repeatedly pulled off this trick by appearing so very plausibly dressed in a three-quarter-length silver fox coat, and by sounding so impeccably British, that nobody doubted her bona fides. Perhaps Pitt had put to unintended use the *Guide*'s advice to 'Keep your accent while you can; most English accents, especially when spoken by a girl, are regarded in America as charming.' By the time police apprehended this daughter of a retired Scotland Yard detective (a pedigree the *Times* related without comment), her charm had unlocked many doors. Twenty-three room keys were found in Pitt's possession, along with an impressive trove of stolen jewellery, furs and other clothing valued at $25,000. Means and opportunity evidently presented no obstacles. But what of motive? The *New York Times* concluded that nothing more psychologically aberrant had driven this crime spree than the perpetrator's 'desire for the fine things'.[131]

Press stories, even less spectacular ones, tend to distort lived reality by accentuating extremes and exaggerating characters into caricatures. What, then, of British brides' *self*-described experience of postwar America? In their stories, clothing and consumption also play a role, but rarely the lead. Most women didn't marry men who could afford to give them a $1,000 clothing budget. In this regard, Avice Wilson was much more typical than the brides showcased in magazine features. Avice had been a teenage dairy-worker when she met her GI boyfriend-then-husband, Johnnie Grasso, a first-generation Italian American immigrant whose family had settled in Lackawanna, a steel town on the edge of Buffalo, New York. When Avice and Johnnie were reunited in New York in August 1946, they spent just a couple of days seeing big city sights and shopping before setting off on the long drive to his family home. Along the way, Avice acquired a couple more 'pretty cotton dresses', better suited to the heat and humidity of an upstate summer. Johnnie also presented her with six pairs of nylons. But thereafter married life required serious scrimping, as the couple strove to establish an independent home and set up a block-making business, struggling (and failing) to keep their marriage afloat.[132]

Decades after she moved to the United States and long after the annulment of her marriage, Avice embarked on a project to gather fellow British GI brides' recollections of their relationships and relocations to America. Many of the questionnaires she amassed, written by women who cast their minds back forty years or more, offer intriguing counterpoints to the glossy coverage of 'war brides' by contemporary media. In the latter, what *husbands* wore rarely received any mention. But men's wardrobe choices could prove consequential. Told to present themselves with care on arrival, wives more pertinently might have been warned to brace for a certain sartorial shock on reunion with their husbands. *Punch* put a satirical spin on this theme with a ditty, 'The GI Brides' Lament'. Urging women to forgive their 'GI Josephs' their 'coats of varied check' and 'letters on their sweaters', *Punch*'s target was the 'loudness' of American menswear in contrast to muted British tweeds and flannels.[133] For many British women, though, it wasn't so much the style as the fact of their husband's civilian apparel that elicited surprise. The man embraced again on a pier in New York – or on a distant railroad platform – sometimes bore scant resemblance to the soldier/lover whose image they'd kept alive during months of separation. By the time wives reached the United States, many couples had spent far more time apart than together. Some could tally their entire relationship in days rather than weeks or months. It speaks to the brevity of their courtships, as well as the density of military regulations constraining wartime romance, that some women had *never* seen their spouses dressed in anything other than uniform until the moment of stateside reunion. Shock could take one of two forms. Delight or disappointment. Avice's questionnaires contain examples of both. 'Handsome!,' Mary Stephenson recalled of the first glimpse of her husband in civvies at Burbank, Ohio. 'Ah the glamour of a uniform!!,' sighed Judy Dockerty, remembering a more deflating reunion with her spouse in Newark, New Jersey.[134]

American uniforms were styled to elongate the legs, broaden the shoulders and slim the waists of servicemen. In addition to enhancing the wearer's physique, uniforms also imparted an intangible mystique as they elevated men into *soldiers*.[135] While some women surely proved immune to the magical thinking inspired by male uniforms, others were more susceptible. Seeing a husband as a civilian for the first time would, at the very least, cast him in a different light. If the glow was less flattering than the aura emitted by the uniform, a reduction in status sometimes resulted from claims about the GI's background being exposed as exaggerations or outright lies. One British woman discovered her spouse's boast that his family owned a 'chain of restaurants' meant they operated baseball ground peanut stands, at one of which she was expected to work.[136]

Unexpected poverty forms a theme of the questionnaires. Although some respondents related wonderment over American abundance, others told a different story. The *War Bride's Guide* only fleetingly alerted brides to the discrepancy between Hollywood's America and the country they'd encounter first-hand. Just a page long, the *Guide*'s section on class tensions and 'unfriendliness between people of different ancestry' was entitled 'Americans Are No Angels'. Its recommended reading on 'The South, civil war and reconstruction' was Margaret Mitchell's *Gone with the Wind*. Scarlett O'Hara, who famously transformed green velvet drapes into a glamorous gown, may have been a poster-girl for 'making do', but she provided less reliable guidance on race relations.[137] Many British women were no better prepared for Jim Crow than for grinding poverty among a white, as well as Black, underclass. Doris Smith from Birmingham, whose parental home boasted a bathroom and two WCs, was taken aback to find that her husband's family small-holding in backwoods Kentucky lacked electricity and plumbing. She took her baths in a tub of water (drawn from a well) in the most private spot available: the smokehouse where meat was cured. Bristolian Mary Brook found comparable conditions in rural Alabama. Her new family was very kind, but she 'couldn't <u>ever</u> eat fried squirrel'. And if Mary imagined that Britons held a monopoly on improvisation, she must've been surprised to find herself taught by a sister-in-law how to sew baby clothes from flour sacks.[138] Social class may have been less ossified, but economic disparities in America were no less pronounced than back home in Britain.

Whether it was American wealth or poverty – or the chasm between them – that came as the greater shock depended on the perspective and background of the British wife as well as the man she'd married. If middle-class Britons struggled to adjust to their American spouses' humbler circumstances, poorer women sometimes found it just as hard to see their poverty reflected back in the disdainful eyes of richer new relations. Some American in-laws didn't trouble to mask – or deliberately conveyed – disparaging judgements about British women's appearance and apparel. Patricia Cade, who emigrated from Wallasey, was asked by her husband's cousin to display the clothes she'd brought over from England. The latter's withering comment about Patricia's 'clod-hopper shoes', standard issue in wartime Britain, cut deep. So deep, in fact, that it remained vivid some four decades later.[139] Clothing and footwear often cued strangers' snap judgements about their wearers. That a verdict was hastily reached and thoughtlessly voiced did nothing to lessen its impact on a demeaned recipient. Stigma could cast a lifelong shadow.

Ever After …

What became of the dress that conducted such intense feeling in late 1947? Soon after the ceremony, Elizabeth's gown joined the display of gifts at St James's Palace. But where it should go next, and what work it would perform, led to disagreement between the royals and the government. Harold Wilson regarded Hartnell's design as a magic key that might unlock the door to American trade. Writing to Sir Ulick Alexander (in the Palace's Privy Purse Office) barely a fortnight after the wedding, Wilson explained the predicament: 'one of the difficulties which have always faced us in the American market has been the absence of "great names" of international standing in British fashion design. The French, who have almost a monopoly of these names, have consequently been able to dictate international fashion – an important industry in itself.' Wilson insisted he understood the 'delicacy' of this request, but asked the Palace to consider allowing the princess's wedding dress to appear in a fashion show staged by Hartnell in New York 'not later than mid-February' 1948. 'It would be an unexampled climax to an exhibition of this kind if it were possible to include the actual dresses worn by Princess Elizabeth and the Bridesmaids.' Replicas would be displayed thereafter, in the United States and elsewhere, as requests flooded in from the Dominions. But only *the* dress, bearing the ineffable imprint of the princess, would yield the desired effect. After its star turn in America's fashion metropolis, the bridal gown would be 'flown straight back to this country'.[140]

The Palace was impervious to this commercial logic, no matter how diplomatically phrased. Perhaps the royals had been put off by Hartnell's cruder talk of 'cashing in in dollars on Princess Elizabeth's wedding outfit' or his plan to market in America 'an astringent perfume for the feet of both sexes' – an unlikely candidate for the royal crest.[141] At any rate, although the Palace consented to a *replica* being shown in New York, it insisted the original stay put. Various ideas passed back and forth about displaying Elizabeth's gown in Edinburgh, Cardiff and Belfast and then, at the Palace's suggestion, in Britain's 'textile areas' – to give people there 'a rather special favour'.[142] Eager to entice more workers into the textile industries, Wilson greeted this proposal warmly. Putting Elizabeth's dress on display, shielded by a protective glass case, in destinations such as Manchester, Preston, Bradford, Leeds and Nottingham would be 'an invaluable stimulant to morale and recruitment in textile industries', he enthused. '[O]ne of the finest examples of British art, skill and workmanship in textiles could help considerably arouse pride and interest in the industries which contributed to its production.'[143] The dress did indeed tour the north, while plans for a fashion show in New York fizzled out amid what one exasperated BoT official described as 'very trying and complicated' negotiations between the Palace, the BoT and the couturier. As for producing replicas for display overseas, this idea ran aground when the Palace declined to foot the bill for six copies at a total price of £6,000. If nothing else, this figure highlights that earlier claims Elizabeth's gown cost a mere £200 had substantially undervalued its expense.[144] Using the Bank of England's historical currency calculator, a dress that cost £1,000 in 1947 would today (in 2024) cost £32,376.40.[145] Then as now, the price of Elizabeth's dress exceeded the annual salary of many British workers.

Hartnell did not take New York by storm in early 1948. Nor did his creation, having magnetized so much attention, make much of an impression on late-forties style, opines Colin McDowell. Jonathan Walford's illustrated history of *Forties Fashion* makes no mention whatsoever of Elizabeth's wedding dress.[146] Perhaps this isn't so surprising. As Hartnell predicted, his gown was too ornate to be recreated in minute detail – or until makers of *The Crown*, possessed of the largest budget in television history, did exactly that in 2016. Validating the historical currency calculator, *The Crown*'s wardrobe department spent a rumoured £30,000 to fabricate the replica worn by Claire Foy in the opening episode of season one.[147] Yet, while strikingly expensive, Elizabeth's gown was not strikingly original. Gowns designed by Hartnell in the 1930s had already employed his trademark motifs of embroidery, appliqué and bead-work. Moreover, the princess's bridal gown was soon overshadowed by another garment created for an even more portentous royal ceremony in 1953: Queen Elizabeth II's coronation. Amid a welter of predictions about the monarchy's longevity prompted by the princess's marriage, with some imagining she'd *never* become queen, no one foresaw that she would ascend to the throne so soon. When King George VI died in February 1952, aged just fifty-six, Hartnell was commissioned to produce Elizabeth's coronation gown. This garment made a deeper imprint than the wedding dress, possibly because millions saw the coronation on television, but had only listened to the wedding ceremony on the radio.[148]

Popular memory of forties bridal attire has been captivated by a very different kind of dress: not encrusted with myriad pearls and crystals, but fashioned from parachute silk. News first emerged during the war that some brides, determined to have their white wedding come what may, were confecting bridal gowns from parachute silk. The most prominently reported early example related to Hollywood star Elyse Knox, who was presented with a damaged parachute by her football player fiancé, Lieutenant Tommy Harmon. Since this canopy had saved Harmon's life when he was shot down over China, Knox wanted to use the silk – bullet-holes and all – for her wedding gown when they married in August 1943: 'It brought him back alive.'[149] Variants on this 'swords-into-ploughshares' theme sprang up in every theatre during the war and after. Brides in Germany and Japan, not just the United States and Britain, married in parachute material.

The parachute wedding dress could mean many things. Converting silk or rayon from martial to marital use put a particularly romantic spin on the familiar motif of war *matériel*'s reincarnation for pacific purposes: a symbol not just of ingenuity trumping adversity, but of love's triumph over hate. Of the many such stories and images preserved in museums and online galleries, one stands out as particularly poignant. Lili Lax, a Czech Jew who survived Auschwitz and other Nazi camps, was among those liberated at Bergen-Belsen in April 1945. At neighbouring Celle DP camp she met and fell in love with a fellow Czech, Ludwig Frydman. When they wed in January 1946 at a synagogue near the camp, Lili wore a dress fashioned from a white rayon parachute, the remnants of which the same seamstress (compensated in cigarettes) turned into a shirt for Ludwig. Unlike Harmon's, this was not a parachute that had saved the groom's life. On the contrary, Ludwig bartered two pounds of coffee and cigarettes for the parachute from a German airman. If a Jewish couple could survive Nazi persecution to marry in rayon from a *Luftwaffe* parachute, there was perhaps no limit to the transformations that could be wrought as objects turned into their antitheses in a refashioned postwar world.

Six months later, Lili's sister married in the same dress, followed by several other Jewish brides. At seventeen, Lili stopped counting.[150]

CONCLUSION

Books are obliged to have conclusions, and authors writing them often feel compelled to conclude their narratives tidily. Needlework involves something comparable. In sewing, one knots or finishes off loose ends. As an eight-year-old, although I'd been taught to sew by my mother, I lacked confidence in my ability to twist a single thread into a knot and submerge its tail invisibly below the fabric's surface. So, I asked my school teacher to 'finish me off' – a request which elicited laughter I was too young to understand. Nearly fifty years later, I know more about how various things are finished off – loose ends, stories, lives, books. But the story of postwar clothing resists the artifice of a neat conclusion. Raw edges *should* be left unfinished. Just as this history of postwar fabric has several points of origin – all during the war – so numerous possible endings present themselves, none tidily. The aftermaths of World War II were chronically, irredeemably messy. Political schisms fuelled further conflicts, fresh displacements, more suffering and ongoing scarcity. Even with the benefit of hindsight, a definitive 'post-' to that war eludes identification, whether our yardstick is renewed tranquillity (peace) or restored national fortunes (prosperity). If historians struggle with periodization, Britons who survived the war and subsequent age of austerity surely found it even harder to pinpoint when a definitive end to 'all that' had arrived.

Reflecting in November 1947 on Princess Elizabeth's marriage to Philip Mountbatten, and what it might retrospectively come to signify, some Mass Observers gave this occasion an optimistic spin. 'It is the one thing since the end of the war which has given the British people unity, it may well prove to be the turning-point in the tide of our fortunes,' opined an RAF airman stationed at Kinloss, which had perhaps sheltered him from the wedding's divisiveness.[1] Some historians likewise identify 1947 as an inflection point in postwar British history. The New Look marked a symbolic, but increasingly material, start to a definitively *post*-war era, proposes Angela Partington.[2] And yet, like British women's hemlines, which fell in increments, not through instantaneous adoption of the 'full Dior', rationing and other restrictions over garments and footwear eased only gradually. 'There was no single finishing line for the shortages of food, clothes and fuel and all the aspects of austerity which gave a dull grey tinge to post-war life,' notes Susan Cooper.[3]

Britons awaited the end of controls with equal measures of frustration and anticipation as months, then years, went by after 1945. With the material rewards of victory all too intangible, Attlee's government began to fear the impact of popular dissatisfaction with queues, coupons, shortages and inflation on its electoral fortunes. Dalton's *annus horrendus* didn't conveniently conclude on 31 December 1947. The following year, to fend off Conservative attacks and irate housewives, Harold Wilson promised a 'bonfire of controls'. His phrase evoked not just annual November fifth festivities but also the celebratory bonfires lit on VE Day, atop which numerous effigies of Hitler went up in flames.[4] There was, however, no culminating day on which all ration books could be burnt. The VE Day analogy was apt in one sense alone. When Wilson announced the end of clothes rationing in March 1949, it felt less euphoric than people who'd spent years waiting for this moment had surely expected, rather like the anticlimactic end of the war in Europe while fighting continued in Asia. As Wilson coyly tore up his clothing ration book for the press photographers, he dampened the celebratory mood with a reminder that Britons should put their own defunct 'little red books' on the kerb for the 'salvage man' – a parsimonious gesture far less gratifying than incinerating obsolete coupons.[5] Henceforth, Britons could purchase clothing and footwear, as well as replacing worn-out bed linen, curtains, towels and hankies, all without coupons. Sweets came off the ration too. But adults, if not children, couldn't fail to notice that restrictions over more nutritious foodstuffs remained in place. Some staples, including meat, would continue to be rationed until 1954, making Britain the last country to end wartime food restrictions.[6]

Figure C.1 *Daily Express* columnist Drusilla Beyfus defies Harold
Wilson's injunction to recycle obsolete clothes rationing books by
setting hers alight, 15 March 1949 (Photo by Express/Getty Images)

The reason why the government decided to terminate clothes
rationing in March 1949 was revealing, though hardly the stuff of jubilant headlines. The cost of new garments had risen so much – 93 per
cent since 1938 – that a substantial number of Britons couldn't afford
to purchase many, or *any*, new garments, whether or not rationing
remained in place.[7] Labour cabinet ministers worried that Washington
would interpret the end of clothing controls to mean that Westminster
had capitalized on Marshall Aid to improve Britons' standard of living, rather than focusing on production for export to earn the dollars
that would help repay American loans. When he announced the end
of clothes rationing, Wilson duly took pains to stress that the export
drive would continue unabated, billing 1949 as 'Lancashire's Year of
Destiny'.[8] He could do so in the sure knowledge there'd be no sudden reorientation of garment production towards the domestic market.
High prices effectively curbed demand, as shoppers were well aware.

The *News Chronicle* accompanied its photo of Wilson cautiously ripping up his coupon book with a story headlined 'Women Say "Very Nice, But –"'. For the government, 'derationing' represented less the ignition of a 'bonfire of controls' than the lighting of a votive candle, with the accompanying prayer that voters would give Labour more time to build the New Jerusalem: a welfare system in which healthcare, pensions and insurance against sickness and unemployment were universal entitlements.[9]

The extent of ongoing British clothing poverty is hinted by a letter folded away in the archives of Oxfam, a postwar entrant into the increasingly crowded field of overseas relief. In May 1949, two months after Wilson's smokeless 'bonfire', George Blake wrote in despair to Oxfam's headquarters from Preston, where destiny had yet to reignite cotton's fortunes. He'd seen an Oxfam advertisement soliciting donations to clothe European refugees and wanted to know whether the charity might spare some garments for *his* family. He was off work sick, living on £2 9s 6d per week, with four school-age children and another baby on the way. 'I have better tried at different places in Preston but I am one of those unlucky persons not to receive anything in the discarded clothes line.' Blake implored his missive's recipient to regard it not as a 'begging letter', but as a token of his family's 'desperate need of clothes'. He remained empty-handed. Oxfam's polite response explained that all clothing donations were sent abroad. Its author instead directed Blake to his local Citizens Advice Bureau, a wartime institution that long outlived its for-the-duration genesis.[10]

The fragility of postwar recovery in 1949 is further underscored if we consider developments beyond Britain. If prosperity remained elusive, so too did peace. This was the year in which the USSR detonated its first atomic bomb, ratcheting up anxiety about the prospect of thermonuclear war.[11] But apprehension about planetary annihilation was accompanied by a parallel response – obliviousness to this prospect, or a wilful determination to repress the unthinkable by turning atomic testing into the referent for something altogether different. How else do we explain the fact that a mere eleven months elapsed between the obliteration of Hiroshima and Nagasaki in August 1945 and French designer Louis Réard's decision to christen his two-piece swimsuit '*le bikini*'? Réard named his creation after Bikini Atoll, where four days earlier the United States had conducted the first of sixty-seven postwar nuclear bomb tests in the Marshall Islands. (Britain held its own independent tests a year later.) Unveiling his 'bikini', Réard simultaneously nodded to fellow French designer Jacques Heim, whose beachfront shop in Cannes sold a two-piece ensemble cheekily named 'Atome', after the 'smallest known particle of matter'. The appalling implications of the atomic age seemingly left them unmoved. Reporters quipped that, since Réard's G-string two-piece was even smaller than Heim's, he had 'split the *atome*'. While the devastation of the Marshall Islands passed largely unremarked, the bikini passed into common currency, just as – thanks to Hollywood – the 'bombshell' had earlier become synonymous with a devastatingly attractive woman.[12]

That atomic fission should impart a frisson to flesh-exposing swimwear is all the more troubling if we contemplate what the atomic bombs – named, with equally troubling insouciance, 'Little Boy' and 'Big Man' – did to the residents of Hiroshima and Nagasaki on whom they were dropped. Some accounts of the bikini's genesis suggest that the name purposely gestured towards the fabric *vestiges* left after an atomic explosion – a moniker bestowed not, then, in ignorance of the bomb's effects but in full sardonic awareness.[13]

The heat from the blast at Hiroshima was so infernal that it seared off clothing in an instant. One Japanese physician, Dr Michihiko Hachiya, was asleep in 'drawers and undershirt' on the sultry morning of 6 August 1945. After a blinding flash of light followed by an ear-splitting implosion, he was stunned to regain consciousness and find himself 'completely naked'. 'How odd! Where were my drawers and undershirt?', he later recalled having thought. With a shard of glass embedded in his neck and a mangled thigh, Hachiya set off for a nearby hospital, his workplace, with his wife. His diary powerfully conveys the surreal horror of surviving a nuclear explosion before its victims understood what had caused their city's devastation and their own bodily anguish. He apologizes to a headless corpse for having tripped over it and, modesty not extinguished, asks a soldier for a towel to cover his nakedness, while all around buildings lie in ruins, fires smouldering among the debris. Stumbling to the hospital, Hachiya is perplexed to find that women passing by with babies are also unclothed. 'Perhaps they had been in the bath,' he speculates. 'But then I saw a naked man, and it occurred to me that, like myself, some strange thing had deprived them of their clothes.' These speechless

Figure C.2 Child survivors of the atomic bombing of Hiroshima wear face masks to block the smell of corpses, 1 October 1945 (Bettmann/ Getty Images)

figures shuffle past – arms awkwardly held out to prevent friction between limbs and torsos. American journalist John Hersey would later describe victims' skin peeling off in 'huge, glove-like pieces' in an account of Hiroshima's destruction that filled the entire 31 August 1946 edition of the *New Yorker*, widely disseminated on both sides of the Atlantic. His graphic simile pointed to an eerie elision of skin and fabric among survivors. Some found that the flower-prints of kimonos had been seared onto their skin. White fabric reflected thermal radiation away from the body, whereas dark areas of cloth conducted heat, leaving an imprint of the garment's pattern burnt onto the wearer's flesh.[14]

This horrifying example of the atomic bomb's unprecedented destructiveness returns us, fittingly, to the prevalence of 'bare life' during and after the war. Clothing, as this book has shown, was an essential precondition for survival, though sometimes the very coverings necessary to protect human existence lethally jeopardized it. Recall the lice, adept at burrowing into garment seams, that spread an epidemic of typhus at Belsen. Raw human need – on an epochal scale – continued long after 1945, as revolution, rebellion, partition and civil war began to unpick European empires and reshape the world order. Millions more refugees soon joined the vast mass of people uprooted during the war and then immobilized in refugee camps that, in time, gained the flimsy solidity of towns improvised from canvas and corrugated metal. Clothing distribution continued to form a prominent part of humanitarian relief, generating wave after wave of appeals – like the one seen in a Sunday paper by George Blake in Preston – urging better-off people in Britain and North America to donate used garments.

One particularly resonant example lies in the work of the United Nations Relief and Works Agency for Palestine Refugees in the Near East (UNRWA). This organization, modelled on the by-then-defunct UNRRA, was established in 1949 to provide basic humanitarian aid to Palestinian refugees who'd fled or been driven from their homes before and during the conflict that engulfed the former British mandate after the State of Israel came into existence in May 1948. Mass displacement, the *Nakba* (or 'catastrophe') to Palestinians, left in tatters the UN's 1947 partition plan for an Arab state to exist alongside Israel, with Jerusalem and Bethlehem under international control. Tattered Arab refugees, many of whom had fled with nothing, sought shelter in the neighbouring states of Jordan, Egypt, Syria and Lebanon.[15] Victor Gollancz, having earlier harnessed his energies to mustering supplies for hungry and threadbare Germans, found a new 'underdog' to champion. In a pamphlet entitled *Why Jews Should Help Arab Refugees*, Gollancz pointedly told readers: 'Arab children are dying; and if they are allowed to die and no attempt, no Jewish attempt, is made to save them, there will be, quite inevitably, such a legacy of hatred as must poison still more virulently middle-Eastern life.' He concluded with a heartfelt entreaty: 'In love, and in the acts that spring from love, is the only salvation.'[16]

As with his campaign on behalf of Germans, Gollancz did not act alone. He encouraged readers of his petition to make donations to a newly founded Jewish Society for Human Service.[17] The British Red Cross likewise prioritized Palestinian refugees. In January 1951, the organization launched an appeal for clothes and bedding with a broadcast on the BBC Home Service. Sir Ronald Storrs (a former military governor of the Palestine mandate) described the 'suffering – spiritual, physical' of some 800,000 refugees as they struggled to subsist in Gaza. Storrs foregrounded the plight of children, quoting a UNESCO official:

> We went to see the refugees – thousands of men and women exposing their suffering in a mood of utter despair beneath a grey winter sky. Children by the hundred – most of them half naked – shoeless and shivering – conveyed the depths of their misery in gestures that were more eloquent than words. They showed us holes in the ground – deep, like wells – where the children were living in total darkness, piled one on top of the other against the icy rock.

Storrs asked listeners for garments and bedding. Anything at all. Blankets; old sheets; towels; bedspreads; lengths of fabric. The desert, he explained, was cold at night. 'We used to say that however many blankets you have over you – if only two – keep one to put under you; against the raw chill that seeps out of the pitiless dead sand. These children have no blankets at all, and hardly any clothing.'[18] A blanket might make the difference between survival or extinction. As we've seen, blankets served humanity in extremis in multiple guises. For refugees, they were variously something to sleep in (and on) or something to wear. The US aid agency CARE produced a pattern for turning a blanket into a woman's suit, stylishly modelled in *Life* magazine in February 1947, though most refugees lacked the wherewithal to pin paper pieces to a blanket, cut them out and sew them together by machine.[19] At Belsen in April 1945, blankets functioned as makeshift stretchers and shrouds. In DP camps, draped over taut pieces of string, blankets formed partitions in dormitories. Oblong pieces of woollen cloth enabled a fiction of privacy – as much as a couple or family could hope for in overcrowded barracks. In Palestine, a blanket might serve as a rudimentary tent, simultaneously roof and walls.[20]

The Red Cross billed its campaign 'Bundles for Palestine', tapping into memories of American 'bundles for Britain' dispatched during the Blitz. Now, better-off Britons could extend the same grace by donating discarded textiles to refugees in Gaza. This role reversal – Britain no longer 'poor cousin' but 'rich relation' – extended only so far, however. Some British politicians saw in Palestinians' plight an opportunity for humanitarianism to serve a more self-interested end. In a parliamentary debate in 1952, with Churchill reinstalled as PM, Conservative MP Capt. Arthur Soames proposed that UNRWA be steered towards ordering garments for Palestinians from Lancashire's ailing cotton mills. Several strands of this book's study of people- and garments-in-motion again intertwine. European Volunteer Workers, plucked from German and Austrian DP camps, had been sent into textile mills in the late 1940s, though the industry's maladies were too chronic to be remedied by an injection of foreign labour alone. Robust export markets were also required and, by the early fifties, British products faced stiff competition from cheaper cotton textiles manufactured by refurbished Japanese mills. Soames discerned a way in which to draw distant sites of duress – from Preston to Palestine – into a reciprocally beneficial relationship. So much the better if the US government, the primary supplier of UNRWA's budget, paid the estimated £2,000,000 it would require to clothe 850,000 Palestinians in Lancashire cotton.[21]

The history of clothing is full of such unexpected entanglements, textiles binding far-flung people in webs of mutuality. During the war and early postwar years, both people and fabric circulated, changed hands and switched identities in staggering numbers. Enlistment in the armed forces, war work in factories or on the land and overseas humanitarianism propelled millions of Britons into motion and, often, into uniform of one sort or another. What people wore – and where their garments came from – altered as prewar trade routes were severed, production shifted towards military apparel, donated garments arrived from overseas and British military surplus in turn set sail for the continent and beyond. To study postwar clothing is thus to appreciate the overlapping trajectories of mobile bodies and textiles in a constant state of circulation, passed from hand to hand and from one use to another. Clothing, as *Making Do* has shown, lay at the heart of interlocking entitlement struggles that required political leaders, military officers and relief workers to decide who got clothed in what, and at whose expense. 'Redress' was often, quite literally, enacted through reallocations of garments – whether, for instance, in the decision to clothe male veterans at female civilians' expense or to compel Germans to surrender garments and bedding for victims of the Third Reich, before they, in turn, were outfitted with dyed military kit.

Relationships between war, the military and clothing were, and remain, intricately knotted. The militarization of civil society after 1945 has attracted a good deal of attention. Many commentators, whether focusing on the United States or Britain, conclude that fashion has fallen victim to rampant militarization. While surplus apparel has saturated everyday life, civilian adaptations of military staples – camouflage fabric, combat boots, cargo pants, bomber jackets, aviator shades – have pervaded street style.[22] Certainly, army surplus shops were a fixture of British high streets throughout the twentieth century. Around the time my mother made my blackout skirt, c. 1981, it was a fad among girls at my school to trade leather satchels or Adidas hold-alls for army surplus canvas shoulder-bags, personalized with CND symbols and favourite two-tone band logos. Millets supplied many of these briefly modish bags. (Mine was a relic of my father's National Service in the 1950s.) The outdoor clothing and equipment retail chain began by selling army and navy surplus after World War I, a role it continued following World War II. Over time, however, both the merchandise and the aura of Millets' shops mutated into something more 'outdoorsy', shedding the suggestion that going camping was akin to going out on manoeuvres.[23]

The 'civilianization' of military kit has received far less comment than the militarization of civilian apparel. Yet, rather than conceiving these as unidirectional processes, it's surely more appropriate to understand them as circular. It's hard, after all, to read the peace sign drawn on a teenage girl's army bag as a sign of insidious military 'mission creep'. One of the biggest surprises I encountered in researching this book wasn't just how commonly but how *completely* military material could be transformed – transcended, even – by human creativity. How was it possible for survivors of Nazi camps to wear *Wehrmacht* apparel? To put on a stormtrooper's boots? To marry in *Luftwaffe* parachute rayon? To turn German uniforms into children's toys; their own striped uniforms into dolls representing *themselves*? I'd imagined some fabric would resist refashioning – too tainted by past associations to touch, even if dyed a different shade, as though toxic associations would continue to bleed through. Yet seemingly not. What's equally clear, though, is that people's capacity to disregard previous ownership of, say, a *Wehrmacht* jacket or boots shouldn't be mistaken for a condition of abjection in which *any* garment would suffice to satisfy raw need. Even in the direst of circumstances, survivors of Nazi genocide who chose garments at 'Harrods' in Belsen were selective. They wanted clothes that, whatever their functional attributes, would enhance appearance: a criterion that applied to donated and requisitioned civilian attire as well as military surplus. At the very least, unbecoming garments had to show potential for reclamation. Individuality, as much as necessity, was the 'mother of invention'. Likewise, when DPs came to Britain as EVWs in the late 1940s, they weren't willing to 'make do' with *anything* offered by the WVS. British relief workers were sometimes exasperated by this pickiness, but government officials – surveying the 'junk' that emerged from 'bundles for Britain' or UNRRA bales – were just as sniffy about garments and shoes that weren't fit for purpose.

Clothing always represented more than 'mere' cover for vulnerable bodies, a source of protection from the elements and insulation from infection. What people wore profoundly shaped their sense of self. To restore and sustain self-esteem – to elicit others' respect, perhaps even their love – only *some* garments passed muster. Clothing was capable of betrayal. Garments and shoes that were hopelessly worn, out of place or out of date, misshapen or ill-fitting could expose their wearer to scorn. No matter how stylish a coat sewn from an UNRRA blanket might appear modelled in *Life*, not everyone whose outwear was improvised from army surplus felt chic to be so attired. If clothing was a medium of exchange, a currency in which postwar rewards and entitlements were tallied, it also formed a yardstick of measurement. Strangers and neighbours alike frequently judged one another by their apparel. As *Making Do* has shown, many sartorial appraisals made in the wake of war were not only unusually sharp but also particularly consequential. Millions of people, trading places and statuses, found these passages mediated by a change of garments. Transitions were thus accompanied by the shock of seeing oneself, or of being seen by others, anew. Not always flatteringly.

Postwar's seemingly rigid binary – between victors and vanquished – proves a wildly insufficient guide to the multiplicity of altered statuses and relationships resulting from the war. For Britain, 'winning' was bound up with the longer-term process of surrendering global dominance. Historians often emphasize that many Britons stubbornly refused to accept altered geopolitical and economic realities for decades after 1945, clinging to fantasies of restored global primacy. This observation is certainly true of a ruling class intent on reinforcing empire against further unravelling. But fewer 'ordinary' Britons, registering postwar alterations as diminutions, seemingly harboured such illusions in the late 1940s. And often reduced circumstances most palpably made themselves felt in what people wore – their clothes and shoes.

'Shabby'. 'Threadbare'. 'Down-at-heel'. No trio of epithets recurs more frequently in descriptions of postwar Britain, whether the appraisals were delivered by Britons or by others, such as Americans scornfully eyeing up British GI brides' hand-stitched attire and clumsy shoes. In 1950, a US diplomat and his spouse co-authored a book about their time in postwar Britain, entitled *Destination Austerity*, as though this were not an economic condition but a geographical location. Noting the profusion of British women in various – but invariably unflatter-ing – civil and military uniforms, Nancie Matthews repeated the verdict of an Italian friend, 'used to the feminine women of his own country': '[T]here seemed to be a third sex in Britain,' androgynous Amazons who appeared to be 'running the country'.[24] (These 'Amazons' created an optical illusion. Women were not ruling the country. The general election of 1945 returned a record crop of female MPs to Parliament, but this unprecedented number amounted to just twenty-four.)

In recent years, the return of austerity, more by ideological choice than as a result of war-induced necessity, has helped fuel a resurgence of interest in forties fashion: a montage of wedge heels, knee-length dresses, wide shoulders and hair quiffed under polka-dotted bandannas, projected to the imaginary strains of Glenn Miller wafting from a canteen radio.[25] 'Make Do and Mend' has likewise been resurrected as a motto for a more sustainable approach to fash-ion as consciousness of looming planetary apocalypse grows. Facsimile reproductions of the original Board of Trade/Ministry of Information booklet first published in 1943 can be found in museum shops.[26]

If we wish to preserve life on earth, we should indeed 'make do' with fewer and more durable garments. But forties fashion nostalgia nevertheless requires caution. It was easier to 'go through your ward-robe', as the Board of Trade entreated, for those with a sizeable closet to browse in search of garments hitherto relegated to the rear that could be refreshed (or 'upcycled' in today's parlance). In the 1940s, wealthier Britons possessed not only more but *better* clothing. As Rose Macauley noted of a tweedily aristocratic character in her portrait of rubble-strewn London, *The World My Wilderness* (1950), 'since all Pamela's clothes were good, and of the kind known as cheaper in the end, they lasted practically for ever'.[27] The rose-tinted aura around the war in main-stream British memory culture has fostered a mistaken belief that the wartime slogan 'Equality of Sacrifice' described a reality rather than an affirmative aspiration. Wartime sacrifices, like postwar rewards, were unevenly distributed. Nella Last, the Cumbrian Mass Observation diarist, made this point succinctly in an entry dated 20 October 1942:

> I used to think the blurb in the papers was true – that the war was levelling people. Not a bit of it. It's making people *more* unequal – the bombed and the not bombed, the free people and the enslaved, the sheltered and the lonely wives and sweethearts, ones with money to throw around and ones with not enough to go round.[28]

Royals aside, Britons received the same basic allocation of clothing coupons, but they did not possess identical incomes or wardrobes. 'Making do' did not make good deeply embedded inequalities.

There's also a troubling mismatch between the recent resurrection of 'making do' as a preservationist mantra and the proliferation of disposable fancy-dress forties costumes available in shops and online. These war-themed outfits raise questions on both environmental and ethical grounds. It's one thing to dress up an infant trick-or-treater as a mini Rosie the Riveter, another to outfit a little girl as Anne Frank – as US big-box chain Target found in 2017 when protestors demanded it remove supplies of these costumes from its stores. Yet these outfits, marketed by online retailer Smiffy as 'World War II Evacuee Girl', can still be bought today. Currently, this get-up sells for £16.99, modelled by a smiling little girl, posing sassily with hand on hip, as though the name label affixed with string to her duffle coat were a detail borrowed from Paddington; as though there were nothing funner than being forcibly evicted from home, parted from loved ones, and sent off to an alien destination and uncertain fate. In Anne Frank's case, that meant dying – starving, naked, terrified of lice – in a Nazi concentration camp.[29]

Looking clear-sightedly at the 1940s confronts us with the duration and depth of distress generated by the mid-twentieth century's engulfing cataclysm. When we contemplate the decade's distinctive garments, we should recall not just the wardrobes but the *war*, in all its appalling destructiveness. Amid, and after, the most catastrophic violence humans had ever inflicted on one another, clothing was always a marker of status, occasionally an agent of death. Sometimes, but only sometimes, it helped restore life, rekindling faith in the possibility of kindness. These phenomena should be remembered, and grieved, as we contemplate what it'll take to refashion our own perennially postwar world.

EPILOGUE

This book began with the transformation of World War II blackout material into a skirt – or, more precisely, it started with my mother making me this garment. It's only fitting, then, to conclude by returning to that scene and to her memory. I began drafting the first chapters of *Making Do* in the immediate aftermath of her death in May 2022, and it's dedicated to her memory. At last, a book of mine on a subject about which she'd eagerly want to read! I've thought often over the past two years about that irony. That only after her death did I turn to a topic that had been one of her life-long passions: clothing. Writing this book has served as a form of therapy and a posthumous tribute. Victor Gollancz's injunction seems especially apt: 'In love, and in the acts that spring from love, is the only salvation.'

Remembering my long-ago discarded blackout skirt, and my own cavalier teenage treatment of it, I've been gripped with remorse of a sort that surely afflicts many of the newly bereaved. Why wasn't my younger self more appreciative of maternal acts of grace? Why wasn't I more curious about my parents' earlier lives? Where, I wondered, once it was too late to ask, did that blackout fabric come from? Did this fabric accompany my mother on the journey that took her from Belfast to Cheshire to Scotland to Suffolk, where this skirt was sewn? Was the blackout material removed from a window in her parental home? Or did she perhaps inherit it, a trousseau of sorts, when she married my father? His father, gassed in the trenches of World War I and deceased before I was born, had owned a drapery shop in Edinburgh. Perhaps my grandfather was left with a glut of unsold blackout fabric in 1945, some of which he later gave to his son's beautiful and beautifully turned-out fiancée.

Immersed in the stuff of the 1940s, I've had an opportunity to plot the co-ordinates of my mother's girlhood on the grid of that global conflict. Her seventh birthday, 12 April 1945, was coincidentally the same day on which Franklin Roosevelt died, and when British and German commanders agreed that Britons would assume control of Bergen-Belsen concentration camp. Three weeks later, readers of the *Manchester Guardian* were entreated to donate blackout curtains for clothing for 'liberated European peasants' – an alternative destiny for the fabric that became my skirt. More diffusely, I've been reminded of how much of my mother's childhood was clouded by the war and crimped by austerity. Contemplating how few new clothes she must've had as a child and in her adolescence has helped me better appreciate her love of clothing and the volume of material she left behind: drawer after drawer of gloves, coats, jackets, knits, scarves, skirts, blouses, unfinished sewing projects and dress patterns, all carefully folded and wrapped in tissue: the accumulation of a life lived under the war's penumbra. More poignantly, my mother's material possessions struck me after her death as expressive of unfulfilled aspiration to lead a different kind of existence – one that would've provided greater scope for her talents, a more expansive stage for her wardrobe of costumes.

Writing this book has helped me come to terms with both my mother's loss and her attitude to clothing. Contemplating wartime loss, postwar alteration and adjustment, has reframed many things in my mind. Most of all, it has taught me a more generous appreciation of why and how garments matter. Clothing was fundamental to my mother's sense of self. And, in that, she was undoubtedly not alone. What we wear defines us and our dreams of surmounting the constrictions of historical circumstance.

ACKNOWLEDGEMENTS

This book is dedicated to the memory of my first and best teacher – my mother, Patricia Carruthers, with love and thanks for all she taught me about sewing, reading, storytelling and the ties between these activities. I wish she could read what I have to say on a topic dear to her heart.

Like every author, I've amassed many debts to archivists who've assisted in locating materials in their collections, delivering files and boxes from climate-controlled storerooms, and then reshelving them again. I thank the staff of the National Archives at Kew; the Bodleian Library, University of Oxford; and the Women's Library, LSE. Neasa Roughan at the Royal College of Nursing Archives, Edinburgh, kindly tracked down material relating to loaned US wedding dresses. At the University of Warwick's Modern Records Centre, many people assisted me over repeat visits. In particular, I'm grateful to Liz Woods, who pointed me towards her mother's own work on women's clothing in Warwickshire in World War II. Special thanks, too, to Naomi Shewan, who helped secure permission from the estate of Sir Victor Gollancz to reproduce an image from his collection of private papers. At the Imperial War Museum, Jane Rosen devoted hours to tracking down relevant collections that I might otherwise have missed. I'm also grateful to her colleague Cian Martin for his assistance with licensing several images from the IWM's collection.

At the University of Warwick, I'm fortunate to work in a department which is so conducive to getting research and writing done.

Heads of Department Rebecca Earle and Tim Lockley signed off on periods of study leave for which I'm immensely grateful. My colleague Rosie Doyle assigned me some wonderful research assistants, and I thank them all for their diligent work: Vicki Banks, Euan Higgins, Sumaiyah Patel and Dee Sheed. Although we often talk in academia of research-led teaching, this book's genesis attests the reciprocal significance of teaching-led research. One of the first finalists who took my 'Postwar' module at Warwick in 2017, Molly Wilson-Smith, unwittingly planted the seed that would grow into this book when she enquired about the feasibility of writing an essay on postwar clothing. Contemplating how one might do so made me appreciate the salience of fabric to so many of the topics my module covered – threads I'd hitherto failed to pull together. Since Molly didn't write that essay in the end, I hope she won't mind that I wrote an entire book inspired by her enquiry!

Several colleagues at Warwick offered encouragement, including Rebecca Earle, Anne Gerritsen, Peter Marshall, Mark Philp and Claire Shaw. Other friends and colleagues generously read, and offered valuable feedback on, chapters or longer portions of the manuscript: Fran Bartkowski, Roberta Bivins, Judith Byfield and Andy Buchanan, to whom I'm also indebted for sharing material related to Emil Mazey. Beth Bailey and Wendy Wasserman both made time available to carefully read the entire manuscript. I'm most appreciative of their enthusiasm for *Making Do* and the detailed suggestions they provided.

At Cambridge University Press, Cecelia Cancellaro responded with welcome excitement to the original proposal, putting me in touch with her colleague Liz Friend-Smith, who has been a champion of this project from the start. I would also like to thank Rosanna Barraclough and Lisa Carter, and the anonymous reviewers who responded so positively to *Making Do*. Steven Holt deserves special credit for his meticulous copy-editing of the manuscript.

Finally, I thank family members in Ireland, Vermont and England for ongoing support. In particular, love and gratitude are owed to my sister Siobhán, who carried heavy burdens with tremendous stoicism and grace during the final years of our mother's life. My biggest debt, as ever, is to my husband, Joe Romano, who understands exactly how much this project has meant to me, and encourages me in all I do. With love and thanks for everything, always.

NOTES

Introduction

1. Ina Zweiniger-Bargielowska, *Austerity in Britain: Rationing, Controls and Consumption, 1939–1955* (Oxford: Oxford University Press, 2000); Christopher Sladen, *The Conscription of Fashion: Utility Cloth, Clothing and Footwear 1941–1952* (Aldershot: Scolar Press, 1995).
2. Julie Summers, *Fashion on the Ration: Style in the Second World War* (London: Profile Books/IWM, 2016); Maggie Wood, *'We Wore What We'd Got': Women's Clothes in World War II* (Exeter: Warwickshire Books, 1989); Geraldine Howell, *Wartime Fashion: From Haute Couture to Homemade, 1939–1945* (London: Bloomsbury Academic, 2013); Geraldine Howell, *Women in Wartime: Dress Studies from Picture Post 1938–1945* (London: Bloomsbury Visual Arts, 2021); Peter McNeil, '"Put Your Best Face Forward": The Impact of the Second World War on British Dress', *Journal of Design History*, 6:4 (1993), 283–99. On 1940s style more generally, Colin McDowell, *Forties Fashion and the New Look* (London: Bloomsbury Publishing, 1997); Jonathan Walford, *Forties Fashion from Siren Suits to the New Look* (London: Thames & Hudson, 2011); Geraldine Biddle-Perry, *Dressing for Austerity: Aspiration, Leisure and Fashion in Postwar Britain* (London: I.B. Tauris, 2017).
3. 'Average Hours Worked and Wages', *The Garment Worker*, 14:3 (March 1945), 52. For 1945 ceiling prices, 'Non-utility Clothing: Women's Outerwear', *Manchester Guardian*, 20 November 1945, p. 5. Statistics relating to clothing costs and waste in 2023 are derived from Waste and Resources Action Programme (WRAP), 'Textiles Market Situation Report 2024', www.wrap.ngo/resources/report/textiles-market-situation-report-2024.
4. Charles Graves, *Women in Green: The Story of the W.V.S.* (London: William Heinemann, 1948), p. 143; 'Profile – Lady Reading', *The Observer*, 24 June 1945, p. 6; James Hinton, *Women, Social Leadership, and the Second World War* (Oxford: Oxford University Press, 2003).
5. Board of Trade/Ministry of Information, *Make Do and Mend* (London: HMSO, 1943), foreword by Hugh Dalton, p. 1. On wartime salvage initiatives more

generally, Peter Thorsheim, *Waste into Weapons: Recycling in Britain during the Second World War* (Cambridge: Cambridge University Press, 2015).

6. Board of Trade/Ministry of Information, *Make Do and Mend*, p. 5.

7. Sladen, *Conscription of Fashion*, p. 21.

8. On hunger and its alleviation in the postwar world, Frank Trentmann and Just Fleming (eds.), *Food and Conflict in Europe in the Age of the Two World Wars* (Basingstoke: Palgrave Macmillan, 2006); Alice Weinreb, '"For the Hungry Have No Past nor Do They Belong to a Political Party": Debates over German Hunger after World War II', *Central European History*, 45:1 (2012), 50–78; Alice Weinreb, *Modern Hungers: Food and Power in Twentieth-Century Germany* (New York: Oxford University Press, 2017); Atina Grossmann, 'Grams, Calories, and Food: Languages of Victimization, Entitlement, and Human Rights in Occupied Germany, 1945–1949', *Central European History*, 44:1 (2011), 118–48; Chris Aldous, 'Contesting Famine: Hunger and Nutrition in Occupied Japan, 1945–1952', *Journal of American–East Asian Relations*, 17:3 (2010), 230–56; Owen Griffiths, 'Need, Greed, and Protest in Japan's Black Market, 1938–1949', *Journal of Social History*, 35:3 (2002), 825–58.

9. Giorgio Agamben, *Homo Sacer: Sovereign Power and Bare Life*, trans. Daniel Heller-Roazen (Stanford, CA: Stanford University Press, 1998).

10. Primo Levi, *The Awakening: A Liberated Prisoner's Long March Home through East Europe*, trans. Stuart Woolf (Boston: Little, Brown and Company, 1965), pp. 40–41.

11. Hanna Rose Shell, *Shoddy: From Devil's Dust to the Renaissance of Rags* (Chicago: University of Chicago Press, 2020), pp. 114–18; Alison Matthews David, *Fashion Victims: The Dangers of Dress Past and Present* (London: Bloomsbury, 2015), pp. 28–39.

12. J. R. Busvine, 'Destruction of Lice in Clothing by Hot and Cold Air', *Bulletin of Entomological Research*, 35:2 (1944), 115–25.

13. Karen Tranberg Hansen, *Salaula: The World of Secondhand Clothing and Zambia* (Chicago: University of Chicago Press, 2000); Andrew Brooks, *Clothing Poverty: The Hidden World of Fast Fashion and Second-Hand Clothes* (London: Zed Books, 2015).

14. 'Clothes from Old Milk Bottles', *SEAC News*, 25 August 1944.

15. Board of Trade/Ministry of Information, *Make Do and Mend*, pp. 3–4.

16. Roland Barthes, *The Fashion System*, trans. Matthew Ward and Richard Howard (Berkeley: University of California Press, 1990 [1983]).

17. Jeremy A. Crang, *Sisters in Arms: Women in the British Armed Forces during the Second World War* (Cambridge: Cambridge University Press, 2020); Lucy Noakes, *Women in the British Army: War and the Gentle Sex, 1907–1948* (London: Routledge, 2006).

18. Nathan Joseph, *Uniforms and Nonuniforms: Communication through Clothing* (New York: Greenwood Press, 1986); Jennifer Craik, *Uniforms Exposed: From Conformity to Transgression* (Oxford: Berg, 2005); Jane Tynan and Lisa Godson (eds.), *Uniform: Clothing and Discipline in the Modern World* (London: Bloomsbury Visual Arts, 2019).

19. Susan L. Carruthers, *The Good Occupation: American Soldiers and the Hazards of Peace* (Cambridge, MA: Harvard University Press, 2016), pp. 65–66; Dan Stone, *The Liberation of the Camps: The End of the Holocaust and Its Aftermath* (New Haven, CT: Yale University Press, 2015).

20. 'Hungry People of Europe', *The Times*, 8 March 1945, p. 3.

21. JCS 1067, 'Directive to Commander in Chief of United States Forces Regarding the Military Government of Germany', 16 April 1945, Office of the Historian, US Government, https://history.state.gov/historicaldocuments/frus1945v03/d351; Carruthers, *Good Occupation*, p. 53.

22. On Mass Observation, James Hinton, *The Mass Observers: A History, 1937–1949* (Oxford: Oxford University Press, 2013); Claire Langhamer, '"Who the Hell Are Ordinary People?": Ordinariness as a Category of Historical Analysis', *Transactions of the Royal Historical Society*, 28 (2018), 175–95; Patricia Malcolmson and Robert Malcolmson (eds.), *The Diaries of Nella Last: Writing in War and Peace* (London: Profile Books, 2012), entry for 21 August 1945, p. 222. *Housewife, 49* debuted on ITV in December 2006, written by and starring Victoria Wood.

23. National Planning Association, *Clothing and Shelter for European Relief*, Planning Pamphlet no. 34 (Washington, DC: National Planning Association, 1944), pp. 1–2.

24. Harry S. Truman letter to Henry J. Kaiser calling upon him to head the Second United National Clothing Collection Campaign, dated 21 August 1945, released 23 September 1945, https://bit.ly/4coKO7U, Harry S Truman Library and Museum.

25. Robert Ross, *Clothing: A Global History* (Cambridge: Polity Press, 2008); Giorgio Riello and Peter McNeil (eds.), *The Fashion History Reader: Global Perspectives* (Abingdon: Routledge, 2010); Giorgio Riello, *Cotton: The Fabric That Made the Modern World* (Cambridge: Cambridge University Press, 2013); Sven Beckert, *Empire of Cotton: A Global History* (London: Allen Lane, 2014).

26. J. B. Priestley, *English Journey* (London: William Heinemann Ltd. & Victor Gollancz, 1934), p. 222.

27. Mary B. Rose (ed.), *The Lancashire Cotton Industry: A History since 1700* (Preston: Lancashire County Books, 1996); John Singleton, *Lancashire on the Scrapheap: The Cotton Industry 1945–1970* (Oxford: Oxford University Press, 1991).

28. *Statistics Relating to the War Effort of the United Kingdom* (Cmd. 6564), (London: HMSO, 1944), CAB 106/315.

29. National Planning Association, *Clothing and Shelter*, p. 7, p. 21.

30. Harold D. Lasswell, *Politics: Who Gets What, When, How* (New York: Whittlesey House, 1936).

31. Raynes Minns, *Bombers and Mash: The Domestic Front 1939–45* (London: Virago, 1980); Gail Braybon and Penny Summerfield, *Out of the Cage: Women's Experiences in Two World Wars* (London: Pandora, 1987); Penny Summerfield, *Women Workers in the Second World War: Production and Patriarchy in Conflict* (London: Routledge, 1989); Crang, *Sisters in Arms*; Noakes, *Women in the British Army*.

32. On wartime hunger, Lizzie Collingham, *The Taste of War: World War II and the Battle for Food* (New York: Penguin Press, 2012). On the politics of food distribution, Margaret Mead, 'Food and Feeding in Occupied Territory', *Public Opinion Quarterly*, 7:4 (1943), 618–28. See also Sladen, *Conscription of Fashion*, p. 21.

33. On the intimately tactile properties of clothing, Sofi Thanhauser, *Worn: A People's History of Clothing* (London: Allen Lane, 2022); Roberto Filippello and Ilya Parkin (eds.), *Fashion and Feeling: The Affective Politics of Dress* (Cham: Palgrave Macmillan, 2023). On worn clothes as prompts to memory, Bethan Bide, 'In Their Shoes: Using Fashion Objects to Explore the Duration and Complexity of Wartime Experiences', *Critical Military Studies*, 7:4 (2021), 418–34.

34. Francesca M. Wilson, *Advice to Relief Workers: Based on Personal Experience in the Field* (London: John Murray/Friends Relief Service, 1945); Francesca M. Wilson, *In the Margins of Chaos: Recollections of Relief Work in and between Three Wars* (London: John Murray, 1944).

35. Andrew Buchanan, 'Globalizing the Second World War', *Past & Present*, 258:1 (2023), 246–81; Andrew N. Buchanan, *From World War to Postwar: Revolution, Cold War, Decolonization, and the Rise of American Hegemony, 1943–1958* (London: Bloomsbury, 2023); Mary Dudziak, *War-Time: An Idea, Its History, Its Consequences* (New York: Oxford University Press, 2012).

36. Of these, the principal organizations were the United Nations Relief and Rehabilitation Administration (UNRRA) and the International Red Cross Organization, which distributed parcels of clothing to POWs and civilian internees.
37. Council of the Clothing Trade Associations, 'Report on Post-war Reconstruction in the Clothing Industries', 2nd edition, 9 December 1943, MSS. 21/5126, Modern Records Centre, University of Warwick (hereafter MRC).
38. Madeleine Ginsburg, 'Rags to Riches: The Second Hand Clothes Trade, 1700–1978', *Costume*, 14:1 (1980), 121–35; Beverly Lemire, 'Peddling Fashion: Salesmen, Pawnbrokers, Taylors, Thieves and the Second-Hand Clothes Trade in England, c. 1700–1800', *Textile History* 22:1 (1991), 67–82; Vivienne Richmond, *Clothing the Poor in Nineteenth-Century England* (Cambridge: Cambridge University Press, 2013). On social class and clothing consumption, Catherine Horwood, *Keeping Up Appearances: Fashion and Class between the Wars* (Stroud: The History Press, 2011); Rachel Worth, *Fashion and Class* (London: Bloomsbury Visual Arts, 2020).
39. Jack Barry Bamford, 'Diary of Five Weeks in New York en route to the Falklands, 1942', p. 39, private papers of J. B. Bamford, documents.5419, Imperial War Museum, London (hereafter IWM).
40. Correspondence in BT 64/1407, TNA.
41. Ashley Jackson, *The British Empire and the Second World War* (London: Hambledon Continuum, 2006), p. 414; Sandra Trudgen Dawson, 'Rubber Shortages on Britain's Home Front', in Mark J. Crowley and Sandra Trudgen Dawson (eds.), *Home Fronts – Britain and the Empire at War, 1939–45* (Woodbridge: Boydell & Brewer, 2017), pp. 59–75; William G. Clarence-Smith, 'The Battle for Rubber in the Second World War: Cooperation and Resistance', in J. Curry-Machado (ed.), *Global Histories, Imperial Commodities, Local Interactions* (Basingstoke: Palgrave Macmillan, 2013), pp. 204–23.
42. Margaret S. Watson, 'Some Aspects of Internment, Hong Kong, January 1942–August 1945', *Social Work*, 3:11 (1946), 260–65; Grace Harvey, *Yangchow Years* (Bridgnorth: Dreamstar Books, 2003), pp. 41–50; private papers of Mrs G. Harvey, documents.13151, IWM; 'Memorandum handed by the Bailiff, on behalf of the Superior Council of the States of Jersey to the Platz Command of the German Forces of Occupation of the Island, for submission to the Competent Military Authority. Aug. 31, 1944' (signed A. M. Coutanche, Bailiff), documents.10573, IWM.
43. On UNRRA's origins and remit, UNRRA, *Helping the People to Help Themselves: The Story of the United Nations Relief and Rehabilitation Administration* (London: HMSO, 1944); Philipp Weintraub, 'UNRRA: An Experiment in International Welfare Planning', *Journal of Politics*, 7:1 (1945), 1–24; George Woodbridge, *U.N.R.R.A.: The History of the United Nations Relief and Rehabilitation Administration* (New York: Columbia University Press, 1950); Jessica Reinisch, 'Internationalism in Relief: The Birth (and Death) of UNRRA', in Mark Mazower, Jessica Reinisch and David Feldman (eds.), *Post-war Reconstruction in Europe: International Perspectives, 1945–1949* (*Past & Present* Supplement no. 6, Oxford, 2011). On the ambiguities of 'rehabilitation', Silvia Salvatici, '"Help the People to Help Themselves": UNRRA Relief Workers and European Displaced Persons', *Journal of Refugee Studies*, 35:3 (2012), 428–51. On the 'Victory Clothing Collection', see correspondence between British Embassy staff in Washington, DC, Foreign Office personnel in London and UNRRA in FO 115/4299 and FO 115/4300, TNA.
44. On UNRRA's acquisition of British army surplus, including the possibility that female American UNRRA personnel would acquire British ATS uniforms, WO 229/43/6, TNA. On the US military's reluctance to let civilians (particularly

civilian women) wear American officers' uniforms, 'Women Abroad Lose Officers' Uniforms', *NYT*, 7 February 1946, p. 17.

45. Anonymous letter to B-Bag, *Stars & Stripes*, 23 July 1945.

46. On UNRRA uniforms and lack of cooperation between relief agencies, see FO 371/51524, TNA. On tension between military personnel and relief workers, Silvia Salvatici, '"Fighters without Guns": Humanitarianism and Military Action in the Aftermath of the Second World War', *European Review of History*, 25:6 (2018), 957–76.

47. 'Dedicated Followers: Uniforms and the Nineteenth-Century Salvation Army's Attitudes to Fashion', Salvation Army International Heritage Centre, https://bit.ly/3WKbBFE.

48. On Quaker objections to military uniform, Jane Tynan, '"Quakers in Khaki": Conscientious Objectors' Resistance to Uniform in World War I Britain', in Stephen Gibson and Simon Mollan (eds.), *Representations of Peace and Conflict* (Basingstoke: Palgrave Macmillan, 2012), pp. 86–102; 'Quakers in WWII', www.quakersintheworld.org/quakers-in-action/301/Friends-Relief-Service-in-WWII.

49. Graves, *Women in Green*, p. 30.

50. On mass displacement, Malcolm J. Proudfoot, *European Refugees: 1939–52* (London: Faber and Faber, 1957); Ben Shephard, *The Long Road Home: The Aftermath of the Second World War* (New York: Alfred A. Knopf, 2011); G. Daniel Cohen, *In War's Wake: Europe's Displaced Persons in the Post-war Order* (New York: Oxford University Press, 2012); Rana Mitter, 'Relocation and Dislocation: Civilian, Refugee, and Military Movement as Factors in the Disintegration of Postwar China, 1945–49', *Itinerario*, 46 (special issue 2) (2022), 193–213; Meredith Oyen, 'The Right of Return: Chinese Displaced Persons and the International Refugee Organization, 1947–56', *Modern Asian Studies*, 49:2 (2015), 546–71. On the delayed return of POWs, Frank Biess, *Homecomings: Returning POWs and the Legacies of Defeat in Postwar Germany* (Princeton: Princeton University Press, 2006); Andrew F. Barshay, *The Gods Left First: The Captivity and Repatriation of Japanese POWs in Northeast Asia, 1945–1956* (Berkeley: University of California Press, 2013); Yokote Shinji, 'Soviet Repatriation Policy, US Occupation Authorities, and Japan's Entry into the Cold War', *Journal of Cold War Studies*, 15:2 (2013), 30–50; Lori Watt, *When Empire Comes Home: Repatriation and Reintegration in Postwar Japan* (Cambridge, MA: Harvard University Press, 2009).

51. *Vogue*, 20 September 1939, quoted by McNeil, '"Put Your Best Face Forward"', p. 288; Anne O'Hare McCormick, 'Winning the Peace: "It Is Our Job"', *NYT*, 30 September 1945, p. 91.

52. Lynda Nead, '"Red Taffeta under Tweed": The Color of Post-war Clothes', *Fashion Theory*, 21:4 (2017), 365–89; Lynda Nead, *The Tiger in the Smoke: Art and Culture in Post-war Britain* (New Haven: Yale University Press, 2017).

1 Victors

1. On British wartime propaganda, Ian McLaine, *Ministry of Morale: Home Front Morale and the Ministry of Information in World War II* (London: Routledge, 1979); Robert MacKay, *Half the Battle: Civilian Morale in Britain during the Second World War* (Manchester: Manchester University Press, 2003); David Clampin, *Advertising and Propaganda in World War II: Cultural Identity and the Blitz Spirit* (London: I.B. Tauris, 2014); Daniel Ussishkin, *Morale: A Modern British History* (New York: Oxford University Press, 2017).

2. Guy Cuthbertson, *Peace at Last: A Portrait of Armistice Day, 11 November 1918* (New Haven: Yale University Press, 2018); Guy Cuthbertson, 'Armistice Attire', Yale University Press blog, 10 December 2018, https://yalebooks.yale.edu/2018/12/10/armistice-attire. On 'Mafficking', Macdonald Hastings, 'This Was VE-Day in London', *Picture Post*, 19 May 1945, p. 6.
3. See correspondence in MEPO 2/6266; WO 204/6730; HO 45/23203; HO 45/25156, TNA.
4. Leman Street Station to Deputy Assistant Commissioner C, 'Cessation of Hostilities in Europe', 13 April 1945, MEPO 2/6266.
5. Mass Observation, *Report on Victory in Europe*, 10 June 1945, p. 7, TC 49, 'Victory Celebrations 1945–46', Mass Observation Archive, University of Sussex, via Mass Observation Online (hereafter MO).
6. Deputy Assistant Commissioner 2 to Deputy Assistant Commissioner A, 11 May 1945; Commissioner of Police of the Metropolis to the Home Secretary, 10 May 1945, MEPO 2/6266.
7. On Allied plans for invasion of the Japanese home islands in 1946, D. M. Giangreco, *Hell to Pay: Operation DOWNFALL and the Invasion of Japan, 1945–1947* (Annapolis, MD: Naval Institute Press, 2009); Nicholas Evans Sarantakes, *Allies against the Rising Sun: The United States, the British Nations, and the Defeat of Imperial Japan* (Lawrence, KS: University Press of Kansas, 2009).
8. Richards Vidmer, 'Britain to Celebrate VE-Day, But Soberly – No One Can Long Forget Terrific Tasks Ahead', *Washington Post*, 8 April 1945, p. B3.
9. Ibid.
10. Clampin, *Advertising and Propaganda*, ch. 6; Matthew Hilton, *Consumerism in Twentieth-Century Britain: The Search for a Historical Movement* (Cambridge: Cambridge University Press, 2003), ch. 5; Paul Addison, *Now the War Is Over: A Social History of Britain 1945–51* (London: Jonathan Cape/BBC, 1985), ch. 2.
11. Letters from Betty Finlay to her mother and aunt dated 4 February 1945, 8 May 1945, 10 August 1945 and 14 August 1945, private papers of Betty Duignan (née Finlay), documents.12644, IWM.
12. Christopher Sladen, *The Conscription of Fashion: Utility Cloth, Clothing and Footwear 1941–1952* (Aldershot: Scolar Press, 1995), pp. 25–42; Helen Reynolds, 'The Utility Garment: Its Design and Effect on the Mass Market 1942–45', in Judy Attfield (ed.), *Utility Reassessed: The Role of Ethics in the Practice of Design* (Manchester: Manchester University Press, 2001), pp. 125–42.
13. Stafford Cripps quoted by Colin Cooke, *The Life of Richard Stafford Cripps* (London: Hodder and Stoughton, 1957), p. 330; Ben Pimlott, *Hugh Dalton* (London: Jonathan Cape, 1985), ch. 13; John Singleton, *Lancashire on the Scrapheap: The Cotton Industry 1945–1970* (Oxford: Pasold Research Fund/ Oxford University Press, 1991), pp. 26–29.
14. 'The Morning after Victory – Still Food Rations', *Daily Mail*, 9 March 1945, p. 3.
15. 'Extension of Clothes Ration Period', *Sunday Times*, 18 March 1945, p. 1.
16. Peter Hennessy, *Never Again: Britain 1945–51* (London: Penguin Books, 2006 [1992]), p. 100.
17. 'Post-war Programmes: Controls Stay – Mr. Dalton', *Sunday Times*, 8 April 1945, p. 5; Eric M. Gamage (Chairman, Retail Distributors' Association) to the editor, 'The Nation's Clothes', *The Times*, 23 February 1945, p. 5; W. T. Caves (Secretary, Wholesale Textile Association) to the editor, 'Clothing Stocks', *The Times*, 27 February 1945, p. 5; Eric M. Gamage to the editor, 'The Nation's Clothes', *The Times*, 1 March 1945, p. 5; Frederick Marsden to the editor, 'Clothing Stocks', *The Times*, 6 March 1945, p. 5.

18. Alison Settle, 'Shopping Joys Will Not Come with Victory', *The Observer*, 8 April 1945, p. 6.

19. '"Dresses from Dust Sheets" Racket Smashed by Mr. Dalton', *Daily Mail*, 21 February 1945, p. 3.

20. On the end of the war in the Pacific, Giangreco, *Hell to Pay*; Sarantakes, *Allies against the Rising Sun*.

21. Thomas L. Stokes, 'Keeping a Tight Belt', *Los Angeles Times*, 6 May 1945, p. A4.

22. National Planning Association, *Clothing and Shelter for European Relief*, Planning Pamphlet no. 34 (Washington, DC: National Planning Association, 1944); Walter A. Waggoner, 'V-E Day to Increase U.S. Price and Supply Problems', *NYT*, 6 May 1945, p. E10.

23. 'Starvation in East Indies', *The Times*, 9 March 1945, p. 3.

24. John Watts, *The Facts of the Cotton Famine* (London: Routledge Library of Industrial Classics, 1968 [1866]); Janam Mukherjee, *Hungry Bengal: War, Famine and the End of Empire* (Oxford: Oxford University Press, 2015); 'Cloth Famine in Bengal', *Times of India*, 23 March 1945, p. 5; 'Grain and Cloth Shortage: Mr. Gandhi's Plan to Solve Problem', *Times of India*, 18 February 1946, p. 8; Yasmin Khan, *The Raj at War: A People's History of India's Second World War* (London: Bodley Head, 2015), p. 297.

25. Harry S. Truman, Statement by the President Commending the Work of the United National Clothing Collection, 4 July 1945, congratulating 7,300 local committees of the United National Clothing Collection for exceeding the goal of amassing 150,000,000 pounds of clothing, https://bit.ly/3M2eOLW.

26. 'Times Sq. Getting Big Clothing Box', *NYT*, 11 April 1945, p. 21; 'Pageant Spurs Clothing Drive as 5,000 in Times Square Look On', *NYT*, 13 April 1945, p. 19.

27. Photographs of Baxter's and Miller's striptease feature in 'Film Noir Photos' blogspot, http://filmnoirphotos.blogspot.com/2017/01/bevy-of-beauties-strip-poker.html; 'Old Clothing Collection for War Victims', *Life*, 2 April 1945, pp. 32–33.

28. Newsreel footage of the camps elicited strong and varied reactions in Britain and the United States. American critic James Agee decried the 'atrocity films' as propaganda intended to stir up anti-German hatred, legitimating a punitive occupation, James S. Agee, 'Films', *The Nation*, 19 May 1945. In some cities in both countries, service personnel compelled civilian moviegoers to remain in theatres to watch newsreels, Barbie Zelizer, *Holocaust Memory through the Camera's Eye* (Chicago: Chicago University Press, 1998), p. 148; Hannah Caven, 'Horror in Our Time: Images of the Concentration Camps in the British Media, 1945', *Historical Journal of Film, Radio, and Television*, 21:3 (2001), 205–53.

29. Andrew Buchanan, 'Domesticating Hegemony: Creating a Globalist Public, 1941–1943', *Diplomatic History*, 45:2 (2021), 301–29; Stephen Wertheim, *Tomorrow the World: The Birth of U.S. Global Supremacy* (Cambridge, MA: The Belknap Press of Harvard University Press, 2020).

30. Relief and War Supplies Dept., British Embassy, Washington, DC to Relief Dept., Foreign Office, London, 7 March 1945, FO 371/51351, TNA. Other correspondence in this file attests UNRRA's shaky start in relief operations and in securing positive publicity. On the second 'Victory Clothing Collection', launched in January 1946, see correspondence between British Embassy staff in Washington, DC, Foreign Office personnel in London and UNRRA in FO 115/4299 and FO 115/4300.

31. 'Clothing Drive', *Washington Post*, 30 January 1945, p. 6.

32. 'V-E Day Clothing Gifts', *NYT*, 9 May 1945, p. 3.

33. David Ogilvy, British Embassy, Washington, DC, to W. J. Hasler, Foreign Office, 27 April 1945, FO 371/51351; Stephen E. Ambrose, *Rise to Globalism: American Foreign Policy since 1938* (Baltimore, MD: Penguin Books, 1971).

34. Liisa Malkki, *The Need to Help: The Domestic Arts of International Humanitarianism* (Durham, NC: Duke University Press, 2015); Silvia Salvatici, '"Help the People to Help Themselves": UNRRA Relief Workers and European Displaced Persons', *Journal of Refugee Studies*, 35:3 (2012), 428–51; Robert H. Bremner, *Giving: Charity and Philanthropy in History* (London: Routledge, 1994); Nicholas Faulkner, 'Guilt, Anger and Compassionate Helping', in Michael Ure and Mervyn Frost (eds.), *The Politics of Compassion* (London: Routledge, 2013), pp. 107–20.

35. David M. Potter, *People of Plenty* (Chicago: University of Chicago Press, 1954); Eleanor Roosevelt, 'My Day, June 20, 1945', Eleanor Roosevelt Papers, Digital Edition, George Washington University, https://www2.gwu.edu/~erpapers/myday/displaydoc.cfm?_y=1945&_f=md000055.

36. Harry S. Truman to Henry J. Kaiser, 21 August 1945, Harry S. Truman Library and Museum, https://bit.ly/4coKO7U; 'Give Clothing', *Parents' Magazine*, 20:12 (1945), 140; 'Victory Clothing Collection for Overseas Relief' advertisement, *Redbook*, 86:3 (1946), 53.

37. Newsreel; 'Children Big Donors in the Clothing Drive', *NYT*, 3 May 1945, p. 23; 'Children to Aid 2 Relief Drives', *NYT*, 17 December 1945, p. 18; Christine Sadler, 'UNRRA Is Their Nearest Approach to Santa Claus', *Washington Post*, 23 December 1945, p. S3; 'Clothes Drive Mark Set by 12-Year-Old', *NYT*, 4 February 1946, p. 19.

38. 'V-E Day Clothing Gifts', *NYT*, 9 May 1945, p. 3.

39. 'Children Big Donors in the Clothing Drive', *NYT*, 3 May 1945, p. 23.

40. Frank Sinatra, 'Things You've Outgrown', Special Release No. 132, Victory Clothing Collection, 7 December 1945, United Nations Archive, UNRRA S-1244-0000-0018-00001.

41. The slogan 'What can you spare that they can wear?' was launched by Eleanor Roosevelt, FO 371/51351.

42. On publicity for UNRRA's clothing drive giving photographic emphasis to Chinese children, FO 371/51351. On the United States and the Philippines, Christopher Capozzola, *Bound by War: How the United States and the Philippines Built America's First Pacific Century* (New York: Basic Books, 2020); Motoe Sasaki, *Redemption and Revolution: American and Chinese New Women in the Early Twentieth Century* (Ithaca, NY: Cornell University Press, 2016).

43. The initial offer of 45,000 pounds of clothing for British Far Eastern colonies was quickly raised to 415,000 pounds, George E. H. Marshall, Acting Director, Clothing, Textiles and Footwear Division, Bureau of Supply, UNRRA, Washington, DC, to R. W. Jackling, 1st Secretary, British Embassy, Washington, DC, 9 March 1946, FO 115/4299, TNA. See also correspondence between UNRRA officials, the British Embassy in Washington, DC, and Foreign and Colonial Office in FO 115/4300, TNA.

44. Marshall to Jackling, 14 February 1946; Jackling to Marshall, 23 February 1946, FO 115/4299. On bathing trunks as shorts, R. Ogilvy, 2nd Secretary, British Embassy, Washington, DC, to David Weintraub, Acting Deputy Director General, UNRRA, 15 May 1945, FO 371/51351. On imperialism and the spread of western-style clothing, Robert Ross, *Clothing: A Global History, Or, The Imperialists' New Clothes* (Cambridge, MA: Polity, 2008).

45. H. W. Shaw (UNRRA) to W. B. Redman, British Supply and Air Commission, New York, 16 March 1946, FO 115/4299; '150 Million Tons of Clothes Gets a Pressing', *New York World Telegram*, 20 June 1945, clipping in FO 371/51351.

46. Sir Mark Young, Governor of Hong Kong, to George Hall, Secretary of State for the Colonies, 27 July 1946, FO 115/4300.

47. Studies of the modern *enactment* of victory, as opposed to military strategies responsible for securing it, are surprisingly few. The most sustained study relates to US pageantry: Sebastian Jobs, *Welcome Home, Boys!: Military Victory Parades in New York City 1899–1946* (Frankfurt am Main: Campus Verlag, 2012). Defeat has attracted far more attention: Wolfgang Schivelbusch, *The Culture of Defeat: On National Trauma, Mourning, and Recovery* (New York: Metropolitan Books, 2003); Jenny Macleod (ed.), *Defeat and Memory: Cultural Histories of Military Defeat in the Modern Era* (Basingstoke: Palgrave Macmillan, 2008); Steven J. Mock, *Symbols of Defeat in the Construction of National Identity* (Cambridge: Cambridge University Press, 2012); Akiko Hashimoto, *The Long Defeat: Cultural Trauma, Memory, and Identity in Japan* (Oxford: Oxford University Press, 2015).

48. 'Justice Has Been Done', *Daily Mail*, 9 May 1945, p. 2.

49. Susan L. Carruthers, *The Good Occupation: American Soldiers and the Hazards of Peace* (Cambridge, MA: Harvard University Press, 2016), p. 72; Rick Atkinson, *The Guns at Last Light: The War in Western Europe, 1944–1945* (New York: Henry Holt, 2013), pp. 544–45; Seth Givens, 'Liberating the Germans: The US Army and Looting in Germany during the Second World War', *War in History*, 21:1 (2013), 33–54.

50. Paul Mattick, 'Obsessions of Berlin', *Partisan Review*, 15:10 (1948), p. 1112, quoted by Irene Guenther, 'Out of the Ruins: Fashioning Berlin, 1945–52', *Fashion Theory*, 21:4 (2017), 391–421 (p. 396).

51. Frank L. Howley, Personal Diary, vol. 2 (1 July 1945–1 July 1946), 'Impression of VJ Day Parade', papers of Frank L. Howley, US Army Military History Institute, Carlisle, PA (hereafter USAMHI); John Maginnis Diary, 7 September 1945, 'VJ Day in Berlin', papers of John Maginnis, USAMHI.

52. Howley, 'Impression of VJ Day Parade'.

53. Maginnis Diary, 7 September 1945.

54. Howley, 'Impression of VJ Day Parade'; 'Allied Victory Parade in Berlin', *Illustrated London News*, 15 September 1945, p. 291; Zhukov and Patton on the reviewing stand, Getty Images, photo ID 119462479.

55. John W. Dower, *Embracing Defeat: Japan in the Wake of World War II* (New York: W. W. Norton, 1999), p. 41; Carruthers, *Good Occupation*, pp. 82–87.

56. William Manchester, *American Caesar: Douglas MacArthur, 1880–1964* (New York: Back Bay Books, 2008), p. 444; Carruthers, *Good Occupation*, p. 86; Clovis E. Byers to family, 1 September 1945, Clovis E. Byers papers, box 30, Hoover Institution Archive, Stanford University, Palo Alto, CA.

57. Rose Cottrell to Pat and Family, 11 May 1945, private papers of Miss Rose G. Cottrell, documents.13128, IWM. On illuminations, Shanti Sumartojo, '"Dazzling Relief": Floodlighting and National Affective Atmospheres on VE Day 1945', *Journal of Historical Geography*, 45 (2014), 59–69.

58. MO, *Victory in Europe*, p. 28. Vivid accounts of VE Day can be found in David Kynaston, *Austerity Britain, 1945–51* (London: Bloomsbury Publishing, 2007), pp. 5–18; Hennessy, *Never Again*, pp. 56–64.

59. MO, *Victory in Europe*, p. 9.

60. MO, *Victory in Europe*, p. 26.

61. On troops being encouraged to greet victory 'in a spirit of sober satisfaction and heartfelt gratitude', WO 204/6730. On fears that VE Day festivity might encourage a 'relaxation of effort in the war against Japan', HO 45/23203.

62. MO, *Victory in Europe*, p. 22.

63. 'Government's Plans for V.E.-Day Celebrations', *Manchester Guardian*, 2 May 1945, p. 5.

64. MO, *Victory in Europe*, p. 49.

65. MO, *Victory in Europe*, p. 50; *British Pathé*'s special issue, 'The Fruits of Victory', 17 May 1945, depicts a life-size Hitler effigy – bearing a sign 'I'VE HAD IT' – being slung up by two gleeful women, www.britishpathe.com/asset/67408.

66. MO, *Victory in Europe*, p. 13.

67. MO, *Victory in Europe*, p. 14. Examples of victory scarves can be found in Jacqueline M. Atkins, *Wearing Propaganda: Textiles on the Home Front in Japan, Britain, and the United States, 1931–1945* (New Haven: Yale University Press, 2005), pp. 236, 359–62.

68. MO, *Victory in Europe*, p. 26. On party hats, see also Hastings, 'This Was VE-Day in London'.

69. MO, *Victory in Europe*, p. 35.

70. Cottrell to Pat and family, 11 May 1945, IWM.

71. The photograph of the bowler-hatted New Zealand sailor is in the IWM collection, www.iwm.org.uk/collections/item/object/205202200.

72. 'Our London Correspondence: V.E.-Day, 1945', *Manchester Guardian*, 9 May 1945, p. 4.

73. This photograph, taken by US Army Signals Corps photographer T. G. Massecar, is catalogued as EA 65799, www.iwm.org.uk/collections/item/object/205125103, IWM; Richard Smith, 'I'm THAT Girl in the Iconic Picture Showing VE Celebrations in Trafalgar Square 70 Years Ago', *Daily Mirror*, 25 June 2015, www.mirror.co .uk/news/uk-news/im-girl-iconic-picture-showing-5949282.

74. MO, *Victory in Europe*, p. 44; ibid., p. 24.

75. MO, *Victory in Europe*, p. 43.

76. 'The Men of War Kiss from Coast to Coast', *Life*, 27 August 1945, pp. 26–27 (p. 27); Brook L. Blower, 'V-J Day, 1945, Times Square', in Brooke L. Blower and Mark Philip Bradley (eds.), *The Familiar Made Strange: American Icons and Artefacts after the Transnational Turn* (Ithaca, NY: Cornell University Press, 2015), pp. 70–87; Aaron Hiltner, *Taking Leave, Taking Liberties: American Troops on the World War II Home Front* (Chicago: University of Chicago Press, 2020), pp. 98–103.

77. Hiltner, *Taking Leave*, p. 101; 'Riots and Looting Mark Bay City's Celebration', *Los Angeles Times*, 16 August 1945, p. 1; An Onlooker, '"Raising a Little Hell"', *Los Angeles Times*, 20 August 1945, p. A4.

78. '26 Die, Many Hurt in 1st U.S. Day of Celebration', *Daily Boston Globe*, 16 August 1945, p. 8; 'Peace Revelers Raped Woman, and Threw Her into Well Alive', *Washington Post*, 21 August 1945, p. 6.

79. MO, *Victory in Europe*, pp. 44–45. On sexual violence in wartime London, Julia Laite, *Common Prostitutes and Ordinary Citizens: Commercial Sex in London, 1885–1960* (Basingstoke: Palgrave Macmillan, 2011), pp. 168–69. Much of the scholarship on sexual violence in wartime Britain focuses on crimes perpetrated, or allegedly committed, by Black American GIs and the racist character of the military judicial system, Mary Louise Roberts, 'The Leroy Henry Case: Sexual Violence and Allied Relations in Great Britain, 1944', *Journal of the History of Sexuality*, 26:3 (2017), 402–23; Stephanie Makowski, 'For the Duration Only: Interracial Relationships in World War II Britain', *Journal of the History of Sexuality*, 29:2 (2020), 222–52.

80. 'A Slap in the Face', *Daily Mail*, 14 August 1945, p. 2.

81. Planning for this event spanned multiple departments: CAB 21/2258; CO 876/81; DO 35/1309; HO 45/20689; HO 326/78; HO 45/202688; HO 45/20689; INF 6/44; WORK 21/203.

82. *HC Deb*, 'Victory Celebrations (Government Decision)', 18 February 1946, *Hansard*, col. 485–86. On the Conservative motion, 'Cancel Victory Parade',

Union Jack, 14 March 1946. For public opinion on what MO termed the 'Peace Parade', MO Topic Collection 49-649733, 'Victory 1946 Attitudes'. On Britons' ambivalence on the day itself, Sydney Jacobson, 'Why We Celebrated', *Picture Post*, 22 June 1946, pp. 7–13.

83. 'Sackcloth March Plan for Victory Parade', *Union Jack*, 25 February 1946; 'Typists, Shopkeepers Plan Protest in Victory Parade', *Guinea Gold*, 5 March 1946.

84. 'Typists, Shopkeepers Plan Protest in Victory Parade', *Guinea Gold*, 5 March 1946.

85. 'May–September Clothing Coupons', *Manchester Guardian*, 19 February 1946, p. 5.

86. MO File Report 2378, 'Victory Celebrations'.

87. 'N.-West Rejects Victory Rejoicing', *Manchester Guardian*, 12 April 1946, p. 3.

88. 'Sinews of Peace', text of an address prepared for delivery by The Right Honourable Winston Churchill, MP, at Westminster College, Fulton Missouri, 5 March 1946, FO 371/51624, TNA; Patrick Wright, *Iron Curtain: From Stage to Cold War* (New York: Oxford University Press, 2009).

89. Anne O'Hare McCormick, 'Beyond the Victory Parade in London', *NYT*, 8 June 1946, p. 19.

90. Angus Calder, *The People's War: Britain, 1939–45* (London: Granada, 1971); Joanna Bourke, *The Second World War: A People's History* (Oxford: Oxford University Press, 2001); Jonathan Fennell, *Fighting the People's War: The British and Commonwealth Armies and the Second World War* (New York: Cambridge University Press, 2019).

91. 'MPs Criticise London Victory Parade', *SEAC News*, 20 April 1946.

92. 'V-Day Marchers: Merchant Navy, Women's Forces and C.D. Forces', *Illustrated London News*, 15 June 1946, p. 652; 'Noel Streatfield', Collecting Books and Magazines, www.collectingbooksandmagazines.com/streat.html.

93. Historians have long challenged the conceit of a plucky 'island nation' with its 'back against the wall': Sonya O. Rose, *Which People's War?: National Identity and Citizenship in Wartime Britain 1939–1945* (Oxford: Oxford University Press, 2003); Wendy Webster, *Mixing It: Diversity in World War Two Britain* (Oxford: Oxford University Press, 2018); Daniel Todman, *Britain's War, 1937–1941: Into Battle* (New York: Oxford University Press, 2016); Daniel Todman, *Britain's War, 1942–1947: A New World* (New York: Oxford University Press, 2020).

94. MO, *Victory in Europe*, p. 21.

95. Ann Temple, 'Grievances or Grumbling?', *Daily Mail*, 7 March 1946, p. 2.

96. MO, 'Victory 1946 Attitudes', p. 29; Eric Newton, 'Sword and Ploughshare: Memorable Scene in the Mall', *Manchester Guardian*, 10 June 1946, p. 4.

97. Robert W. Rydell, *All the World's a Fair: Visions of Empire at American International Expositions, 1876–1916* (Chicago: University of Chicago Press, 1984); Paul A. Kramer, 'Making Concessions: Race and Empire Revisited at the Philippine Exposition, St. Louis, 1901–1905', *Radical History Review*, 73 (1999), 74–114; John McAleer and John M. Mackenzie (eds.), *Exhibiting the Empire: Cultures of Display and the British Empire* (Manchester: Manchester University Press, 2015).

98. 'Nazi P.o.W.s Build Park', *The Star*, 9 April 1946, clipping in HO 45/20689. For numbers of colonial troops from different countries, Circular Unnumbered (2), Confidential, 'Victory Celebrations', 14 March 1946, CO 876/81.

99. According to one service newspaper, colonial troops' drinking water was drawn from the Serpentine; 'Hyde Park Camp for Victory Parade Troops', *Union Jack*, 6 April 1946. For a photograph of East African troops ironing their clothes in Kensington Gardens, www.iwm.org.uk/collections/item/object/205202317. See also *British Pathé*, 'Empire Troops at Camp', 9 July 1946, www.britishpathe.com/asset/94821.

100. Hugh Massingham, 'London's Millions See Stirring Pageant of Empire and Allies', *Manchester Guardian*, 9 June 1946, p. 6. See also the two-page spread featuring 'faces of empire', 'The World in London: Representatives of Our Overseas Allies Who Will March in the Victory Day Parade', *Illustrated London News*, 8 June 1946, pp. 616–17.

101. Betty Finlay to her mother and aunt, 25 August 1945.

102. Lynda Nead, *The Tiger in the Smoke: Art and Culture in Post-war Britain* (New Haven: Yale University Press, 2017), pp. 147–49; Lynda Nead, '"Red Taffeta under Tweed": The Color of Post-war Clothes', *Fashion Theory*, 21:4 (2017), 365–89.

103. Julia Herrick, 'Shortage of Good Dress Materials', *Sunday Times*, 11 March 1945, p. 6.

104. Mrs Violet Walton to Joseph Walton, 17 April 1945, private papers of Mrs V. E. Walton, documents.18852, IWM.

105. Guy Ramsey, 'The Family of Britain', *Daily Mail*, 10 June 1946, p. 3.

106. For an overview of the impact of war on Britain's empire, John Darwin, *The Empire Project: The Rise and Fall of the British World-System, 1830–1970* (Cambridge: Cambridge University Press, 2009), pp. 514–65. On British reactions to 'Zionist terrorism' in Palestine, David Leitch, 'Explosion at the King David Hotel', in Michael Sissons and Philip French (eds.), *Age of Austerity* (Oxford: Oxford University Press, 1986), pp. 45–67.

107. MO File Report 2378, 'Victory Celebrations', p. 2.

108. Herbert Ellison, 'War-Dazed England Is Becoming "Land of Tired Oldsters"', *Washington Post*, 9 December 1945, p. B1; Bevin quoted by Hennessy, *Never Again*, p. 221.

109. Rose Cottrell to Pat, Mun, Dad & Everybody, 11 June 1946, IWM.

110. 'London's Victory Day Celebration', *Manchester Guardian*, 10 June 1946, p. 5; 'Victory Celebrations: Special Supplement', *The Times*, 10 June 1946, p. 1.

2 Survivors

1. William A. Davis, 'Typhus at Belsen I: Control of the Typhus Epidemic', *American Journal of Hygiene*, 46:1 (1947), 66–83; W. R. F. Collis, 'Belsen Camp: A Preliminary Report', *BMJ*, 1:4405 (1945), 814–16; F. M. Lipscomb, 'Medical Aspects of Belsen Concentration Camp', *The Lancet*, 246:6367 (1945), 313–15.

2. Scholars disagree over the efficacy of the relief operation: Joanne Reilly, *Belsen: The Liberation of a Concentration Camp* (London: Routledge, 1998); E. Trepman, 'Rescue of the Remnants: The British Emergency Relief Operation in Belsen Camp 1945', *Journal of the Royal Army Medical Corps*, 147:3 (2001), 281–93; Ben Shephard, *After Daybreak: The Liberation of Belsen, 1945* (London: Pimlico, 2006); Paul Weindling, '"Belsenitis": Liberating Belsen, Its Hospitals, UNRRA and Selection for Re-emigration, 1945–1948', *Science in Context*, 19:3 (2006), 401–18; Jane Brooks, '"The Nurse Stoops Down ... For Me": Nursing the Liberated Persons at Bergen-Belsen', in Jane Brooks and Christine F. Hallett (eds.), *One Hundred Years of Wartime Nursing Practices, 1954–1953* (Manchester: Manchester University Press, 2015), pp. 211–31.

3. Jo Reilly, David Cesarani, Tony Kushner and Colin Richmond (eds.), *Belsen in History and Memory* (London: Frank Cass, 1997); Hannah Caven, 'Horror in Our Time: Images of the Concentration Camps in the British Media, 1945', *Historical Journal of Film, Radio, and Television*, 21:3 (2001), 205–53; Toby Haggith, 'The Filming of the Liberation of Bergen-Belsen and Its Impact on the Understanding of the Holocaust', *Holocaust Studies*, 12:1 (2006), 89–122.

4. Christine Lattek, 'Bergen-Belsen: From "Privileged" Camp to Death Camp', in Jo Reilly, David Cesarani, Tony Kushner and Colin Richmond (eds.), *Belsen in History and Memory* (London: Frank Cass, 1997), pp. 37–71.

5. Alice Lok Cahana quoted in 'Bergen-Belsen', Holocaust Encyclopedia, United States Holocaust Memorial Museum (hereafter USHMM), https://encyclopedia .ushmm.org/content/en/article/bergen-belsen.

6. Hanna Lévy-Hass, *Inside Belsen*, trans. Ronald Taylor (Brighton: Harvester Books, 1982), pp. 51–69; Anita Lasker-Wallfisch, 'A Survivor's Memories of Liberation', *Holocaust Studies*, 12:1 (2006), 22–26 (pp. 24–25); Lieutenant Colonel Mervyn Gonin, 'The RAMC at Belsen Concentration Camp', lecture transcript, private papers of Lt Col. M. W. Gonin, documents.3713, IWM.

7. Paul Kemp, 'The British Army and the Liberation of Bergen-Belsen', *Holocaust Education*, 5:2–3 (1996), 134–48; Reilly, *Belsen*, pp. 19–49; Shephard, *After Daybreak*, pp. 24–42; Ben Flanagan and Donald Bloxham (eds.), *Remembering Belsen: Eyewitnesses Record the Liberation* (London: Vallentine Mitchell, 2005), pp. 6–20.

8. Effie Barker to father (Lt Col. Frederick Barker) and brother (Gilbert Welch Barker), 27 April 1945, private papers of Miss E. L. Barker, documents.10541, IWM.

9. Molly Silva Jones, 'From a Diary Written in Belsen', p. 1, in private papers of Miss J. McFarlane, documents.9550, IWM; Jean McFarlane, 19 April–14 May 1945, McFarlane papers.

10. Silva Jones, 'From a Diary', p. 1; Alan MacAuslan, 'One Month at Belsen', transcript memoir, p. 2, private papers of Dr A. MacAuslan, documents.3042, IWM.

11. Michael Hargrave, 'Diary of a Medical Student in Belsen Concentration Camp, May, 1945', entry for 18 May, p. 60, private papers of Dr M. J. Hargrave, documents.7272, IWM. Others estimated the height of the pile to be even higher. For instance, Catholic chaplain Rev. Fr. Edmund Swift tallied the mound of footwear at 15′, cited in Flanagan and Bloxham (eds.), *Remembering Belsen*, p. 17. The *Illustrated London News* devoted a two-page spread to a line drawing of this scene, 'As Doré Might Have Conceived It: Belsen Camp, Where Prisoners Were Scientifically Exterminated', *Illustrated London News*, 5 May 1945, pp. 472–73.

12. MacAuslan, 'One Month at Belsen', p. 5.

13. Peter Horsey, 'Diary', private papers of Dr P. J. Horsey, documents.1345, IWM. See also FRS (Friends Relief Service), Reports of Team 100 at Belsen Camp, June 1945, p. 2 in private papers of E. Hall Williams, documents.2420, IWM; Lt Col. J. A. D. Johnston, RAMC, 'Administrative Report – Belsen Concentration Camp', in Barker papers.

14. McFarlane, 19 April–14 May 1945, p. 8; Marian Blackman, 'Stories Told of Camp I', private papers of Miss M. J. Blackman, documents.11454, IWM.

15. Arnold Horwell letter to wife, 30 April 1945, private papers of Dr A. R. Horwell, documents.1164, IWM. Sister K. J. Elvidge described survivors as using 'the dead bodies as pillows'; letter to 'my darlings', 26 May 1945, cited in Flanagan and Bloxham (eds.), *Remembering Belsen*, p. 20.

16. Gonin, 'RAMC at Belsen', p. 6.

17. Silva Jones, 'From a Diary', p. 8. On child survivors, W. R. F. Collis, 'Some Paediatric Problems Presented at Belsen Camp', *BMJ*, 1:4442 (1946), 273–75; Robert Collis and Han Hogerzeil, *Straight On* (London: Taylor & Francis Group, 2010 [1947]). On the fate of infants after the Holocaust more generally, Tara Zahra, *The Lost Children: Reconstructing Europe's Families after World War II* (Cambridge, MA: Harvard University Press, 2011).

18. Gonin, 'RAMC at Belsen', p. 6.

19. 'Belsen – An Account Based on Official Reports of the Uncovering by the British Army of the Belsen Concentration Camp and of the Action Taken during the Vital Days to Minimize the Suffering of the 60,000 Inmates', Supplement of *British Zone Review*, 13 Oct. 1945, in McFarlane papers.

20. Silva Jones, 'From a Diary', p. 1, p. 8.

21. Evelyn Bark, *No Time to Kill* (London: Robert Hale, 1961), p. 50.

22. Hargrave, 'Diary of a Medical Student', entry for 3 May 1945.

23. MacAuslan, 'One Month at Belsen', p. 6.

24. Lt Col. Johnston noted that the 'females [were] in worse condition than the men, their clothing generally, if they have any, only filthy rags', Johnston, 'Administrative Report'.

25. Claudia Theune, 'Clothes as Expression of Action in Former Concentration Camps', *International Journal of Historical Archaeology*, 22:3 (2018), 492–510; Sofia Pantouvaki, 'Narratives of Clothing: Concentration Camp Dress as a Companion to Survival', *International Journal of Fashion Studies*, 1:1 (2014), 19–37; Lizou Fenyvesi, 'Reading Prisoner Uniforms: The Concentration Camp Prisoner Uniform as a Primary Source for Historical Research', in *Textile Narratives & Conversions: Proceedings of the 10th Biennial Symposium of the Textile Society of America, October 11–14, Toronto, Ontario* (2006), https://digitalcommons.unl.edu/tsaconf/341; Noah Benninga, 'The Bricolage of Death: Jewish Possessions and the Fashioning of the Prisoner Elite in Auschwitz–Birkenau, 1942–1945', in Leora Auslander and Tara Zahra (eds.), *Objects of War: The Material Culture of Conflict and Displacement* (Ithaca, NY: Cornell University Press, 2018), pp. 189–220.

26. Theune, 'Clothes as Expression of Action', p. 498.

27. Maj. William A. Davis, 'Typhus at Belsen Camp', p. 5, in Horsey papers.

28. MacAuslan, 'One Month at Belsen', pp. 14–15.

29. 'Belsen Prisoner or SS Man? Strange Story of an "Ordinary" German', *Manchester Guardian*, 20 October 1945, p. 6. For Schmitz's testimony: www.bergenbelsen.co.uk/pages/trial/trial/trialdefencecase/Trial_040_Schmitz.html.

30. Terence McQuillin, RAMC, 'Relief of Bergen-Belsen, April/May 1945', pp. 11–12, private papers of T. C. McQuillin, documents.3187, IWM.

31. Silva Jones, 'From a Diary', p. 8. Horsey likewise registered that 'a few are fairly well dressed', Horsey, 'Diary', 3 May 1945. Capt J. Gant noted that some women even had silk stockings, 'It is assumed that these have only been in a few days', cited in Flanagan and Bloxham (eds.), *Remembering Belsen*, p. 18.

32. Pte E. Fisher, RAMC, 'A Soldier's Diary of Belsen', p. 4, private papers of E. Fisher, documents.3056, IWM. On Fisher's background, Shephard, *After Daybreak*, p. 106.

33. Silva Jones, 'From a Diary', p. 8. One of the medical students made a similar observation, Humphrey Kidd, Diary, 2 May 1945, private papers of H. B. Kidd, documents.2691, IWM.

34. Susan L. Carruthers, 'Compulsory Viewing: Concentration Camp Film and German Re-education', *Millennium: Journal of International Studies*, 30:3 (2001), 733–59. On film and re-education more generally, Jennifer Fay, *Theaters of Occupation: Hollywood and the Reeducation of Postwar Germany* (St Paul, MN: University of Minnesota Press, 2008); Cora Sol Goldstein, *Capturing the German Eye: American Visual Propaganda in Occupied Germany* (Chicago: University of Chicago Press, 2009).

35. M. F. Beardwell, *Aftermath* (Ilfracombe: Arthur M. Stockwell, n.d. c. 1953), p. 43.

36. Horwell, letter to wife, 30 April 1945; 'Belsen – An Account Based on Official Reports', p. 8.

37. Johnston, 'Administrative Report'; Capt. J. Gant, 21 Light Field Ambulance BLA, cited in Flanagan and Bloxham (eds.), *Remembering Belsen*, p. 17; Miss J. Rudman,

9th General Hospital, letter to Bill, 14 May 1945, cited in Flanagan and Bloxham (eds.), *Remembering Belsen*, p. 30.

38. R. W. Thompson, 'S.S. Women Tied Dead to Living: Belsen Horror', *Sunday Times*, 22 April 1945, p. 5.
39. MacAuslan, 'One Month at Belsen', pp. 15–16.
40. Davis, 'Typhus at Belsen Camp', p. 5.
41. Dr Fritz Leo, 'The Concentration Camp for Sick People at Bergen Belsen', p. 2, in Barker papers, IWM.
42. Shephard, *After Daybreak*, p. 17.
43. See, among many other photographs, BU 5465, BU 3722, BU 3765 and BU 3813 in the IWM collection.
44. Davis, 'Typhus at Belsen Camp', p. 5.
45. Gonin, 'RAMC at Belsen', p. 6. See also Kidd, 'Diary', 2 May 1945, IWM.
46. Johnston, 'Administrative Report', p. 2.
47. Horsey, 'Diary', 8 May 1945.
48. Hargrave, 'Diary of a Medical Student', 7 May 1945, p. 32.
49. 'Belsen – An Account Based on Official Reports', p. 4.
50. Gonin, 'RAMC at Belsen', p. 6. Silva Jones describes a 'cold anger with those primarily responsible, the Germans', Silva Jones, 'From a Diary', p. 2, while McQuillin relates how some colleagues treated Germans contemptuously whereas he preferred the Swiss advice 'to treat Germans coldly but properly', McQuillin, 'Relief of Bergen-Belsen', p. 13.
51. Hargrave, 'Diary of a Medical Student', 4 May 1945, p. 24.
52. Shephard, *After Daybreak*, p. 113; Bark, *No Time to Kill*, p. 52.
53. Gonin, 'RAMC at Belsen', p. 9.
54. McFarlane, 19 April–14 May 1945, p. 6.
55. Douglas Brock Peterkin, 'Observations on the Outbreak of Louse-Borne Typhus Fever at Belsen Concentration Camp, April, 1945', PhD thesis, University of Edinburgh (1947), pp. 79–80.
56. McFarlane, 19 April–14 May 1945, p. 6.
57. Barker, letter, 23 March 1945.
58. MacAuslan, 'One Month at Belsen', p. 4.
59. Peterkin, 'Observations', p. 54.
60. Ward, letter to mother, 11 May 1945; McFarlane, 19 April–14 May 1945, p. 9.
61. Horsey, 'Preliminaries', pp. 1–2.
62. MacAuslan, 'One Month at Belsen', p. 1.
63. Hargrave, 'Diary of a Medical Student', 6 May 1945, p. 30; MacAuslan, 'One Month at Belsen', p. 37; Horsey, Diary, 3 May 1945; Irene Guenther, *Nazi Chic? Fashioning Women in the Third Reich* (Oxford: Berg, 2004).
64. Peterkin, 'Observations', p. 58.
65. McQuillin, 'Relief of Bergen-Belsen', p. 4.
66. Horsey, Part IV, 'The Hospital Squares', XI.
67. A British army photographer noted a reaction at odds with McQuillin's perception, namely that, despite the RAMC badge, patients were frightened of men in typhus suits; Sgt Oakes quoted by Caven, 'Horror in Our Time', p. 218.
68. 'Belsen – An Account Based on Official Reports', p. 7.
69. Silva Jones, 'From a Diary', p. 4.
70. Ibid., p. 6.
71. Gonin, 'RAMC at Belsen', p. 10. On the tardy dispatch of UNRRA clothing from the United States, 'Belsen Inmates to Get Relief', *NYT*, 21 November 1945, p. 8.
72. 'Belsen – An Account Based on Official Reports', p. 7.

73. Military government correspondence relating to the clothing levy in Germany, operated between 1945 and 1946, can be found in FO 1032/582 and FO 1013/1490, TNA. Journalists in Germany alerted readers to this material form of reparation: 'SS for Mines: "Belsen Levy" on Clothing', *Daily Mail*, 14 May 1945, p. 1; 'Clothes Levy for Belsen Victims: Allies Poetic Justice', *Western Daily Press and Bristol Mirror*, 14 May 1945, p. 1; 'Ruling Germany', *Dundee Courier*, 17 May 1945, p. 2.

74. Ward, letter to mother, 15 May 1945.

75. MacAuslan, 'One Month at Belsen', p. 4.

76. On the double standards and different euphemisms that distinguished relief workers' 'liberating' or 'organizing' supplies from DPs' 'stealing' or 'looting', UNRRA worker Muriel Heath, interview with Lyn E. Smith, 11 September 1998, www.iwm.org .uk/collections/item/object/80019861, IWM; Sharif Gemie, Fiona Reid and Laure Humbert, *Outcast Europe: Refugees and Relief Workers in an Era of Total War 1936–48* (London: Continuum, 2012), pp. 183–85. On DPs more generally, Ben Shephard, *The Long Road Home: The Aftermath of the Second World War* (New York: Alfred A. Knopf, 2011); G. Daniel Cohen, *In War's Wake: Europe's Displaced Persons in the Post-war Order* (New York: Oxford University Press, 2012).

77. Ward, letter to mother, 11 May 1945.

78. Gonin, 'RAMC at Belsen', p. 10.

79. Ward, letter to mother, 14 August 1945. On marriage and procreation in DP camps, Atina Grossmann, *Jews, Germans, and Allies: Close Encounters in Occupied Germany* (Princeton: Princeton University Press, 2007), pp. 184–98.

80. Provision of Clothing and Blankets for Military Government Purposes, Control Commission, BAOR (British Army of the Rhine),13 September 1945, FO 1032/582.

81. Report on Liaison Visit by Maj. P. C. E. Russell on 12 September to 30 Corps District to Investigate DP Clothing Situation, FO 1032/582.

82. Report on Clothing Situation in 8 Corps Area in DP Camps, 15 September 1945, FO 1032/582.

83. Jo Reilly, 'Cleaner, Carer and Occasional Dance Partner? Writing Women Back into the Liberation of Bergen-Belsen', *Holocaust Education*, 5:2–3 (1996), 157–58.

84. MacAuslan, 'One Month at Belsen', p. 37. For a similar complaint about unattached shoes, but blaming 'some stupid man called Kaiser [organizer of the United National Clothing Collection], in America, who had the idea of sending trucks through the street and people threw in shoes', see Heath interview with Smith.

85. Collis and Hogerzeil, *Straight On*, p. 54; Beardwell, *Aftermath*, p. 54.

86. Silva Jones, 'From a Diary', p. 7.

87. On soldiers supplying this nickname, Eryl Hall Williams, *A Page in the History of Relief: London – Antwerp – Belsen – Brunswick, 1944–46* (York: Sessions Book Trust), p. 36. For footage (shot by Sgt Hewitt in May 1945) of survivors being taken by ambulance and selecting clothes at 'Harrods', a destination marked by jaunty handmade signs, see https://collections.ushmm.org/search/catalog/irn1001293, USHMM.

88. Mary Kessell, German Diary, August–October 1945, entry for VJE (VJ Day in Europe) night, private papers of Miss M. Kessell, documents.18803, IWM.

89. Kessell, German Diary, 13 August 1945.

90. Beth Clarkson, 'Clothing in Hospital Section', FRS Reports on Team 100 at Belsen Camp, June 1945, in E. Hall Williams papers. In a pamphlet for novices, Quaker veteran Francesca Wilson cautioned against the old 'Lady Bountiful attitude' – 'a hangover from the Victorian age when the rich needed the poor' – but traces of it still remained, Francesca M. Wilson, *Advice to Relief Workers: Based on Personal Experience in the Field* (London: John Murray and Friends Relief Service, 1944), p. 7.

91. 'Richard Dimbleby's Despatch of 17 April 1945', in Ben Flanagan and Donald Bloxham (eds.), *Remembering Belsen: Eyewitnesses Record the Liberation* (London: Vallentine Mitchell, 2005), pp. xi–xiii; Stone, *Liberation of the Camps*, p. 82. On the 'dejudaized' character of Dimbleby's text, no full copy of which remains extant, Judith Petersen, 'Belsen and a British Broadcasting Icon', *Holocaust Studies*, 13:1 (2007), 19–43.

92. On the various reasons and rationalizations for Jews' omission or marginalization in contemporary accounts of Belsen, see Reilly, *Belsen*, p. 51; Tony Kushner, *The Holocaust and the Liberal Imagination: A Social and Cultural History* (Oxford: Blackwell, 1994), pp. 214–15; Caven, 'Horror in Our Time', p. 229; Petersen, 'Belsen and a British Broadcasting Icon', pp. 26–28.

93. Barker, letter, 15 May 1945.

94. Some Jewish relief workers and military personnel also replicated these tropes in which perceptions of class played a structuring role. See, for example, the letters of Major Irving Heymont, who kept his Jewish faith hidden both from his US Army colleagues and from the Jewish survivors over whom he presided at Landsberg DP Camp in Bavaria, Irving Heymont papers, RG-19.038, USHMM, https://bit .ly/4dvutPS. For a discussion of Heymont, Carruthers, *Good Occupation*, pp. 175–81.

95. Beardwell, *Aftermath*, p. 51.

96. Ward, letter to mother, 21 May 1945.

97. Beardwell, *Aftermath*, pp. 54–55.

98. Collis and Hogerzeil, *Straight On*, p. 54.

99. Ward, letter to mother, 14 June 1945. Clarkson described the index card system to register who received what, Clarkson, 'Clothing in Hospital Section'.

100. Ward, letter to mother, 23 June 1945.

101. Ibid., 22 June 1945.

102. Gonin, 'RAMC at Belsen', pp. 9–10; Shephard, *After Daybreak*, pp. 83–84.

103. Reilly, *Belsen*, pp. 39–40. Not surprisingly, Jewish relief workers took umbrage at the *Express*'s characterization of Belsen and the *News Chronicle*'s claim that the camp had been 'converted into a great health restoring centre'. See Jewish Committee for Relief Abroad, *Volunteers' Newsletter*, September–October 1945, p. 3, Rose Henriques Archive, Wiener Library, London.

104. Ward, letter to mother, 21 May 1945.

105. Barker, letter, 15 May 1945; part of this letter was printed, under the headline 'Evelyn to Brenda', in the *Devon and Exeter Gazette*, 8 June 1945, p. 3.

106. Sgt Oakes quoted by Caven, 'Horror in Our Time', p. 219.

107. Clarkson, 'Clothing in Hospital Section'.

108. Barker, letter, 21 May 1945.

109. The caption sheet accompanying a photograph showing the interior of 'Harrods', taken by Sgt Hewitt on 16–17 May 1945, states that UNRRA worker Mrs H. Tanner is helping 'a woman choose suitable dress for future dates'; BU 6365, www.iwm.org.uk/collections/item/object/205194187, IWM.

110. Eryl Hall Williams, diary, entries for 19 and 21 May 1945. He departed from Belsen on 25 May. In an oral history interview with Lyn E. Smith, recorded on 30 March 1995, he says a little more about 'Harrods', interview 15323, reel 4, IWM. In striking contrast, *Picture Post* printed a story about Belsen, accompanied by pen and ink sketches of male survivors getting outfitted at 'Harrods', 'Victim and Prisoner', *Picture Post*, 22 September 1945, pp. 16–17.

111. Gonin, 'RAMC at Belsen', p. 11. This passage, mischaracterized as a 'diary entry', was later adopted by the artist Banksy as inspiration for his 'Holocaust lipstick' series. See also Mark Celinscak, *Distance from the Belsen Heap: Allied Forces and*

the Liberation of a Nazi Concentration Camp (Toronto: University of Toronto Press, 2015), p. xv.

112. Hargrave, 'Diary of a Medical Student', 8, 9, 11, 18 and 23 May 1945.
113. McFarlane, 19 April–14 May 1945, pp. 16–17; Barker, letter, 21 May 1945.
114. MacAuslan, 'One Month at Belsen', p. 47.
115. Horwell, letter to wife, 4 May 1945; Horwell, letter, 11 May 1945.
116. Col. H. L. W. Bird, 'Notes on Belsen Camp, 18 May 1945', in McFarlane papers.
117. On UNRRA and repatriation, Cohen, *In War's Wake*; George Woodbridge, *UNRRA: The History of the United Nations Relief and Rehabilitation Administration* (New York: Columbia University Press, 1950). On the preferences of Jewish survivors, Zeev W. Mankovitz, *Life between Memory and Hope* (Cambridge: Cambridge University Press, 2002); Sharon Kangisser Cohen, 'Choosing a *Heim*: Survivors of the Holocaust and Post-war Immigration', *European Judaism: A Journal for the New Europe*, 46:2 (2013), 32–54.
118. Clarkson, 'Clothing in Hospital Section'.
119. 'Text of Report to the President on Conditions among Refugees in Western Europe', *NYT*, 30 September 1945, p. 38.
120. Leonard Dinnerstein, 'America, Britain and Palestine: The Anglo-American Committee of Inquiry and the Displaced Persons, 1945–1946', *Diplomatic History* 4:3 (1980), 283–302; Arieh J. Kochavi, 'The Struggle against Jewish Immigration to Palestine', *Middle Eastern Studies* 34:3 (1998), 146–67; Avinoam Patt, '"The People Must Be Forced to Go to Palestine": Rabbi Abraham Klausner and the She'erit Hapletah in Germany', *Holocaust and Genocide Studies* 28:2 (2014), 240–76.
121. 'Bergen-Belsen Displaced Persons Camp', Holocaust Encyclopedia, USHMM, https://encyclopedia.ushmm.org/content/en/article/bergen-belsen-displaced-persons-camp.
122. Appendix 8, 'Jane's Work for RT/100 among the Jews', in Williams, *A Page in the History of Relief*, p. 117.
123. Ward, letter, 14 June 1945.
124. Jane Leverson, 'Report on DP Centre Lingen', 6 June 1945, in Horwell papers.
125. British UNRRA worker Rhoda Dawson also noted the making of toys from *Wehrmacht* uniforms at another DP camp, Rhoda Dawson, 'The Stagnant Pool: Work among Displaced Persons in Germany, 1945–47', p. 67 in private papers of Mrs R. N. Bickerdike, documents.3277, IWM. The British Red Cross Museum & Archives preserves a doll made by a survivor at Belsen, dressed in striped fabric, given to Red Cross relief worker Enid Fordham, catalogued as 1535/4, and two others in Polish traditional costume, also presented to Fordham, 1535/3 and 1535/5. The IWM collection includes two dolls, produced at Belsen, wearing striped fabric from survivors' camp clothing, catalogued as EPH10142 and EPH10141.2.

3 Veterans

1. Montague Burton to Raymond Burton, 11 August 1944, Burton letter LEEWW: 2001.875.1.18, Second World War Experience Centre, Otley.
2. Eric M. Sigsworth, *Montague Burton: The Tailor of Taste* (Manchester: Manchester University Press, 1990), p. 124.
3. M. Burton to R. Burton, 11 August 1944.
4. Burton to Sir Cecil Weir, 31 July 1944; Weir to Burton, 3 August 1944, BT 64/954, TNA; Danielle Sprecher, 'Demob Suits: One Uniform for Another? Burtons and the Leeds Multiple Tailors' Production of Men's Demobilization Tailoring after the Second World War', *Costume*, 54:1 (2020), 108–30.

5. Burton to Weir, 31 July 1944. On wartime production problems faced by British clothing manufacturers and those based in Leeds more particularly, Katrina Honeyman, *Well-Suited: A History of the Leeds Clothing Industry 1850–1990* (Oxford: Oxford University Press, 2000); Sigsworth, *Montague Burton*, ch. 7.
6. Sigsworth, *Montague Burton*, p. 112. On demobilization, Rex Pope, 'British Demobilization after the Second World War', *Journal of Contemporary History*, 30:1 (1995), 65–81; Alan Allport, *Demobbed: Coming Home after the Second World War* (New Haven: Yale University Press, 2009).
7. The derivation of the phrase is disputed. Alternative origin stories suggest that the 'Monty' in question was Field Marshall Sir Bernard Montgomery, 'full' referring to his preferred breakfast. See Julia Cresswell, *The Penguin Dictionary of Clichés* (London: Penguin, 2000); *The Full Monty*, dir. Peter Cattaneo, 1997.
8. David Hughes, 'The Spivs', in Michael Sissons and Philip French (eds.), *Age of Austerity 1945–1951* (Oxford: Oxford University Press, 1986 [1963]), pp. 69–88.
9. On Norman Wisdom, John Hall, 'Pagliacci in a Demob Suit', *The Guardian*, 31 July 1971, p. 9; 'Object of the Week – Demob Suit on Loan', 9 November 2017, Leeds. gov.uk, https://news.leeds.gov.uk/news/object-of-the-week-demob-suit-on-loan.
10. This figure was based on a projection of outfitting three million men (one million fewer than eventually received clothing); Treasury Inter Service Committee, draft minute of the 470th Meeting, 9 November 1943, BT 64/936.
11. Sir Harry Shackleton quoted in 'Still Fewer Suits for Civilians: Effect of Quicker Demobilisation', *Manchester Guardian*, 6 December 1945, p. 5.
12. Minute by Churchill to Dalton, 14 April 1945, DALTON/2/7/7, papers of Hugh Dalton, The Women's Library, LSE.
13. Wendy Ugolini, 'The Great War, Demobilisation and "Civvy Clothes"', blog post, https://bit.ly/4chiBji; Rachel Neal, 'From Khaki to Civvies: The First World War, Demobilisation and the Narratives of Men's Dress', PhD thesis, De Montfort University, 2022.
14. 'Their "Last Hours" Are Happy Ones', *United Services Review*, 9 July 1945.
15. Ministry of Supply, Confidential Memorandum on Civilian Clothing for Demobilised Servicemen, 18 August 1943, BT 64/936, TNA.
16. At an inter-departmental meeting, Maj. Gen. Hoare opined that the main problem had been measurements 'taken by amateurs'. Extract from the Minutes of the 31st Meeting of the Standing Committee on Demobilisation held on 31 August 1943, WO 32/9945, TNA.
17. Confidential Memorandum on Civilian Clothing for Demobilised Servicemen, 18 August 1943, BT 64/936.
18. Sir Thomas Barlow, Observations on Sir Arnold Overton's Letter to the War Office on Clothing for the Demobilised Men (c. 31 August 1943), BT 64/936.
19. Mass Observation (MO), *The Journey Home* (London: John Murray, 1944), p. 91.
20. Ibid., p. 28.
21. Adam R. Seipp, *The Ordeal of Peace: Demobilization and the Urban Experience in Britain and Germany* (Farnham: Ashgate, 2009), pp. 142–45. On race riots in 1919, Jacqueline Jenkinson, *Black 1919: Riots, Racism and Resistance in Imperial Britain* (Liverpool: Liverpool University Press, 2009); Ray Costello, *Black Tommies: British Soldiers of African Descent in the First World War* (Liverpool: Liverpool University Press, 2017); Jane L. Chapman, *African and Afro-Caribbean Repatriation, 1919–1922* (Basingstoke: Palgrave, 2018).
22. George Mosse's thesis regarding veterans' 'brutalization' and the coarsening consequences for national politics (particularly the rise of fascism in interwar Germany) has been much debated. George Mosse, *Masses and Man: Nationalist and Fascist Perceptions of Reality* (Detroit: Wayne State University Press, 1987); Mark Edele

and Robert Gerwarth, 'The Limits of Demobilization: Global Perspectives on the Aftermath of the Great War', *Journal of Contemporary History*, 50:1 (2015), 3–14; Lorenzo Benadusi, 'Brutalization and the Civilizing Process: An Ongoing Debate between Mosse and Elias', *Journal of Contemporary History*, 56:4 (2021), 950–66. On shell-shock, Tracey Loughran, *Shell-Shock and Medical Culture in First World War Britain* (Cambridge: Cambridge University Press, 2017).

23. William Lemkin, 'How Britain Provided a Complete Outfit for Her Demobilised Servicemen', *The Outfitter Export* (July 1947), p. 45.

24. Geraldine Biddle-Perry, *Dressing for Austerity: Aspiration, Leisure and Fashion in Postwar Britain* (London: I.B. Tauris, 2017), pp. 45–47; Allport, *Demobbed*, p. 119; *HC Deb*, 'Discharged Army Personnel (Clothing Allowance)', 9 December 1943, *Hansard*, cc. 1664–72.

25. Treasury, Inter-Service Committee, War Office Memo #1357, Provision of Clothing for Military Personnel on Demobilisation, 22 March 1944, BT 64/936; Minute by R. W. Baldwin, 11 November 1943, BT 64/936; Minutes of Meeting Held Saturday 28 June 1943 at Portland House on the Question of Clothing for Demobilised Service Men, BT 64/936.

26. Christopher Sladen, *The Conscription of Fashion: Utility Cloth, Clothing and Footwear 1941–1952* (Aldershot: Scolar Press, 1995), p. 22; Peter McNeil, '"Put Your Best Face Forward": The Impact of the Second World War on British Dress', *Journal of Design History*, 6:4 (1993), 283–99 (pp. 285–86); *HC Deb*, 'Austerity Suits', 6 April 1944, *Hansard*, cc. 2210–49.

27. J. B. Lintott to Arnold Overton, 17 January 1944, BT 64/936.

28. 'Your Demob Suit Will Be Pre-war Style', *Air Force News*, 1 February 1944. The disposal of army surplus clothing was a complex and contested issue. Garment manufacturers still bristled at the dent to their business suffered as a result of government liquidation of surplus material after the Great War, Council of Clothing Trade Associations, 'Report on Post-war Reconstruction in the Clothing Industry', 9 December 1943, pp. 14–16, MSS.21/5126, MRC.

29. Minute by R. W. Baldwin, 'Clothing for Demobilised Soldiers', 2 October 1943, BT 64/936.

30. Dennis Rooke and Alan D'Egville, *Call Me Mister! A Guide to Civilian Life for the Newly Demobilised* (London: William Heinemann, 1946), pp. 12–13.

31. Army Council Secretariat, Standing Committee on Demobilisation, Minutes of 32nd Meeting, 6 September 1943, BT 64/936.

32. Officers received a cash allowance (set at £35 in 1942), but this did not cover the steadily rising cost of uniforms and other expenses, such as mess subscriptions, Jeremy A. Crang, *The British Army and the People's War 1939–1945* (Manchester: Manchester University Press, 2000), p. 25; 'Army and ATS Officers' Jackets', *The Garment Worker*, 14:2 (1945), 33; John Berger quoted by McNeil, '"Put Your Best Face Forward"', p. 288.

33. Hopkinson to Hugh Dalton, 24 December 1943, BT 64/936.

34. Lemkin, 'How Britain Provided', p. 47.

35. Hopkinson to Dalton; Hopkinson quoted in 'Cash, Coupons for Girls', *SEAC News*, 4 April 1944.

36. Arnold (Board of Trade) to F. C. Bovenschen (War Office), 30 August 1943, BT 64/936.

37. Correspondence in AVIA 22/465.

38. Barlow, Observations on Sir Arnold Overton's Letter.

39. Army Council Secretariat, 6 September 1943, BT 64/936.

40. Extract from minutes of the 136th Meeting of the Executive Committee of the Army Council, 12 November 1943, WO 32/9945.

41. A. H. Clough (Treasury Chambers) to K. Lyon, War Office, 28 October 1943, WO 32/9945.

42. Reconstruction Committee, R (43) 5, Provision of Civilian Clothing and Retention of Uniform on Demobilisation, 6 December 1943, BT 64/936.

43. Minute by R. W. Baldwin, 11 November 1943, BT 64/936; Executive Committee of the Army Council, Provision of Civilian Clothing for Soldiers on Demobilisation. Memo by chairman for consideration by committee at their meeting of November 1943, WO 32/9945.

44. War Cabinet. Reconstruction Committee. Provision of Civilian Clothing and Retention of Uniform on Demobilisation, Memorandum by the President of the Board of Trade, 15 December 1943, CAB 124/423.

45. Hanna Rose Shell, *Shoddy: From Devil's Dust to the Renaissance of Rags* (Chicago: University of Chicago Press, 2020).

46. 'Khaki Going into Your Autumn Suit', *SEAC News*, 14 May 1946.

47. Memorandum by the President of the Board of Trade, 15 December 1943, CAB 124/423.

48. Minutes of meeting held Saturday 28 June 1943, at Portland House on the question of Clothing for Demobilised Service Men, BT 64/936.

49. Hettie Grimstead, 'London Letter', *Los Angeles Times*, 12 May 1946, p. C1.

50. J. B. Priestley, *Three Men in New Suits* (London: Heinemann, 1945), p. 23.

51. Anon., 'Review: Three Men in New Suits', *Washington Post*, 26 August 1945, p. S5; J. D. Beresford, 'Books of the Day: New Novels, Review of Priestley and Waugh', *Manchester Guardian*, 1 June 1945, p. 3.

52. Priestley, *Three Men in New Suits*, 3rd impression (July 1946), 'Author's Note'.

53. 'MPs to See "Monstrosity" Suit for Soldiers Given on Discharge', *Evening Standard*, 8 January 1944, BT 64/936. See also Cyril Martin, 'This Is the Army's "Victory" Suit"', *Daily Mail*, 12 January 1944, p. 3.

54. Geraldine Howell, *Wartime Fashion: From Haute Couture to Homemade, 1939–1945* (London: Bloomsbury, 2012), pp. 132–35.

55. Allport, *Demobbed*, pp. 121–22; Lemkin, 'How Britain Provided', p. 47. This attention to service paid off. During the Olympia 'dress rehearsal', reporters gushed over carefully selected assistants who displayed 'courtesy of a kind uncommon now in "Civvy Street"', 'Suits for Soldiers', *Manchester Guardian*, 20 February 1945, p. 3.

56. A. Conley, 'A Call for Increased Effort in the Garment Trades', *The Garment Worker*, 14:2 (1945), 23–24; Kay quoted by A. Conley, 'This Is Your Job', *The Garment Worker*, 14:11 (1945), 209.

57. 'First Day of Demobilisation: Efficient Organisation Paves the Way Back to "Civvy Street"', *Manchester Guardian*, 19 June 1945, p. 3; MO, *Journey Home*, p. 102.

58. *British Pathé*, 'Demob', 28 June 1945, www.britishpathe.com/asset/67464.

59. 'The Thin Man Returns – with Fat Man', *Daily Mail*, 19 January 1946, p. 3; 'Rehabilitation of the Disabled', *The Garment Worker*, 14:1 (1945), 13–14.

60. 'Demob Suit Same for All Ranks', *Air Force News*, 24 October 1944.

61. 'Film Star Demobbed', *Tripoli Times*, 4 September 1945; 'Monty Picks Demob Suit', *Air Force News*, 27 November 1945; 'Monty Picks Demob Suit', *Daily Mail*, 15 November 1945, p. 3.

62. 'A Store Where "The Customer Is Always Right"', *Manchester Guardian*, 8 December 1945, p. 3; 'Still More Demob. Suits Wanted', *The Garment Worker*, 15:1 (1946), 9.

63. Alan Bryett, interview with Peter Hart, April 2004, www.iwm.org.uk/collections/item/object/80024309, IWM; '"Savile Row" Demob Suits for 2s. 6d. Tips: Troops Beat the "Bribe" Patrol', *Daily Mail*, 17 December 1945, p. 3.

64. Bill Hunt, 'Ask Him If He's Lucky: An Account of My Time in the RAF, 1942–47', unpublished typescript memoir (n.d. c. 2000–2002), p. 238, private papers of Flight Lieutenant W. G. Hunt, documents.27242, IWM.

65. Bert Scrivens, interview with Peter Hart, February 2007, www.iwm.org.uk/collections/item/object/80028277, IWM.

66. Robert Ellison, interview with Harry Moses, 1999, www.iwm.org.uk/collections/item/object/80017743, IWM.

67. 'Bribe Patrols Watch Demob Suit Racket', *SEAC News*, 31 December 1946.

68. HC Collins to the editor, 'Clothing Issue', *Manchester Guardian*, 21 December 1945, p. 4.

69. William Cowans, interview with Harry Moses, 1997, www.iwm.org.uk/collections/item/object/80016748, IWM.

70. Edward (Ted) Grey, interview with Harry Moses, 1995, www.iwm.org.uk/collections/item/object/80016183, IWM. See also George Bland, interview with Harry Moses, 1997, who recalls spivs offering '30 bob', www.iwm.org.uk/collections/item/object/80016745, IWM.

71. Thomas Bruce Jackson, interview with Peter Hart, September 2003, www.iwm.org.uk/collections/item/object/80023579, IWM; Monty Fish, interview with Peter Hart, November 2007, www.iwm.org.uk/collections/item/object/80030206, IWM. One knowledgeable MO diarist noted in October 1945 'quite a few of the new demobilisation suits in pawn', Simon Garfield, *Our Hidden Lives: The Remarkable Diaries of Post-war Britain* (London: Ebury Press, 2005), p. 115.

72. 'Is That All?', *Union Jack*, 16 May 1947. On the theft of material for 1,000 demob suits, 'Big Haul of Demob Suit-Cloth', *Union Jack*, 29 December 1945; 'Burglar Chooses Demob Suit', *Dundee Courier*, 13 July 1946, p. 2.

73. Don Mitchard, interview with Peter Hart, April 2005, www.iwm.org.uk/collections/item/object/80028279, IWM.

74. Albert Cameron, interview with Peter Hart, 1992, www.iwm.org.uk/collections/item/object/80017433, IWM.

75. Hunt, 'Ask Him If He's Lucky', p. 239.

76. Hunt, 'Ask Him If He's Lucky', p. 239. On the extent of embitterment in and towards the armed forces, Alan Allport, *Browned Off and Bloody-Minded: The British Soldier Goes to War, 1939–1945* (New Haven: Yale University Press, 2015).

77. '24 Clothing Coupons to Last Eight Months', *Manchester Guardian*, 22 August 1945, p. 5. On sharing coupons, 'Demobilisation Coupons: A Study of the Way These Clothing Coupons Were Being Used, for the Board of Trade', RG 23/79, TNA.

78. 'The Civvy Suit', *The Times*, 8 October 1945, p. 5.

79. Linsey Robb, '"The Cushy Number": Civilian Men in British Post-war Representations of the Second World War', in Linsey Robb and Juliette Pattinson (eds.), *Men, Masculinities and Male Culture in the Second World War* (Basingstoke: Palgrave, 2018), pp. 169–88. On conscripted miners receiving what they regarded as 'pocket money', 'Grievances of "Bevin Boys"', *The Times*, 20 January 1944, p. 8. That they were not issued demob suits has been highlighted in recent projects to memorialize their service, 'Remembering the Bevin Boys in the Second World War', Amgueddfa Cymru, https://museum.wales/articles/1020/Remembering-the-Bevin-Boys-in-the-Second-World-War.

80. Lucy Noakes, *Women in the British Army: War and the Gentle Sex, 1907–1948* (London: Routledge, 2006); Jeremy A. Crang, *Sisters in Arms: Women in the British Armed Forces during the Second World War* (Cambridge: Cambridge University Press, 2020).

81. Gail Braybon and Penny Summerfield, *Out of the Cage: Women's Experiences in Two World Wars* (London: Pandora, 1987); Penny Summerfield, *Women Workers in the Second World War: Production and Patriarchy in Conflict* (London: Routledge, 1989).

82. Men did not, of course, hold identical opinions about their kit. For some poorer men, their army boots, underwear and overcoats were the first such items they had ever had, Emma Newlands, 'The Body and Becoming a Soldier in Britain during the Second World War', in Douglas E. Delaney, Mark Frost and Andrew L. Brown (eds.), *Manpower and Armies of the British Empire in the Two World Wars* (Ithaca, NY: Cornell University Press, 2021), pp. 144–59 (p. 147). More style-conscious enlistees sometimes complained that battledress made men look like 'a sack of potatoes tied in the middle'; Allport, *Browned Off*, p. 81.

83. J. B. Priestley, *British Women Go to War* (London: Collins, 1943); Noakes, *Women in the British Army*, p. 109.

84. Julie Summers, *Fashion on the Ration: Style in the Second World War* (London: Profile Books, 2016), pp. 154–74; Pat Kirkham, 'Fashion, Femininity and "Frivolous" Consumption in World-War-Two Britain', in Judy Attfield (ed.), *Utility Reassessed: The Role of Ethics in the Practice of Design* (Manchester: Manchester University Press, 2001), pp. 143–56; Jane Waller and Michael Vaughan-Rees, *Women in Wartime: The Role of Women's Magazines 1939–1945* (London: Macdonald Optima, 1987).

85. ATS veterans quoted by Noakes, *Women in the British Army*, p. 108. See also Emma Treleaven, 'Standard and Supremely Smart: Luxury and Women's Service Uniforms in World War II', *Luxury*, 5:2 (2018), 107–28.

86. Mattie E. Treadwell, *The Women's Army Corps* (Washington, DC: Center of Military History, United States Army, 1991), p. 198, p. 199. See also Melissa A. McEuen, *Making War, Making Women: Femininity and Duty on the American Home Front, 1941–1945* (Athens, GA: University of Georgia Press, 2011).

87. Crang, *Sisters in Arms*, pp. 201–11; Noakes, *Women in the British Army*, pp. 133–41.

88. Minutes of Meeting held Saturday 28 June 1943.

89. Joanna Bourke, 'The Great Male Renunciation: Men's Dress Reform in Inter-war Britain', *Journal of Design History*, 9:1 (1996), 23–33.

90. Barlow, Observations on Sir Arnold Overton's letter.

91. *HC Deb*, 'Demobilised Women (Clothing Grants)', 21 March 1944, *Hansard*, vol. 398. On 'cheering' greeting Grigg's announcement, 'Cash, Coupons for Girls', *SEAC News*, 4 April 1944.

92. On siren suits, Howell, *Wartime Fashion*, pp. 67–69. Profumo quoted by Noakes, *Women in the British Army*, p. 137.

93. Crang, *Sisters in Arms*, p. 207; Biddle-Perry, *Dressing for Austerity*, p. 60; 'Year's Delay Hits Clothing Exports', *The Observer*, 27 January 1946, p. 5.

94. Treasury Inter-Service Committee, War Office Memorandum #1358, Arrangements in Regard to the Provision of Civilian Clothing for ATS on 'Demobilisation' or 'Release', 25 March 1944, BT 64/936.

95. Ord Johnstone to Kenneth Lyon, 6 June 1944, BT 64/936.

96. Alison Settle, 'Clothing Fears of Girls in Uniform: Shortage after Demobilisation', *The Observer*, 6 May 1945, p. 7.

97. Maureen Pilling, 'Women Only', *Air Force News*, 6 November 1945; Biddle-Perry, *Dressing for Austerity*, pp. 76–78.

98. Dorothy Rolfe (née Davies), Discharge Papers from WLA; MS memoir (n.d.); Private papers of Mrs D. Rolfe, documents.1121, IWM.

99. 'Square Deal Demand for the Land', *Air Force News*, 28 May 1946.

100. On WLA demobilization, BT 64/1464, TNA.

101. Neil J. Diamant, Martin Crotty and Mark Edele, *The Politics of Veteran Benefits in the Twentieth Century: A Comparative History* (Ithaca, NY: Cornell University Press, 2020), ch. 5.

102. Stephen Lovell, *The Shadow of War: Russia and the USSR, 1941 to the Present* (Oxford: Wiley-Blackwell, 2010), p. 2.

103. Reuters, 'Disbanding Red Army Girls', *Manchester Guardian*, 28 June 1945, p. 8; Robert Dale, *Demobilized Veterans in Late Stalinist Leningrad* (London: Bloomsbury Academic, 2015), p. 22; Robert Dale, 'Rats and Resentment: The Demobilization of the Red Army in Postwar Leningrad, 1945–50', *Journal of Contemporary History*, 45:1 (2010), 113–33; Evgenii D. Moniushko, *From Leningrad to Hungary: Notes of a Red Army Soldier, 1941–46* (London: Routledge, 2004), p. 138.

104. Martin Crotty and Mark Edele, 'Total War and Entitlement: Towards a Global History of Veteran Privilege', *Australian Journal of Politics and History*, 59:1 (2013), 15–32; Mark Edele, 'The Soviet Culture of Victory', *Journal of Contemporary History*, 54:4 (2019), 780–98.

105. 'Needs of Veterans Puzzle Clothiers', *NYT*, 17 July 1945, p. 17; Nancy McInerny, 'The Woman Vet Has Her Headaches, Too: A Job, a Place to Live, Other People, Clothes: All of These Demand Difficult Adjustment', *NYT Sunday Magazine*, 30 June 1946, p. 18, pp. 38–39.

106. Michael D. Gambone, *The Greatest Generation Comes Home: The Veteran in American Society* (College Station, TX: Texas A&M University Press, 2005); Suzanne Mettler, *Soldiers to Citizens: The GI Bill and the Making of the Greatest Generation* (New York: Oxford University Press, 2005); Robert Francis Saxe, *Settling Down: World War II Veterans' Challenge to the Postwar Consensus* (Basingstoke: Palgrave Macmillan, 2007); Robert F. Jefferson, '"Enabled Courage": Race, Disability, and Black World War II Veterans in Postwar America', *Historian*, 65:5 (2003), 1102–24.

107. On the emergence of the postwar welfare state, Peter Hennessy, *Never Again: Britain 1945–1951* (London: Penguin Books, 2006 [1992]); David Kynaston, *Austerity Britain, 1945–51* (London: Bloomsbury Publishing, 2007).

108. Miriam Phelan, 'A Full Monty', in Rosalind McKever and Claire Wilcox (eds.), *Fashioning Masculinities: The Art of Menswear* (London: V&A Publishing, 2022), pp. 186–91 (p. 191). On demobilization clothing's role in standardizing the suit as classless British menswear, see also Honeyman, *Well-Suited*, p. 2; Sprecher, 'Demob Suits'.

109. Biddle-Perry, *Dressing for Austerity*, p. 40.

110. Sir Cecil Weir, 16 August 1944, BT 64/954.

111. Extract from the minutes of the 31st Meeting of the Standing Committee on Demobilization, 31 August 1943, WO 32/9945.

112. 'Children to Go Short of Clothes: "Demob" Rush', *Daily Mail*, 5 October 1944, p. 3.

113. Mark Roodhouse, *Black Market Britain 1939–1955* (Oxford: Oxford University Press, 2013); Donald Thomas, *An Underground at War: Spivs, Deserters, Racketeers and Civilians in the Second World War* (London: John Murray, 2003).

114. Historians disagree over the extent of wartime black market activity, partly because definitions of what constituted black marketeering varied, but also because some illicit trade passed below the radar of officials attempting to suppress it, Ina Zweiniger-Bargielowska, *Austerity in Britain: Rationing, Controls and Consumption, 1939–1955* (Oxford: Oxford University Press, 2000); Roodhouse, *Black Market Britain*.

115. Ivor Brown, 'This Picking and Stealing', *The Observer*, 25 November 1945, p. 4.

4 Protestors

1. Official reports variously tally the number of West Indian RAF men on board from 1,200 to 1,400. Naval message from NOIC (Naval Officer in Charge) Trinidad to Commander-in-Chief, Jamaica, 21 May 1946, ADM 1/19941, TNA.

2. Naval message from Master *Bergensfjord* and Officer Commanding Troops to Garrison Commander NCA (North Caribbean Area), 22 May 1946, ADM 1/19941.

3. 'Report of Voyage, Glasgow to Jamaica', Leif Hansen, Master, SS *Bergensfjord*, CO 137/866/9, TNA.

4. Ivorall Davis, '3 Ship's Crew Shot by Jamaica RAF in Gun Riot at Sea', *Public Opinion*, 25 May 1946; 'RAF Men Landed under Rifles and Guns', *Daily Gleaner*, 26 May 1946, p. 1.

5. 'Report on Arrival of SS *Bergensfjord* in Jamaica', CO 137/866/10, TNA.

6. Davis, '3 Ship's Crew Shot'. See also 'No Riot But Free for All Fight', *Daily Gleaner*, 26 May 1946; 'Armed Soldiers Greet Returning Troopship', *Daily Express* (Jamaica), 23 May 1946.

7. 'Three Shot in Riot aboard Troopship', *Daily Mail*, 24 May 1946, p. 1. Some local papers also carried short reports, attributing the riot to the umbrage West Indian veterans had taken to 'insulting remarks' made about their 'English wives' by crew members, 'Fight on Troopship', *Nottingham Evening Post*, 24 May 1946, p. 1; 'Fight aboard Troopship', *Derby Daily Record*, 24 May 1946, p. 8; 'Jamaicans Fight with Crew in Troopship', *Gloucestershire Echo*, 24 May 1946, p. 1.

8. Information from the *Bergensfjord*'s passenger manifest, BT 27/1580, TNA.

9. A. B. Acheson, Colonial Office, to Air Vice Marshal Sir John Cordingley, 27 July 1946, AIR 20/9051, TNA; NOIC, Trinidad, 21 May 1946, ADM 1/19941; Sir J. Huggins to Secretary of State for the Colonies, 5 June 1946, CO 137/866/9; Hugh Foot to Seel, 11 June 1946, CO 137/866/9.

10. RAF veteran Hedley Jones devotes one paragraph in an account of his postwar career to his journey on the *Bergensfjord*, attributing trouble to 'insulting remarks' made by armed Norwegian 'security police', to which Jamaican airmen took umbrage; Hedley Jones, 'The Jones High Fidelity Audio Power Amplifier of 1947', *Caribbean Quarterly*, 56:4 (2010), 97–107 (p. 102). A slightly longer account is provided by Dudley Thompson, a Jamaican RAF officer called upon to quell the disturbance that, he was told, had arisen because white Trinidadians accused Black Jamaicans of behaving badly in England, 'causing many racial incidents there'. See Dudley J. Thompson, *From Kingston to Kenya: The Making of a Pan-Africanist Lawyer* (Dover, MA: The Majority Press, 1993), p. 33. Squadron Leader R. A. Webster, Senior Accountant Officer, RAF Jamaica, 'West Indian Airman [sic] – Allowance in lieu of Civilian Clothing', 4 June 1946, CO 137/866/10.

11. David Duncan, *Mutiny in the RAF* (London: Socialist History Society, 1999); Daniel Garcia, 'Class and Brass: Demobilization, Working Class Politics and American Foreign Policy between World War and Cold War', *Diplomatic History*, 34:4 (2010), 681–98; Angel Alcalde and Xosé M. Núnez Seixas, *War Veterans and the World after 1945: Cold War Politics, Decolonization, Memory* (London: Routledge, 2018); Martin Crotty, Neil J. Diamant and Mark Edele, *The Politics of Veteran Benefits in the Twentieth Century: A Comparative History* (Ithaca, NY: Cornell University Press, 2020). On Civil Rights, Thomas A. Guglielmo, 'A Martial Freedom Movement: Black G.I.s' Political Struggles during World War II', *Journal of American History*, 104:4 (2018), 879–903; Kimberley L. Phillips, *War! What Is It Good For?: Black Freedom Struggles and the U.S. Military from World War*

II to Iraq (Chapel Hill: University of North Carolina Press, 2012); Matthew F. Delmont, *Half American: The Heroic Story of African Americans Fighting World War II at Home and Abroad* (New York: Penguin, 2022). On African veterans and nationalist politics, David Killingray with Martin Plaut, *Fighting for Britain: African Soldiers in the Second World War* (Woodbridge: James Currey, 2010); Gregory Mann, *Native Sons: West African Veterans and France in the Twentieth Century* (Durham, NC: Duke University Press, 2006); Judith A. Byfield, Carolyn A. Brown, Timothy Parsons and Ahmad Alawad Sikainga (eds.), *Africa and World War II* (New York: Cambridge University Press, 2015).

12. Garcia, 'Class and Brass'; R. Alton Lee, 'The Army "Mutiny" of 1946', *Journal of American History*, 53:3 (1966), 555–71.

13. Susan L. Carruthers, *The Good Occupation: American Soldiers and the Hazards of Peace* (Cambridge, MA: Harvard University Press, 2016), pp. 191–94; Lee, 'The Army "Mutiny"', 558–59; Michael Timonin, '"We Had All Tried to Act Like Ladies, But We Weren't Getting Anywhere": The Bring Back Daddy Clubs and the Demobilization of 1945', in Mark J. Crowley and Sarah Trudgen Dawson (eds.), *Women's Experiences of the Second World War: Exile, Occupation and Everyday Life* (Woodbridge: Boydell & Brewer, 2021), pp. 162–65.

14. AP, 'Baby Clothes Used as Threat', *NYT*, 19 December 1945, p. 17.

15. 'Baby Shoes Plead for Return of G.I.s', *New York Herald Tribune*, 9 January 1946, p. 3A.

16. John C. Sparrow, *History of Personnel Demobilization in the United States Army* (Washington, DC: Office of the Chief of Military History, Department of the Army, 1951); Jack Stokes Ballard, *The Shock of Peace: Military and Economic Demobilization after World War II* (Washington, DC: University Press of America, 1983), pp. 73–116.

17. Carruthers, *Good Occupation*, pp. 200–17.

18. L. E. W., 'Conditions Overseas', letter to the editor, 22 November 1945, *Manchester Guardian*, 12 December 1945, p. 4.

19. 'Over 700 Casualties in Bombay Riots', *Times of India*, 23 February 1946, p. 1; Alan Allport, *Demobbed: Coming Home after the Second World War* (New Haven: Yale University Press, 2009), pp. 41–44; Duncan, *Mutiny in the RAF*.

20. AP, 'Senators Hear G.I. Describe Army Waste', *Los Angeles Times*, 14 January 1946, p. 1. Relatively little has been written on the subject of disposal of army surplus after the war, given the magnitude of the task: John B. Olverson, 'Legal Aspects of Surplus War Property Disposal', *Virginia Law Review*, 31:3 (1945), 550–612; Sam Lebovic, 'From War Junk to Educational Exchange: The World War II Origins of the Fulbright Program and the Foundations of American Cultural Globalism, 1945–50', *Diplomatic History*, 37:2 (2013), 280–312; Gwen Sinclair, 'Jeeps, Communists, and Quonset Huts: World War II Surplus Disposal in the Territory of Hawai'i', *Hawaiian Journal of History*, 50 (2016), 121–40; Alex Souchen, *War Junk: Munitions Disposal and Postwar Reconstruction in Canada* (Vancouver: University of British Columbia Press, 2020).

21. Robert Trumbull, 'Soldiers Report Waste in Manila: Protests Abroad and at Home on GI Discharge Delays', *NYT*, 14 January 1946, p. 9; AP, 'Senator, GI Clash on Army Surplus: Committee Member Appeals to Colonel to Curb Sergeant at Philippine Hearing', *NYT*, 15 January 1946, p. 5.

22. Record of a Meeting between the Secretary of War, the Honorable Robert P. Patterson, and a Committee Representing Soldiers Stationed in Manila, P.I., January 17, 1946, Emile Mazey Papers, Wayne State University, Detroit, MI, p. 26 (with thanks to Andrew Buchanan for sharing this material).

23. Differential rates of pay sometimes caused strikes and mutinies by colonial troops, Killingray and Plaut, *Fighting for Britain*, p. 127, p. 210. This racialized injustice has drawn more recent press attention, Jack Losh, 'African British Army Paid Less Than White Soldiers', *The Guardian*, 13 February 2019, www.theguardian.com/world/2019/feb/13/african-british-army-paid-less-than-white-soldiers.

24. On British officialdom's attitudes towards Black British colonial subjects, Gavin Schaffer, 'Fighting Racism: Black Soldiers and Workers in Britain during the Second World War', *Immigrants & Minorities*, 28:2–3 (2010), 246–65; Marika Sherwood, *Many Struggles: West Indian Workers and Service Personnel in Britain (1939–45)* (London: Karia Press, 1985). As early as 1942, British officials considered the postwar 'concentration' and repatriation of non-white troops, lest they become a 'social problem', DO 35/674/5, TNA. By 1945, plans were afoot to develop a land-resettlement scheme to 'rehabilitate' ex-servicemen in Jamaica, CO 137/866/6.

25. On recruitment in British African colonies, Killingray and Plaut, *Fighting for Britain*, pp. 35–81. On dissatisfaction with the material rewards of soldiering, ibid., pp. 191–92. Recruitment to the Indian Army touted the advantages of service in terms of 'free rations, clothes, and games'; Yasmin Khan, *The Raj at War: A People's History of India's Second World War* (London: Bodley Head, 2015), p. 23.

26. Tony Kushner, '"Without Intending Any of the Most Undesirable Features of a Colour Bar": Race Science, Europeanness and the British Armed Forces during the Twentieth Century', *Patterns of Prejudice*, 3:4 (2012), 339–74. On parallel experiences of Black men in the Navy, Frances Houghton, '"Alien Seamen" or "Imperial Family"?: Race, Belonging and British Sailors of Colour in the Royal Navy, 1939–47', *English Historical Review*, 137:588 (2022), 1429–61.

27. Quoted by Roger Lambo, 'Achtung! The Black Prince: West Africans in the Royal Air Force, 1939–46', *Immigrants & Minorities*, 12:3 (1993), 145–63 (pp. 146–49).

28. Other men and women arrived from the Caribbean to undertake different kinds of work. By October 1944, nearly 1,000 Caribbean and African civilian workers had come to Britain: 350 technicians from the West Indies recruited by the Ministry of Labour to work in Merseyside; 300 members of the British Honduras Forestry Unit in Edinburgh and Newcastle; and 350 West African industrial workers who came to the UK 'on their own initiative', Lambo, 'Achtung', p. 160; Robert N. Murray, *Lest We Forget: The Experiences of World War II Westindian Ex-Service Personnel* (Hertford: Hansib Publications, 1996), pp. 73–84.

29. Grant quoted by Stephen Bourne, *Under Fire: Black Britain in Wartime, 1939–45* (Cheltenham: The History Press, 2020), p. 143.

30. 'Note of a Conference Held at the Colonial Office on the 18th November 1944 to Consider the Question of the Disposal of Civilian Colonial War Workers in the United Kingdom', CO 876/77.

31. 'Provision for the Repatriation of Persons Who Normally Resided Abroad', DO 35/674/5; 'West Indian Technicians and Trainees', 10 September 1946, LAB 26/134, TNA.

32. 'Girl Told to Leave a Hospital: Visit to Coloured Airmen', *Daily Mail*, 28 February 1946, p. 1. On racist tensions around West Indian RAF personnel and white women, Wendy Webster, *Mixing It: Diversity in World War II Britain* (Oxford: Oxford University Press, 2018), pp. 197–99, pp. 207–209; Hazel Carby, 'Becoming Modern Racialized Subjects: Detours through Our Pasts to Produce Ourselves Anew', *Cultural Studies*, 23:4 (2009), 624–57 (pp. 644–49). On the tensions surrounding the courtship and marriage of her Jamaican RAF father to her white Welsh-born mother, Hazel V. Carby, *Imperial Intimacies: A Tale of Two Islands* (London: Verso, 2019).

33. See correspondence in AIR 20/9051. On volatile relations between West Indians and white American personnel, Graham Smith, *When Jim Crow Met John Bull: Black American Soldiers in World War II Britain* (London, I.B. Tauris, 1987), pp. 85–87; Peter Fryer, *Staying Power: The History of Black People in Britain* (London: Pluto Press, 2018), pp. 303–305; Neil A. Wynn, '"Race War": Black American GIs and West Indians in Britain during the Second World War', *Immigrants & Minorities*, 24:3 (2006), 324–46.

34. Stansgate to G. N. Bell, 13 December 1945, AIR 20/9051; 'Coloured Airmen "Besieged" in Camp', *Daily Mail*, 8 February 1946, p. 1; 'RAF "Clash" with Jamaicans at Surrey Aerodrome', *Manchester Guardian*, 9 February 1946, p. 5.

35. Air Marshal Grahame Donald to Under Secretary of State, Air Ministry, 3 October 1945, AIR 20/9051. On concentrating men at a 'selected station with no WAAF element', P. S. to A. M. P., 14 January 1946, AIR 20/9051.

36. Donald to Slessor, 30 November 1945, AIR 20/9051.

37. One of the earliest scholars of West Indian and West African migration to post-war Britain noted this imperial tendency to teach students in the colonies 'to value the standards of the imperial country and their connexion to it; to announce with pride *Civis Romanus sum*, or its twentieth-century equivalent', Michael Banton, 'Recent Migration from West Africa and the West Indies to the United Kingdom', *Population Studies*, 7:1 (1953), 2–13 (p. 2).

38. Stansgate to Bell, 13 December 1945.

39. G. N. Hall to Stansgate, 10 January 1946, AIR 20/9051.

40. Draft letter from Stansgate to Hall, 15 February 1946, AIR 20/9051.

41. Hall to Stansgate, 10 January 1946.

42. Minute by Slessor, 23 May 1946, AIR 20/9051.

43. 'Armed Soldiers Greet Returning Troopship', *Daily Express* (Kingston), 23 May 1946, p. 1.

44. Hansen, 'Report of Voyage'. During the war, some British servicemen mutinied over appalling conditions aboard troopships, Geoffrey Field, '"Civilians in Uniform"; Class and Politics in the British Armed Forces, 1939–1945', *International Labor and Working Class History*, 80 (2011), 121–47 (pp. 130–32).

45. 'Conditions of Troop Mess Decks', 25 May 1946, Leif Hansen, CO 137/866/10; 'Report on Events in the SS *Bergensfjord* during Its Voyage from Glasgow to Kingston', CO 137/866/9.

46. The spectre of intimacy between Black men and white women cast a long shadow over the West Indians' service in Britain and this episode in particular. Revealingly, some brief press stories on the *Bergensfjord* in British local newspapers attributed the trouble to 'insulting remarks' about the RAF men's 'English wives' made by crew members – a different manifestation of racialized sexual anxiety; see 'Fight aboard Troopship' and 'Fight on Troopship'. None of the TNA archival files contains any reference to the veterans having British wives, nor did Jamaican reporters advance this possible explanation for violence aboard the ship.

47. Brig. Julian Jefferson to Under Secretary of State for War, 'Riots on SS *Bergensfjord*', 28 May 1946, CO 137/866/10.

48. Hansen, 'Report of Voyage'.

49. Hansen, 'Report of Voyage'; 'Report by Officer Commanding Troops, SS *Bergensfjord*', May 24, 1946, CO 137/866/10.

50. 'Report by Officer Commanding Troops'; Staff Officer (Intelligence) Jamaica to CIC, '*Bergensfjord* Incident', 14 June 1946, ADM 1/19941.

51. On the discrepancy between servicemen's views of protest and the services' construction of 'mutiny' as a potentially capital offence, Field, '"Civilians in Uniform"',

p. 130; Keith Grint, *Mutiny and Leadership* (Oxford: Oxford University Press, 2021); 'Report by Officer Commanding Troops'.

52. Staff Officer (Intelligence), 14 June 1946.

53. On the 'howling' mob, 'Report by Officer Commanding Troops'. Jefferson complained that Hansen 'exaggerated', Jefferson, 28 May 1946. See also Staff Officer (Intelligence) to CIC, 'Narrative of HMT *Bergensfjord* Incident, 21–23 May 1946', ADM 1/19941.

54. Interview with Mrs Jackson, wife of Lt Jackson, RNVR (Royal Naval Volunteer Reserve); Evidence of Lt Cordery, RNVR, ADM 1/19941.

55. Gregory to NOIC, Trinidad, 20 May 1946, ADM 1/19941.

56. Cordingley to Acheson, 9 July 1946, AIR 20/9051.

57. Capt. F. W. Thatcher, CC Troops, HT *Bergensfjord*, to HQ, NCA, 'Additional Report', 25 May 1946, p. 3, CO 137/866/9.

58. R. A. Webster to Under Secretary of State, Air Ministry, 4 June 1946, CO 137/866/9; Telegram from Squadron Leader Webster, Port of Spain, 17 May 1946, CO 137/866/9.

59. Telegram from Webster, 17 May 1946, CO 137/866/9; Government Notices, 'Royal Air Force: Civilian Clothing Allowance on Discharge', *Daily Gleaner*, 25 May 1946, p. 18.

60. Black South Africans were shown films depicting this transformation; Louis Grundlingh, 'The Military, Race, and Resistance: The Conundrums of Recruiting Black South African Men during the Second World War', in Judith A. Byfield, Carolyn A. Brown, Timothy Parsons and Ahmad Alawad Sikainga (eds.), *Africa and World War II* (New York: Cambridge University Press, 2015), pp. 71–88 (p. 75). The photographic record of recruitment into Britain's Indian Army fixates on recruits' partially naked bodies, turned into smartly attired soldiers, 'Behind the Photographs: Indian Army Recruitment in the Second World War', Imperial War Museum, www.iwm.org.uk/research/research-projects/provisional-semantics/behind-the-photographs. On the protest over boots in Sierra Leone, Killingray and Plaut, *Fighting for Britain*, p. 129.

61. R. H. Kakembo, *An African Soldier Speaks* (London: Edinburgh House, 1946), p. 9. On the sexual allure of military uniform, Mary Nombulelo Ntabeni, 'Military Labour Mobilisation in Colonial Lesotho during World War II, 1940–1943', *Scientia Militaria: South African Journal of Military Studies*, 36:2 (2008), 36–59 (pp. 46–47). Women's attraction to men in uniform figures as a motif of Rosanna Amaka's novel set in wartime Nigeria, Rosanna Amaka, *Rose and the Burma Sky* (London: Doubleday, 2023).

62. Martin Francis, *The Flyer: British Culture and the Royal Air Force, 1939–1945* (Oxford: Oxford University Press, 2011), p. 1, p. 24.

63. Murray, *Lest We Forget*, p. 122.

64. Joyce Egginton, *They Seek a Living* (London: Hutchinson, 1957), p. 51.

65. R. Fane, 'The Return of the Soldier: East Africa', *Journal of the Royal African Society*, 43:171 (1944), 56–60 (pp. 56–57).

66. Kakembo, *An African Soldier Speaks*, pp. 27–28.

67. Timothy Parsons, 'The Consequences of Uniformity: The Struggle for the Boy Scout Uniform in Colonial Kenya', *Journal of Social History*, 40:2 (2006), 361–83 (p. 367); Hal Brands, 'Wartime Recruiting Practices, Martial Identity and Post-World War II Demobilization in Colonial Kenya', *Journal of African History*, 46:1 (2005), 103–25 (p. 123).

68. Tracey Connolly, 'Emigration from Ireland to Britain during the Second World War', in Brian Girvin and Geoffrey Roberts (eds.), *Ireland and the Second World War: Politics, Society and Remembrance* (Dublin: Four Courts, 2000), pp. 52–53.

On Irish poverty during the 1940s and the country's black market in Irish military apparel, Bryce Evans, *Ireland during the Second World War: Farewell to Plato's Cave* (Manchester: Manchester University Press, 2015), pp. 73–74.

69. Bernard Kelly, *Returning Home: Irish Ex-Servicemen after the Second World War* (Dublin: Merrion, 2012), p. 153.

70. Memorandum by the Secretary of State for Dominion Affairs, 'The Wearing of Uniform by Members of the United Kingdom Forces When Visiting Eire on Leave', 17 October 1939, CAB 67/1/38, TNA; W.M. 52 (3), 'Eire. Wearing of Uniform by Members of the United Kingdom Forces When on Leave', October 19, 1939, CAB 65/1/52, TNA.

71. Army Council Secretariat, Standing Committee on Demobilisation, Minutes of 32nd Meeting, 6 September 1943, BT 64/936.

72. Banton, 'Migration from British Colonies', p. 9. On the varied views of RAF veterans about staying in Britain or going back, Murray, *Lest We Forget*, pp. 126–30.

73. Murray, *Lest We Forget*, p. 129.

74. Air Ministry personnel, having expected only 10 per cent of West Indian airmen would apply for training courses offered by the Colonial Office, were surprised that 60 per cent did so, of whom 50 per cent were accepted; P.S. to A.M.P., 'West Indian Ground Personnel', 12 October 1946, AIR 20/9051.

75. C. L. R. James, 'The Case for West Indian Self-Government', in Anna Grimshaw (ed.), *The C. L. R. James Reader* (Oxford: Blackwell, 1992), p. 52. On the politics of clothing more generally in Jamaica, Steeve O. Buckridge, *The Language of Dress: Resistance and Accommodation in Jamaica, 1760–1890* (Kingston: University of West Indies Press, 2004).

76. Carby, *Imperial Intimacies*, pp. 47–48.

77. For illustrations of the Windsor and Butler garments, see Carolina A. Miranda, 'Zoot Suit: How the Bold Look Made History and Continues to Influence Fashion', *LA Times*, 13 June 2023, https://lat.ms/3YA7jDA.

78. Shane White and Graham White, *Stylin': African-American Expressive Culture, from Its Beginnings to the Zoot Suit* (Ithaca, NY: Cornell University Press, 1999), pp. 248–62; Harvey R. Neptune, *Caliban and the Yankees: Trinidad and the United States Occupation* (Chapel Hill: University of North Carolina Press, 2007), p. 106; Steve Chibnall, 'Whistle and Zoot: The Changing Meanings of a Suit of Clothes', *History Workshop*, 20:1 (1985), 56–81; Kathy Peiss, *Zoot Suit: The Enigmatic Career of an Extreme Style* (Philadelphia: University of Pennsylvania Press, 2011).

79. Patrick Leigh Fermor, *The Traveller's Tree: A Journey through the Caribbean Islands* (London: John Murray, 2005 [1950]), pp. 175–76. Neptune's *Caliban and the Yankees* (pp. 121–22) alerted me to Fermor's description.

80. Jacqueline Jenkinson, *Black 1919: Riots, Racism and Resistance in Imperial Britain* (Liverpool: Liverpool University Press, 2009), p. 164.

81. Noga Marmor, 'A Place in the Empire: Gibraltar Camp in Jamaica and the British Imperial Order, 1940–47', *Journal of Imperial and Commonwealth History*, 50:3 (2022), 571–600.

82. Philip Sherlock, *Norman Manley* (London: Macmillan, 1980), pp. 144–45; Huggins to Hall, 5 June 1946, CO 137/866/9.

83. 'Embittered at Welcome', *Daily Gleaner*, 25 May 1946. An earlier story noted the 'short, almost cryptic, official statement', which said nothing about the disorder's probable cause, which the *Gleaner* speculated sprang from 'intense disaffection between Jamaicans and the English officers and attendants on the ship', 'Two Officers, One Sailor Shot as RAF Men Battle Troopship's Crew', *Daily Gleaner*, 23 May 1946, p. 1.

84. 'Military Probe Begun, Arrests Are Reported', *Daily Express* (Jamaica), 25 May 1946, p. 1.

85. For instance, Mike Phillips and Trevor Phillips, *Windrush: The Irresistible Rise of Multi-racial Britain* (London: HarperCollins, 1998) and, for a critique of such teleological narratives, Tony Kushner, *The Battle of Britishness: Migrant Journeys, 1685 to the Present* (Manchester: Manchester University Press, 2014).

86. 'Our London Correspondence', *Manchester Guardian*, 18 June 1948, p. 4; 'Jamaican Emigrants Arrive: A Thames Greeting', *Manchester Guardian*, 22 June 1948, p. 5.

87. *Daily Mirror*, 23 June 1948, quoted by Royal Museums Greenwich, 'The Story of the Windrush', www.rmg.co.uk/stories/windrush-histories/story-of-windrush-ship.

88. Lynda Nead, '"Red Taffeta under Tweed": The Color of Post-war Clothes', *Fashion Theory*, 21:4 (2016), 365–89; Lynda Nead, *The Tiger in the Smoke: Art and Culture in Post-war Britain* (New Haven: Yale University Press, 2017), pp. 151–97; Stuart Hall, 'Reconstruction Work: Images of Post-war Black Settlement', in Charlotte Brunsdon (ed.), *Writings on Media: History of the Present* (Durham, NC: Duke University Press, 2021), pp. 78–94; Teleica Kirkland, 'Performative Elegance: The Windrush Generation, Fashion and the Politics of Respectability', in Royce Mahawatte and Jacki Wilson (eds.), *Dangerous Bodies: New Global Perspectives on Fashion and Transgression* (Cham: Palgrave Macmillan, 2023), pp. 147–66. On the significance of sartorial style to West Indians in Britain, Beryl Gilroy, *Black Teacher* (London: Faber & Faber, 2021 [1976]); Carol Tulloch, *The Birth of Cool: Style Narratives of the African Diaspora* (London: Bloomsbury, 2020 [2016]), pp. 171–98; Elli Michaela Young, '"It Was Jamaica Style, and They Didn't Have Anything Like That in England": An Oral History of Self-Fashioning', in Sarah A. Lichtman and Jilly Traganou (eds.), *Design, Displacement, Migration: Spatial and Material Histories* (New York: Routledge, 2023), pp. 153–63.

89. BBC Caribbean Service, *Going to Britain?* (c. 1959), p. 11, British Library, www.bl.uk/collection-items/bbc-pamphlet-going-to-britain. The section on clothing was written by E. N. Burke, Adviser on Community Development for the Commissioner for the West Indies, British Guiana and British Honduras, Clair Wills, *Lovers and Strangers: An Immigrant History of Post-war Britain* (London: Allen Lane, 2017), pp. 18–19.

90. The number of passengers on the *Windrush* has often been misstated, but the National Archive passenger manifest tallies 1,027, of whom more than 800 gave their most recent address as somewhere in the Caribbean, https://blog.national archives.gov.uk/the-empire-windrush-passenger-list. On stowaways wearing RAF uniforms, 'Jamaicans Gaoled Here', *Essex Chronicle*, 25 June 1948, p. 1. Tellingly, a majority of the 'Windrush Profiles' featured on the Windrush Foundation website are biographies of veterans, https://windrushfoundation.com.

91. Royal Air Force Museum, '"Pilots of the Caribbean": Volunteers of African Heritage in the Royal Air Force', www.rafmuseum.org.uk/research/online-exhibitions/pilots-of-the-caribbean; 'Answering the Call', www.rafmuseum.org .uk/research/online-exhibitions/pilots-of-the-caribbean/answering-the-call. See also Kushner, 'Without Intending', pp. 344–49.

92. Donald to Slessor, 30 November 1945. Slessor quoted by Lambo, 'Achtung!', n. 44, p. 163.

93. RAF veteran Sam King's memoir briefly covers his postwar experiences in Britain. Turned down for a course in plumbing and assigned to a Coventry camp to learn carpentry, King departed Britain on the *Almanzora* in November 1947, returning on the *Windrush* six months later, Sam King, *Climbing Up the Rough Side of the Mountain* (Leicestershire: Upfront Publishing, 2004), pp. 65–73, pp. 89–95.

94. Lydia Lindsey, 'Halting the Tide: Responses to West Indian Immigration to Britain, 1946–1952', *Journal of Caribbean History*, 26:1 (1992), 62–96 (p. 63).

95. Lori Watt, *When Empire Comes Home: Repatriation and Reintegration in Postwar Japan* (Cambridge, MA: Harvard University Press, 2009); Tessa Morris-Suzuki, *Borderline Japan: Foreigners and Frontier Controls in the Postwar Era* (Cambridge:

Cambridge University Press, 2010); Matthew R. Augustine, 'Dividing Islanders: The Repatriation of "Ryūkyūans" from Occupied Japan', in Christine de Matos and Mark E. Caprio (eds.), *Japan as the Occupier and Occupied* (Basingstoke: Palgrave Macmillan, 2015).

96. Lindsey, 'Halting the Tide'. On 'Anglo-Saxon stock', Kathleen Paul, *Whitewashing Britain: Race and Citizenship in the Postwar Era* (Ithaca, NY: Cornell University Press, 2018).

97. Bernard Kelly, '"Masters in Their Own House": Britain and the 1946 Ex-Service Free Passage Scheme', *Journal of Imperial and Commonwealth History*, 44:1 (2016), 121–39. Churchill quoted by Kathleen Paul, '"British Subjects" and "British Stock": Labour's Postwar Imperialism', *Journal of British Studies*, 34:2 (1995), 233–76 (p. 267). On the logic of strengthening Britain's white 'racial bonds' with the Empire/Commonwealth, Paul, *Whitewashing Britain*.

98. M. A. Bevan quoted by Clive Harris, 'Post-war Migration and the Industrial Reserve Army', in Winston James and Clive Harris (eds.), *Inside Babylon: The Caribbean Diaspora in Britain* (London: Verso, 1993), pp. 9–54 (p. 21).

99. Lindsey, 'Halting the Tide', p. 67.

100. On Jamaican veterans being prompted to migrate to the United States as temporary farmworkers, T. E. Sealey (for Harold Moody), The League of Coloured Peoples, London, to Secretary of State for the Colonies, 30 May 1946, CO 137/866/6.

5 Germans

1. UP, 'Monty Says German Gals All Out for Teasing', *Beachhead News*, 22 June 1945; 'Leave Your Helmet On', *Time*, 2 July 1945, p. 25. For a critique of this trope, Susanne zur Nieden, 'Erotic Fraternization: The Legend of German Women's Quick Surrender', in Karen Hagemann and Stefanie Schüler-Springorum (eds.), *Home/Front: The Military, War and Gender in Twentieth Century Germany* (Oxford: Berg, 2002), pp. 297–310. On the fraternization ban, Susan L. Carruthers, *The Good Occupation: American Soldiers and the Hazards of Peace* (Cambridge, MA: Harvard University Press, 2016), pp. 111–31; Petra Goedde, *GIs and Germans: Culture, Gender, and Foreign Relations, 1945–1949* (New Haven: Yale University Press, 2003), pp. 71–72.

2. 'Why Germans Are Shunned: The Price of Guilt: F.-M. Montgomery on Troops' Attitude', *Daily Mail*, 11 June 1945, p. 1.

3. Our Military Correspondent, 'The Allies in Germany: Non-fraternisation', *Manchester Guardian*, 7 June 1945, p. 5.

4. 'Fratting', *Daily Mail*, 4 June 1945, p. 2; Daniel Lerner, 1st Lt, Editor, German Civilian Intelligence, 'Notes on a Trip through Occupied Germany', 18 April 1945, to Chief of Intel, PWD/SHAEF (Psychological Warfare Division, Supreme Headquarters Allied Expeditionary Force), Papers of Richard Crossman MP, MSS.154/3/PW/1/67-71, MRC. See also Cpl Debs Myers, 'Germany's Steep Road', *Yank*, 17 August 1945.

5. Percy Knauth, 'Fraternization: The Word Takes On a Brand-New Meaning in Germany', *Life*, 2 July 1945, p. 26; 'German Girls: U.S. Army Boycott Fails to Stop GIs from Fraternizing with Them', *Life*, 23 July 1945, p. 35; Carruthers, *Good Occupation*, pp. 113–15; Ann Elizabeth Pfau, *Miss Yourlovin: GIs, Gender, and Domesticity during World War II* (New York: Columbia University Press, 2008), ch. 3, www.gutenberg-e.org/pfau/chapter3.html. *British Pathé* attempted to reassure newsreel viewers that the 'average Tommy' was not tempted by German women's charms, even after the lifting of the 'frat ban', 'Fraternising – Frat Ban On – Frat Ban Off', 2 August 1945, www.britishpathe.com/asset/67544. Released on the same day

and incorporating some identical footage, Paramount's newsreel was (more realistically) entitled 'Fraternisation Wins the Day', www.britishpathe.com/asset/218053.

6. Lerner, 'Notes on a Trip'.

7. The US re-education film *Die Todesmühlen* (*Death Mills*) mocked Germans' apparent jauntiness on setting off, as though on a picnic. On this and other re-educative films' use of images of the camps, Susan L. Carruthers, 'Compulsory Viewing: Concentration Camp Film and German Re-education', *Millennium: Journal of International Studies*, 30:3 (2001), 733–59; Cora Sol Goldstein, *Capturing the German Eye: American Visual Propaganda in Occupied Germany* (Chicago: University of Chicago Press, 2009). On the genre of 'confrontation' photographs, Dagmar Barnouw, *Germany 1945: Views of War and Violence* (Bloomington: Indiana University Press, 1996), ch. 1.

8. Lee Miller, 'GERMANY … out of the German Prison', *Vogue*, 1 May 1945, p. 143.

9. Poirier reported in *Union Jack* (Eastern Italy edition), 2 May 1945.

10. Patrick Gordon Walker, *The Lid Lifts* (London: Victor Gollancz, 1945), p. 78.

11. Irene Guenther, *Nazi Chic?: Fashioning Women in the Third Reich* (Oxford: Berg, 2004),

12. Nathaniel Parker Weston, 'Photographs of Jewish Clothing in Nazi Germany and the Shoah: Visual Records of Economic Assaults, Exploitation, and Plunder', *Textile*, 21:3 (2022), 701–19. For footage of newly liberated camps recording Allied soldiers handling piles of children's clothes, as well as mountains of shoes and suitcases, see *British Pathé*, www.britishpathe.com/asset/206738.

13. Gordon Walker, *The Lid Lifts*, p. 68. After a visit to Dachau, one SHAEF official explained how the system operated: 'Clothes were turned over to the local agency of Deutsche Textil- und Bekleidungswerke, GmbH, a private corporation whose stockholders were SS officials, which reclaimed and repaired garments (with the use of unpaid prison labor), and then resold them to the camp clothing depot for the use of other prisoners', William Harlan Hale, SHAEF PWD, 'Dachau Concentration Camp, Report on a Two-Day Visit, 1–2 May [1945]', Crossman papers, MSS.154/3/PW/1/1-3.

14. *Die Todesmühlen* (*Death Mills*), dir. Hanuš Burger, US Signal Corps (1945), https://catalog.archives.gov/id/36082, RG 111, Records of the Office of the Chief Signal Officer, National Archives and Record Administration (NARA), United States.

15. Rhoda Dawson, *The Stagnant Pool: Work among Displaced Persons in Germany 1945–1947*, in private papers of Mrs R. N. Bickerdike, documents.3277, IWM; 'Mixing with Germans: Fraternization Ban Relaxed', *The Times*, 16 July 1945, p. 3.

16. Mindful of UNRRA's limited remit – to aid only Allied populations and those liberated from Axis control – SHAEF set out a typology of people in need of assistance and who had responsibility for their care, SHAEF, Administrative Memorandum Number 39 (Revised 16 April 1945), 'Displaced Persons and Refugees in Germany', reproduced as Appendix B in Malcolm Proudfoot, *European Refugees, 1939–52: A Study in Forced Population Movement* (London: Faber & Faber, 1957), pp. 445–69.

17. Paul Betts, *Ruin and Renewal: Civilising Europe after the Second World War* (London: Profile Books, 2020), p. 113.

18. Guenther, *Nazi Chic?*, pp. 219–20. During the war, British publications periodically alerted readers to the impoverishment of German wardrobes due to dire shortages of wool and cotton. See, for example, an illustrated story, sardonically entitled 'What the Well-Dressed German Wears', *Picture Post*, 18 December 1943, pp. 18–19.

19. Guenther, *Nazi Chic?*, p. 221.

20. Our Special Correspondent, 'Seizure of Clothing in Germany: Soldiers to Surrender Civilian Wear', *The Times*, 15 January 1945, p. 4.

21. Our Military Correspondent, SHAEF, 'Uniforms for the Volkssturm: Nazi Salvage Drive', *Manchester Guardian*, 10 March 1945, p. 6.

22. Martin Caiger-Smith, *The Face of the Enemy: British Photographers in Germany 1944–1952* (Berlin: Dirk Nishen Publishing, 1988), pp. 34–35.

23. Anonymous, *A Woman in Berlin. Eight Weeks in the Conquered City: A Diary*, trans. Philip Boehm (New York: Metropolitan Books, 2005), p. 9, p. 3.

24. Ibid., p. 158.

25. Ibid., p. 161. On Nazi flags transformed into red kerchiefs, Ruth Andreas-Friedrich, *Battleground Berlin: Diaries 1945–1948*, trans. Anna Boerresen (New York: Paragon House Publishers, 1990), entry for 1 May 1945, p. 11.

26. Elizabeth Heineman, '"The Hour of the Woman: Memories of Germany's "Crisis Years" and West German National Identity', *American Historical Review*, 101:2 (1996), 354–95; Irene Guenther, 'Out of the Ruins: Fashioning Berlin, 1945–1952', *Fashion Theory*, 21:4 (2017), 391–421; Mila Ganeva, 'Fashion amidst the Ruins: Revisiting the Early Rubble Films *And the Heavens Above* (1947) and *The Murderers Are among Us* (1946)', *German Studies Review*, 37:1 (2014), 61–85; Mila Ganeva, *Film and Fashion amidst the Ruins of Berlin: From Nazism to the Cold War* (Rochester, NY: Camden Press, 2018).

27. On looting by Germans, Lerner, 'Notes on a Trip'.

28. Ruth Andreas-Friedrich diary entry for 30 August 1943, quoted by Guenther, *Nazi Chic?*, p. 231

29. HQ BAOR, Memo, 29 August 1945, FO 1032/582.

30. Gordon Walker, *The Lid Lifts*, p. 78.

31. 'Protocol of the Proceedings of the Berlin Conference', 1 August 1945, *Foreign Relations of the United States: Diplomatic Papers, The Conference of Berlin (The Potsdam Conference)*, 1945, Vol. II, https://history.state.gov/historicaldocuments/frus1945Berlinv02/d1383. The figure of ten million displaced is offered by Peter Gatrell, *The Unsettling of Europe: The Great Migration, 1945 to the Present* (London: Penguin Books, 2020), p. 24, drawing on Jacques Vernant, *The Refugee in the Postwar World* (London: Allen & Unwin, 1953), pp. 95–96. Other scholars give significantly higher estimates. Francis Graham-Dixon proposes that, by the mid 1950s, around 15 million ethnic Germans had been expelled, with 12.5 million settling to the west of their former homes, Francis Graham-Dixon, *The Allied Occupation of Germany: The Refugee Crisis, Denazification and the Path to Reconstruction* (London: Bloomsbury Academic, 2020 [2013]), p. 5.

32. R. M. Douglas, *Orderly and Humane: The Expulsion of the Germans after the Second World War* (New Haven: Yale University Press, 2012); David W. Gerlach, *The Economy of Ethnic Cleansing: The Transformation of the German–Czech Borderlands after World War II* (Cambridge: Cambridge University Press, 2017).

33. Stig Dagerman, *German Autumn*, trans. Robin Fulton Macpherson (Minneapolis: University of Minnesota Press, 2011 [1947]), p. 5.

34. Matthew Frank, *Expelling the Germans: British Opinion and Post-1945 Population Transfer in Context* (Oxford: Oxford University Press, 2008).

35. Ruth Dudley Edwards, *Victor Gollancz: A Biography* (London: Victor Gollancz, 1987), p. 401.

36. Victor Gollancz, *What Buchenwald Really Means* (London: Victor Gollancz, 1945); Dudley Edwards, *Victor Gollancz*, p. 402.

37. Matthew Frank, 'The New Morality – Victor Gollancz, "Save Europe Now" and the German Refugee Crisis, 1945–46', *Twentieth Century British History*, 17:2 (2006), 230–56; Dudley Edwards, *Victor Gollancz*, pp. 401–64.

38. Dudley Edwards, *Victor Gollancz*, p. 406.

39. On 'civilization' – and its redemption – as a dominant discursive motif, Betts, *Ruin and Renewal*.

40. Peggy Duff, *Save Europe Now, 1945–1948: Three Years Work* (London: self-published pamphlet, 1948), MSS.157/SEN/1/7, MRC.

41. Victor Gollancz, German visit notebooks, October–November 1946, Papers of Sir Victor Gollancz, MSS.157/8/GE2-7, MRC.

42. Victor Gollancz, 'Germany Revisited II – Clothes and Houses', *Manchester Guardian*, 12 September 1947, p. 4.

43. Diary of Brigadier John Barraclough, Military Governor, North Rhine Province, Control Commission for Germany (British Element), 1945–1950, MSS.21/3533, MRC; Dagerman, *German Autumn*, pp. 19–20.

44. Victor Gollancz to Ruth Gollancz, 5 October 1946, quoted by Dudley Edwards, *Victor Gollancz*, p. 435.

45. Victor Gollancz to Ruth Gollancz, 9 October 1946, quoted by Dudley Edwards, *Victor Gollancz*, p. 437.

46. Frank Trentmann and Just Fleming (eds.), *Food and Conflict in Europe in the Age of the Two World Wars* (Basingstoke: Palgrave Macmillan, 2006); Alice Weinreb, '"For the Hungry Have No Past nor Do They Belong to a Political Party": Debates over German Hunger after World War II', *Central European History*, 45:1 (2012), 50–78; Alice Weinreb, *Modern Hungers: Food and Power in Twentieth-Century Germany* (New York: Oxford University Press, 2017); Atina Grossmann, 'Grams, Calories, and Food: Languages of Victimization, Entitlement, and Human Rights in Occupied Germany, 1945–1949', *Central European History*, 44:1 (2011), 118–48.

47. J. R. L. A., 'Life in Berlin', *Manchester Guardian*, 13 July 1946, p. 4. On Germans taking their shoes to be repaired one at a time to reduce the risk of a pair being stolen, 'Shoe Shortage in Germany: Lack of Materials', *Manchester Guardian*, 8 July 1947, p. 8.

48. Gollancz journal entry for 18 November 1946, German visit notebooks, MSS.157/8/GE.

49. Victor Gollancz, *In Darkest Germany* (London: Victor Gollancz, 1947). The photographs are filed as MSS.157/12/GE/1/1-132 and MSS.157/12/GE/2, Papers of Sir Victor Gollancz, MRC. For a discussion of these images, Jessica Medhurst, 'Representing and Repetition: Victor Gollancz's *In Darkest Germany* and the Metonymy of Shoes', *German Life and Letters*, 69:4 (2016), 468–84.

50. J. D. Salinger, 'For Esmé – with Love and Squalor', *The New Yorker*, 31 March 1950, p. 28.

51. H. G. Wells, 'This Misery of Boots' (1905), https://gutenberg.net.au/ebooks13/1303681h.html.

52. Gollancz, *In Darkest Germany*, p. 53.

53. Medhurst, 'Representing and Repetition'; on photography as an unreliable witness, Susan Sontag, *Regarding the Pain of Others* (New York: Picador, 2003).

54. Stephen Spender, *European Witness* (London: Hamish Hamilton, 1946), p. 143.

55. Victor Gollancz, 'A Visit to Dusseldorf', letter to the editor, *The Times*, 5 November 1946, p. 5.

56. Dagerman, *German Autumn*, p. 7.

57. Gollancz, *In Darkest Germany*, p. 54. Gollancz continued to elaborate this theme in public talks and letters on his return home. See Our London Staff, 'A Picture of German Youth', *Manchester Guardian*, 16 December 1946, p. 6; 'Shoe Shortage in Germany', *Manchester Guardian*, 8 July 1947, p. 8; Gollancz, 'Germany Revisited II'.

58. On US military government officers' responses to barefoot Italians, Carruthers, *Good Occupation*, pp. 42–43.

59. Betts, *Ruin and Renewal*, pp. 116–17; Heide Fehrenbach and Davide Rodogno (eds.), *Humanitarian Photography: A History* (Cambridge: Cambridge University Press, 2015); Sharon Sliwinski, *Human Rights in Camera* (Chicago: University of

Chicago Press, 2011); Johannes Paulmann (ed.), *Humanitarianism and Media: 1900 to the Present* (Oxford: Berghahn Books, 2018).

60. Jeffrey Feldman, 'The Holocaust Shoe. Untying Memory: Shoes as Holocaust Memorial Experience', in Edna Nahshon (ed.), *Jews and Shoes* (New York: Berg, 2008), pp. 119–30 (p. 123); Moshe Pearlman, *The Capture and Trial of Adolf Eichmann* (London: Weidenfeld & Nicolson, 1963), p. 304.

61. AP, 'Tattered Sandals Accuse Eichmann', *Los Angeles Times*, 4 May 1961, p. 8.

62. 'An Auschwitz Memorial: Relics of the German Death Camp', *Manchester Guardian*, 21 July 1947, p. 6. By 1961, the museum had devoted a bin 'as big as a moderate room' to adults' shoes and another to children's shoes, Robert S. Bird, 'Visitor Overwhelmed by Nazi Horror Camp', *Los Angeles Times*, 9 April 1961, p. 17.

63. Victor Gollancz, 'The British Zone', letter to the editor, *The Times*, 15 November 1946, p. 5.

64. Dudley Edwards, *Victor Gollancz*, pp. 469–70.

65. 'Clothing for Relief Abroad', *Manchester Guardian*, 12 December 1946, p. 4. On the ongoing operations of British Jewish relief workers in Germany, Tom Sampson, 'Anglo-Jewish Humanitarianism and the Jewish Relief Unit', *German History*, 40:2 (2022), 220–38.

66. 'British Rule in Germany', unsigned review of *In Darkest Germany*, *Times Literary Supplement*, 1 February 1947, p. 60.

67. Major Guy Lloyd, '"In Darkest Germany": The Tory Who Stands with Mr Gollancz', *Daily Mail*, 28 January 1947, p. 4.

68. The records of Save Europe Now are held by the Modern Records Centre, MSS.157/3/SEN/1/1-181. 'Parcels to Germany: New Channels for Gifts to Individuals', *Manchester Guardian*, 10 January 1947, p. 3.

69. Duff, *Save Europe Now*, p. 5. Petitions sent to the government by concerned individuals and various organizations, urging a more lenient policy to alleviate German suffering, can be found in FO 371/58164, TNA; on the first shipment of SEN parcels, FO 938/269, TNA.

70. 'Children's Footwear Shortage: Mothers' Vain Search', *The Times*, 5 October 1945, p. 2.

71. 'Scandal of the Shoes', *Daily Mail*, 30 November 1945, p. 1. On Britain's footwear situation, Christopher Sladen, *The Conscription of Fashion: Utility Cloth, Clothing and Footwear 1941–1952* (Aldershot: Scolar Press, 1995), ch. 4. On substitutes for leather in the construction of footwear in Britain and elsewhere, Jonathan Walford, *Forties Fashion: From Siren Suits to the New Look* (London: Thames & Hudson, 2011), pp. 114–25.

72. 'Old Tyres Make New Soles', *Daily Mail*, 16 January 1945, p. 3.

73. 'Cripps Says Children Are Better Shod', *Daily Mail*, 28 November 1945, p. 3; 'The Big Shoe Scandal: Cripps Admits "Great Worry"', *Daily Mail*, 4 December 1945, p. 1; 'The Great Shoe Scandal: Bristol and the Makers Tell Cripps', *Daily Mail*, 8 December 1945, p. 1; 'Guilty, Sir Stafford!', *Daily Mail*, 4 December 1945, p. 2.

74. 'No Shoes – No School', *Daily Mail*, 6 December 1945, p. 1; 'Children Cannot Go to School', *Daily Mail*, 14 December 1945, p. 3; 'The Shoe Scandal', *Daily Mail*, 1 December 1945, p. 1.

75. British HQ (Germany), 'Old Clothes for Germans: Appeal to Leave-Men', *Manchester Guardian*, 31 December 1946, p. 8; 'Food and Clothes for Germany: Army Chaplain's Appeal', *The Times*, 23 August 1947, p. 7.

76. 'Aid for German Children', *Manchester Guardian*, 18 February 1947, p. 6; 'Gifts for Germans', *Manchester Guardian*, 14 December 1946, p. 5.

77. Walter Meyer to Pickford, 8 July 1947, private papers of Reverend C. Pickford, documents.27257, IWM.

78. Allbrich Drewitz to Pickford, 14 August 1947.

79. Ada Oestreich to Pickford, 4 October 1947; Oestreich to Pickford, 4 December 1947.

80. Records of the Association for Moral and Social Hygiene, 3AMS/B/07/27, box 065, The Women's Library, LSE. On sexual barter in Germany and elsewhere, Carruthers, *The Good Occupation*, ch. 4; *A Foreign Affair*, dir. Billy Wilder (1948).

81. Lilli Lilienfeld to Miss Hollitscher, 12 May 1953, 5BFW/12/19, box 152, Records of the British Federation of University Women, The Women's Library, LSE.

82. Duff, *Save Europe Now*, p. 10.

83. Zeev W. Mankowitz, *Life between Memory and Hope: The Survivors of the Holocaust in Occupied Germany* (Cambridge: Cambridge University Press, 2007); Anna Holian, *Between National Socialism and Soviet Communism: Displaced Persons in Postwar Germany* (Ann Arbor: University of Michigan Press, 2011); Ben Shephard, *The Long Road Home: The Aftermath of the Second World War* (New York: Alfred A. Knopf, 2011); G. Daniel Cohen, *In War's Wake: Europe's Displaced Persons in the Post-war Order* (New York: Oxford University Press, 2012).

84. SHAEF, 'Displaced Persons and Refugees in Germany'.

85. MG Iserlohn, 'Clothing Levy – Issue to Cover Essential Needs for Months Jan.–Mar. [19]46', 4 December 1945, FO 1013/1490, TNA; HQ MG Dusseldorf, 'Release of Clothing for Refugees', 29 December 1945, FO 1013/1490.

86. K Det. MG Siegburg to 808 Det. Cologne, 'Supplies', 7 December 1945, FO 1013/1490.

87. Provision of Clothing and Blankets for Mil Gov Purposes, 'Statement for Issue to German Authorities (To be Translated into GERMAN before Issue of This Instruction). Notice. Textiles – Levy of Manufactured Articles', 13 September 1945, FO 1032/582.

88. Notes on Talk with Miss Hewitt of FRS, Oberhausen, 2 November 1946, MSS.151/3/GE/1/14/1-37, MRC.

89. Report on the Clothing Situation in 8 Corps Area, FO 1032/582.

90. Gollancz, *In Darkest Germany*, p. 55.

91. Econ Div Econ 1, CCG (British Element), Minden, 'Availability of Clothing and Bedding in the British National Zone of GERMANY', p. 3, 3 January 1946, FO 1032/582. 'Report on the Production of Sanitary Towels in the British Zone', 28 November 1946, FO 1027/84, TNA.

92. HQ MG North Rhine Region, 'Sitrep on Clothing Levy at Jan. 26 1946', FO 1013/1490.

93. Mil Gov Command, 'Clothing Levy', 24 January 1946, FO 1032/582'; 'Availability of Clothing and Bedding in the British National Zone of GERMANY', p. 3.

94. The POW population figure is from Christopher Knowles, *Winning the Peace: The British in Occupied Germany, 1945–1948* (London: Bloomsbury Academic, 2017), p. 13.

95. 'Allied Control Council Making Progress: Unity among Four Powers Maintained', *Manchester Guardian*, 31 August 1945, p. 8; Reuters, 'Ban on Uniforms', *South China Morning Post*, 5 April 1946, p. 2.

96. Lt Col. S. A. Rillington, HQ MG Land North Rhine-Westphalia, 'Uniform Worn by DPs', 27 August 1946, FO 1052/386, TNA. On WO fears of kit falling into the 'wrong hands', Telegram from CONFOLK, 'Battledress Garments', 23 November 1946, FO 1032/582.

97. 'Immerse Yourself in the History of DYLON since 1946', www.dylon.co.uk/all-about-dylon/our-history.html.

98. Julie Summers, *Fashion on the Ration: Style in the Second World War* (London: Profile Books, 2016), p. 137.

99. See correspondence in FO 1032/582.

100. Rillington, 'Uniform Worn by DPs'; MG Westfalen Region, 'Dyed Battledress', 13 July 1946; Capt. J. W. Lucas, HQ MG Schleswig Holstein Region, 'Battledress for PWX', 25 July 1946, FO 1052/386.

101. Zonal Executive Offices, CCG Bad Salzuflen, 'Uniforms Worn by PWX', 19 September 1946, FO 1052/386.

102. HG MG Hansestadt Hamburg, 'DP Maintenance – Clothing', 10 October 1946; 'Tents into Shoes', *News Guardian*, 19 April 1946; 'Footwear for Germans', *Manchester Guardian*, 7 November 1946, p. 3. On MG's plans to resume local footwear manufacture, Peter Wilson, Controller of Leather Industries, 'Footwear Production in the British Zone', 25 June 1946, FO 1032/582.

103. Knowles, *Winning the Peace*, pp. 49–51.

104. See discussions in FO 943/531; FO 1032/1021, TNA.

105. On offloading Board of Trade surplus into the British Zone, FO 943/578, TNA; 'Germans to Buy "Old Look" Clothes', *Manchester Guardian*, 3 April 1948, p. 5. Britain also imported US military surplus into the British Zone; FO 1014/711, TNA.

106. Adelheid Rasche and Christina Thomson, *Christian Dior in Germany 1947–1957* (Stuttgart: Arnoldsche, 2007).

107. Guenther, 'Out of the Ruins', p. 414; Ganeva, *Film and Fashion*, pp. 121–44.

108. 'Berlin Style Show Has a Paris Aroma', *NYT*, 12 March 1946, p. 22. Ganeva notes that the first 'peacetime fashion tea' in Berlin was hosted in a private apartment as early as September 1945; Ganeva, *Film and Fashion*, p. 3.

109. Donald Bloxham, *Genocide on Trial: War Crimes Trials and the Formation of Holocaust History and Memory* (Oxford: Oxford University Press, 2001); Kim C. Priemel and Alexa Stiller (eds.), *Reassessing the Nuremberg Military Tribunals: Transitional Justice, Trial Narratives and Historiography* (Oxford: Berghahn Books, 2014); John J. Michalczyk, *Filming the End of the Holocaust: Allied Documentaries, Nuremberg and the Liberation of the Concentration Camps* (London: Bloomsbury, 2016); Christian Delage, *Caught on Camera: Film in the Courtroom from the Nuremberg Trials to the Trials of the Khmer Rouge*, ed. and trans. Ralph Schoolcraft and Mary Byrd Kelly (Philadelphia: University of Pennsylvania Press, 2014).

110. Rebecca West, 'Greenhouse with Cyclamens I (1946)', in *A Train of Powder: Six Reports on the Problem of Guilt and Punishment in Our Time* (Chicago: Ivan R. Dee, 2000 [1955]), p. 3, p. 10, pp. 27–28.

111. Reuters, 'GI's See Fashion Show: Red Cross Girls in Nuremberg Parade to Cheers', *NYT*, 30 March 1946, p. 11.

112. On the importance the Allies attached to the trial's dramaturgy, including conspicuous deployment of Black American Military Police as guards for war criminals, such as Otto Ohlendorf, see Werner Sollors, *The Temptation of Despair: Tales of the 1940s* (Cambridge, MA: The Belknap Press of Harvard University Press, 2014), p. 187.

113. James Derriman, *Pageantry of the Law* (London: Eyre & Spottiswoode, 1955); Gary Watt, 'Law Suits: Clothing as the Image of Law', in Leif Dahlberg (ed.), *Visualizing Law and Authority: Essays on Legal Aesthetics* (Berlin: De Gruyter, 2012), pp. 23–47.

114. Our Special Correspondent, 'War Trials to Start To-day', *Manchester Guardian*, 20 November 1945, p. 5.

115. Our Special Correspondent, 'Surviving Nazi Leaders in the Dock', *Manchester Guardian*, 21 November 1945, p. 5.

116. Janet Flanner, 'Letters from Nuremberg', letter dated 15 March 1946, in Janet Flanner, *Janet Flanner's World: Uncollected Writings 1932–1975*, ed. Irving Drutman (New York: Harvest/Harcourt Brace Jovanovich, 1981), p. 114.

117. West, 'Greenhouse with Cyclamens I', p. 5.

118. 'Surviving Nazi Leaders in the Dock'.

119. Nuremberg cartoon, 'How Much Better We Would Have Done It', https://bit.ly/3Aom9mI.

120. David Low, 'A Cartoonist's Impressions of Nuremberg Trial: Accused "Very Ordinary Looking"', *Manchester Guardian*, 12 December 1945, p. 5.

121. Raymond Daniell, 'German General Cites Army Crimes', *NYT*, 8 January 1946, p. 10.

122. Flanner, 'Letters from Nuremberg', letter dated 22 March 1946, p 120.

123. West, 'Greenhouse with Cyclamens I', p. 16.

124. Flanner, 'Letters from Nuremberg', letter dated 22 March 1946, p. 119.

125. West, 'Greenhouse with Cyclamens I', p. 16.

126. On the verdicts, UK National Archives, https://blog.nationalarchives.gov.uk/death-hanging-nuremberg-trials.

127. 'Sinews of Peace', text of an address prepared for delivery by The Right Honorable Winston Churchill, MP, at Westminster College, Fulton Missouri, 5 March 1946, FO 371/51624, TNA.

128. Flanner, 'Letters from Nuremberg', letter dated 22 March 1946, p. 109; Patrick Wright, *Iron Curtain: From Stage to Cold War* (New York: Oxford University Press, 2009).

129. Flanner, 'Letters from Nuremberg', letter dated 22 March 1946, p. 119.

130. Francine Hirsch, 'The Soviets at Nuremberg: International Law, Propaganda, and the Making of the Postwar Order', *American Historical Review*, 113:3 (2008), 701–30 (p. 723).

131. *Ninotchka*, dir. Ernst Lubitsch (1939); *Silk Stockings*, dir. Rouben Mamoulian (1957). For a critique of the reigning western paradigm which held that a socialist society could not be a consumerist society, see David Crowley and Susan E. Reid, 'Introduction: Pleasures in Socialism?', in David Crowley and Susan E. Reid (eds.), *Pleasures in Socialism: Leisure and Luxury in the Eastern Bloc* (Evanston, IL: Northwestern University Press, 2010), pp. 12–61. On fashion in the eastern bloc, Djurdja Bartlett, *FashionEast: The Spectre That Haunted Socialism* (Cambridge, MA: MIT Press, 2010).

132. George Orwell, *Nineteen Eighty-Four: A Novel* (London: Secker & Warburg, 1949).

133. David Riesman, 'The Nylon War', *Common Cause*, 4:7 (1951), 279–85; Walter L. Hixson, *Parting the Curtain: Propaganda, Culture, and the Cold War, 1945–1961* (New York: St. Martin's Press, 1998); Susan E. Reid, 'Who Will Beat Whom? Soviet Popular Reception of the American National Exhibition in Moscow, 1959', *Kritika: Explorations in Russian and Eurasian History*, 9:4 (2008), 855–904.

134. Dr Hensel to HQ MG Düsseldorf, 'Providing Consumers' Goods', 5 November 1946, MSS.157/3/SEN/3/30-46.

135. Michael J. Hogan, *The Marshall Plan: America, Britain, and the Reconstruction of Western Europe, 1947–1952* (New York: Cambridge University Press, 1987); Benn Steil, *The Marshall Plan: Dawn of the Cold War* (New York: Oxford University Press, 2021).

136. Paul Bretherton, 'There's Chic Again in Berlin's Ruins', *Daily Mail*, 6 November 1947, p. 2.

137. C. C. S. Newton, 'The Sterling Crisis of 1947 and the British Response to the Marshall Plan', *Economic History Review*, 37:3 (1984), 391–408; Henry Pelling, *Britain and the Marshall Plan* (New York: St. Martin's Press, 1988).

6 Workers

1. 'It's a Long Queue (20,000 strong) and It Has a Turning', *Daily Mail*, 30 September 1946, p. 3. Mass Observation (MO), 'A Report on BRITAIN CAN MAKE IT Exhibition', 26 November 1946, File Report 2241, p. 9.
2. The precise total was 1,432,369, Diane Bilbey, 'Statistics, Statistics', in Diane Bilbey (ed.), *Britain Can Make It: The 1946 Exhibition of Modern Design* (London: Paul Hoberton Publishing/V&A Publishing, 2019), pp. 52–59 (p. 52).
3. 'Britain Can Make It', *The Times*, 14 September 1946, p. 8.
4. The 1940 Ministry of Information/GPO documentary, directed by Humphrey Jennings and narrated by US journalist Quentin Reynolds, initially produced as *London Can Take It*, was screened elsewhere in a shortened version as *Britain Can Take It!*, www.iwm.org.uk/collections/item/object/1060022010, IWM. See Anthony Aldgate and Jeffrey Richards, *Britain Can Take It: British Cinema in the Second World War* (London: I.B. Tauris, 2007).
5. 'Britain Can Make It', *Picture Post*, 19 October 1946, p. 23.
6. Edwina Ehrman, 'Women's Fashions', in Diane Bilbey (ed.), *Britain Can Make It: The 1946 Exhibition of Modern Design* (London: Paul Hoberton Publishing/V&A Publishing, 2019), pp. 122–29 (p. 122); Alison Settle, 'From a Woman's Viewpoint', *The Observer*, 6 October 1946, p. 7.
7. A Woman Correspondent, 'Women's Side of the "Britain Can Make It" Exhibition', *Manchester Guardian*, 24 September 1946, p. 8.
8. 'Britain Can Make It', *Picture Post*, 19 October 1946, p. 23; MO, 'A Report on BRITAIN CAN MAKE IT', pp. 13–15.
9. D. H. J. of Chelsea to the editor, *The Times*, 6 October 1946, p. 4.
10. Graham Stanford, 'A Girl in Britain's "Glamour Shop"', *Daily Mail*, 24 September 1946, p. 3.
11. MO, 'A Report on BRITAIN CAN MAKE IT', p. 15.
12. 'Available: now 1, soon 2, later 3', *The Ambassador: The British Export Journal for Fashions and Textiles*, 10 (October 1946).
13. MO, 'A Report on BRITAIN CAN MAKE IT', p. 11.
14. By 1946, Utility goods were widely praised for stylish designs and high-quality fabrics that belied the dispiriting name, Alison Settle, 'From a Woman's Viewpoint', *The Observer*, 8 December 1946, p. 7.
15. George Schuster, 'Are We TOO FEW For the Job?', *Picture Post*, 19 April 1947, pp. 21–23.
16. Kathleen Paul, *Whitewashing Britain: Race and Citizenship in the Postwar Era* (Ithaca, NY: Cornell University Press, 2018), p. 4.
17. Paul, *Whitewashing Britain*, p. 25; Wendy Webster, *Imagining Home: Gender, 'Race' and National Identity, 1945–64* (Abingdon: Routledge, 1998).
18. John Singleton, 'Planning for Cotton', *Economic History Review*, 43:1 (1990), 62–78 (p. 62). Cripps quoted in 'Nation's Effort: Sir S. Cripps Suggests Tasks for Women', *Manchester Guardian*, 10 July 1948, p. 3.
19. Singleton, 'Planning for Cotton', pp. 69–70.
20. Priestley predicted in 1933 that 'not all the reorganization and rationalisation and trade agreements and tariffs and embargoes in the world will bring back to Lancashire what Lancashire has lost', J. B. Priestley, *English Journey* (Manchester: Harper North, 2023 [1934]), pp. 334–35. A social survey conducted in Lancashire in 1948 found that 56 per cent of respondents lacked confidence in the future of the cotton industry, William Crofts, *Coercion or Persuasion?: Propaganda in Britain after 1945* (London: Routledge, 1989), p. 134.

21. Singleton, 'Planning for Cotton', p. 71.

22. John Singleton, *Lancashire on the Scrapheap* (Oxford: Oxford University Press, 1991), p. 48.

23. Crofts, *Coercion or Persuasion?*, p. 153.

24. Ibid., pp. 110–67; Susan L. Carruthers, '"Manning the Factories": Propaganda and Policy on the Employment of Women, 1939–1947', *History*, 75:244 (1990), 232–56 (pp. 248–52). For recruitment materials, see INF 13/127; INF 13/136; INF 13/137, TNA.

25. The poster can be found in LAB 8/1485, TNA, www.nationalarchives.gov.uk/education/resources/attlees-britain/womens-employment, reproduced in Clair Wills, *Lovers and Strangers: An Immigrant History of Post-war Britain* (London: Penguin, 2018), p. 31; Crofts, *Coercion or Persuasion?*, p. 116; Carruthers, 'Manning the Factories'.

26. Alison Settle, 'Wives Must Go Back to the Cotton Mills', *The Observer*, 22 April 1945, p. 5.

27. F. Zweig, *Women's Life and Labour* (London: Victor Gollancz, 1952), p. 133.

28. Priestley, *English Journey*, p. 167; Political and Economic Planning, 'Employment of Women', *Planning*, 15:285 (1948), MO File Report 3017, p. 44.

29. Crofts, *Coercion or Persuasion?*, p. 113.

30. Zweig, *Women's Life and Labour*, p. 35. For a different appreciation of mill girls' public image in the interwar years, Rebecca Conway, 'Making the Mill Girl Modern?: Beauty, Industry and the Popular Newspaper in 1930s' England', *Twentieth Century British History*, 24:4 (2013), 518–41.

31. 'Clothing and the War Effort', *The Garment Worker*, 14:1 (1945), p. 15, MSS.192/TGW/3/1/12, MRC; Margaret Stewart and Leslie Hunter, *The Needle Is Threaded: The History of an Industry* (London: Heinemann/Newman Neame, 1964), p. 209.

32. Bernard Sullivan, 'Clothing Industry Creates Absenteeism', *The Garment Worker*, 14:6 (1945), 116–17 (p. 116).

33. 'Mr Dalton Speaks on Clothing Trade Problems', *The Garment Worker*, 14:4 (April 1945), 64.

34. *Cotton Come Back*, dir. Donald Alexander, Data Film Productions (1946), https://player.bfi.org.uk/free/film/watch-cotton-come-back-1946-online. For the shooting script, NF 34/291, TNA.

35. 'Rt. Hon. Sir Stafford Cripps, Chancellor of the Exchequer, speaking at a press conference in London, 29 Jan. 1948', LAB 12/513.

36. Crofts, *Coercion or Persuasion?*, pp. 126–27.

37. F. Zweig, *Productivity and Trade Unions* (Oxford: Basil Blackwell, 1951), p. 157.

38. Gail Braybon and Penny Summerfield, *Out of the Cage: Women's Experiences in Two World Wars* (London: Pandora, 1987), p. 267.

39. Crofts, *Coercion or Persuasion?*, p. 92.

40. MO, *The Journey Home* (London: John Murray, 1944), p. 56. On changing attitudes towards courtship and marriage, Selina Todd, *Young Women, Work, and Family in England 1918–50* (Oxford: Oxford University Press, 2005), pp. 217–23; Claire Langhamer, *The English in Love: The Intimate Story of an Emotional Revolution* (Oxford: Oxford University Press, 2013).

41. On the 'double burden', Braybon and Summerfield, *Out of the Cage*; Penny Summerfield, *Women Workers in the Second World War: Production and Patriarchy in Conflict* (London: Routledge, 1989); Laura King, 'How Men Valued Women's Work: In and Outside the Home in Post-war Britain', *Contemporary European History*, 28:4 (2019), 454–68. On housework routines in Lancashire, Zweig, *Women's Life and Labour*, p. 20.

42. Patricia Malcolmson and Robert Malcolmson (eds.), *Nella Last's Peace: The Post-war Diaries of Housewife*, 49 (London: Profile Books, 2008), diary entry for 10 January 1946, p. 71, and *passim*.

43. Zweig, *Women's Life and Labour*, p. 154.

44. Singleton, *Lancashire on the Scrapheap*, p. 57.

45. 'Employment of Women', p. 38, p. 42.

46. Paul, *Whitewashing Britain*, p. 48.

47. Diana Kay and Robert Miles, *Refugees or Migrant Workers?: European Volunteer Workers in Britain, 1946–1951* (London: Routledge, 1992), pp. 34–35.

48. On 'Balt Cygnet', J. A. Tannahill, *European Volunteer Workers in Britain* (Manchester: Manchester University Press, 1958), pp. 19–22; Linda McDowell, 'Narratives of Family, Community and Waged Work: Latvian European Volunteer Worker Women in Post-war Britain', *Women's History Review*, 31:1 (2004), 23–55; Linda McDowell, *Hard Labour: The Forgotten Voices of Latvian Migrant Volunteer Workers* (London: University College London Press, 2005), pp. 100–104; Emily Gilbert, *Rebuilding Post-war Britain: Latvian, Lithuanian and Estonian Refugees in Britain, 1946–51* (Barnsley: Pen & Sword Books, 2017), pp. 75–78, 80–88.

49. Tannahill, *European Volunteer Workers*, p. 38.

50. Ibid., pp. 22–23.

51. On the consequential nature of these distinctions, Diana Kay and Robert Miles, 'Refugees or Migrant Workers? The Case of the European Volunteer Workers in Britain (1946–1951)', *Journal of Refugee Studies*, 1:3–4 (1988), 214–36. On UNRRA's interactions with MoL personnel, 'Operation Westward Ho Progress Reports', FO 1052/370, TNA.

52. UN archives, S-1450-0000-0195-00001, Employment of DPs in Great Britain. On deportation, Tannahill, *European Volunteer Workers*, p. 40; Kay and Miles, *Refugees or Migrant Workers?*, pp. 47–49. In 1948, the MoL continued to be concerned about its ability to deport unsatisfactory EVWs after an eighteen-month probationary period, LAB 213/1005.

53. Margaret McNeill, *By the Rivers of Babylon: A Story of Relief Work among the Displaced Persons of Europe* (London: Bannisdale Press, 1950), pp. 200–201; Ben Shephard, *The Long Road Home: The Aftermath of the Second World War* (New York: Alfred A. Knopf, 2011), pp. 328–48.

54. MoL recruitment poster/booklet reproduced by Elizabeth Stadulis, 'The Resettlement of Displaced Persons in the United Kingdom', *Population Studies*, 5:3 (1952), 207–37 (p. 214).

55. Kathryn Hulme, *The Wild Place* (Lexington, MA: Plunket Lake Press, 2021 [1953]), pp. 163–68; Francesca M. Wilson, *Aftermath: France, Germany, Austria, Yugoslavia, 1945 and 1946* (London: Penguin Books, 1947), pp. 134–53.

56. Margaret McNeill, 'The Will to Work', *Manchester Guardian*, 10 October 1947, p. 3.

57. Kay and Miles, 'Refugees or Migrant Workers?', p. 220. After 1 July 1947, recruitment was restricted to single individuals unaccompanied by dependants and with no promise of future family reunification, Tannahill, *European Volunteer Workers*, p. 46.

58. McDowell, *Hard Labour*, p. 100. More rigorous medical examinations that included pregnancy tests were only carried out on 10 per cent of recruits, Kay and Miles, *Refugees or Migrant Workers?*, p. 58. On the separation of couples, Tannahill, *European Volunteer Workers*, p. 45.

59. McNeill, *By the Rivers of Babylon*, p. 202.

60. *British Pathé*, 'People in Camera', 24 April 1947, www.britishpathe.com/asset/54159.

61. Tannahill, *European Volunteer Workers*, p. 27.

62. McNeill, *By the Rivers of Babylon*, pp. 202–203.

63. Hulme, *The Wild Place*, p. 164.

64. 'Fate of the Refugees', *The Times*, 14 September 1948, p. 5. Janet Flanner quoted this editorial in her letter for the *New Yorker*, Janet Flanner, 'Aschaffenburg, October 20, 1948', in Janet Flanner, *Janet Flanner's World: Uncollected Writings 1932–1975*, ed. Irving Drutman (New York: Harvest Books/Harcourt, Brace Jovanovich, 1981), p. 153. See also Wills, *Lovers and Strangers*, p. 40.

65. Susan L. Carruthers, *Cold War Captives: Imprisonment, Escape, Brainwashing* (Berkeley: University of California Press, 2009), ch. 4. On Soviet propaganda, Tannahill, *European Volunteer Workers*, p. 41. On the MoL's recognition that EVWs were not 'slave workers', Kay and Miles, 'Refugees or Migrant Workers?', p. 227.

66. Paul, *Whitewashing Britain*; Webster, *Imagining Home*, pp. 25–44; Ian R. G. Spencer, 'The Open Door, Labour Needs and British Immigration Policy, 1945–55', *Immigrants and Minorities*, 15:1 (1996), 22–41.

67. Wilson, *Aftermath*, p. 152. On the inadequacy of screening in Austrian DP camps, which let former SS men into the EVW scheme, IRO Regional Employment Officer to Brigadier Marshall, 'Report on My Visit to Seedorf Camp', 14 July 1947, FO 1052/371, TNA. The MoL adamantly asserted that 'collaborators, quislings and war criminals are never given D.P. status and are not, therefore, found amongst these European Volunteer Workers', Ministry of Labour and National Service, *Workers from Abroad* (1948), p. 4, MSS.271/T/30/3, MRC.

68. 'An Essential Import', *The Times*, 10 February 1947, p. 5. On the determinants of empathy, Laura J. Hilton, 'Who Was "Worthy"?: How Empathy Drove Policy Decisions about the Uprooted in Occupied Germany, 1945–1948', *Holocaust and Genocide Studies*, 32:1 (2018), 8–28.

69. Graham Stanford, 'DP – A Name That Haunts Europe', *Daily Mail*, 8 June 1948, p. 2. The stigmatizing connotations of the label were present as soon as the coinage came into common use in the spring of 1945. A reporter noted in August 1945 that DP 'is not a title of honour in the British zone of occupation in Germany today … [Rather] it represents a headache for which no aspirin can be found', 'The "Displaced Person": How He Appears to the British Soldier', *Manchester Guardian*, 31 August 1945, p. 4.

70. MoL, 'Publicity for the Education of Popular Opinion on Foreign Workers', Minutes of the First Meeting, held 1 October 1947 to 'consider ways and means of educating public opinion to acceptance of Foreign Workers (EVWs and Poles) into life of the nation', LAB 12/513, TNA.

71. 'Finding Homes for D.P.s' Families', *Manchester Guardian*, 9 December. 1947, p. 6. Likewise, the *Hull Daily Mail* billed 'European voluntary workers' as the 'new, and kinder name, for displaced person', 'Hopes for New Life at Hull Camp', *Hull Daily Mail*, 31 May 1947, p. 3.

72. Minute by George Isaacs, 2 September 1947, Minutes of meeting on 1 October 1947, LAB 12/513.

73. Tony Kushner argues persuasively that antisemitic riots in Britain should not be attributed solely to feeling stoked up by events in Palestine, Tony Kushner, 'Anti-Semitism and Austerity: The August 1947 Riots in Britain', in Panikos Panayi (ed.), *Racial Violence in Britain in the Nineteenth and Twentieth Centuries* (Leicester: Leicester University Press, 1996), pp. 150–70.

74. MO, 'Report on Attitudes to Palestine and the Jews', File Report 2515 (1947), p. 54; Sydney Jacobson, 'The Emigrants to England', *Picture Post*, 31 May 1947, p. 9. British officials perhaps reassured themselves that their exclusionary policy wasn't driven by prejudice but reflected Jewish DPs' own disinclination to undertake

work in textiles or mines. Ruth Fellner (Jewish Refugees Committee, London) to Hanne Bernhard-Rath, Jewish Relief Unit (Germany), 28 March 1947; Operation Westward Ho!: Scheme and Executive Instruction. Emigration and Visits to the UK, 1946–8: Work Permits, Wiener Library.

75. The notion that Britain was an ethnically homogeneous 'island nation' was shared by white Britons across the political spectrum. When the *Windrush* docked at Tilbury on 22 June 1948, eleven Labour MPs wrote to Attlee in alarm, protesting that an 'influx of coloured people domiciled here is likely to impair the harmony, strength and cohesion of our public and social life', quoted by Webster, *Imagining Home*, p. 25.

76. MoL, *Workers from Abroad*, pp. 5–6. Distribution of 20,000 copies of this pamphlet was discussed by the Committee for the Education of Public Opinion on Foreign Workers, 12 May 1948, LAB 12/513.

77. Wilson, *Aftermath*, p. 153.

78. Wills, *Lovers and Strangers*, pp. 23–24; Kathy Burrell, *Moving Lives: Narratives of Nation and Migration among Europeans in Post-war Britain* (Aldershot: Aldgate, 2006); Clive Harris, 'Post-war Migration and the Industrial Reserve Army', in Winston James and Clive Harris (eds.), *Inside Babylon: The Caribbean Diaspora in Britain* (London: Verso, 1993), pp. 9–54; David Olusoga, *Black and British: A Forgotten History* (London: Macmillan, 2016), pp. 490–94.

79. See, for instance, a letter from Learie Constantine to the editor, 'Coloured Colonial People', *Manchester Guardian*, 27 March 1951, p. 4; Wills, *Lovers and Strangers*, p. 10.

80. Paul, *Whitewashing Britain*, p. 65. See also Linda McDowell, 'Constructions of Whiteness: Latvian Women Workers in Post-war Britain', *Journal of Baltic Studies* 38:1 (2007), 85–107 (p. 110); Simon Phillips, Michele Abendstern and C. Hallett, '"They More or Less Blended in with Society": Changing Attitudes to European Migrant Workers in Post-war Lancashire', *Immigrants & Minorities*, 25:1 (2007), 49–72. On whiteness and Britishness more generally, Paul Gilroy, *There Ain't No Black in the Union Jack* (London: Routledge Classics, 2002 [1987]).

81. Paul, *Whitewashing Britain*, p. 122; Laura Price, 'Immigrants and Apprentices: Solutions to the Post-war Labour Shortage in the West Yorkshire Wool Industry, 1945–1980', *Textile History*, 45:1 (2014), 32–48 (p. 35).

82. 'Dressmaker' was one of the most frequently stated professions of the approximately 300 female paying passengers on the *Windrush*, Lisa Berry-Waite, 'Women on Board the Empire Windrush', UK National Archives, 14 June 2023, https://blog.nationalarchives.gov.uk/women-on-board-the-empire-windrush.

83. Cripps, press conference, 29 January 1948, LAB 12/513. 'Friendliness' was also emphasized in the MoL booklet for trade unionists, which encouraged them to 'revive the spirit of hospitality and friendship which flourished in former times', *Workers from Abroad*, p. 7. Strikingly, the MoL took a different tack in addressing EVWs, warning them of British 'reserve and our apparent slowness to make friends'; Ministry of Labour and National Service, *To Help You Settle in Britain: A Handbook for European Volunteer Workers* (1948), MSS.126/TG/RES/X/718/1.

84. White Paper, 'Economic Survey for 1947' (Cmd. 7046), para. 125, LAB 12/513. This language was replicated verbatim in an MoL circular distributed to trade unions in April 1947; ML Cir. 59/1, 24 April 1947, MSS.292/103.2/1, MRC.

85. Stadulis, 'The Resettlement of Displaced Persons', p. 226.

86. 'Cotton's Big Part in Export Drive: Sir Stafford Cripps Calls on Industry for Prompt Effort', *Manchester Guardian*, 17 September 1947, p. 6.

87. Clair Wills, *The Best Are Leaving: Emigration and Post-war Irish Culture* (Cambridge: Cambridge University Press, 2014), pp. 154–55; Clair Wills, 'Digs and Lodging Houses: Literature, Ruins, and Survival in Postwar Britain', *Éire-Ireland*, 52:3–4 (2017), 57–74. On clothing poverty in 1940s Ireland, Bryce Evans, *Ireland during the Second World War: Farewell to Plato's Cave* (Manchester: Manchester University Press, 2015), pp. 73–74. On the circulation to Ireland of clothes sent from relatives who had emigrated to the United States, Enda Delaney, *The Irish in Post-war Britain* (Oxford: Oxford University Press, 2007), ch. 1.

88. Kay and Miles, *Refugees or Migrant Workers?*, pp. 76–79.

89. On the recruitment of German women, MoL National Joint Advisory Board, 'Employment of Foreign Workers', NJC 23, MSS.292/103.2/1, MRC. Between 1945 and 1951, some 60,000 Germans settled in the UK, Johannes-Dieter Steinert and Inge Weber-Newth, 'The Legacy of War: Germans in Post-war Britain', in Johannes-Dieter Steinert and Inge Weber-Newth (eds.), *European Immigrants in Britain 1933–1950* (Munich: K. G. Saur, 2003), pp. 201–218. On the parallel scheme to import Italian women workers, LAB 26/244, TNA.

90. On these arrangements, LAB 26/202, TNA.

91. On MoL liaison with the WVS regarding EVWs' clothing, LAB 26/202, LAB 26/235, TNA.

92. MoL Regional Office, Manchester to Miss Boyes, Welfare Department, 17 June 1947, LAB 26/202.

93. On Irish migrants in Wales, BT 64/801, TNA.

94. Patricia Malcolmson and Robert Malcolmson (eds.), *The Diaries of Nella Last: Writing in War & Peace* (London: Profile Books, 2012), p. 292, p. 228. WVS staff also recorded 'resentment at Poles buying up second hand clothing', Miss Johnson, WVS HQ, 22 October 1947, LAB 12/513.

95. On women fleeing, or being deported, from their homes with no shoes and only the clothes they wore, Wendy Webster, 'Defining Boundaries: European Volunteer Worker Women in Britain and Narratives of Community', *Women's History Review*, 9:2 (2000), 257–76 (pp. 65–66).

96. MoL, 'Report of the Conference of Assistant Regional Controllers Responsible for Welfare Work and of Regional Welfare Officers Held at Headquarters on Thursday, 29 January, 1948', 'Issue of Clothing', p. 5, LAB 12/513.

97. Brig. A. C. Todd, PW & DP Division to Secretariat 'G', 60 HQ CCG Lubbecke, 8 July 1947, FO 1052/371; Col. C. R. Chambers, PW & DP Division, to Lt-Col. Billington, PWDP Branch, Land North Rhine/Westphalia, 1 July 1947, FO 1052/371.

98. E. Philip, Welfare Officer, Townhead Mill Co., Rochdale, 26 September 1947, LAB 26/202. On sharing a single coat, Webster, 'Defining Boundaries', p. 269. On women arriving in Wigan without underclothes, Copy of a Minute Recording the Proceedings of the Regional Board for Industry, 16/48, 'Clothing for EVW's', LAB 26/202.

99. Tannahill, *European Volunteer Workers*, p. 66.

100. 'Provision of Clothing for European Volunteer Workers', LAB 26/230.

101. Note of a meeting on 14 July 1947, between Miss Boyes and Mr Morley (MoL) and Mr Robinson and Mr Chambers (Ministry of Supply), 'concerning complaints which had been received regarding the inferior quality and shrunken nature of many of the garments which had been purchased from Ministry of Supply for issue to E.V.Ws.', LAB 26/202. On women refusing to accept inferior apparel, Minutes of the Conference on Welfare of Poles and EVWs at WVS HQ, 20 April 1948, 'Holding Hostels for EVWs', LAB 26/235.

102. Webster, 'Defining Boundaries', pp. 267–68. The WVS volunteers also registered male EVWs who were 'very self-conscious about their inferior clothes', so much

so that they refused to enter Britons' homes 'until they had been able to buy others', Minutes of the Conference on Welfare of Poles and EVWs at WVS HQ, 20 April 1948, 'Holding Hostels for EVWs', LAB 26/235.

103. Lady Reading to Mr W. L. Buxton (MoL), 7 August 1947, LAB 26/235; Minutes of the Conference on Welfare of Poles and EVWs held at WVS HQ, 4 March 1949, LAB 26/235.

104. Minutes of the Conference on Welfare of Poles and EVWs at WVS HQ, 4 March 1949, LAB 26/235.

105. Extensive correspondence on EVWs' clothing, cash allowances, coupons and eligibility for the Industrial Ten can be found in LAB 26/202.

106. Minutes of the Conference on Welfare of Poles and EVWs at WVS HQ, 20 April 1948, 'Holding Hostels for EVWs', LAB 26/235.

107. Extract from letter of 21 May 1947 from Miss Candy, MoL Southern Regional Office, LAB 26/202.

108. The need to guard clothing against 'pilfering' is a recurrent theme of correspondence with MoL regional officers in LAB 26/202; Minutes of the Conference on Welfare of Poles and EVWs at WVS HQ, 4 March 1949, 'Welfare of Poles and EVWs in Employment', LAB 26/235.

109. Jordanna Bailkin, *Unsettled: Refugee Camps and the Making of Multicultural Britain* (Oxford: Oxford University Press, 2020).

110. MoL, Publicity for the Education of Popular Opinion on Foreign Workers, 1 October 1947, LAB 12/513.

111. On malicious rumours swirling around the hostels, Sydney Jacobson, 'Our Immigrants Are Settling In', *Picture Post*, 17 January 1948, p. 16. The best way of countering such misconceptions was discussed by the MoL, Minutes of meeting held on 5 December 1947 to discuss publicity for education of opinion on foreign workers, LAB12/513.

112. Stadulis, 'The Resettlement of Displaced Persons', p. 227.

113. James Hinton, 'Self-Help and Socialism in the Squatters' Movement of 1946', *History Workshop*, 25:1 (1988), 100–126; Tannahill, *European Volunteer Workers*, p. 46.

114. Mrs Bernice Dungworth to TUC, 1 February 1948, MSS.292/103.2/1, MRC.

115. Secretary, Organisation Department, TUC, to Mrs B. E. Dungworth, 3 February 1948, MSS.292/103.2/1.

116. Dungworth to TUC, 5 February 1948, MSS.292/103.2/1.

117. Kay and Miles, *Refugees or Migrant Workers?*, pp. 116–17; 'Let Them Be Displaced', *Daily Mirror*, 20 July 1948, p. 2.

118. 'European Labour in Cotton Mills: Need to Avoid Large Concentrations', *Financial Times*, 9 September 1947, p. 4.

119. 'Lancashire's Big Labour Problem: Growing Opposition to Foreign Workers', *Financial Times*, 3 July 1948, p. 5.

120. Maud Bülbring, 'Post-war Refugees in Great Britain', *Population Studies*, 8:2 (1954), 99–112 (p. 104).

121. Bülbring, 'Post-war Refugees', p. 108.

122. 'Settling D.P. Volunteers in Cotton Mills', *The Observer*, 21 December 1947, p. 5.

123. Bülbring, 'Post-war Refugees', p. 107.

124. '"Foreign Workers Trying to Take Upper Hand": Landlords Form Protection Society', *Manchester Guardian*, 18 February 1949, p. 3.

125. On shock at the lack of indoor sanitation, Tannahill, *European Volunteer Workers*, p. 67; EVW quoted by Webster, 'Defining Boundaries', p. 271.

126. Latvian EVW quoted by McDowell, *Hard Labour*, p. 117.

127. Ibid., p. 116.

128. Precise figures broke down as follows: boot and shoe manufacture (63); clothing: wholesale (57); cotton (7,564); flax spinning and weaving (13); hosiery (265); jute (175); rayon (1,000); wool (3,173), Tannahill, *European Volunteer Workers*, p. 133.

129. Webster, 'Defining Boundaries', p. 263; Minutes of a meeting held on 5 December 1947 at the Ministry of Labour to discuss publicity for the education of popular opinion on foreign workers, LAB 12/513; Stadulis, 'The Resettlement of Displaced Persons', p. 216; 'Displaced Persons in the Mills: A Successful Scheme', *The Times*, 13 January 1948, p. 2.

130. 'Women Weavers Won't Teach Foreigners', *Daily Mirror*, 3 April 1948, p. 5.

131. On the Ministry of Health's attitude, MH 55/1578; Kay and Miles, 'Refugees or Migrant Workers?', p. 223. On additional clothing needs of pregnant women, LAB 26/202.

132. Barbara Reeve to NCUMC, 23 February 1948, Folder 5/OPF/2/5/a, Box 059, Records of the National Council for One Parent Families, The Women's Library, LSE (hereafter NCUMC).

133. Manchester Diocesan Council for Moral Welfare Work, 25 May 1949, NCUMC.

134. Gloucester Diocesan Association for Moral Welfare Work, 11 May 1949, NCUMC.

135. Blackburn Diocesan Council to NCUMC, 11 March 1948, NCUMC.

136. Extract from Gainsborough Narrative Report, March 1950, 'Welfare of German Girls', LAB 26/235.

137. Manchester Diocesan Council for Moral Welfare Work, 25 May 1949, NCUMC.

138. Miss Mary Elliott (Superintendent & Outdoor Worker), Hamilton House, Rugby to Miss Raynes, 14 May 1949, NCUMC.

139. Anne Ashley, General Secretary, Edinburgh Council of Social Service, 13 June 1949, NCUMC.

140. *HC Deb*, 'European Volunteer Workers', *Hansard*, 10 May 1949, Vol. 464, cc 1637. Tannahill gives a significantly higher figure of 538 EVWs deported by 31 December 1950; *European Volunteer Workers*, p. 129.

141. Statistics from Tannahill, *European Volunteer Workers*, p. 133.

142. Extract from monthly narrative report from Malvern, Worcestershire, for May 1947, 'Displaced Persons' Camp', LAB 26/235. Concerts featuring EVW performers were held in other locations; 'Ukrainian Folk Song Recital', *Hull Daily Mail*, 12 April 1948, p. 3.

143. McNeill, *By the Rivers of Babylon*, p. 209.

144. Jacobson, 'Our Immigrants Are Settling In', p. 16.

145. *Code Name: Westward Ho!*, dir. Mary Beales, COI, 1949, https://player.bfi.org.uk/free/film/watch-code-name-westward-ho-1949-online?play-film.

146. Stadulis, 'The Resettlement of Displaced Persons', p. 228.

147. 'E.V.Ws. in Atherton', sent by WVS to Miss Boyes (MoL), 7 October 1949, LAB 26/235.

148. Paul, *Whitewashing Britain*, p. 125.

7 Brides

1. UP, 'Elizabeth's Gown Most Closely Guarded Secret since Radar', *Los Angeles Times*, 24 September 1947, p. 5.

2. For a comparison with the D-Day landings, Robert Musel, 'Veil of Secrecy Hides Princess' Bridal Dress', *Washington Post*, 9 October 1947, p. B5. For the atomic analogy, Eli Goldston, 'Design Pirates May Copy Princess' Wedding Gown Unhampered by Law', *Lawyer & Law Notes*, 2:2 (1948), 30–32 (p. 30); 'The Fashionable "Incident"', *Manchester Guardian*, 27 October 1947, p. 3.

3. Musel, 'Veil of Secrecy'. On the engagement, Ben Pimlott, *The Queen: Elizabeth II and the Monarchy* (London: HarperPress, 2012), pp. 122–25; Edward Owens, 'Love, Duty and Diplomacy: The Mixed Response to the 1947 Engagement of Princess Elizabeth', Frank L. Müller and Heidi Mehrkens (eds.), *Royal Heirs and the Uses of Soft Power in Nineteenth-Century Europe* (London: Palgrave Macmillan, 2016), pp. 223–40.

4. Joan Skipsey, 'Notes on a Coming Wedding', *NYT Sunday Magazine*, 26 October 1947, p. 50.

5. Norman Hartnell, *Silver and Gold: The Autobiography of Norman Hartnell* (London: V&A Publishing, 2019 [1955]), p. 114.

6. AP, 'One Peek, No Story: Reporters Get First "Briefing" on Royal Wedding Dress', *NYT*, 7 October 1947, p. 30.

7. Robert Musel, 'The Secret's Out: Elizabeth Will Marry in Lustrous White Satin', *Washington Post*, 25 October 1947, p. B3.

8. 'Princess's Gown (as Reported from Rome)', *Daily Mail*, 12 November 1947, p. 1. The *Evening Standard* decided *not* to run photos it claimed to have obtained a week before the ceremony, reportedly for fear of a public backlash that it had disrespected Elizabeth's wishes, Edward Owens, *Monarchy, Mass Media and the British Public, 1932–53* (London: University of London Press, 2019), p. 319. Local British newspapers, as well as the international press, published sketches on the wedding day: see, for instance, 'Today's Royal Wedding the World Is Watching', *The Cornishman*, 20 November 1947, p. 5; 'Elizabeth's Gown Set with Pearls: Sketches of Gowns Designed for the Royal Wedding in London Today', *NYT*, 20 November 1947, p. 13.

9. H. Gunn to Lord Beaverbrook, 19 November 1947, quoted by Owens, *Monarchy, Mass Media and the British Public*, p. 319.

10. Musel, 'The Secret's Out'.

11. Anonymous acquaintance of the princess quoted by Skipsey, 'Notes on a Coming Wedding', p. 51; Hartnell, *Silver and Gold*, p. 113.

12. 'Copy of Gown Speeded; Embroiderers Finish Duplicate of Princess' Bridal Dress', *NYT*, 24 November 1947, p. 29.

13. Goldston, 'Design Pirates', p. 32.

14. Owens, *Monarchy, Mass Media and the British Public*, p. 318.

15. Correspondence in BT 64/1026, TNA.

16. *British Pathé*, 'Silk for Princess's Wedding Dress', 6 October 1947, www.britishpathe.com/asset/79355; 'Where English Silk Was Made for Incorporation in Princess Elizabeth's Wedding Train: Lullingstone Silk Farm, Kent, Founded in 1932', *Illustrated London News*, 11 October 1947, pp. 410–11; '... And the People Who Made It', *Picture Post*, 22 November 1947, pp. 11–13.

17. Hartnell, *Silver and Gold*, p. 112. Sandro Botticelli, 'Spring' (or 'Primavera'), c. 1480, Le Gallerie degli Uffizi, Florence, www.uffizi.it/en/artworks/botticelli-spring.

18. Correspondence about Hartnell's lapses can be found in BT 64/4146, TNA.

19. Cyril Garbett, Archbishop of York, quoted by Pimlott, *The Queen*, p. 139.

20. Frank Mort, 'Love in a Cold Climate: Letters, Public Opinion and Monarchy in the 1936 Abdication Crisis', *Twentieth Century British History*, 25:1 (2014), 30–62.

21. Dalton quoted by Peter Hennessy, *Never Again: Britain 1945–51* (London: Penguin Books, 2006 [1992]), p. 277.

22. Hennessy, *Never Again*, p. 290.

23. Yasmin Khan, *The Great Partition: The Making of India and Pakistan* (New Haven: Yale University Press, 2017); Haimanti Roy, *Partitioned Lives: Migrants, Refugees and Citizens in India and Pakistan, 1947–1965* (Delhi: Oxford University Press, 2013).

24. Pimlott, *The Queen*, pp. 111–19.

25. On Scotland Yard and security against terrorists, UP, 'Elizabeth's Edict on Stockings Breaks Tradition', *Washington Post*, 15 November 1947, p. 3. On the end of empire in Palestine, Rory Miller (ed.), *Britain, Palestine and Empire: The Mandate Years* (London: Routledge, 2010); Motti Golani, *Palestine between Politics and Terror, 1945–1947* (Waltham, MA: Brandeis University Press, 2013).

26. Spyridon Plakoudas, *The Greek Civil War: Strategy, Counterinsurgency and the Monarchy* (London: I.B. Tauris, 2017); Gioula Koutsopanagou, *The British Press and the Greek Crisis, 1943–1949: Orchestrating Cold-War Consensus in Britain* (London: Palgrave Macmillan, 2020).

27. On Philip's lineage, Pimlott, *The Queen*, pp. 94–97; Owens, 'Love, Duty and Diplomacy', pp. 225–26; Owens, *Monarchy, Mass Media and the British Public*, pp. 299–300.

28. 'Lt. Philip – 17 Years Ago', *Daily Mirror*, 20 November 1947, p. 1.

29. Anonymous Huddersfield man quoted by Philip Ziegler, *Crown and People* (Newton Abbot: Readers Union, 1979), p. 81.

30. Bevin's antisemitism has been much debated, and sometimes disputed, by historians, Raphael Langham, 'The Bevin Enigma: What Motivated Ernest Bevin's Opposition to a Jewish State in Palestine', *Jewish Historical Studies*, 44 (2012), 165–78.

31. MO, Directive Questionnaire December 1947, respondent 3844.

32. Ina Zweiniger-Bargielowska, *Austerity in Britain: Rationing, Controls, and Consumption, 1939–1955* (Oxford: Oxford University Press, 2000), pp. 215–18.

33. MO's Directive Questionnaire for December 1947 framed the fourth question: 'How do you feel about the royal wedding?' My analysis draws on more than 300 responses to this directive.

34. MO, Directive Questionnaire December 1947, respondent 4162, respondent 3015.

35. MO, Directive Questionnaire December 1947, respondent 3898.

36. MO, Directive Questionnaire December 1947, respondent 3861.

37. MO, Directive Questionnaire December 1947, respondent 3848.

38. MO, Directive Questionnaire December 1947, respondent 4256.

39. Dior quoted by Claire Wilcox, *The Golden Age of Couture: Paris and London 1947–57* (London: V&A Publishing, 2008), p. 39.

40. Marjorie Backett, 'Paris Forgets This Is 1947', *Picture Post*, 27 September 1947, p. 26, p. 27.

41. On the allure of the 'New Look' to working-class women, Carolyn Steedman, *Landscape for a Good Woman: A Story of Two Lives* (London: Virago, 1986); Angela Partington, *Popular Fashion and Working-Class Affluence* (London: Routledge, 2007). MO found primarily negative verdicts on the New Look (seven out of every ten) in response to a 'stop press' question tacked onto its September 1947 Directive, canvassing views on the 'skirt length controversy'. But MO registered attitudes softening over time, in tandem with lengthening hemlines, MO, 'A Report on the New Look', file report 3095 (March 1949).

42. MO, Directive Questionnaire September 1947, respondent 4256.

43. Molly Cochrane, letter to the editor, 'Skirts', *New Statesman and Nation*, 27 September 1947, p. 252; MO, Directive Questionnaire September 1947, respondent 4292; respondent 3782.

44. On the undergirding required to achieve the appropriate silhouette, 'The New Under Look', *Picture Post*, 10 April 1948, p. 14; Ridealgh quoted by Christopher Sladen, *The Conscription of Fashion: Utility Cloth, Clothing and Footwear 1941–1952* (Aldershot: Scolar Press, 1995), p. 77. Ridealgh is disparaged as a 'robust grandmother with a North Country background' by Pearson Phillips, 'The New

Look', in Michael Sissons and Philip French (eds.), *Age of Austerity, 1945–1951* (Oxford: Oxford University Press, 1986 [1963]), pp. 117–36 (pp. 131–32). In the same vein, Ross refers to another MP, Bessie Braddock, who castigated the New Look as 'the ridiculous whim of idle people', as a 'Liverpudlian battle-axe of a Labour politician', Robert Ross, *Clothing: A Global History, Or, The Imperialists' New Clothes* (Cambridge: Polity Press, 2008), p. 141. For Ridealgh's intervention in favour of an 'austerity wedding', *HC Deb*, 6 August 1947, *Hansard*, Vol. 441.

45. MO, Directive Questionnaire September 1947, respondent 4255.
46. Elizabeth Wilson, *Adorned in Dreams: Fashion and Modernity* (London: I.B. Tauris, 2003), p. 226.
47. *British Pathé*, 'Harold Wilson at Home', 6 October 1947, www.britishpathe.com/asset/69118. The same issue also depicted work on Elizabeth's dress, 'Silk for Princess's Dress', www.britishpathe.com/asset/79355.
48. MO, Directive Questionnaire September 1947, respondent 3789. This man was either channelling or parroting George Orwell, who had written, 'If the new fashion prevails it is obvious that the well to do will find the labour and the means to renovate their wardrobes whereas the majority of working girls will not. This may again tend to widen the gulf between the classes', quoted by Wilson, *Adorned in Dreams*, p. 226.
49. MO, Directive Questionnaire September 1947, respondent 4277.
50. MO, Directive Questionnaire September 1947, respondent 3789.
51. 'Wary Princess to Compromise on Skirt Style', *Los Angeles Times*, 27 October 1947, p. 2.
52. '"Sinister Spies" Lurk in Dress Industry', *Union Jack*, 9 August 1947.
53. Julie Summers, *Fashion on the Ration: Style in the Second World War* (London: Profile Books, 2016), p. 177; David Kynaston, *Austerity Britain, 1945–51* (London: Bloomsbury Publishing, 2007), p. 258; Beatrice Behlen, '"Does Your Highness Feel Like a Gold Person or a Silver One?" Princess Margaret and Dior', *Costume*, 46:1 (2012), 55–74.
54. *HC Deb*, Churchill, 'Marriage of Princess Elizabeth', *Hansard*, 22 October 1947, Vol. 443. Pimlott delivers a glowing verdict on the wedding's popularity, Pimlott, *The Queen*, pp. 141–43, while Hennessy deems it 'a wonderful and hyperbole-laden diversion from austerity', Hennessy, *Never Again*, p. 332. Owens finds the monarchy 'largely successful in creating an image of the royal lovers that engendered strong, positive forms of empathy', Owens, *Monarchy, Mass Media and the British Public*, p. 274. Kynaston emphasizes mixed feelings, Kynaston, *Austerity Britain*, pp. 243–45.
55. MO, Directive Questionnaire December 1947, respondent 4153; in a similar vein, respondent 4162; Owens, *Monarchy, Mass Media and the British Public*, pp. 313–14.
56. *HC Deb*, Gallacher, 'Marriage of Princess Elizabeth', *Hansard*, 22 October 1947, Vol. 443; Paul P. Kennedy, 'Red M.P. Disrupts House on Wedding: Gallacher Angers Commons by Jibes at Mountbatten – Congratulations Voted', *NYT*, 23 October 1947, p. 11.
57. AP, 'Only a Bridal Gown: Princess Elizabeth Forgoes Trousseau Due to "Conditions"', *Washington Post*, 19 August 1947, p. 1; Editorial, 'What, No Royal Trousseau?', *NYT*, 20 August 1947, p. 20.
58. Skipsey, 'Notes on a Coming Wedding', p. 50.
59. Ulick Alexander to Miss Kilroy, 29 January 1947, BT 64/4194, TNA. This file also contains an itemized list of the princess's wardrobe for the tour and each garment's coupon value. On Africans' responses to the tour, Hilary Sapire, 'African Loyalism and Its Discontents: The Royal Tour of South Africa, 1947', *Historical Journal*, 54:1 (2011), 215–40.

60. Ina Zweiniger-Bargielowska, 'Royal Rations', *History Today*, 1 December 1993, pp. 13–15.
61. Elizabeth Bowen, *The Heat of the Day* (London: Vintage, 2015 [1948]), p. 382.
62. Mary Delane, 'Women and Life', *Sunday Times*, 16 November 1947, p. 7. The Palace told the BoT that it was not responsible for a Press Association report which categorically denied that the Royals had received any more coupons than other subjects, BT 64/4194.
63. Robert McCrum, 'The Masterpiece That Killed George Orwell', *The Observer*, 10 May 2009, www.theguardian.com/books/2009/may/10/1984-george-orwell; MO, Directive Questionnaire December 1947, respondent 3889.
64. MO, Directive Questionnaire December 1947, respondent 3848.
65. Chicago Daily News Foreign Service, 'Britons Send Clothing Coupons to Elizabeth', *Los Angeles Times*, 9 September 1947, p. 1.
66. MO, Directive Questionnaire December 1947, respondent 4238.
67. MO, Directive Questionnaire December 1947, respondent 3793; respondent 4098; Kynaston, *Austerity Britain*, p. 244.
68. The Royal Collection Trust, custodian of the monarchy's art collection, states that 'the young Princess Elizabeth had to save clothing coupons to purchase material for her dress' without mention of the extra allowance, 'The wedding of Princess Elizabeth and Prince Philip, Westminster Abbey', https://bit.ly/46F9F69; Summers, *Fashion on the Ration*, p. 176.
69. In 1941–2, the royal family and their household staff received a total of 4,750 coupons, rising to 8,250 for 1947–8, exclusive of the allowance for Elizabeth's dress, BT 64/4193.
70. Correspondence in BT 64/4192; 'Coupons for the Royal Wedding', *Manchester Guardian*, 23 October 1947, p. 5.
71. '20 Disgusted Young Ladies' to BoT Clothing Coupon Dept., 23 October 1947, BT 64/4192.
72. MO, Directive Questionnaire December 1947, respondent 1478.
73. On Philip queuing for extra clothing coupons, John O. Cotton, 'When a Princess Marries', *Maclean's*, 15 November 1947, p. 12.
74. UP, 'Royal Gown to Cost $5,000, Experts Say', *NYT*, 8 October 1947, p. 22.
75. AP, 'Elizabeth's Gown to Cost Under $800', *NYT*, 9 October 1947, p. 29.
76. Marion Crawford, *The Little Princesses* (London: Cassell, 1950), p. 113, quoted by Pimlott, *The Queen*, p. 133.
77. MO Directive Questionnaire December 1947, respondent 3524; respondent 3527. Respondent 1048 called the expenditure 'a great insult to people trying to bear with austerity living', as did respondent 1688. See also Winifred E. Groom letter to the editor, 'The Royal Trousseau', *Picture Post*, 2 August 1947, p. 5.
78. MO, Directive Questionnaire December 1947, respondent 4250.
79. MO, Directive Questionnaire December 1947, respondent 4312; Betty Spencer Shew, *Royal Wedding* (London: MacDonald & Evans, 1947), p. 92.
80. MO, Directive Questionnaire December 1947, respondent 3613. One male Londoner entertained 'the ribald idea that there might be something in it if they really treated the affair as a fertility ceremony, and, as in South Germany, had the pair go to bed together in the Glass Coach in full public view – possibly with a bottle of wine poured over him, and a bag of flour over her, at some stage', respondent 3806.
81. MO, Directive Questionnaire December 1947, respondent 4214.
82. For discussion between the Cabinet and Palace on the bank holiday question, PREM 8/656, TNA.
83. Owens, *Monarchy, Mass Media and the British Public*, p. 276, pp. 319–20.

84. MO, Directive Questionnaire December 1947, respondent 2928; respondent 1054; respondent 1682; respondent 3960; Owens, *Monarchy, Mass Media and the British Public*, pp. 313–14.
85. MO, Directive Questionnaire December 1947, respondent 3843.
86. MO, Directive Questionnaire December 1947, respondent 4312; respondent 1980.
87. MO, Directive Questionnaire December 1947, respondent 3806; respondent 3814.
88. MO, Directive Questionnaire December 1947, respondent 3861.
89. MO, Directive Questionnaire December 1947, respondent 3798.
90. MO, Directive Questionnaire December 1947, respondent 1362.
91. MO, Directive Questionnaire December 1947, respondent 3884; see also respondents 3809, 4272 and 2756.
92. MO, Directive Questionnaire December 1947, respondent 3642; see also respondent 4189.
93. 'A Royal Wedding Brings Joy to Britain', *Life*, 1 December 1947, pp. 31–43 (p. 32).
94. 'A Royal Wedding Brings Joy to Britain'. See also A. J. Liebling's satirical take on the hyperbolic excess of much American reportage on the wedding finery, A. J. Liebling, 'A Ringside Seat at the Wedding', *New Yorker*, 29 November 1947, www.newyorker.com/magazine/1947/12/06/a-ringside-seat-at-the-wedding.
95. Drew Middleton, 'Worn, Shabby Britons Thrill to Cavalry, Bands, Coaches', *NYT*, 21 November 1947, p. 1, p. 5.
96. Herbert L. Matthews, '80 Pairs of Nylons Sent to Elizabeth', *NYT*, 29 October 1947, p. 13. On the threadbare carpets and chairs at Buckingham Palace, see also Skipsey, 'Notes on a Coming Wedding', p. 10.
97. Inter-departmental discussion of arrangements for the display of gifts can be found in WORK 19/1076, TNA.
98. *Marriage of HRH The Princess Elizabeth and Lieutenant Philip Mountbatten, RN, List of Wedding Gifts* (London: St James's Palace, 1947), p. 114; Lisa Trivedi, *Clothing Gandhi's Nation: Homespun and Modern India* (Bloomington: Indiana University Press, 2007).
99. 'Trousseau Gift Flown to Princess', *Washington Post*, 14 November 1947, p. C9.
100. Charles Yarbrough, 'Washington Mother to Attend Elizabeth's Afternoon Party at St. James's Tuesday', *Washington Post*, 15 November 1945, p. 1, p. 3.
101. Lois Guerrieri, 'Takeoff for Royal Wedding Is Breathtaking Experience', *Washington Post*, 16 November 1947, p. M1; Charles E. Davis, '5 Guerrieris "Keep House", Let Mother Go to Royal Party', *Washington Post*, 16 November 1947, p. M3; Murrey Marder, 'Guerrieris Carry On in Mother's Absence', *Washington Post*, 17 November 1947, p. B1; 'Guerrieri Girl Misses Mother on Birthday', *Washington Post*, 18 November 1947, p. 8. Recorded as item 181, it appears as 'Green taffeta gown' in the official *List of Wedding Gifts*, p. 15.
102. Lois Guerrieri, 'D.C. Mother Sees Sights in London', *Washington Post*, 20 November 1947, p. 1, p. 4; 'Princess Elizabeth Will Be Wed in Pearl-Bedecked Ivory Satin', *Washington Post*, 10 November 1947, p. 1, p. 4.
103. Charles Yarborough, 'D.C. "Cinderella" Back in N.Y. from Princess' Wedding Fete', *Washington Post*, 23 November 1947, p. M18.
104. 'WAAF Weddings White: Military Brides Get Model Gowns from Benefactor', *NYT*, 30 June 1943, p. 12; 'For WRENS Only: Bridal Gowns for Hire', *Manchester Guardian*, 11 August 1943, p. 4; Hope Ridings Miller, 'Why Give Bridal Dresses for British But Not American Girls? Here's Why!', *Washington Post*, 28 January 1944, p. 6.
105. Hartnell, *Silver and Gold*, p. 106.
106. 'Uniforms vs. Gowns', *Stars & Stripes*, 4 May 1944.

107. Barbara Cartland, 'How I Want to Be Remembered', typescript ms., pp. 33–34, Barbara Cartland papers, GB 106, 7BCA, box 1, The Women's Library, LSE.

108. UP, 'American Wedding Gowns Shown for Use in Britain', *NYT*, 2 May 1944, p. 22; 'Women Mob Bride in Gown Sent by Mrs. Roosevelt', *Los Angeles Times*, 4 June 1944, p. 6.

109. Private papers of Mrs D. Rolfe (née Davies), documents.1121, IWM. By July 1946, Gainsborough Pictures claimed that 1,739 brides had 'gone to the altar in Gainsborough wedding dresses', *Kinematograph Weekly*, 26 September 1946, p. xlvi; Barbara Wace, 'British Film Studio Rents Gowns to Couponless Brides', *Washington Post*, 8 July 1947, p. B9.

110. Royal College of Nursing Council Minutes, 1944–6, RCN 2/1, Royal College of Nursing Archives, Edinburgh.

111. Genevieve Reynolds, 'U.S. Clubwomen Send Bridal Gowns to Britain', *Washington Post*, 31 October 1944, p. 87.

112. 'Circulating Set of Bridal Costumes Sent to British Girls' Forces by Women's Clubs', *NYT*, 29 January 1944, p. 8.

113. David Reynolds, *Rich Relations: The American Occupation of Britain, 1942–1945* (London: Phoenix Press, 2000 [1995]).

114. Reynolds, *Rich Relations*, pp. 200–15, pp. 262–83.

115. On patchy records, Reynolds, *Rich Relations*, pp. 420–21. Zeiger puts the documented total of British wives at more than 70,000, of whom at least 36,390 entered the United States between 1946 and 1950, Susan Zeiger, *Entangling Alliances: Foreign War Brides and American Soldiers in the Twentieth Century* (New York: New York University Press, 2010), p. 87. On the military's attempts to deter enlisted men's marriages, Susan L. Carruthers, *Dear John: Love and Loyalty in Wartime America* (New York: Cambridge University Press, 2022), ch. 1.

116. Kathleen Paul, *Whitewashing Britain: Race and Citizenship in the Postwar Era* (Ithaca, NY: Cornell University Press, 2018), p. 25.

117. Reynolds, *Rich Relations*, pp. 413–28; Zeiger, *Entangling Alliances*, pp. 81–87.

118. 'The War Brides', *NYT*, 5 February 1946, p. 20. More generally on British wives' reception in the US, Barbara G. Friedman, *From the Battlefront to the Bridal Suite: Media Coverage of British War Brides, 1942–1946* (Columbia, MO: University of Missouri Press, 2007). For scenes of German POWs performing 'menial tasks', *British Pathé*, 'London to Tidworth', 28 January 1946, www.britishpathe.com/asset/82789.

119. On the centrality of consumption to the framing of the 'war bride story' in the United States, Zeiger, *Entangling Alliances*, pp. 147–50; *British Pathé*, 'School for Brides', 15 October 1945, www.britishpathe.com/asset/83046.

120. Mrs Avice R. Wilson, 'A GI Bride's Jottings', p. 2, private papers of Mrs A. R. Wilson, documents.3403, IWM.

121. Good Housekeeping, *A War Bride's Guide to the U.S.A.* (London: Collins & Brown, 2006 [1945]), p. 12. Margaret Franklin's memoir mentions this booklet as 'invaluable', Margaret Franklin, 'Memories of My Life in America by Margaret A Franklin', typescript ms., private papers of Mrs M. A. Franklin, documents.12497, IWM.

122. Fred Urquhart, *The Last GI Bride Wore Tartan* (Edinburgh: Serif Books, 1947).

123. During and after the war, the BoT constantly reviewed eligibility criteria for extra clothing coupons awarded to Britons preparing to leave the country; see discussions in BT 64/801; 'Americans Must See You Shabby', *Manchester Guardian*, 11 October 1945, p. 3.

124. Margaret Paroutaud, 'Is Your Marriage Really Necessary? (A War-Bride's Story)', typescript ms., 1984, private papers of Mrs M. D. Paroutaud, documents.1896, IWM.

125. Bessie Hackett, 'Trains Speed British Brides to GI Mates', *Washington Post*, 12 February 1946, p. 2.
126. Bessie Hackett, 'Waving Greetings to America: 2334 GI Brides Arrive in N.Y. on Giant Liner', *Washington Post*, 11 February 1946, p. 1; 'Queen Mary Makes 5th War-Bride Trip', *NYT*, 22 April 1946, p. 22.
127. Iris Ashley Knowles, 'No Queues, No Stinting: Why This Is Paradise for GI Brides', *Washington Post*, 17 February 1946, p. S1; Lee E. Graham, 'Yank on a Pedestal', *NYT Sunday Magazine*, 13 April 1947, p. SM152.
128. Good Housekeeping, *War Bride's Guide*, p. 23.
129. Jessamyn West, 'Meet an Overseas War Bride', *Ladies' Home Journal*, August 1946, pp. 127–32, pp. 194–95. See also Joyce R. Brandt, 'A GI Bride "at Home"', *NYT Sunday Magazine*, 17 March 1946, p. SM15.
130. Two young British brides, one bound for Cowan, Tennessee, the other for Escondido, California, reportedly missed their trains from New York Penn Station for this reason; 'War Brides Linger at Shop Windows', *NYT*, 13 February 1946, p. 29; Zeiger, *Entangling Alliances*, p. 146.
131. 'Ex-War Bride Liking "Fine Things" Held in $25,000 Hotel Room Thefts', *NYT*, 5 January 1947, p. 1; '$10,000 Bail Is Fixed for English GI Bride', *NYT*, 6 January 1947, p. 10; 'Ex-War Bride Is Held in High Bail as Thief', *NYT*, 8 January 1947, p. 48. See Zeiger on this case and other crimes, including murder, perpetrated by British women, Zeiger, *Entangling Alliances*, pp. 148–49. On the case of Bridget Waters, convicted of manslaughter, see FO 600/38, TNA.
132. Wilson, 'A GI Bride's Jottings'.
133. *Punch* quoted by Gertrude Samuels, 'Forty Thousand GI Brides Appraise Us', *NYT Sunday Magazine*, 1 December 1946, p. SM11.
134. Mary Mowrer (née Stephenson) questionnaire; Judy Bond (née Dockerty) questionnaire, 'Questionnaires Filled In by Women Who Married American Servicemen and Emigrated to the USA Following the Second World War', documents.15325, IWM. Reynolds recounts one woman hoping that her husband wouldn't appear on the dock in a zoot suit, and another who registered her husband as 'a stranger' on seeing him for the first time in civilian attire, Reynolds, *Rich Relations*, p. 422, p. 428.
135. Jennifer Craik, *Uniforms Exposed: From Conformity to Transgression* (Oxford: Berg, 2005).
136. Reynolds, *Rich Relations*, p. 423.
137. Good Housekeeping, *War Bride's Guide*, pp. 26–27, p. 35. On Scarlett O'Hara's dress, 'Museum Musings – The Curtain Dress from Gone with the Wind', James Madison Museum of Orange County Heritage, 17 January 2021, https://bit .ly/3YJMUMj.
138. Doris Smith (née Parman) questionnaire; Mary Brook (née Kearley) questionnaire, documents.15325, IWM.
139. Patricia Cade (née McMahon) questionnaire, documents.15325, IWM.
140. Harold Wilson to Sir Ulick Alexander, 2 December 1947, BT 64/1026, TNA.
141. Minute by Ord Johnstone, 26 November 1947, BT 64/1026.
142. Major Harvey (Private Secretary to the Queen) to Wilson, 9 December 1947; John Colville (Private Secretary to Princess Elizabeth) to Wilson, 23 January 1948, BT 64/1026.
143. Wilson to Colville, 3 February 1948; Colville to Wilson, 4 February 1948, BT 64/1026.
144. The *Manchester Guardian* printed the dress's itinerary after its display in Edinburgh, Cardiff and Belfast: Glasgow, Liverpool, Bristol, Preston, Leicester, Nottingham, Manchester, Bradford, Leeds and Huddersfield, 'Royal Wedding Dress for Tour Again', *Manchester Guardian*, 31 May 1948, p. 4. On the cost of

the replicas, minute by Ord Johnstone, 15 December 1947, BT 64/1026. On the Palace not paying, Miss Lane to Colville, 16 February 1948, BT 64/1026.

145. Calculated on 6 February 2024 using the Bank of England calculator, www .bankofengland.co.uk/monetary-policy/inflation/inflation-calculator.

146. C. McDowell, *Forties Fashion and the New Look* (London: Bloomsbury, 1997), p. 188; Jonathan Walford, *Forties Fashion: From Siren Suits to the New Look* (London: Thames & Hudson, 2011).

147. Sarah Lindig, 'This Is How Much It Cost to Replicate Queen Elizabeth's Wedding Dress for The Crown', *Harper's Bazaar*, 6 November 2016, https://bit.ly/4csssTo.

148. The V&A's digital archive contains several examples of evening dresses designed by Hartnell prior to 1947 featuring elaborate beading and embroidered tracery. That Hartnell took greater pride in Elizabeth's Coronation garb than he did in her bridal attire is suggested by the greater space devoted to the former in his memoir, Hartnell, *Silver and Gold*, pp. 118–35.

149. 'Elyse Knox to Be Wed in Harmon's Parachute', *Los Angeles Times*, 18 March 1944, p. 6; 'Hollywood', *Cockatoo*, 21 March 1944. For another story of a dress fashioned from a parachute that had saved the groom's life, see Smithsonian, 'Parachute Wedding Dress', www.si.edu/newsdesk/snapshot/parachute-wedding-dress.

150. 'Wedding gown made from a white rayon parachute worn by multiple Jewish brides in a DP camp', USHMM, https://collections.ushmm.org/search/catalog/irn13648. On Ludwig's shirt, https://collections.ushmm.org/search/catalog/irn13545. For a parallel story of a Polish DP's bridal dress fashioned from an American parachute, see www.chicagohistory.org/exhibiting-a-post-world-war-ii-wedding-dress. The IWM possesses another parachute wedding dress worn by a Polish bride liberated at Belsen, whose husband (Sgt Norman Turgel) arrested Josef Kramer, www.iwm.org.uk/collections/item/object/30081821.

Conclusion

1. MO, Directive Questionnaire for December 1947, respondent 4150.

2. Angela Partington, 'The Days of the New Look: Working-Class Affluence and the Consumer Culture', in Jim Fyrth (ed.), *Labour's Promised Land?: Culture and Society in Labour Britain 1945–51* (London: Lawrence & Wishart, 1995), pp. 247–63 (p. 247).

3. Susan Cooper, 'Snoek Piquante', in Michael Sissons and Philip French (eds.), *Age of Austerity, 1945–1951* (Oxford: Oxford University Press, 1986 [1963]), pp. 23–42 (p. 41).

4. Christopher Sladen, *The Conscription of Fashion: Utility Cloth, Clothing and Footwear 1941–1952* (Aldershot: Scolar Press, 1995), p. 80.

5. Henry Irving, 'The Birth of a Politician: Harold Wilson and the Bonfire of Controls, 1948–9', *Twentieth Century British History*, 25:1 (2014), 87–107 (pp. 100–102); 'Mr. Wilson Tears 'Em Up', *News Chronicle*, 15 March 1949, p. 1.

6. Ina Zweiniger-Bargielowska, *Austerity in Britain: Rationing, Controls, and Consumption, 1939–1955* (Oxford: Oxford University Press, 2000), pp. 86–87.

7. A Woman Correspondent, 'No Big Buying Rush Expected', *Manchester Guardian*, 15 March 1949, p. 5.

8. Discussions in LAB 14/455, TNA; BT 64/4272, TNA; 'Clothing Demand and Supply in Reasonable Balance', *Manchester Guardian*, 15 March 1949, p. 2; 'Clothes off Ration', *Manchester Guardian*, 15 March 1949, p. 5; *British Pathé*, 'Clothes Rationing Comes to an End', 17 March 1949, www.britishpathe.com/asset/120143; BBC Archive, 'Clothes Rationing Ends', 16 March 1949, www .bbc.co.uk/videos/c1rrzwwq4ono.

9. Irving, 'Birth of a Politician'; David Kynaston, *Austerity Britain, 1945–51* (London: Bloomsbury Publishing, 2007), pp. 297–98; 'Women Say "Very Nice, But –"', *News Chronicle*, 15 March 1949, p. 1.

10. George Blake to Dear Sirs, n.d.; unsigned letter to George Blake, 11 May 1949, Oxfam papers, MS. Oxfam DIR/2/3/2/1, Bodleian Library, University of Oxford.

11. Robert S. Norris and William M. Arkin, 'Soviet Nuclear Testing, August 29, 1949–October 24, 1990', *Bulletin of the Atomic Scientists*, 54:3 (1998), 69–71.

12. Steve Brown, 'Archaeology of Brutal Encounter: Heritage and Bomb Testing on Bikini Atoll, Republic of the Marshall Islands', *Archaeology in Oceania*, 48:1 (2013), 26–39 (pp. 28–29).

13. Brown, 'Archaeology of Brutal Encounter', p. 29. Another definition, offered by *Webster's Third International Dictionary*, holds that the name 'bikini' derives 'from the comparison of the effects wrought by a scantily clad woman to the effects of an atomic bomb', quoted by James Cameron, '23 Nuclear Explosions Later', *New York Times Sunday Magazine*, 1 March 1970, pp. 219–20.

14. Michihiko Hachiya, *Hiroshima Diary: The Journal of a Japanese Physician, August 6–September 30, 1945*, trans. and ed. Warner Wells (Chapel Hill: University of North Carolina Press, 1995 [1955]), pp. 3–4; John Hersey, *Hiroshima* (New York: Bantam Books, 1966 [1946]), p.59. For photographs of garments and the scars left by kimono patterns, Ishiuchi Miyako, *Postwar Shadows* (Los Angeles: J. Paul Getty Museum, 2015).

15. Benny Morris, *The Birth of the Palestinian Refugee Problem* (Cambridge: Cambridge University Press, 1987); Ilana Feldman, *Life Lived in Relief: Humanitarian Predicaments and Palestinian Refugee Politics* (Berkeley: University of California Press, 2018).

16. Victor Gollancz, 'Why Jews Should Help Arab Refugees', (n.d.), papers of Sir Victor Gollancz, MSS.157/3/SS/10/1-34, MRC. This text is undated, but Gollancz refers to a column, 'Plight of Arab Refugees', in *The Times*, 30 October 1948, p. 3.

17. Jewish Society for Human Service papers, MSS.157/3/JS/1/1-216, MRC.

18. Script of Sir R. Storrs' BBC radio appeal, delivered 3 January 1951, FO 371/91406, TNA.

19. 'Blanket Fashions: Army's Spare Bedcovers Become Clothes for Needy in Europe', *Life*, 17 February 1947, pp. 71–72.

20. Rhoda Dawson, *The Stagnant Pool: Work among Displaced Persons in Germany, 1945–47*, p. 28, private papers of Mrs R. N. Bickerdike, documents.3277, IWM.

21. *HC Deb*, Captain Soames, 'Textile Industry', 26 March 1952, *Hansard*, Vol. 498, cc. 465–67; 'Threat to Future of Textile Trades', *The Times*, 27 March 1952, p. 4. See also discussion in PREM 11/198, TNA.

22. On militarization, Cynthia H. Enloe, *Maneuvers: The International Politics of Militarizing Women's Lives* (Berkeley: University of California Press, 2000). On military fashion, Jane Tynan and Lisa Godson (eds.), *Uniform: Clothing and Discipline in the Modern World* (New York: Bloomsbury Publishing, 2019); B. Sutton, 'Fashion of Fear: Securing the Body in an Unequal Global World', in Erynn Masi de Casanova and Afsan Jafar (eds.), *Bodies without Borders* (New York: Palgrave Macmillan, 2013), pp. 75–99.

23. On the history of Millets, https://tinyurl.com/4s2842ed.

24. Herbert Matthews and Nancie Matthews, *Assignment to Austerity: An American Family in Britain* (Indianapolis: Bobbs-Merrill Company, 1950), p. 236.

25. Owen Hatherley, *The Ministry of Nostalgia: Consuming Austerity* (London: Verso Books, 2017).

26. Board of Trade/Ministry of Information, *Make Do and Mend* (London: HMSO, 1943).

27. Rose Macauley, *The World My Wilderness* (London: Virago, 2018 [1950]), p. 74.

28. Patricia Malcolmson and Robert Malcolmson (eds.), *Nella Last's Peace: The Post-war Diaries of Housewife, 49* (London: Profile Books, 2008), diary entry for 20 October 1942, p. 191.

29. Katie Reilly, 'US Retailers Remove Anne Frank Costume', *Time*, 16 October 2017, https://time.com/4985058/anne-frank-halloween-costume-holocaust; Smiffys, World War II Evacuee Girl, https://tinyurl.com/387n47bw.

INDEX

Entries with page numbers in italics are for figures.